THE CULTURAL IDENTITY OF
SEVENTEENTH-CENTURY WOMAN

'Nature hath placed an eminency in the male over the female.'
William Gouge

'We oftener enslave men than men enslave us. They seen to govern the world, but we really govern the world, in that we govern men.'
Margaret Cavendish

This anthology brings together extracts from a wide variety of seventeenth-century sources to illustrate the ways in which the cultural notion of 'woman' was then constructed. Although the dominant ideology was unquestionably patriarchal, and many of its manifestations were misogynistic and determined to keep women in their place, it was also diverse, self-questioning, contradictory and committed to loving rather than authoritarian relations between the sexes.

Two hundred passages are topically arranged to represent the chief contexts in which women were anatomized, described, admonished, berated, imaged, exemplified, lectured and eulogized. Subjects covered include: the female body and sexuality; the significance of female beauty; female vices and virtues; marriage, adultery and divorce; wifely and maternal duties; women's work and involvement in public affairs; and women's role as the inspiration and object of artistic imagination. Four final sections illustrate subversive ideas, transgressive behaviour and radical challenges to patriarchalism which anticipate later feminist arguments. Each chapter has a helpful introduction which highlights the major issues and supplies a context for the extracts.

This fascinating collection of opinions from both men and women will prove an invaluable sourcebook, enabling informed discussion of the key issues of gender roles, sexuality and identity in the seventeenth century.

N. H. Keeble is Reader in English at the University of Stirling. His publications include *Richard Baxter: Puritan Man of Letters* (1982) and *The Literary Culture of Nonconformity in Later Seventeenth-Century England* (1987).

THE CULTURAL IDENTITY
OF SEVENTEENTH-CENTURY
WOMAN

A reader

Compiled and edited by N. H. Keeble

London and New York

First published 1994
by Routledge
11 New Fetter Lane, London EC4P 4EE

Simultaneously published in the USA and Canada
by Routledge
29 West 35th Street, New York, NY 10001

© 1994 N. H. Keeble

Typeset in Garamond by Florencetype Ltd, Stoodleigh, Devon

Printed and bound in Great Britain by Clays Ltd, St Ives plc

British Library Cataloguing in Publication Data
A catalogue record for this book is available from the British Library

Library of Congress Cataloging in Publication Data
The cultural identity of seventeenth-century woman: a reader/
edited by N. H. Keeble.
p. cm.
Includes bibliographical references (p.) and index.
1. Women–Europe–History–17th century–Sources.
2. Sex role–Europe–History–17th century–Sources.
3. Patriarchy–Europe–History–17th century–Sources.
I. Keeble, N. H.
HQ1587.C85 1994
305.4′094′09032–dc20 94–4517

ISBN 0–415–10481–5 (hbk)
0–415–10482–3 (pbk)

CONTENTS

CONTENTS

Part III 'Feminisms'

ACKNOWLEDGEMENTS

Grateful acknowledgement to copyright holders is made as follows: poems by Anne Bradstreet are reprinted by permission of the publishers from *The Works of Anne Bradstreet*, ed. Jeannine Hensley, Cambridge, Mass.: Harvard University Press, copyright 1967 by the President and Fellows of Harvard College; passages from John Bunyan's *Miscellaneous Works*, vol. III, ed. J. Sears McGee (1987) and vol. IV, ed. T. L. Underwood (1989), from Bunyan's *The Life and Death of Mr. Badman*, ed. James F. Forrest and Roger Sharrock (1988), from Thomas Campion's *Works*, ed. Percival Vivian (1909), from Thomas Carew's *Poems*, ed. Rhodes Dunlap (1949), from John Donne's *Paradoxes, Problems, Essayes and Characters*, ed. Helen Peters (1980), from John Evelyn's *Diary*, ed. E. S. de Beer (1955), from Robert Herrick's *Poetical Works*, ed. L. C. Martin (1963), from Lucy Hutchinson's *Memoirs of the Life of Colonel Hutchinson*, ed. James Sutherland (1973), from Samuel Jeake's *Astrological Diary*, ed. Michael Hunter and Annabel Gregory (1988), from Ralph Josselin's *Diary*, ed. Alan Macfarlane (1976), from *The Memoirs of Anne, Lady Halkett, and Ann, Lady Fanshawe*, ed. John Loftis (1979), from *Eighteenth-century Women Poets*, ed. Roger Lonsdale (1989), from Richard Lovelace's *Poems*, ed. C. H. Wilkinson (1930), from Andrew Marvell's *Poems and Letters*, ed. H. M. Margoliouth, rev. Pierre Legouis and E. E. Duncan-Jones (1971) and from William Shakespeare's *Complete Works*, ed. Stanley Wells and Gary Taylor (1988) are reprinted by permission of Oxford University Press; passages from Robert Burton, *The Anatomy of Melancholy*, ed. Holbrook Jackson, 3 vols, Everyman's Library (1932) by permission of David Campbell Publishers; passages from Margaret Cavendish, *New Blazing World and Other Writings*, ed. Kate Lilley (1992) by permission of Pickering & Chatto (Publishers) Ltd; the passage from *The Chamberlain Letters*, ed. Elizabeth McClure Thomson (1965) by permission of John Murray (Publishers) Ltd and The Putnam Publishing Group; the passage from *The Journal of George Fox* ed. J. L. Nickalls (1975) by permission of the Library Committee of London Yearly Meeting of the Religious Society of Friends; the passage from *Her Own Life: autobiographical writings by seventeenth-century*

Englishwomen, ed. Elspeth Graham, Hilary Hinds, Elaine Hobby and Helen Wilcox (1989) by permission of Routledge Ltd; passages from *The Poems of John Milton*, ed. John Carey and Alastair Fowler (1968) by permission of Longman Group UK; passages from *The Complete Prose Works of John Milton*, vol. II, ed. Ernest Sirluck (1959) by permission of Yale University Press; poems from *The Collected Works of Katherine Philips, the Matchless Orinda*, vol. I, ed. Patrick Thomas (1990) by permission of Stump Cross Books; the passage from *The Puritans: a sourcebook of their writings*, ed. Perry Miller and Thomas H. Johnson (copyrighted 1938; reprinted as a Harper Torchbook, 1963) by permission of Harper-Collins Publishers; poems from *The Poems of John Wilmot, Earl of Rochester*, ed. Keith Ward (1984) by permission of Basil Blackwell Ltd.

Every attempt has been made to obtain permission from the copyright-holders to reproduce the following copyrighted material: the passages from *The Women's Sharp Revenge: five women's pamphlets from the Renaissance*, ed. Simon Shepherd, published by Fourth Estate Ltd (1985); the passage from Bathsua Makin's *Essay to Revive the Antient Education of Gentlewomen*, introd. Paula L. Barbour, published by the University of California Press for the Augustan Reprint Society (1980); passages from *A Collection of Ranter Writings from the 17th Century*, ed. Nigel Smith, published by Junction Books Ltd (1983); the passage from Thomas Middleton's *Women beware Women*, ed. Roma Gill, published by Ernest Benn Ltd (1968).

INTRODUCTION

I say, that both male and female are cast in one same mould: instruction and custom excepted, there is no great difference between them. [22*]
(Montaigne, *The Essayes*)

Nowhere does Michel de Montaigne's percipience more clearly distinguish him from his age than in his recognition that the identities and status of men and women are culturally constructed, not God-given, immutable, 'natural' facts. Such immunity to ideological prejudice is, however, rare. Montaigne's essays appeared in English in John Florio's translation in 1603, but throughout the seventeenth century in England, as in France, the overwhelmingly dominant view continued to be that men and women are, by their creation, of a different order of being. This difference between the sexes was invariably conceived and presented hierarchically: man and woman were, in Milton's words, 'Not equal, as their sex not equal seemed' (2)*. Since she was 'betwixt a man and a child' (43), and generally more child-like than man-like, woman owed deference, obedience and service to man. 'Here is her glory, even to be under him', as John Bunyan succinctly put it (97).

Despite the recent example of Queen Elizabeth to show just what a woman might do when *she* was over *him*, the conviction that woman is weaker, inferior and in need of masculine guidance was voiced as firmly by women, even individual and able women, as by men. Although herself a translator of Lucretius and author of a work of systematic theology, Lucy Hutchinson, for example, held that women should watch over themselves carefully and 'embrace nothing rashly' since their natural 'imbecility' is such that 'the most knowing' woman is inferior in knowledge and judgement 'to the masculine understanding of men' (26). To challenge this order was to invite condemnation for insubordination, wilfulness and pride. Any encroachment by a woman upon the masculine spheres of scholarship and politics and any publication of female opinions had consequently to make its

---

* Parenthetical numbers refer to the extracts in this anthology.

ix

way apologetically, disclaiming self-assertiveness and any intention to 'equalize women to men' (28).

In the Christian tradition of Western Europe the proof text for this belief is, of course, Genesis (1). Seventeenth-century women were never allowed to forget that they were the daughters of Eve, that they carried her guilt, and that any insubordination on their part was a mark of un-regeneracy. It was a reading of Genesis greatly indebted to St Paul (e.g. 3). His admonitory presence is felt whenever woman's place falls for dis-cussion (e.g. 71). His is the authority to be countered (e.g. 8) by those who would argue for a larger and more liberal conception of woman's role than that permitted by Margaret Cavendish's axiom, 'man is made to govern commonwealths, and women their private families' (27). As that suggests, woman's place was domestic: 'it becometh her to keep home' (93). The notion of a good woman was indistinguishable from the notion of a good wife, and a good wife does not roam. Within marriage, she lost her legal identity as a separate person (92) and she was recom-mended so to devote herself to fulfilling her husband's wishes as to lose her own will in his. Sir Thomas Overbury concluded his character of a good wife with the terse aphorism, 'She is he' (4). Any argument against this restrictiveness had to deal not only with St Paul but also with those misogynistic passages in the Old Testament wisdom literature which identify any desire to stray beyond the home as one mark of a whore, characterize woman as man's temptress, and depict her as morally weak and duplicitous, if not innately evil (47, 56). 'The Devil doth easier fasten with them than with men' (3).

Despite the frequency with which the Bible was adduced in its support, this is not, of course, an emphasis peculiar to the Judaeo-Christian tradition. On the contrary, it is characteristic of all recorded societies; perhaps it is definitive of society. Seventeenth-century commentators found the pagan moralists quite as much to their purpose. Aristotle, Plato and Seneca are names frequently invoked. As William Gouge put it, 'the heathen by the light of Nature' realized that there was 'an eminency in the male over the female' (96). From the Platonic tradition, however, derived another, con-trary, conception of woman, imaging her not as vicious but as an ideal of physical and spiritual beauty who grants the male onlooker a glimpse of the divine (31, 32, 33). As man excels in judgement, so woman excels in beauty (35). This was a train of thought particularly serviceable to courtiers for whom wooing and seduction afforded a ready and recognized means by which to deploy and display their accomplishments, in verse if not in fact. Not infrequently, their idealism was spliced with a strand of Ovidian libertinism (161). Theirs is a love poetry curiously uninterested in women and much preoccupied with the poets' own sexual nature and desires. Though women poets might find other voices and other attitudes (82, 175–8), after John Donne male love poets hardly found any other way to talk of, or to, women before the decline of love as a poetic subject (and courtly accomplishment) during the last quarter of the century.

The record does, however, also show women refusing to reconcile the discrepancy between the prevailing ideology and their own experience and aspirations in favour of the former. There was an awareness that what the medical profession explained as the biologically inevitable weaknesses of woman's nature and incapacity of mind were, in truth, no such thing: campaigning for the education of women, Bathsua Makin asserted, in accents very like Montaigne's, that 'Custom, when it is inveterate, hath a mighty influence: it hath the force of Nature itself' (28). As a result of the exceptional and compelling circumstances of Civil War and under the impetus of the radicalism of Puritan enthusiasm, such discordant notes are sounded particularly during the Interregnum (134, 135). For less obvious reasons, and from women at the centre of polite society, they are also to be heard in a noticeably sustained way during the last quarter of the century, defending women as 'Education's, more than Nature's fools' (190). There are besides occasional sympathetic commentaries on what women endure to be heard from men throughout the century, though that sympathy is never allowed to threaten patriarchal imperatives (20, 21, 46).

It is the purpose of the extracts which follow to make available a representative selection from the primary material illustrative of these and related concepts and attitudes. They are intended to provide evidence and contexts for the discussion of ideas about woman's nature, place and duty during the period and for the consideration of literary and historical issues concerning women. Although some of the extracts are written by women, this is not an anthology illustrative of seventeenth-century women's experiences; it is an anthology illustrative of seventeenth-century ways of conceptualizing, describing, characterizing and presenting women and their experiences. To this end, the extracts are arranged topically, covering the main, but by no means all, the prevailing images and notions of woman. These primary themes are briefly described and something of the main import of the extracts, and of the relationships between them, is indicated in the introductory sections to each chapter, but, in the way of texts and of human discourse, the extracts do not, in fact, each conveniently confine themselves to a single topic. They are more richly suggestive than either the chapter headings or the introductory comments indicate, often touching extracts in other chapters at a number of points. To allow comparison of passages scattered through the book and to facilitate cross-reference, the extracts are numbered in one sequence. The source and date (of publication, unless otherwise stated) is given in brief at the beginning of each extract; full details, and listings of all those extracts from any one source, may be found in the bibliography. For ease of reading, spelling, capitalization and punctuation are standardized and modernized throughout; titles, however, are given in the form of the originals.

INTRODUCTION

As it deals with the evidence of texts, this anthology draws upon the records left by the literate, that is, by the gentry, professional and commercial classes, church and court. The cultural life of those below the station of yeomen, of cottagers, agricultural workers, labourers and vagrants, though undoubtedly controlled by the organs of church and state, was probably not defined by them but by oral and folkloristic traditions. It probably differed considerably from that detailed here, but, in the nature of the case, it cannot be represented in an anthology of this sort. A selection of reports of it left by the literate could be compiled, but such third-party accounts would preserve the attitudes and assumptions of the onlookers rather than of those they observed. Statistical evidence, from which social historians can infer something of popular culture, is not, of course, amenable to anthologization.

I am grateful to Professor Helen Wilcox for having supported the original idea for this anthology and to a number of colleagues for their help during its compilation. I owe more than she probably realizes to conversations with Tina Webberley. David Bebbington, Robin Sowerby and Roderick Watson have kindly answered particular queries. Valerie Allen looked over and commented on the introductions to the chapters, much to their advantage. What was originally a very baggy selection of extracts was greatly improved and tightened up by the care with which the reader appointed by Routledge read through my typescript. Though we still differ on some points of emphasis and interpretation, I owe a great debt to the rigour with which this reader pruned out dead wood. The responsibility for remaining infelicities and errors, and for the selection of extracts, is, of course, my own.

I gratefully acknowledge the award by the Carnegie Trust for the Universities of Scotland of a research grant towards travelling costs incurred in preparing this anthology.

NHK

1

IN THE BEGINNING: MALE AND FEMALE

It has been characteristic of human societies since at least the Bronze Age that, despite being widely separated in time and space and adopting a diversity of manners and customs, they oppose the idea of the female to that of the male, according precedency to the male and a secondary, derivative or subordinate status to the female. In the European tradition it is to the Genesis creation myth (1) that this conviction most commonly appeals for justification. Genesis in fact recounts two distinct creation stories, distinguished by Biblical scholars since the late nineteenth century as belonging to the separate source traditions which lie behind the writings which came to form the Pentateuch (Skinner (1930), pp. xliii–lxv; Speiser (1964), pp. xx–xliii). The *P* (or Priestly) narrative (i.1 to ii.4a) is a good deal less discriminatory than the second (ii.4b to iii.24) *J* narrative (Jahvist or Yahwist, from the Hebrew word *Yahweh* which this tradition prefers to *Elohim* as the name of God). Like their predecessors, however, seventeenth-century commentators paid far more attention to the creation of Eve from Adam's rib in the latter than they did to the simultaneous creation of male and female in the former ('male and female created he *them*') which grants apparently equal authority to man and to woman ('let *them* have dominion over the fish of the sea . . .'). The second *J* narrative proved more service-able: in the subsequent creation of Eve was found evidence of woman's secondary status (115: III.§3), in the rib proof of her crooked nature (9), in the story of the Fall reason to blame her for all the ills of humankind, and in the curse placed upon her, as in Adam's naming of the beasts before Eve's creation, evidence of her intellectual inferiority and her subordination to man. 'The fallen angel knew what he did when he made his assault upon the woman. His subtlety told him that the woman was the weaker vessel [I Pet. iii.7]' (138. For summary accounts of seventeenth-century interpretations of Genesis see Turner (1987); more generally, see Philips (1984)). These inferences continued to be the commonplaces they had been throughout the Middle Ages, whether muted, as in Milton's verse equivalent of the idealized human forms of Renaissance painting and sculpture (2), or tenaciously pressed home, as they are by Bunyan (3). Bunyan's

1

marked sympathy for Adam as the victim of a 'woeful tragedy' is matched by his determination to draw from the narrative the moral that women should obey their husbands. The point was never more tersely put than by Sir Thomas Overbury: 'For she is he' (4). This is John Swan's inference, too, though more gently put (5). He wrestles also with a perennial difficulty: since Paul so often associates the image of God with masculinity (e.g. Rom. viii.29; I Cor. xi.7; Coloss. ii.10), in what sense is woman formed in the image of God?

There were views more positive to women, even, where perhaps they are not expected, in the marginal glosses to the Calvinist Geneva Bible (1560), which continued to be used, especially in Puritan circles, until the second half of the seventeenth century (6). There were dissident voices too, some-times convinced. That Geneva gloss is picked up by both Esther Sowernam (7) and Rachel Speght (8; cf. 79), who realise the egalitarian force of the *P* narrative. Though rarely so convinced as these pamphlets, there were other dissident voices (e.g. 9), but they were barely registered by the prevailing ideology. Blame for the Fall was rarely meted out equally to both Adam and to Eve. The century was far less impressed by the perfection of Paradise through the creation of Eve than it was haunted by the loss of Paradise through her lamentable weakness.

~

1 Holy Bible 'Authorized' King James Version (1611)

Genesis I

26. And God said, Let us make man in our image, after our likeness: and let them have dominion over the fish of the sea . . . and over every creeping thing that creepeth upon the earth.
27. So created man in his own image, in the image of God created he him; male and female created he them.
28. And God blessed them, and God said unto them, Be fruitful, and multiply, and replenish the earth, and subdue it: and have dominion over the fish of the sea, and over the fowl of the air, and over every living thing that moveth upon the earth.
29. And God said, Behold, I have given you every herb bearing seed, which is upon the face of all the earth, and every tree . . . yielding seed; to you it shall be for meat.
30. And to every beast of the earth, and to every fowl of the air, and to every thing that creepeth upon the earth, wherein there is life, I have given every green herb for meat; and it was so.
31. And God saw every thing that he had made, and, behold, it was very good. And the evening and the morning were the sixth day.

II

1. Thus the heavens and the earth were finished, and all the host of them . . .

7. And the Lord God formed man of the dust of the ground, and breathed into his nostrils the breath of life; and man became a living soul.

8. And the Lord God planted a garden eastward in Eden; and there he put the man whom he had formed.

9. And out of the ground made the Lord God to grow every tree that is pleasant to the sight, and good for food; the tree of life also in the midst of the garden, and the tree of knowledge of good and evil . . .

15. And the Lord God took the man, and put him into the garden of Eden to dress and to keep it.

16. And the Lord God commanded the man, saying, Of every tree of the garden thou mayest freely eat:

17. But of the tree of knowledge of good and evil, thou shalt not eat of it: for in the day that thou eatest thereof thou shalt surely die.

18. And the Lord God said, It is not good that the man should be alone; I will make him an help meet for him.

19. And out of the ground the Lord God formed every beast of the field, and every fowl of the air; and brought them unto Adam to see what he would call them; and whatsoever Adam called every living creature, that was the name thereof.

20. And Adam gave names to all cattle, and to the fowl of the air, and to every beast of the field; but for Adam there was not found an help meet for him.

21. And the Lord God caused a deep sleep to fall upon Adam, and he slept: and he took one of his ribs, and closed up the flesh instead thereof.

22. And the rib, which the Lord God had taken from man, made he a woman, and brought her unto the man.

23. And Adam said, This is now bone of my bones, and flesh of my flesh: she shall be called Woman, because she was taken out of Man.

24. Therefore shall a man leave his father and his mother, and shall cleave unto his wife: and they shall be one flesh.

25. And they were both naked, the man and his wife, and were not ashamed.

III

1. Now the serpent was more subtle than any beast of the field which the Lord God had made. And he said unto the woman, Yea, hath God said, Ye shall not eat of every tree of the garden?

2. And the woman said unto the serpent, We may eat of the fruit of the trees of the garden:

3. But of the fruit of the tree which is in the midst of the garden, God hath said, Ye shall not eat of it, neither shall ye touch it, lest ye die.

4. And the serpent said unto the woman, Ye shall not surely die.

5. For God doth know that in the day ye eat thereof, then your eyes shall be opened, and ye shall be as gods, knowing good and evil.

6. And when the woman saw that the tree was good for food, and that it was pleasant to the eyes, and a tree to be desired to make one wise, she took of the fruit thereof, and did eat, and gave also to her husband with her; and he did eat.

7. And the eyes of them both were opened, and they knew that they were naked; and they sewed fig leaves together; and made themselves aprons.

8. And they heard the voice of the Lord God walking in the garden in the cool of the day: and Adam and his wife hid themselves from the presence of the Lord God amongst the trees of the garden.

9. And the Lord God called unto Adam, and said unto him, Where art thou?

10. And he said, I heard thy voice in the garden, and I was afraid, because I was naked; and I hid myself.

11. And he said, Who told thee that thou wast naked? Hast thou eaten of the tree, whereof I commanded thee that thou shouldest not eat?

12. And the man said, The woman whom thou gavest me to be with me, she gave me of the tree, and I did eat.

13. And the Lord God said unto the woman, What is this that thou has done? And the woman said, The serpent beguiled me, and I did eat.

14. And the Lord God said unto the serpent, Because thou hast done this, thou art cursed above all cattle, and above every beast of the field; upon thy belly shalt thou go, and dust shalt thou eat all the days of thy life:

15. And I will put enmity between thee and the woman, and between thy seed and her seed; it shall bruise thy head, and thou shalt bruise his heel.

16. Unto the woman he said, I will greatly multiply thy sorrow and thy conception; in sorrow thou shalt bring forth children; and thy desire shall be to thy husband, and he shall rule over thee.

17. And unto Adam he said, because thou hast hearkened unto the voice of thy wife, and hast eaten of the tree, of which I commanded thee, saying, Thou shalt not eat of it: cursed is the ground for thy sake; in sorrow shalt thou eat of it all the days of thy life;

18. Thorns also and thistles shall it bring forth to thee; and thou shalt eat the herb of the field.

19. In the sweat of thy face shalt thou eat bread, till thou return unto the ground; for out of it wast thou taken: for dust thou art, and unto dust shalt thou return.

20. And Adam called his wife's name Eve; because she was the mother of all living . . .

22. And the Lord God said, Behold, the man is become as one of us, to know good and evil: and now, lest he put forth his hand, and take also of the tree of life, and eat, and live for ever:

23. Therefore the Lord God sent him forth from the garden of Eden, to till

the ground from whence he was taken.

24. So he drove out the man; and he placed at the east of the garden of Eden Cherubims, and a flaming sword which turned every way, to keep the way of the tree of life.

2 John Milton, *Paradise Lost* (1667), IV.288–324

Two of far nobler shape erect and tall,
Godlike erect, with native honour clad
In naked majesty seemed lords of all,
And worthy seemed, for in their looks divine
The image of their glorious maker shone,
Truth, wisdom, sanctitude severe and pure,
Severe but in true filial freedom placed;
Whence true authority in men; though both
Not equal, as their sex not equal seemed;
For contemplation he and valour formed,
For softness she and sweet attractive grace,
He for God only, she for God in him:
His fair large front and eye sublime declared
Absolute rule; and hyacinthine locks
Round from his parted forelock manly hung
Clustering, but not beneath his shoulders broad:
She as a veil down to the slender waist
Her unadorned golden tresses wore
Dishevelled, but in wanton ringlets waved
As the vine curls her tendrils, which implied
Subjection, but required with gentle sway,
And by her yielded, by him best received,
Yielded with coy submission, modest pride,
And sweet reluctant amorous delay.
Nor those mysterious parts were then concealed,
Then was not guilty shame, dishonest shame
Of nature's works, honour dishonourable,
Sin-bred, how have ye troubled all mankind
With shows instead, mere shows of seeming pure,
And banished from man's life his happiest life,
Simplicity and spotless innocence.
So passed they naked on, nor shunned the sight
Of God or angel, for they thought no ill.
So hand in hand they passed, the loveliest pair
That ever since in love's embraces met,
Adam the goodliest man of men since born
His sons, the fairest of her daughters Eve.

3 John Bunyan, *An Exposition on the First Ten Chapters of Genesis* (1692; written 1680s?), ii.428–40

Chapter III

[Gen. iii.2] 'And the woman said.' Indeed, the question was put to her, but the command was not so immediately delivered to her: 'The Lord God commanded the man' (Gen. ii.16). This therefore I reckon a great fault in the woman, an usurpation, to undertake so mighty an adversary, when she was not the principal that was concerned therein; nay, when her husband who was more able than she, was at hand, to whom also the law was given as chief. But for this act, I think it is, that they are now commanded silence, and also commanded to learn of their husbands (I Cor. xiv.34,35). A command that is necessary enough for that simple and weak sex. Though they see it was by them that sin came into the world, yet how hardly are some of them to this day dissuaded from attempting unwarrantably to meddle with potent enemies, about the great and weighty matters that concern eternity (I Tim. ii.11–15) . . .

[Gen. iii.16] 'I will greatly multiply thy sorrows', &c. This is true, whether you respect the woman according to the letter of the text, or as she was a figure of the church; for in both senses their sorrows for sin are great, and multiplied upon them: the whole heap of the female sex know the first, the church only knows the second . . .

'And thy desire shall be to thy husband, and he shall rule over thee.' Doubtless the woman was, in her first creation, made in subordination to her husband, and ought to have been under obedience to him. Wherefore, still that had remained a duty, had they never transgressed the commandment of God; but observe, the duty is here again not only enjoined, and imposed, but that as the fruit of the woman's sin; wherefore, that duty that before she might do as her natural right by creation, she must now do as the fruits of her disobedience to God. Women therefore, whenever they would perk it and lord it over their husbands, ought to remember, that both by creation and transgression they are made to be in subjection to their own husbands. This conclusion makes Paul himself: 'Let (saith he) the woman learn in silence with all subjection. But I suffer not a woman to teach, nor to usurp authority over the man, but to be in silence; for Adam was first formed, then Eve; and Adam was not deceived but the woman being deceived, was in the transgression' (I Tim. ii.11–14).

[Gen. iii.17] God having laid his censure upon the woman, he now proceedeth and cometh to her husband, and also layeth his judgment on him . . .

'Because thou hast harkened to thy wife.' Why? Because therein he left his station and headship, the condition which God had appointed him, and gave way to his wife to assume it, contrary to the order of creation, of her relation, and of her sex; for if God had made Adam lord and chief, who ought to have taught his wife, and not to have become her scholar?

Hence note, that the man that suffereth his wife to take his place, hath already transgressed the order of God.

'Because thou hast harkened to the voice', &c. Wicked women, such as Eve was now, if harkened unto, are 'the snares of death' to their husbands [Eccles. vii.26]; for, because they are weaker built, and because the Devil doth easier fasten with them than with men, therefore they are more prone to vanity and all misorders in the matters of God, than they [i.e. the men], and so, if harkened unto, more dangerous upon many accounts: 'Did not Solomon King of Israel sin by these things? yet among many nations was there no king like him, who was beloved of his God, nevertheless even him did outlandish women cause to sin' (Neh. xiii.26). 'But there was none like unto Ahab, which did sell himself to work wickedness in the sight of the Lord, whom Jezebel his wife stirred up' (I Kgs. xxi.25).

Hence note further, that if it be thus dangerous for a man to harken to a wicked wife, how dangerous is it for any to harken unto wicked whores, who will seldom yield up themselves to the lusts of beastly men but on condition they will answer their ungodly purposes! What mischief by these things hath come upon souls, countries and kingdoms, will here be too tedious to relate.

'Because thou hast harkened to the voice of thy wife, and hast eaten of the tree.' That is, from the hand of thy wife; for it was she that gave him to eat: 'Therefore', &c. Although the scripture doth lay a great blot upon women, and cautioneth man to beware of these fantastical and unstable spirits, yet it limiteth man in his censure. She is only then to be rejected and rebuked, when she doth things unworthy her place and calling. Such a thing may happen, as that the woman, not the man, may be in the right (I mean, when both are godly), but ordinarily it is otherwise (Gen. xxi.12). Therefore the conclusion is, let God's word judge between the man and his wife, as it ought to have done between Adam and his, and neither of both will do amiss; but contrariwise, they will walk in all the commandments of God without fault (Luke i.6) . . .

[Gen. iii.20] By this act Adam returneth to his first station and authority in which God had placed him, from which he fell when he became a scholar to his wife; for to name the creatures was in Adam a note of sovereignty and power . . .

4 Sir Thomas Overbury, *A Wife* (1614), pp. 3–4

A Good Woman

A Good Woman is a comfort, like a Man. She lacks of him nothing but heat. Thence is her sweetness of disposition, which meets his stoutness more pleasantly; so wool meets iron easier than iron, and turns resisting into embracing. Her greatest learning is religion, and her thoughts are on her own sex, or on men, without casting the difference. Dishonesty never comes nearer than her ears, and then wonder stops it out, and saves virtue the labour. She leaves the neat youth telling his luscious tales, and puts back the serving-man's putting forward with a frown: yet her kindness is free enough to be seen, for it hath no guilt about it; and her mirth is clear, that you may look through it into virtue, but not beyond. She hath not behaviour at a certain, but makes it to her occasion. She hath so much knowledge as to love it; and if she have it not at home, she will fetch it; for this sometimes in a pleasant discontent she dares chide her sex, though she use it never the worse. She is much within, and frames outward things to her mind, not her mind to them. She wears good clothes, but never better; for she finds no degree beyond decency. She hath a content of her own, and so seeks not an husband, but finds him. She is indeed most, but not much to description, for she is direct and one, and hath not the variety of ill. Now she is given fresh and alive to a husband, and she doth nothing more than love him, for she takes him to that purpose. So his good becomes the business of her actions, and she doth herself kindness upon him. After his, her chiefest virtue is a good husband. For she is he.

5 [John Swan], *Speculum Mundi* (1635), pp. 499–501

The Creation of Man, being Created Male and Female according to the Image of God: together with the Institution of Marriage . . .

Moses addeth that 'male and female created he them' [Gen. i.27], to show that Woman as well as Man was partaker of the same image [of God], the last that had it and yet the first that lost it, for though she were the last in creation, yet first in transgression, as the Scripture speaketh.

But perhaps you will think the Apostle denieth this, saying, 'The man is the image and glory of God, but the Woman is the glory of the man' (I Cor. xi.7). In which it must be considered that the Apostle denieth not the Woman, as she is a creature, to be made in the image of God, but speaking as she is a wife, and considering of them by themselves, he [i.e. Man] then is more honourable and must have the pre-eminence, in which, the Woman is rightly called the glory of the Man, because she was made for him, and put in subjection to him.

A woman's rule should be in such a fashion
Only to guide her household, and her passion:
And in her obedience never's out of season,
So long as either husband lasts, or reason.
Ill thrives the hapless family that shows
A cock that's silent, and a hen that crows.
I know not which live more unnatural lives,
Obeying husbands, or commanding wives.

But to come more nearly to the creation of Woman . . . It was from the side of Man that Woman came, builded up out of a rib taken from thence; not made out of any part of his head, which (if we seek the meaning in a mystery) shows that she must not overtop or rule her husband, nor yet made out of any part of his foot, to show that man may not use her as he pleaseth, not trample or contemn her; but made out of a rib, taken from his side, and near his heart, that thereby he might remember to nourish, love and cherish her, and use her like bone of his bone, and flesh of his flesh [Gen. ii.23].

And being thus made she is married to Adam by God himself, who brought her unto him to show . . . the sacred authority of marriage and of parents in marriage; a mutual consent and gratulation followeth likewise between the parties, lest any one should tyrannically abuse his fatherly power and force a marriage without either love or liking. And thus are two made one flesh, in regard of one original, equal right, mutual consent, and bodily conjunction [Gen. ii.24].

6 Holy Bible, 'Geneva' version (1560), marginal gloss on Gen. ii.22

Signifying that mankind was perfect when the woman was created, which before was like an imperfect building.

7 Esther Sowernam, *Ester hath Hang'd Haman* (1617), pp. 93–4

It appeareth, by that sovereignty which God gave to Adam over all the creatures of sea and land, that man was the end of God's creation: whereupon it doth necessarily, without all exception, follow that Adam, being the last work, is therefore the most excellent work of creation. Yet Adam was not so absolutely perfect but that, in the sight of God, he wanted an helper. Whereupon God created the woman, his last work, as to supply and make absolute that imperfect building which was unperfected in man, as all divines do hold, till the happy creation of the woman. Now of what estimate that creature is and ought to be, which is the last work, upon whom the Almighty set up his last rest – whom he made to add perfection to the end of all creation – I leave rather to be acknowledged by others than resolved by myself . . .

9

That delight, solace and pleasure, which shall come to man by woman, is prognosticated by that place wherein woman was created: for she was framed in Paradise, a place of all delight and pleasure. Every element hath his creatures, every creature doth correspond the temper and the inclination of that element wherein it hath and took his first and principal *esse* or being. So that woman neither can or may degenerate in her disposition from that natural inclination of the place in which she was first framed: she is a Paradisian, that is, a delightful creature, born in so delightful a country.

When woman was created God brought her unto Adam, and then did solemnise that most auspicious marriage betwixt them with the greatest majesty and magnificence that heaven or earth might afford. God was the father which gave so rich a jewel; God was the priest which tied so inseparable a knot. God was the steward which provided all the pleasures, all the dainties, all the blessings which his divine wisdom might afford, in so delightful a place.

The woman was married to Adam as with a most sure and inseparable band; so with a most affectionate and dutiful love Adam was enjoined to receive his wife, as is noted in the [Geneva] bible printed 1595 [in a note on Gen. ii.24: 'So that marriage requireth a greater duty of us toward our wives, than otherwise we are bound to show to our parents'].

There is no love (always excepting the transcending love) which is so highly honoured, so graciously rewarded, so straightly commanded, or which being broken is so severely punished, as the love and duty which children owe to their parents. Yet this love, albeit never so respective, is dispensed withal in respect of that love which a man is bound to bear to his wife. 'For this cause', saith Adam (as from the mouth of God), 'shall a man leave his father and mother, and cleave only to his wife'. The word 'cleave' is uttered in the Hebrew with a more significant emphasis than any other language may express – such a cleaving and joining together which admitteth no separation. It may be necessarily observed that that gift of the woman was most singularly excellent, which was to be accepted and entertained with so inestimable a love, and made inseparable by giving and taking the ring of love, which should be endless.

Now, the woman taking view of the garden, she was assaulted with a serpent of the masculine gender; who, maliciously envying the happiness in which man was at this time, like a mischievous politician he practised, by supplanting of the woman, to turn him out of all. For which end he most craftily and cunningly attempted the woman: and telleth her that therefore they were forbidden to eat of the fruit, which grew in the midst of the garden, that in eating they should not be like unto God. Whereupon the woman accepted, tasted and gave to her husband. In accepting the serpent's offer, there was no sin: for there was no sin till the fruit was eaten. Now, albeit I have undertaken the defence of women, and may in that respect be favoured in taking all advantages I may to defend my sex.

There are many pregnant places in the scripture which might be alleged to extenuate the sin of the woman in respect of the sin of Adam: it is said, (Eccles. xxv[.24]) 'Sin had his beginning in woman'; *ergo*, his fullness in man.

St. Paul saith (Rom. v[.12]): 'By one man's sin death came into the world', without mention of the woman. The same St. Paul writeth to the Corinthians [xv.22], to whom he affirmeth 'that all die in Adam', in which the fullness and effects of sin are charged upon Adam alone: not but that woman had her part in the tragedy, but not in so high a degree as the man.

8 Rachel Speght, *A Mouzell for Melastomus* (1617), pp. 65–70

Almighty God, who is rich in mercy (Ephes. ii.4), having made all things of nothing and created man in his own image (Coloss. iii.30 [*recte* 10]) (that is, as the Apostle expounds it, 'In wisdom, righteousness and true holiness'; making him lord over all (Ephes. iv.24)), to avoid that solitary condition that he was then in, having none to commerce or converse withal but dumb creatures, it seemed good unto the Lord that as of every creature he had made male and female, and man only being alone without mate, so likewise to form an help-meet for him. Adam for this cause being cast into a heavy sleep (Gen. ii.20), God, extracting a rib from his side, thereof made, or built, woman – showing thereby that man was an imperfect building afore woman was made; and, bringing her unto Adam, united and married them together.

Thus the resplendent love of God toward man appeared, in taking care to provide him an helper before he saw his own want and in providing him an helper as should be meet for him. Sovereignty had he over all creatures, and they were all serviceable unto him . . .

True it is (as is already confessed) that woman first sinned, yet find we no mention of spiritual nakedness till man had sinned. Then it is said, 'Their eyes were opened' (Gen. iii.7), the eyes of their mind and conscience . . . as if sin were imperfect and unable to bring a deprivation of a blessing received, or death on all mankind, till man (in whom lay the active power of generation) had transgressed. The offence, therefore, of Adam and Eve is by St. Austin thus distinguished: 'the man sinned against God and himself, the woman against God, herself and her husband'; yet in her giving of the fruit to eat had she no malicious intent towards him, but did therein show a desire to make her husband partaker of that happiness which she thought by their eating they should both have enjoyed. This her giving Adam of that sauce wherewith Satan had served her, whose sourness, afore he had eaten, she did not perceive, was that which made her sin to exceed his. Wherefore, that she might not of him who ought to honour her (I Pet. iii.7) be abhorred, the first promise that was made in paradise God makes to woman: that by her seed should the serpent's head be broken (Gen. iii.15). Whereupon Adam calls her Hevah [i.e. Eve], Life, that as the woman had been an

11

occasion of his sin so should woman bring forth the Saviour from sin, which was in the fullness of time accomplished (Gal. iv.4). By which was manifested that he is a Saviour of believing women no less than of men . . . So that by Hevah's blessed seed, as St. Paul affirms, it is brought to pass that 'male and female are all one in Christ Jesus' (Gal. iii.28) . . .

The efficient cause of woman's creation was Jehovah the Eternal, the truth of which is manifest in Moses his narration of the six days' works, where he saith 'God created them male and female' (Gen. i.28 [recte 27]) . . . That work then cannot choose but be good, yea very good, which is wrought by so excellent a workman as the Lord: for he, being a glorious Creator, must needs effect a worthy creature . . .

Secondly, the material cause, or matter whereof woman was made, was of a refined mould, if I may so speak. For man was created of the dust of the earth (Gen. ii.7), but woman was made of a part of man after that he was a living soul. Yet was she not produced from Adam's foot, to be his too low inferior; nor from his head to be his superior; but from his side, near his heart, to be his equal: that where he is lord, she may be lady. And therefore saith God concerning man and woman jointly: 'Let them rule over the fish of the sea, and over the fowls of the heaven, and over every beast that moveth upon the earth' (Gen. i.26). By which words he makes their authority equal, and all creatures to be in subjection unto them both. This, being rightly considered, doth teach men to make such account of their wives as Adam did of Eve: 'This is bone of my bone, and flesh of my flesh' (Gen. ii.23); as also, that they neither do or wish any more hurt unto them than unto their own bodies. For men ought to love their wives as themselves, because he that loves his wife loves himself (Ephes. v.28): and never man hated his own flesh (which the woman is) unless a monster in nature.

Thirdly, the formal cause, fashion and proportion, of woman was excellent. For she was neither like the beasts of the earth, fowls of the air, fishes of the sea, or any other inferior creature; but man was the only object which she did resemble. For as God gave man a lofty countenance that he might look up to heaven, so did he likewise give unto woman . . . And (that more is) in the image of God were they both created; yea, and to be brief, all the parts of their bodies, both external and internal, were correspondent and meet each for other.

Fourthly and lastly, the final cause or end for which woman was made was to glorify God, and to be a collateral companion for man to glorify God, in using her body and all the parts, powers and faculties thereof as instruments for his honour.

9 [Richard Brathwait], Ar't Asleepe Husband? (1640), pp. 3–5

Yet it may be objected, Man deserves precedency because in his creation he had priority. It is confessed; yet might Woman seem (if we may safely incline to the opinion of some rabbis) to have pre-eminence in the manner of her creation. For, whereas dust gave Man his composition, Woman took hers from Man's perfection. Yea, but the matter she was made of, foretold what she would be. She was made of a crooked subject, a rib, and out her crooked disposition (will some say, who stand ill-affected to the Salic state) she will not stick to tyrannize over a sheepish husband, and give him *rib-roast*. A poor objection! An equal and ingenious exposition would rather frame this conclusion: that the subject whereof she was made begot not in her a crookedness, but pliability of nature, ever ready to bend her will and apply her affection to the mould of Man; not cruelly to domineer, but constantly to adhere to her mate . . . But will some harsh Timonist or woman-hater say, 'Well had it been for the world, if there had never been an Eve in the world; it was her consent that brought a stain to the perfection and integrity of our state'. Yet for all this, if you will believe that ancient Cabbalist, who showed himself an exquisite discourser and discusser of conjectural causes, he will tell you that in his opinion, the Woman showed not so much levity in consenting to the serpent as the Man did facility in giving ear to the Woman. She expostulated the cause with the Serpent ere she consented, whereas he, without more ado, weakly received what she so unhappily offered.

Part I
FEMALE NATURE, CHARACTER AND BEHAVIOUR

2

BODY

The practice and findings of experimental anatomy constituted the most significant sixteenth-century advances in medicine, but these discoveries made little impact upon professional thinking until very late in the seventeenth century, and they hardly affected the popular idea of the body until the eighteenth (Maclean (1980), pp. 28–9). Regardless of such accurate anatomical descriptions as those of the Italian Andreas Vesalius (1543) or such discoveries as William Harvey's of the circulation of the blood (1628), the dominant cultural ideas of the period continued to construe the human body in terms of its constituent 'humours', as the Middle Ages had done. The names of the ancient physicians Hippocrates and Galen continue to be invoked throughout the seventeenth century, with a reverence 'difficult now to understand' (Eccles (1982), p. 17; Siraisi (1990), p. 84; see also Laqueur (1990), pp. 151, 170, 265–6, and Temkin (1973) pp. 134–92 for the durability of Galenic medicine). They are still being adduced in the 1690s, in a period we too blandly think of as predominantly rational and scientific, long after that key event in the history of modern science, the founding of the Royal Society in 1662.

The body of Aristotelian and Galenic lore received by the seventeenth century imaged the body as a series of dualities, parallels and combinations (10). Its 'subtle knot', in John Donne's phrase in 'The Ecstasy', is tied by the spirits, which animate, nourish and drive it (11), but its determining constituents are its four fluid humours. These derived their four essential qualities – heat, coldness, dryness and moisture – from the four elements of which it was believed everything was made (fire, air, earth and water). Each humour, located in a particular organ, was associated with a colour: sanguine (blood) with red; phlegmatic (liver) with white; choleric (gall) with yellow; melancholic (spleen) with black (11). To the four humours, and their various combinations, bodily health or illness and psychological temperament were attributed (see further Eccles (1982), pp. 17–22). This was a way of thinking which understood sexual identity less in terms of difference than in terms of similarities, likenesses and mirror images. It entertained what Thomas Laqueur has called a 'one-sex model' of human biology (Laqueur

17

(1986), pp. 2–3; see further Laqueur (1990), ch. 3 and *passim*). Woman was analogically related to man; in gynaecological texts, physical organs peculiar to her were presented in terms of male organs and were often supposed to perform the same functions (so, for example, the clitoris is described as a penis, the ovaries as testes (12)). Woman was distinguished from man less by her difference than by her insufficiency: she is an inferior or lesser or incomplete man.

The hierarchical nature of humoral physiology, which valued heat over coldness, dryness over moisture, was able to explain woman's inferiority, first, by pointing to the debilitating moistness and coldness of the female body (Maclean (1980), pp. 30–4). 'Heat was the cause of vigour, strength, courage and intellect, and thus it followed that men were naturally superior to women in all these respects' (Eccles (1982), p. 26); the occasional possession of such masculine traits by a woman was attributed to her having an unusual degree of vitalizing body heat and a hot temperament. Woman's inferiority was explicable, secondly, in terms of the disadvantageous circum-stances of her conception and generation (Maclean (1980), pp. 31–2). The Aristotelian idea that fully developed foetuses issued in male children was still current; females were thought of as the product of incomplete develop-ment caused by insufficient generative heat in the womb. Even though the notion sits awkwardly with the Christian belief in the divine creation of both male and female as perfect beings, women were regarded as physiologically 'failed males' (Maclean (1980), pp. 8–9; Brown (1988), p. 10). Evidence of this imperfect development was to be found not only in woman's want of physical strength but in such signs as her internal genital organs which the coldness and moistness of the womb had prevented from developing and extending outside the body, like a man's (Maclean (1980), pp. 31, 32–3; Laqueur (1990), p. 4). To these associations were added age-old prejudices against the sinister or left side. Males were the product of hot sperm from the right testicle deposited on the right (hotter) side of the womb, where the foetus was carried. Females, on the other hand, were produced by cold sperm from the inferior left testicle, were debilitated by insufficient heat in the womb, and were carried on the left side (13). In male-authored texts these signs, circumstantially developed, are taken to indicate the sex of an unborn child (13, 15). Application to women's own experience would promptly have shown them to be erroneous, but it was to 'divers learned men' (15) that appeal continued to be made. Upon their authority, the opposing aberrations of effeminacy and the virago could be explained: while a perfect man was produced by male sperm and a foetus carried on the right (male) side of the womb, and a woman by the contrary, male sperm deposited on the left (female) side of the womb would result in an effeminate man and female sperm deposited on the right side, a virago (Maclean (1980), p. 38).

As this suggests, the process of conception and generation was imperfectly

18

understood. Though the physician Thomas Gibson, drawing on Harvey's *Exercitationes de generatione animalium* (1651), is moving towards a correct identification of the ovaries and their function, he judiciously avoids all discussion of conception as 'too philosophical' for his anatomical treatise (12). In Aristotelian thought, woman contributed nothing to generation save the womb or context and nourishment. In Galen, conception was the product of the combination of male and female seed (a view with implications for the understanding of female sexuality; see chapter 3). The latter is the commoner view (14), though throughout our period both are held, sometimes in awkward combination (Eccles (1982), pp. 37–8). Whatever the particular line taken, the characteristic emphasis is that the male contribution is hot, and therefore active and dynamic, the female cold, and so passive and receptive; the man is 'agent', the woman 'patient' (12, 13). The microscope allowed the existence of sperm to be demonstrated in the 1670s and the hypothesis of the ovum was at the same time convincingly argued, but it was another two centuries before ovulation and fertilization began to be understood. Only then did the purpose and causes of menstruation become apparent (see Laqueur (1990), ch. 5). In our period, menstruation was variously explained as the voiding of unused seed (*menstruum*), or of *menses* (the matter from which, in some Aristotelian accounts, the foetus is formed by the animating effect of the male seed), and of excess blood which the woman's cold nature had failed to absorb (14, 16; Wood (1981), pp. 716–17). It was associated with the curse of Genesis iii.16 (Maclean (1980), pp. 39–40; Wood (1981), p. 713), as were gynaecological complaints generally and the suffering of childbirth in particular, and it retained something of the sense of pollution and uncleanness evident in the Levitical taboos (16), though there are warnings against associating menses with excrement (14; Delaney *et al.* (1976), pp. 33–9). In accordance with humoral thought, infertility was attributed to the coldness of the womb (14), though William Whately is of a different opinion (16), and cures were designed to increase its heat, often in conjunction with the treatments of sympathetic magic (13), for the woman's disposition and imagination were thought to have a powerful effect both upon conception and upon the development of the foetus (13). Monstrous or deformed births were also attributed to copulation shortly before or during menstruation when the female seed had degenerated into a noxious state (Wood (1981), pp. 715–16); intercourse early in a woman's cycle, while the *menses* were fresh and receptive, was thought most likely to result in conception (13).

The one organ distinctively and peculiarly the woman's was the womb. It was thought of almost as a separate organism within the woman, with a will, if not quite a life, of its own (Maclean (1980), pp. 40–2; Eccles (1982), p. 28). She was wholly at its mercy. Added to the debilitating effect of her predominantly cold and damp humour, this still further weakened her, psychologically as well as biologically. To the womb and its humoral complexion were attributed a whole series not only of physical ills but of mental aberrations and temperamental defects (14), particularly those quintessentially female complaints, irrationality, uncontrollable passion (15) and hysteria or 'womb disease' (the word derives from the Greek for 'womb'), also known during this period as 'the mother' (Kahn (1986), pp. 33–4)). It desired conception, and would open to suck in male seed, closing to retain it (13, 14). If frustrated, its resentment caused physical and psychological disorder. To it was also attributed woman's sexual appetite (see chapter 3).

10 Galen, *Certain Workes of Galens* (1586), p. 25

The Office of a Chirurgeon

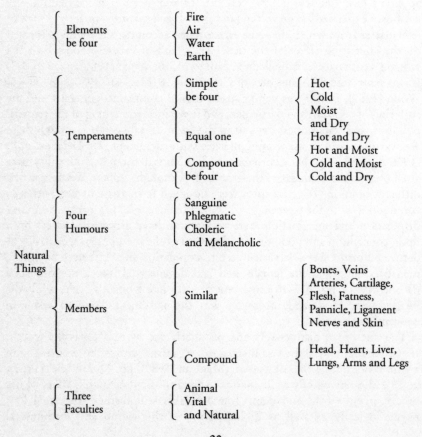

Operations or Actions	Animal	Feeling and Moving
	Vital	Beating of the Pulse and Breathing
	Natural	Generation Auction and Nutrition

Spirits be three	Animal Vital Natural	in	the Brain the Heart the Liver

11 Robert Burton, *Anatomy of Melancholy* (1621–51), I.i.2(2) [I.147–8]

Humours. Spirits

A humour is a liquid or fluent part of the body, comprehended in it, for the preservation of it, and is either innate and born with us, or adventitious and acquisite. The . . . four first primary humours, coming and proceeding from the first concoction in the liver . . . some divide . . . into profitable and excrementitious humours: *pituita* and *blood* profitable; the other two excrementitious . . .

Blood, is a hot, sweet, temperate, red humour, prepared in the mesaraic veins, and made of the most temperate parts of the chylus in the liver, whose office is to nourish the whole body, to give it strength and colour, being dispersed by the veins, through every part of it. And from it spirits are first begotten in the heart, which afterwards by the arteries are communicated to the other parts.

Pituita or *phlegm* is a cold and moist humour, begotten of the colder part of the chylus (or white juice coming of the meat digested in the stomach) in the liver; his office is to nourish and moisten the members of the body, which as the tongue, are moved, that they be not over dry.

Choler [or bile] is hot and dry, bitter, begotten of the hotter parts of the chylus, and gathered to the gall. It helps the natural heat and senses, and serves to the expelling of excrements.

Melancholy [or black choler, black bile], cold and dry, thick, black, and sour, begotten of the more fæculent part of nourishment, and purged from the spleen, is a bridle to the other two hot humours, blood and choler, preserving them in the blood, and nourishing the bones. These four humours have some analogy with the four elements, and to the four ages of man.

To these humours you may add *serum*, which is the matter of urine, and those excrementitious humours of the third concoction, *sweat* and *tears*.

Spirit is a most subtle vapour which is expressed by the blood, and the

21

instrument of the soul, to perform all his actions, a common tie or medium between the body and the soul . . . Of these spirits there be three kinds, according to the three principal parts, *brain, heart, liver*: *natural, vital, animal*. The natural are begotten in the liver, and thence dispersed through the veins, to perform those natural actions. The vital spirits are made in the heart of the natural, which by the arteries are transported to all the other parts: if these spirits cease, then life ceaseth, as in a syncope or swooning. The animal spirits formed of the vital, brought up to the brain, and diffused by the nerves to the subordinate members, give sense and motion to them all.

12 [Thomas Gibson], *Anatomy of Humane Bodies Epitomized* (1682), pp. 136–43, 145–7, 156–60, 163

OF THE GENITALS IN WOMEN

Of Women's Testicles, or Ovaria

Women's testicles differ much from men's . . . their situation is not without the body, as in men, but in the inner cavity of the abdomen, one each side, two fingers' breadth from the bottom of the womb, to whose sides they are knit by a strong ligament . . . their substance appears whitish, but is wholly different from the substance of men's testicles, for men's . . . are composed of seminary vessels . . . but women's do principally consist of a great many membranes and small fibres, loosely united to one another, among which there are several little bladders . . . full of clear liquor. The liquor contained in these bladders had always been supposed by the followers of Hippocrates and Galen to be seed stored up in them, as if they supplied the place of the *vesiculæ seminæ* [seminal sacs] in men. But from Dr. [William] Harvey downwards many learned physicians and anatomists (according to Aristotle) have denied all seed to women. Of which the said Dr. Harvey thus discourses, *De ovi materia, exercit.* 34: 'some women send forth no such humour as is called seed, and yet is not conception thereby necessarily frustrated; for I have known several women (says he) that have been fruitful enough without such emission; yea, some that, after they begun to emit such humour, though indeed they took greater pleasure in copulation, yet grew less fruitful than before. There are also infinite instances of women who, though they have pleasure *in coitu* [in sexual intercourse], yet send forth nothing, and notwithstanding, conceive. I greatly wonder that they that think this emission necessary to generation have not observed that the humour is cast out, and issues most commonly from out the clitoris and orifice of the privity, very seldom from any depth within the neck of the womb, but never within the womb itself, so as that it should there be mixed with the man's seed; and that it is not ropy and oily like seed, but serous, like urine. Now, to what purpose should that be cast out, whose use is necessarily required within? . . .'. And, indeed, whatever that humour be that the more salacious women emit in copulation (of which afterwards) it cannot be that which is contained in these *vesiculæ* [small sacs or cysts], both because it is sent forth in greater quantity than that it can be supplied from them, and also the *vesiculæ* are destitute of any such pores or passages whereby the liquor contained in them might issue out . . . We must therefore subscribe to that new but necessary opinion that supposes these little bladders to contain nothing of seed, but that they are truly eggs, analogous to those of fowl and other creatures, and that the testicles (so called) are not truly so, nor have any such office as those of men, but are indeed an *ovarium* [egg container] wherein these eggs are nourished by the sanguinary vessels dispersed through them, and from whence one or more (as they are fecundated by the man's seed) separate, and are conveyed into the womb by the two *fallopiæ* [fallopian tubes] . . .

Of the Vasa Deferentia in Women, or their Oviducts

. . . having withal rejected the opinion of women's having seed, and affirmed that that which makes the conception is one of those *vesiculæ* in the *testes*, dropping from thence and conveyed into the womb, we must enquire by what way they can pass . . . for *vasa deferentia* [vessels which allow passage downwards] we assign those ducts that Fallopius in his anatomical observations calls *tubæ* [tubes] . . . their use is, in a fruitful copulation, to grant a passage to a more subtle part of the masculine seed (or to a seminal air) towards the *testes*, to bedew the eggs contained in them, which eggs (one or more), being by that means fecundated (or ripened, as it were) and dropping off from the *testis* . . . are received by the extremity of the *tubæ* and carried along their inner cavity to the womb . . .

Of the Uterus or Womb, and its Neck

. . . The uterus or womb is usually divided into four parts: the *fundus*, or bottom; *os internum*, or cervix; the *vagina*; and the *sinus pudorus*, or outward privity . . .

This [the *fundus*] in a special manner is called the womb, because all the rest seem to be made for its sake . . . it is also called the *matrix*, from its being the mother to conserve and nourish the *foetus* . . .

. . . what women emit from the clitoris in copulation [some] think to be true semen . . . But . . . who can think Nature so prodigal of so spiritous and noble a liquor as seed, as to ordain it to be shed at the orifice of the *pudendum*, and so to be quite lost, and never mixed with the man's, which is ejected into the bottom of the womb? But we have above denied all seed to women, and therefore believe that the liquor they emit is only for the lubrication of the *vagina* to cause the greater pleasure *in coitu* . . .

Of the Vagina

It has the name *vagina*, or sheath, because it receives the penis like a sheath . . .

It has many arteries and veins . . . these vessels bring plenty of blood hither in the venereal congress, which, heating and puffing up the *vagina*, increaseth the pleasure and hinders the man's seed from cooling before it reach the *uterus* . . .

Of the Pudendum Muliebre, or Woman's Privity

. . . These parts are called by the general name of *pudenda* because, when they are bared, they bring *pudor*, or shame, upon a woman . . .

The great chink is called *cunnus* by Galen, . . . to conceive; by Hippocrates, *natura*. It is also called *vulva* [wrapper, covering], *porcus* [pig], *concha* [mussel], and by many other names that fancy has imposed upon it . . .

. . . in the upper part of the *pudendum* does a part jet out a little that is called *clitoris* . . . that signifies lasciviously to grope the *pudendum*. It is otherwise called *virga* [twig, rod], for it answers to a man's yard [i.e. penis] in shape, situation, substance, repletion with spirits and erection, and differs from it only in length and bigness. In some it grows to that length as to hang out from betwixt the lips of the privity. Yea, there are many stories of such as have had it so long and big as to be able to accompany with other women like unto men, and such are called *fricatrices* [women who rub], or otherwise *hermaphrodites*; who it is not probable are truly of both sexes, but only the *testes* fall down into the *labia*, and this clitoris is preternaturally extended . . .

. . . we will note further that in some Eastern countries it uses to be so large that for its deformity and the hindrance it gives to copulation, they use to cut it quite out, or hinder its growth by searing it, which they improperly call circumcision . . .

Of a Conception

. . . in the first place, there occurs the man's seed, which is the active principle or efficient cause of the *foetus* . . . and as to the manner of its fecundating the *ovum*, we omit that as being too philosophical for this place. In the next place, therefore, we must come to the matter or passive principle of the *foetus*, and this is an *ovum* impregnated by the man's seed . . .

13 William Sermon, *The Ladies Companion* (1671), pp. 7–15, 18–20, 23, 25–7, 181–4, 198–201

How to Make Women Fruitful

. . . If the cause proceed from the coldness and overmuch humidity or moistness of the womb, which oftentimes it doth, take cardamum grains, cubebs, white ginger, of each two drams, make it all into fine powder, and give to the woman two drams thereof, and presently after let her sit over the bath as followeth:

Take six or seven skeins of raw yarn, boil it in water, and good store of wood ash; then put the pot under some stool, having a hole in the middle thereof, through which let the woman receive the fume up into her privy parts; being covered warm, let her sweat, and when she riseth from the bath, let her sweat in bed also . . . then let her dry herself, and presently let her good husband do his best endeavours . . .

Another Bath

Take camomile, wild thyme, featherfew, privet and the tops of juniper, of each one handful, boil them in a pot of water close covered, then set a stool in the tub, which stool must have a hole in the midst thereof, then set the pot with the herbs under, and let the fumes thereof ascend up into the womb. This bath must be made use of three times, once every day, beginning the next day after her courses are stopped, and if it happens that she sweat, let her dry herself with warm clothes, and two hours after let her lie with her husband . . .

An Excellent Potion for to Cause Conception

. . . Or, eat every morning one newly laid egg for twenty-eight days together, but let the eggs be taken from such hens that have no cock to go that time with them.

Or, take of the slime that a hare will have about his mouth when he eateth mallows, and drink it in wine; two hours after lie with your husband . . .

Or, give to the woman without her knowledge the womb of a hare to eat, or burn the same to powder and give it to her in wine to drink, just after she hath received the fume of tormentil roots boiled in rain water. This being done, let her accompany with her husband, and she will forthwith conceive . . .

Or, take the pizzle of a bull being well dried and grated to powder . . .

Or, hold to the place of conception a little before the act of copulation civet, musk or ambergris; the man may also put a small quantity of either upon the end of his yard. It will not only draw down the womb but will cause the woman to conceive, and after the act let her smell to some of the aforesaid ingredients, for by so doing the womb will be drawn upward and the seed injected therein retained . . .

Wild carrot seed hanged about the left arm of the woman above the elbow causeth conception.

Or, take the shift and all clothes that have been made use of during the time of the woman's monthly purgation, and wash them out in new milk, and give the milk to sucking pigs, and hang up the clothes so washed upon a hedge, etc., in the air, some time, day or night, by which means women become fruitful . . . Women are most subject to conceive a day, two or three after their courses are for the present stopped, at which time they ought not (if they desire children) to use the act of copulation too often, for that makes the womb slippery and more subject to open than to shut, etc., which indeed is the chief reason that ladies of pleasure have so few children . . .

How to Know whether a Woman be with Child or Not

. . . Such symptoms as may be taken from the husband are as followeth, *viz.*

If he find an extraordinary delight in the enjoyment of the wife in the time of copulation, and at the same time feels a kind of sucking or drawing at the end of his yard, and if he returns from the wars of Venus not over-moist, are true signs that the woman is conceived . . .

The significations which may properly be taken from the wife are more infallible or certain . . .

If the wife shall receive a great contentment in the company of her husband and from her natural parts (whether they remain dry or moist) there issue nothing forth, though it is not necessary that those parts should always continue dry, since the womb retaineth only that which is fit for the confirmation of the child.

Also, if she hath at the same time a gaping and stretching, and discerns within her a quivering and shaking . . . and a disquietness or rumbling about the lower part of the belly, which is, because the womb shuts itself together to entertain the matter of generation which it hath sucked or drawn in . . . Likewise . . . her belly fallen and somewhat flat, and in a short time after perceive it to swell or grow bigger . . . and her monthly courses not found to appear . . .

But these signs are not so infallible or certain as others are. The most true . . . are collected from the child's stirring in the womb . . .

How to Know whether a Woman be with Child of a Boy or a Girl

. . . First, you may observe that young women commonly are rather with child of a male than a female. The reason is, because they are hotter than older women, which was well observed by Aristotle . . .

Many observe the like cometh to pass when the conception shall be when the wind is in the South, and then for the most part they bring forth daughters. And when . . . in the North, they bring forth sons . . .

Hippocrates, the prince of physicians, saith that . . . if the right breast be harder than the left, the nipple hard and red, and more high . . . it is a sign the woman is conceived of a male child. Also, a woman that goeth with a boy, the right side of her belly is more copped and bigger than the left, and there the child stirreth first . . .

The male child lieth high above the navel by reason of its heat. The female at the bottom of the belly by reason of its coldness and ponderosity . . .

Many observe that if a woman be with child of a boy, that she hath the pulse of her right side higher, stronger and thicker than her left. And she is subject to reach out her right hand more frequently than the left. In going, she sets forth the right foot always foremost; her right breast bigger than the left; her right eye more brighter and large . . .

Of the Vasa Præparantia [generative vessels], or Seminal Veins and Arteries in Men

The privy members are of two kinds, of the male and female, and so it was thought fit for procreation; for this action requireth an agent and a patient, seed and menstrual blood.

The first is the seat of the plasmatic spirit; the second affordeth supply of matter to the spirit, to extract forth the wonderful frame of the regions and parts of the little world . . .

The stones in Latin are called *testes*, because they testify one to be a man . . . they are two in number, their figure is oval. The right is hotter, and better concocteth the seed, and by Hippocrates is called the begetter of the male. The left stone is more full . . . Yet the seed which is there elaborated is more waterish and cold . . . and begetteth the female . . .

Of the Genitals or Privy Members in Women

The genitals in women have four distinct parts, to wit: the *cunnus*; the womb; the stones; and the spermatic vessels.

The *cunnus* is that part which offers itself to the sight. In it there are eleven parts remarkable . . .

The fifth is called the clitoris . . . as it doth represent the yard of a man, so it suffereth erection and falling, and may properly be called a woman's yard; and in many women it is well known to be as long as a man's, and doth very much trouble them in the act of generation, etc. . . .

Of the Womb

The womb was appointed by Nature to be the field thereof to receive the seed of man and woman . . .

It hath two parts, the *os uteri*, the mouth of the womb, and the *fundus*, the bottom . . .

The mouth . . . though in the act of generation it may be so opened that it will receive the *glans* of a man's yard, yet after conception it is so closely shut that it will not admit the point of a needle; but when a woman is in labour it so openeth that it makes way for the child . . .

Hippocrates saith that those women which are conceived with child have the orifice of the womb shut and closed up so that the air might not get in and corrupt the seed, and that the heat thereof might not go forth.

14 Nicholas Culpeper, *Directory for Midwives* (1662), pp. 20–7, 67–8, 106–7, 115–16, 131–2, 152–3

Of the Knowledge of the Temper of the Womb

. . . a beard in women shows that they have a hot womb and hot stones: it comes with the beginning of the terms [periods], and when the breasts swell, and is hard to be seen.

Aristotle saith, that some women have hairs in their chin when their courses stop, and when they have a hot womb and stones . . .

Also, when terms come forth at twelve years of age, it is a sign of a hot womb and when they last long, the blood is red, hot, but not very much . . . If it be hot and moist, they flow plentifully, and last till fifty. If it be hot and dry, the blood is yellow, thin and sharp, and pricks the privities.

If it be cold and moist, the blood comes late forth, with difficulty, and it is whitish and thin. If it be cold and dry, the terms come forth very late, and with difficulty, and seldom continue till forty, and the blood is thick and little.

The third sign is from lechery, for they who have hot wombs desire copulation sooner and more vehemently and are much delighted therewith. They who are cold, do the contrary. The hot and moist are not tired with much venery. The hot and dry have great lust, and a frenzy if they want it; but they are quickly tired because there are but few spirits. If it be cold and moist, they are not soon lecherous and are easily satisfied; and if they miscarry often the womb is made colder, and they delight not in the sport: but copulation doth them good and makes them more youthful. If it be cold and dry, they desire not a man in a long time, and take no delight, because the spirits are few.

The fourth sign is from conception, for the hot conceive often, and bring forth males or viragoes, if the seed of the man agree with it. The cold doth the contrary.

A hot and moist womb is very fruitful . . .

Hot and dry are fruitful, but not so much as the former . . .

Cold and moist are hard to conceive . . . when they are young, and the seed of the man is hot and dry, they conceive males, but seldom well-shaped or healthful . . .

A cold and dry womb is commonly barren, and if they conceive, the man's seed is hot and moist, they bring forth females; and if males, they are tall and quickly look old.

Of the Flux of the Terms

By divine providence the blood which is voided every month is kept in when there is a child, for if it be its nature, it is not idle, but only superfluous, till they conceive, nor is it more an excrement than seed or milk.

The terms commonly begin at fourteen and then the hair appears on the privities, the breasts swell and women begin to be lecherous; and the blood can no longer stay in the veins, but breaks out at the veins of the womb . . .

They are called by some *flowers*, because they go before conception, as flowers do before fruit . . .

Of the Symptoms from the Womb, and Mother-fits in General

It is not to be expressed what miserable diseases women are subject to, both virgins and others, from the womb and its consent with other parts. For when terms or blood are stopped, there are great symptoms, and while they putrefy, or get evil qualities, the symptoms are grievous and almost inexpressible . . .

. . . As Galen saith, the mother or hysterical passion is one name, but hath under it many symptoms . . .

Of the Frenzy of the Womb

It is a great and foul symptom of the womb, both in virgins and widows, and such as have known men. They are mad for lust, and infinite men, and lie down to them; and it differs from salacity because in that there is no delirium.

It is an immoderate desire of venery that makes women almost mad, or a delirium from an immoderate desire of venery . . .

The immediate cause is plenty of hot and sharp seed against Nature, but next unto that which is natural. It is a little biting, swelling, and forcing Nature to let it out by lechery . . . The part first affected is the womb in the *nympha* [labia], which grows hot and swells, but the *nymphæ* are not properly the seat of venery, but the clitoris, which was called by the same name anciently . . .

29

The outward causes are hot meats spiced, strong wine, and the like, that heat the privities, idleness, pleasure and dancing, and reading of bawdy histories . . .

Of Barrenness, and Want of Conception

. . . Conception is of fruitful seed spent by a man and mixed with a woman's seed to perfection, for the making of a child by the retentive and altering faculty of the womb. Hence, it is necessary that both seeds be fruitful, that is, hot, full of spirits, and well tempered, and a fit subject for a soul, and that both spend at a time, and there be mixed and retained together, to produce a child.

Also, the sucking of the womb is necessary, and that it should lay it up and embrace it, so that there be no space between the seed and the womb . . . Moreover, there must be blood in readiness to get the child, or besprinkle it when it is first framed, and to nourish it after . . .

Of Monsters

Histories tell of many monsters brought forth by women . . .

Histories witness that a monster may be from human seed and the seed of a beast. It is seldom, for the forming faculty doth not err of itself but is seduced by the imagination, or frustrated of its ends, from a fault of the spirits, the heat or matter. Therefore, imagination is the cause of monsters. For histories mention that women with child, by beholding men in vizards [masks], have brought forth monsters with horns and beaks and cloven feet . . .

And though doctors cannot cure monsters, they are to admonish women with child not to look upon monsters, and to strengthen their spirits and heat, and to keep the seed and blood right, and not to allow copulation in time of their terms, lest any monstrous birth should be from much and impure blood.

15 [N.H.], *The Ladies Dictionary* (1694), pp. 123–4, 234

Conception: . . . Censure us not, ladies, as if we intended to salute your ears with anything that can be in the least imputed immodest, by the wise and discreet, and it is to those we chiefly address ourselves; but there are some things that may appear at first blush to border upon it, when indeed there is no such thing in reality, and are so necessary to be known by young ladies, when their conditions call for assistance, that we could not reasonably omit them . . . The signs are gentle pains of the head, swimming or dazzling of the eyes. The eyes sometimes swell and become dim or dusky colour, much of their former brightness fading for a time. The veins wax redder than usual,

and strut with the abundance of blood; the eyes sink in, and the eyebrows
grow loose, sometimes little pimples suddenly arise in the face and eyes
glisten with various colours. The veins between the eyes and the nose will be
extended with blood and those under the tongue look greenish. The neck
will flush with heat and the backbone seem cold. The veins and arteries
swell, and the pulses are observed more easily. Many times the veins of the
breast look black and in a while turn yellow. The nipples look red more than
usual, and to conclude there's desiring of things sometimes not fit for food,
puking and the like . . . we come now to a nicer point, which we should be
difficultly brought to undertake were we not warranted by divers learned
men, who have given their opinions about it. They tell us if it be a male child,
that when it is come to some perfection in the womb, the right eye of the
mother would to appearance move swifter, and sparkle more than the other.
The right pap rise and swell more than the left, and become harder, the
nipple sooner changing colour . . . when the infant first stirs it is more active
and strong . . . on the right side . . . when she goes, though she regard it not,
she commonly sets her right leg first . . . Contrary are the symptoms of the
females . . .

Furor uterinus: an unseemly distemper which is wont to seize upon maids,
especially those of ripe years, and sometimes widows too. They who are
troubled with it throw off the veil of common modesty and decency, and
delight only in lascivious, obscene discourses. They covet a man greedily,
and even furiously, and omit no inviting temptations that may induce them
to satisfy their desires. The cause seems to be in the seminal juice, which,
being exalted to the highest degree of maturity, drives the maids into a kind
of fury, which is conspicuous every year in some brutes, as in cats, bulls,
bucks, does, harts.

16 [William Whately], *A Bride-Bush* (1617), pp. 43–5

I come now to such [duties] as concern the marriage bed, which are as
needful to be known as the former, because offences in that kind are more
capital and dangerous, though not so public. Their matrimonial meetings
must have these three properties. First, it must be cheerful; they must
lovingly, willingly and familiarly communicate themselves unto themselves,
which is the best means to continue and nourish their mutual natural love,
and by which the true and proper ends of matrimony shall be attained in best
manner: for the husband is not his own, but the wife's, and the wife the
husband's. Secondly, their meeting must be sanctified. Paul saith, meat,
drink and marriage are good, being sanctified in prayer [I Tim. iv.3–5]. Men
and women must not come together as brute creatures and unreasonable
beasts, through the heat of desire, but must see their maker in that his
ordinance, and pray his blessing solemnly as at meals (the Apostle speaks of

both alike) that marriage may indeed be blessed unto them. To sanctify the marriage bed, and use it reverently with prayer and thanksgiving, will make it moderate, and keep them from growing weary each of other (as in many it falls out) and cause that lust shall be assuaged which else shall be increased by these meetings. Propagation and chastity, the two chief ends of marriage, are best attained by prayer and thanksgiving in the use thereof, without which they will hardly come, or not with comfort. Neither is it more than needs, to see God in that which so nearly toucheth ourselves, as the hope of posterity; him, as the increase of his kingdom. Thirdly, their nuptial meetings must be seasonable, and at lawful times. There is a season when God and Nature seioynes [scions, i.e. grafts] man and wife in this respect. The woman is made to be fruitful, and therefore also more moist and cold of constitution. Hence it is that their natural heat serves not to turn all their sustenance into their own nourishment, but a quantity redounding is set apart in a convenient place to cherish and nourish the conception, when they shall conceive. Now this redundant humour (called their flowers or terms) hath (if no conception be) it[s] monthly issue or evacuation (and in some oftener) unless there be extraordinary stoppings and obstructions, lasting for six or seven days in the most. Sometimes also this issue, through weakness and infirmity of nature, doth continue many more days. Always after childbirth there is a larger and longer emptying, because of the former retention, which continueth commonly for four, five or six weeks, and in some longer. Now in all these three [sic] times and occasions it is simply unlawful for a man to company with his own wife. The Lord tells us so, Lev. xv.19, 25, also xviii.19, also xx.18. Of which places it is needful that married people should take notice, to which I send them. Neither let women think themselves disgraced because I have laid this matter open in plain but modest speeches. Where God threatens death to the offender, can the minister be faithful if he do not plainly declare the offence? This fault is by God condemned to the punishment of death, Lev. xx.18. Bear then with necessary plainness. And let no woman grieve that the cause of her fruitfulness is known, when she rejoiceth to be found fruitful. Say not, that I may let them read it. Can the minister so discharge his office, of giving men warning that they sin not, because they may read it? But if any through niceness or otherwise, do take snuff at this openness (for immodest and obscene speech they have heard none), they shall argue themselves guilty of the sin which they would not have known, and show rather a willingness to commit evil than prove it evil to teach that plainly which God hath plainly revealed to be known.

3

SEXUALITY

For Nicholas Culpeper (14) there was clearly a direct connexion between the state of the womb and the degree of a woman's sexual desire. Lasciviousness, it appears, is less subject to her will than to physiological predetermination. Woman was consequently presented by medical treatises as at the mercy of her womb. Its voraciousness and insatiability can lead to nymphomania (14, 15); satisfaction of its desire to breed is a biological necessity; denial can lead to dementia and depression. The common remedy for this complaint in young women was that prescribed by Robert Burton: marriage, 'to give them content in their desires' (17). This conviction that woman is a sexual being drew support from ideas about generation. If conception required discharge of female as well as of male seed, then sexual excitement and orgasm is as necessary for its release in the woman as in the man; simultaneous orgasm yields the greatest chance of conception: both should 'spend at a time' (14; see Laqueur (1986), pp. 1–16, and Laqueur (1990), index *s.v.* Orgasm, for full accounts of the relation between orgasm and conception in the Galenic tradition). The clitoris, first described in the medical literature of Western Europe in 1559 (Laqueur (1990), pp. 64–6, but see also p. 98), was consequently assigned an important, indeed, essential, role in generation since without sexual excitement there could be no conception (Eccles (1982), pp. 29, 34; see ibid., pp. 26–42, for a full account of ideas on generation, sexuality and the female productive system). No heed is paid in medical texts to the contrary evidence of women's own experience, even when (as they occasionally were) written by a woman.

These views happily chimed with English Protestantism's rejection of the ascetic and monastic tradition of Roman Catholicism. In an early anticipation of a Gothic motif, Burton presents nunneries as tyrannical and corrupting institutions in which sexual frustration leads to perverse practices, which, for him, include lesbianism (17). Protestantism generally, and Puritanism in particular, were a good deal less anxious about, and more realistically sympathetic towards, sexual desire than the celibate tradition of Rome. Despite the notable exceptions of Augustine and Aquinas, who held that concupiscence and lust, not sexuality itself, were the result of the Fall,

33

the Church Fathers and Medieval Schoolmen had in general been hostile to the idea that sexual relations were part of God's conception of unfallen humanity (Brown (1988), pp. 399–400; Wood (1981), pp. 11–12). In contrast, Protestant treatises characteristically present sexuality not as innately evil, nor as a consequence of the Fall, but as part of the divine scheme and according to the will of God (see e.g. 79). The most signal instance in our period is Milton, who in *Paradise Lost* goes out of his way to insist on (marital) sexual relations in Eden, and to distinguish his image of prelapsarian bliss from both courtly libertinism and indulgence on the one hand, and from the Roman (monastic) ascetic tradition on the other; it is the latter which he explicitly damns as Satanic: 'who bids abstain / But our destroyer, foe to God and man?' (18). This is a direct repudiation of the old Medieval view that sexual pleasure, even within marriage, is at best deeply suspect (Stone (1977), pp. 499–500; see at large, Brooke (1989)). In *Paradise Lost* it is the 'sum of earthly bliss' to make love within the nuptual bower (VIII.510–22; for sexuality and sexual relations in Milton see Turner (1987) and Walker (1988)).

This positive image of sexual relations is, however, constantly under threat from a contrary thrust. Though the moralistic and homiletic literature is as ready as the medical to admit female sexuality as right and proper, it is also sensitive to the dangers of concupiscence. As the archangel Raphael admonishes Adam, 'In loving thou dost well, in passion not' (*Paradise Lost*, VIII.588). The weight of tradition stretching from Moses left the moral and homiletic literature in no doubt where lay the likeliest temptation to deviate from this ideal of moderation. Its excoriations of lust (see chapter 6), drawing on the powerful Old Testament diatribes against harlots and admonitions to avoid the lure of seductive women, have often a misogynistic tone to them. So, too, have the denunciations of antifeminist satire which seem often to express a fear of the destructive power of female sexuality.

Contrary views are, however, to be met with. In Shakespeare revulsion at the innate evil of the female body is the mark not of common sense but of derangement, of male insecurity and of tragic misjudgement of women (19; on women in Shakespeare see Davies (1986), pp. 105–74, Dusinberre (1975), French (1982), and Jardine (1983)). In the extract from Richard Baxter (20) it is not woman who is presented to the implied male reader as a specially dangerous temptation but his own desires. Sharply aware that when restraint is not exercised it is commonly women who are the victims ('used worse by men than dogs are'), Baxter's humane temper recognizes patriarchy's oppression of women and looks to marriage as a protection for 'half the world' against the ravages of the male. Similarly, in his summary and expository account of the law as it bears on the rights and status of women, Thomas Edgar (on his identity and the provenance and purpose of his book, see Prest (1991)) is in no doubt that it is men, not women, in whom sexual desire rages uncontrollably: were it not for 'the rampier of laws', no woman above the age of twelve 'should be able to escape ravishing' (21).

'We frame sins not according to their nature but our interest': Montaigne's aphorism explodes patriarchy's claim to assert moral absolutes (22). Montaigne was a sixteenth-century Frenchman, but, through John Florio's early seventeenth-century translation, his extraordinarily acute, subtle, elusive and self-reflexive *Essays* became part of England's cultural stock. No commentator is more sensitively aware than he of the cultural pressure exerted upon women, or of the self-interested hypocrisy of the commonplaces circulated about woman's nature and her sexual appetite. His mockery of the phallus suggests that he insists on woman's omnivorous sexual appetite less out of conviction than to point up the injustice of the double standard (on which see the introduction to chapter 8). His acknowledgement that, if not satisfied, the womb's greed will cause disorder, is common enough (cf. 17); much rarer is his drawing of a parallel between the womb and the penis which puts man and woman on an equal footing.

If denial of sexuality to women and the notion that there is something unfeminine about desire belong to a later period (on this whole subject see Laqueur (1990), and cf. Eccles (1982), pp. 32–4), the inception of more restrictive codes of decorum and propriety, especially in relation to sexual matters and the manners of polite society, can be detected in the later decades of the seventeenth century. Though clearly intended by its publisher, the entrepreneurial bookseller John Dunton, for an upper-class market, *The Ladies Dictionary* of 1694 sees no indecorousness in containing an entry on the clitoris, but its entry on *Conception* (15) does self-consciously defer to female sensibilities which are expected to blush at references to generation; and the entry cannot bring itself to mention the most obvious sign of conception, cessation of menstruation. Indeed, its designation of its readers as 'ladies', or the 'fair sex', signals the notion of sexual difference to which it now subscribes.

---

17 Robert Burton, *Anatomy of Melancholy* (1621–51), I.iii.2(4) [I.414–19]

Symptoms of Maids', Nuns' and Widows' Melancholy

. . . The causes are assigned out of Hippocrates . . . and those old *gynæciorum scriptores* [writers on gynaecology] . . . heart and brain offended with those vicious vapours which come from menstruous blood . . . the whole malady proceeds from that inflammation putridity, black smoky vapours, etc., from thence comes care, sorrow, and anxiety, obfuscation of spirits, agony, desperation and the like, which are intended or remitted, *si amatorius accesserit ardor* [if the passion of love is aroused], or any other violent object or perturbation of mind. This melancholy may happen to widows, with much care and sorrow, as frequently it doth, by reason of a sudden alteration of their accustomed course of life, &c., to such as lie in child-bed *ob suppressam purgationem* [because of a suppressed period], but to nuns and more ancient maids, and some barren women, for the causes above said, 'tis more familiar . . .

. . . The several cures of this infirmity, concerning diet, which must be very sparing, phlebotomy, physic, internal, external remedies, are at large in great variety . . . But the best and surest remedy of all, is to see them well placed and married to good husbands in due time; *hunc illæ lachrymæ* [hence those tears], that's the primary cause, and this the ready cure, to give them content in their desires. I write not this to patronize any wanton, idle flirt, lascivious or light housewives, which are too forward many times, unruly, and apt to cast away themselves on him that comes next, without all care, counsel, circumspection and judgement. If religion, good discipline, honest education, wholesome exhortation, fair promises, fame and loss of good name, cannot inhibit and deter such (which to chaste and sober maids cannot choose but avail much) labour and exercise, strict diet, rigour and threats may more opportunely be used, and are able of themselves to qualify and divert an ill-disposed temperament. For seldom should you see an hired servant, a poor handmaid, though ancient, that is kept hard to her work, and bodily labour, a course country wench troubled in this kind, but noble virgins, nice gentlewomen, such as are solitary and idle, live at ease, lead a life out of action and employment, that fare well in great houses and jovial companies, ill-disposed peradventure of themselves, and not willing to make any resistance, discontented otherwise, of weak judgment, able bodies and subject to passions . . . such for the most part are misaffected, and prone to this disease. I do not so much pity them that may otherwise be eased but those alone that out of a strong temperament, innate constitution, are violently carried away with this torrent of inward humours, and though very modest of themselves, sober, religious, virtuous and well given (as many so distressed maids are) yet cannot make resistance, these grievances will appear, this malady will take place, and now manifestly shows itself, and may not otherwise be helped . . .

. . . I . . . will . . . add a word or two *in gratiam virginum et viduarum* [on behalf of maids and widows], in favour of all such distressed parties, in commiseration of their present estate. And as I cannot choose but condole their mishap that labour of this infirmity, and are destitute of help in this case, so must I needs inveigh against them that are in fault, more than manifest causes, and as bitterly tax those tyrannizing pseudo-politicians, superstitious orders, rash vows, hard-hearted parents, guardians, unnatural friends, allies (call them how you will), those careless and stupid overseers, that out of worldly respects, covetousness, supine negligence, their own

36

private ends (*cum sibi sit interim bene* [being themselves comfortably situated in the meanwhile]) can so severely reject, stubbornly neglect, and impiously contemn, without all remorse and pity, the tears, sighs, groans, and grievous miseries of such poor souls committed to their charge. How odious and abominable are those superstitious and rash vows of Popish monasteries, so to bind and enforce men and women to vow virginity to lead a single life against the laws of Nature, opposite to religion, policy, and humanity, so to starve, to offer violence, to suppress the vigour of youth, by rigorous statutes, severe laws, vain persuasion, to debar them of that to which, by their innate temperature, they are so furiously inclined, urgently carried, and sometimes precipitated, even irresistibly led, to the prejudice of their souls' health, and good estate of body and mind . . . 'Better marry than burn' saith the Apostle [I Cor. vii.9], but they are otherwise persuaded . . . what fearful maladies, feral diseases, gross inconveniences come to both sexes by this enforced temperance, it troubles me to think of, much more to relate, those frequent abortions and murdering of infants in their nunneries . . . their notorious fornications, those *spintrias* [male prostitutes], *tribadas* [lesbians], *ambubaias* [immoral women], etc., those rapes, incests, adulteries, masauprations [masturbations], sodomies, buggeries of monks and friars . . .

18 John Milton, *Paradise Lost* (1667), IV.737–73

into their inmost bower
Handed they went; and eased the putting off
These troublesome disguises which we wear,
Straight side by side were laid, nor turned I ween
Adam from his fair spouse, nor Eve the rites
Mysterious of connubial love refused;
Whatever hypocrites austerely talk
Of purity and place and innocence,
Defaming as impure what God declares
Pure, and commands to some, leaves free to all.
Our maker bids increase, who bids abstain
But our destroyer, foe to God and man?
Hail wedded love, mysterious law, true source
In Paradise of all things common else.
By thee adulterous lust was driven from men
Among the bestial herds to range, by thee
Founded in reason, loyal, just, and pure,
Relations dear, and all the charities
Of father, son, and brother first were known.
Far be it, that I should write thee sin or blame,
Or think thee unbefitting holiest place,
Perpetual fountain of domestic sweets,

37

Whose bed is undefiled and chaste pronounced,
Present, or past, as saints and patriarchs used.
Here Love his golden shafts employs, here lights
His constant lamp, and waves his purple wings
Reigns here and revels; not in the bought smile
Of harlots, loveless, joyless, unendeared,
Casual fruition, nor in court amours
Mixed dance, or wanton mask, or midnight ball,
Or serenade, which the starved lover sings
To his proud fair, best quitted with disdain.
These lulled by nightingales embracing slept,
And on their naked limbs the flowery roof
Showered roses, which the morn repaired.

19 William Shakespeare, *Cymbeline* (written 1610–11?), II.v.1–35

Is there no way for men to be, but women
Must be half-workers? We are bastards all,
And that most venerable man which I
Did call my father was I know not where
When I was stamped. Some coiner with his tools
Made me a counterfeit; yet my mother seemed
The Dian of that time: so doth my wife
The nonpareil of this. O vengeance, vengeance!
Me of my lawful pleasure she restrained,
And prayed me oft forbearance; did it with
A pudency so rosy the sweet view on't
Might well have warmed old Saturn; that I thought her
As chaste as unsunned snow. O all the devils!
This yellow Giacomo in an hour – was't not? -
Or less – at first? Perchance he spoke not, but
Like a full-acorned boar, a German one,
Cried 'O!' and mounted; found no opposition
But what he looked for should oppose and she
Should from encounter guard. Could I find out
The woman's part in me – for there's no motion
That tends to vice in man but I affirm
It is the woman's part; be it lying, note it,
The woman's; flattering, hers; deceiving, hers;
Lust and rank thoughts, hers, hers; revenge, hers;
Ambitions, covetings, change of prides, disdain,
Nice longings, slanders, mutability,
All faults that man can name, nay, that hell knows,
Why, hers in part, or all, but rather all –

For even to vice
They are not constant, but are changing still
One vice but of a minute old for one
Not half so old as that. I'll write against them,
Detest them curse them, yet 'tis greater skill
In a true hate to pray they have their will.
The very devils cannot plague them better.

20 Richard Baxter, *A Christian Directory* (1673), I.viii.5 [III.103–4]

Directions against Fornication and all Uncleanness

. . . Besides Scripture, God hath planted in Nature a special pudor and modesty to restrain this sin: and they that commit it do violate the law of Nature, and sin against a witness and condemner that is within them . . . Nature hideth the obscene parts, and teacheth man to blush at the mention of any thing that is beyond the bounds of modesty. Say not that it is mere custom, for the vitiated nature of man is not so over precise, nor the villainy of the world so rare and modest, but before this day it had quite banished all restraints of this sin, above most others, if they could have done it, and if God had not written the law which condemneth it very deep in Nature, with almost indelible characters. So that in despite of the horrid wickedness of the earth, though mankind be almost universally inclined to lust, yet there be universal laws and customs restraining it; so that except a very few savages and cannibals like beasts, there is no nation on the earth where filthiness is not a shame, and modesty layeth not some rebukes upon uncleanness . . .

And God hath not put this law into man's nature without very great cause, albeit the implicit belief and submission due to him should satisfy us, though we knew not the causes particularly, yet much of them is notorious to common observation: as that if God had not restrained lust by laws, it would have made the female sex most contemptible and miserable, and used worse by men than dogs are. For, first, rapes and violences would deflower them, because they are too weak to make resistance; and if that had been restrained, yet the lust of men would have been unsatisfied, and most would have grown weary of the same woman whom they had abused, and taken another; at least, when she grew old they would choose a younger, and so the aged women would be the most calamitous creatures upon earth. Besides that lust is addicted to variety, and groweth weary of the same; the fallings out between men and women, and the sicknesses that make their persons less pleasing, and age, and other accidents, would expose them almost all to utter misery. And men would be the law-makers, and therefore would make no laws for their relief, but what consisted with their lusts and ends. So that half the world would have been ruined, had it not been for the laws of matrimony, and such other as restrain the lusts of men.

Also there would be a confused mixture in procreation, and no men would well know what children are their own: which is worse than not to know their lands or houses . . .

Hereby all natural affection would be diminished or extinguished: as the love of husband and wife, so the love between fathers and children would be diminished.

And consequently the due education of children would be hindered, or utterly overthrown. The mothers, that should first take care of them, would be disabled and turned away, that fresh harlots might be received, who would hate the offspring of the former. So that by this means the world and all societies, and civility would be ruined, and men would be made worse than brutes, whom Nature had either better taught, or else made for them some other supply. Learning, religion, and civility would be all in a manner extinct, as we see they are among those few savage cannibals that are under no restraint . . .

21 [T[homas] E[dgar] (ed.)], *The Lawes Resolutions of Womens Rights* (1632), pp. 375–80

Of Rape

She remaineth from henceforth a widow, giving herself to alms and deeds of charity, and of this good mind are many of our widows, which purpose constantly to live out the residue of their days in a devout remembrance of their dear husbands departed, to whom perhaps they made vows never to marry again after their deaths. But to what purpose is it for women to make vows, when men have so many millions of ways to make them break them? And when sweet words, fair promises, tempting, flattering, swearing, lying will not serve to beguile the poor soul, then with rough handling, violence, and plain strength of arms, they are, or have been heretofore, rather made prisoners to lust's thieves than wives and companions to faithful, honest lovers, so drunken are men with their own lusts, and the poison of Ovid's false precept,

Vim licet appellant, vis est ea grata puellis
[It is lawful to appeal to force; violence is by young women]
[*Ars amatoria*, i.673]

that if the rampier of laws were not betwixt women and their harms, I verily think none of them, being above twelve years of age and under an hundred, being either fair or rich, should be able to escape ravishing . . .

22 Montaigne, *The Essayes* (1603), III.v, pp. 512–17, 531, 537

Upon some Verses of Virgil [Aeneid, VIII.387–92, 404–6]

. . . women are not altogether in the wrong when they refuse the rules of life prescribed to the world, for so much as only men have established them without their consent. There is commonly brawling and contention between them and us. And the nearest consent we have with them, is but stormy and tumultuous. In the opinion of our author [Virgil], we herein use them but inconsiderately. After we have known that without comparison they are much more capable and violent in love's effects than we, as was testified by the ancient priest [Tiresias], who had been both man and woman, and tried the passions of both sexes:

> Venus huic erat utraque nota.
> Of both sorts he knew venery.
>   (Ovid, *Metamorphoses*, III.323)

And have moreover learned by their own mouth, what trial was made of it, though in divers ages, by an emperor [Proculus] and an empress [Messalina] of Rome, both skilful and famous masters in lawless lust and unruly wantonness. For he in one night deflowered ten Sarmatian virgins, that were his captives; but she really did in one night also answer five and twenty several assaults, changing her assailants as she found cause to supply her need, or suit her tastes,

> *adhuc ardens rigide tentigine vulve*
> *Et lassata viris, nondum satiata, recessit.*
> [still burning with a vagina hardened by lust she
> retired, exhausted by men, but not yet satisfied]
>   (Juvenal, *Satires*, VI.129–30)

. . . Now, after we have believed (say I) and preached thus much, we have for their particular portion allotted them [i.e. women] continency as their last and extreme penalty. There is no passion more importunate than this, which we would have them only to resist. Not simply as a vice in itself, but as abomination and execration, and more than irreligion and parricide; whilst we ourselves [i.e. men] without blame or reproach offend in it at our pleasure. Even those amongst us who have earnestly laboured to overcome lust have sufficiently vowed what difficulty, or rather, irresistible impossibility they found in it, using nevertheless material remedies to tame and weaken and cool the body. And we on the other side would have them [i.e. women] sound, healthy, strong, in good liking, well-fed and chaste together, that is to say, both hot and cold . . .

The gods (saith Plato) have furnished man with a disobedient, skittish and tyrannical member [i.e. the penis], which like an untamed, furious beast, attempteth by the violence of his appetite to bring all things under his beck. So have they allotted women another [i.e. the womb] as insulting, wild and fierce, in nature like a greedy, devouring and rebellious creature, who if when he craveth it, he be refused nourishment, as impatient of delay, it enrageth, and infusing that rage into their bodies, stoppeth their conduits, hindreth their respiration and causeth a thousand kinds of inconveniences

41

. . . peradventure it were a more chaste and commodiously fruitful use, betimes to give them [women] a knowledge and taste of the quick, than according to the liberty and heat of their fantasy, suffer them to guess and imagine the same. In lieu of true essential parts, they by desire surmise, and by hope substitute, others, three times as extravagant . . . What harm cause not those huge drafts or pictures [of penises], which wanton youths with chalk or coals draw in each passage, wall or stairs of our great houses? whence cruel contempt of our natural store is bred in them [women, when they see them in the flesh]. Who knoweth whether Plato ordaining amongst other well instituted commonwealths that men and women, old and young, should in their exercises or gymnastics present themselves naked one to the sight of another, aimed at that or no? The Indian women who daily without interdiction view their men all over, have at least wherewith to assuage and cool the sense of their seeing . . . In sum, we lure and every way flesh them; we incessantly inflame and excite their imagination; and then we cry out, *but oh, but oh, the belly*! Let us confess the truth: there are few amongst us that fear not more the shame they may have by their wives' offences than by their own vices; or that cares not more (oh wondrous charity!) for his wife's than his own conscience . . . Oh impious estimation of vices! Both we and they are capable of a thousand more hurtful and unnatural corruptions than is lust or lasciviousness. But we frame vices and weigh sins not according to their nature but according to our interest; whereby they take so many different unequal forms. The severity of our laws makes women's inclination to that vice more violent and faulty than its condition beareth and engageth it to worse proceedings than is their cause . . .

I wot not whether Caesar's exploits or Alexander's achievements exceed in hardiness the resolution of a beauteous young woman, trained after our manner, in the open view and uncontrolled conversation of the world, solicited and battered by so many contrary examples, exposed to a thousand assaults and continual pursuits, and yet still holding herself good and unvanquished. There is no point of doing more thorny, nor more active, than this of not doing. I find it easier to bear all one's life a cumbersome armour on his back, than a maidenhead. And the vow of virginity is the noblest of all vows, because it is the hardest. *Diaboli virtus in lumbris est*: 'the Devil's power is in the loins', saith Saint Jerome. Surely we have resigned the most difficult and vigorous devoir of mankind to women, and quit them the glory of it, which might stead them as a singular motive to opinionate themselves therein, and serve them as a worthy subject to brave us, and trample underfeet that vain pre-eminence of valour and virtue we pretend over them . . .

. . . We are in well nigh all things partial and corrupted judges of their [women's] actions, as no doubt they are of ours. I allow of truth as well when it hurts me, as when it helps me. It is a foul disorder that so often urgeth them unto change, and hinders them from settling their affection on any one subject, as we see in this goddess [Venus], to whom they impute so many changes and several friends. But withal, it is against the nature of love not to be violent and against the condition of violence to be constant. And those who wonder at it, exclaim against it, and in women search for the cause of this infirmity as incredible and unnatural, why see they not how often, without any amazement and exclaiming, themselves are possessed and infected with it? . . .

. . . To conclude this notable commentary, escaped from me by a flux of babbling . . . *I say, that both male and female are cast in one same mould; instruction and custom excepted, there is no great difference between them* . . . it is much more easy to accuse the one sex, than to excuse the other. It is that which some say proverbially, 'Ill may the kiln call the oven burnt tail'.

4

MIND AND SOUL

The commonly received opinion that woman's mental ability is inferior to man's derived partly from the force of Aristotelian tradition and humoral biology, and partly from theological tradition. Regarding her as an imperfect man the former expected her to be possessed of less able faculties. This is the starting point for Margaret Cavendish's apologia in 27. That woman was created second raised theological difficulties concerning the precise sense in which she was formed in the image of God rather than of man (see Paul in I Cor. xi.7, alluding to Gen. i.26–7). Her spiritual status could hence be regarded as problematic: in Eph. iv.13 the apparently exclusive 'man' (in the Vulgate Latin version, *vir*, man, not *homo*, human being) is used to designate a regenerate and perfected person (Maclean (1980), pp. 12–14). Consequently, 'problems were made, whether or no / Women had souls' (193). This issue is generally raised with witty or rhetorical rather than serious theological point, as it is by Donne (23), but in the English Midlands in 1647 the Quaker leader George Fox encountered it as a convinced opinion (24). Rationality was regarded as a property of the human soul; if woman's spiritual status is in any doubt, so must her mental be. John Winthrop's cautionary anecdote (25) is typically confident of the difference between the mental abilities of the sexes. Educated and intelligent women themselves internalized this ideological prejudice (26). This seems to be the case even with that remarkable and individualistic woman Margaret Cavendish, Duchess of Newcastle (for whom see Jones (1988); Todd (1989), pp. 55–68). The contrariness and tonal uncertainty of the extract from the preface to *The Worlds Olio* (27; discussed in Hobby (1988), pp. 190–1, 195–7) illustrate the tension which arises when an imaginative and impassioned female intelligence is wedded to political and social conservatism. The Duchess advances a 'feminist' argument to the effect that 'in Nature we have as clear an understanding as men', only to agree that 'there is great difference betwixt the masculine brain and the feminine' and to adduce an extended list of evidences of women's inferiority and incapacity.

Bathsua Makin's analysis is far steadier. Recognizing that the 'natural' is all too often culturally constructed to serve prevailing interest she explains women's mental incapacity as a consequence of educational neglect and social expectation rather than natural fact (28; cf. 190, 194, 195, 198). She was much influenced by the Utrecht scholar Anna Marie van Schurman, renowned throughout Europe for her learning (Wilson and Warnke (1989), pp. 164–70), whose *De ingenii muliebris* was Englished in 1659 as *The Learned Maid* (on Makin see Brink (1980), pp. 86–100; Wilson and Warnke (1989), pp. 286–93; Hobby (1988), pp. 198–203). Presented as an answer to the objections put in a friend's letter (which is prefaced) Makin's *Essay to Revive the Antient Education of Gentlewomen* conveniently summarizes contemporary prejudices against intellectual endeavour in women. Its adoption of a male persona may also illustrate their force (a woman's voice would carry no authority), though there is no firm supporting evidence that the *Essay* is indeed by Makin (Hobby (1988), p. 200). Remarkable and courageous though the *Essay* undoubtedly is, it is 'the modesty of the proposal' which is 'its central identifying feature' (ibid.). Though its collection of Classical, Biblical, mythical and historical precedents establishes that women do indeed have the mental capacity to learn, it promotes their education only in order that they may be better wives and mothers. There is no suggestion that women might pursue learning for its own sake or engage in such academic or political careers as were open to men. *The Ladies Dictionary* is similarly aware of patriarchal self-interest. Though it adopts the feminist arguments advanced in the last decade or two of the century (see chapter 17), their force is dissipated by the ingratiating and patronizing tone of its polite address to the 'fair sex' (29).

---

23 John Donne, *Paradoxes, Problemes, Essayes and Characters* (1652; written 1603–10), pp. 28–9

Problem vii:
Why Hath the Common Opinion Afforded Women Souls?

It is agreed that we have not so much from them as any part of either of our mortal souls of sense or growth; and we deny souls to others equal to them in all but speech, for which they are beholding only to their bodily instruments, for perchance an ape's heart or a goat's or a fox's or a serpent's would speak just so if it were in the breast and could move the tongue and jaws. Have they so many advantages and means to hurt us (for even their loving destroys us) that we dare not displease them, but give them what they will, and so, when some call them angels, some goddesses, and the Peputian heretics make them bishops, we descend so much with the stream to allow them souls? Or do we somewhat in this dignifying them, flatter princes and personages that are so much governed by them? Or do we, in that easiness and prodigality wherein we daily lose our own souls, allow souls to we care not whom, and so labour to persuade ourselves that sith a woman hath a soul, a soul is no great matter? Or do we but lend them souls, and that for use, since they for our sakes give their souls again, and their bodies to boot? Or perchance because the Devil, who doth most mischief, is all soul, for conveniency and proportion because they would come near him, we allow them some soul . . . only to make them capable of damnation?

24 George Fox, *The Journal* (dictated 1675), pp. 8–9

After this, I met with a sort of people that held women have no souls, adding in a light manner, no more than a goose. But I reproved them and told them that was not right, for Mary said, 'My soul doth magnify the Lord, and my spirit hath rejoiced in God my saviour' [Luke i.46–7].

25 John Winthrop, *Journal* (written 1630–49), I.140

13 April 1645: Mr. [Edward] Hopkins, the governor of Hartford upon Connecticut, came to Boston, and brought his wife with him (a godly young woman, and of special parts) who was fallen into a sad infirmity, the loss of her understanding and reason, which had been growing upon her divers years, by occasion of her giving herself wholly to reading and writing, and had written many books. Her husband, being very loving and tender of her, was loath to grieve her; but he saw his error, when it was too late. For if she had attended her household affairs, and such things as belong to women, and not gone out of her way and calling to meddle in such things as are proper for men, whose minds are stronger, etc., she had kept her wits, and might have improved them usefully and honourably in the place God had set her. He brought her to Boston, and left her with her brother, one Mr. Yale, a merchant, to try what means might be had here for her. But no help could be had.

26 Lucy Hutchinson, *Principles of the Christian Religion* (written 1640s?), pp. 5–6

. . . as our sex, through ignorance and weakness of judgement (which in the most knowing women is inferior to the masculine understanding of men), are apt to entertain fancies, and [be] pertinacious in them, so we ought to watch ourselves, in such a day as this, and to embrace nothing rashly; but as our own imbecility is made known to us, to take heed of presumption in ourselves, and to lean by faith upon the strength of the Lord.

27 Margaret Cavendish, *The Worlds Olio* (1655), preface to the reader, sigs A4–A5v

It cannot be expected I should write so wisely or wittily as men, being of the effeminate sex, whose brains Nature hath mixed with the coldest and softest elements. And to give my reason why we cannot be so wise as men, I take leave and ask pardon of my own sex, and present my reasons to the judgement of truth. But I believe all of my own sex will be against me out of partiality to themselves, and all men seem to be against me out of a compliment to women or at least for quiet and ease' sake, who know women's tongues are like stings of bees, and what man would endure our effeminate monarchy to swarm about their ears, for certainly he would be stung to death? So I shall be condemned of all sides, but truth, who helps to defend me. True it is our sex make great complaint that men from their first creation usurped a supremacy to themselves, although we were created equal by Nature, which tyrannical government they have kept ever since, so that we could never come to be free, but rather more and more enslaved, using us either like children, fools, or subjects, that is, to flatter or threaten us, to allure or force us to obey, and will not let us divide the world equally with them, as to govern and command, to direct and dispose as they do; which slavery hath so dejected our spirits as we are become so stupid that beasts are but a degree below us, and men use us but a degree above beasts, whereas in Nature we have as clear an understanding as men, if we were bred in schools to mature our brains, and to manure our understanding that we might bring forth the fruits of knowledge. But to speak truth, men have great reason not to let us into their government, for there is great difference betwixt the masculine brain and the feminine, the masculine strength and the feminine. For could we choose out of the world two of the ablest brained and strongest body of each sex, there would be great difference in the understanding and strength, for Nature hath made man's body more able to endure labour, and man's brain more clear to understand and contrive than woman's; and as great a difference there is between them, as there is between the longest and strongest willow compared to the strongest and largest oak. Though they are both trees, yet the willow is but a yielding vegetable, not fit nor proper to build houses and ships, as the oak . . . or men and women may be compared to the blackbirds, where the hen can never sing with so strong and loud a voice, nor so clear and perfect notes, as the cock. Her breast is not made with that strength to strain so high. Even so, women can never have so strong judgment nor clear understanding nor so perfect rhetoric, to speak orations with that eloquence, as to persuade so forcibly, to command so powerfully, to entice so subtly, and to insinuate so gently and softly into the souls of men. Or they may be compared to the sun and moon, according to the description in the Holy Writ, which saith, God made two great lights, the one to rule the day, the other the night [Gen. i.4–5]; so man is made to govern commonwealths, and women their private families . . . And if it be as philosophers hold, that the moon hath no light but what it borrows from the sun, so women have no strength nor light of understanding, but what is given them from men. This is the reason we are not great mathematicians, arithmeticians, logicians, geometricians, cosmographers . . . this is the reason we are not skilful soldiers, political statists, dispatchful secretaries or conquering Caesars; but our government would be weak, had we not masculine spirits and counsellors to advise us . . . neither would there be such commerce of nations as there is, nor would there be so much gold and silver and other minerals fetched out of the bowels of the earth if there were none but effeminate hands to use the pickaxe and spade, nor so many cities built if there were none but women labourers to cut out great quares of stone . . . neither would there be such steeples and pyramids, as there have been in this world if there were no other than our tender feet to climb, nor could our brains endure the height, we should soon grow dizzy and fall down drunk with too much thin air . . . It is true education and custom may add something to harden us, yet never make us so strong as the strongest of men, whose sinews are tougher, and bones stronger, and joints closer and flesh firmer, than ours are, as all ages have shown. What woman was ever so strong as Samson, or so swift as Hazael [*recte* Jehu: see II Kgs. ix.20]? Neither have women such tempered brains as men, such high imaginations, such subtle conceptions, such fine inventions, such solid reasons, and such sound judgment, such prudent forecast, such constant resolution, such quick sharp and ready flowing wits. What woman ever made such laws as Moses, Lycurgus, or Solon did? . . . It was not a woman that invented the perspective glasses to pierce into the moon . . . Wherefore women can have no excuse, or complaints of being subject, as a hindrance from thinking, for thoughts are free, those can never be enslaved, for we are not hindered from studying, since we are allowed so much idle time that we know not how to pass it away, but may as well read in our closets, as men in their colleges. And contemplation is as free to us as to men to beget clear speculation. Besides, most scholars marry and their heads are so full of their school lectures, that they preach them over to their wives when they come home, so that they know as well what was spoke, as if they had been there. And though most of our sex are bred up to the needle and spindle, yet some are bred in the public theatres of the world, wherefore if Nature had made our brains of that same temper as men's, we should have had as clear speculation, and have been as ingenious and inventive as men, but we find she hath not, by the effects. And that we may see by the weakness of our actions, the constitution of our bodies, and by our knowledge, the temper of our brains, by our unsettled resolutions, inconstant to our promises, the perverseness of our wills, by our facile natures, violent in our passions, superstitious in our devotions. You may know our humours: we have more wit than judgment, [we are] more active than industrious, we have more courage than conduct, more will than strength, more curiosity than secrecy, more vanity than good housewifery, more complaints than pains, more jealousy than love, more tears than sorrow, more stupidity than patience, more pride than affability, more beauty than constancy, more ill nature than good. Besides, the education and liberty of conversation which men have, is both unfit and dangerous to our sex, knowing that we may bear and bring forth branches from a wrong stock, by which every man would come to lose the property of their own children. But Nature, out of love to the generation of men, hath made women to be governed by men, giving them strength to rule, and power to use their authority. And though it seem to be natural that generally all women are weaker than men, both in body and understanding, and that the wisest woman is not so wise as the wisest of men, wherefore not so fit to rule, yet some are far wiser than some men . . . women by education may come to be far more knowing and learned than some rustic and rude bred men. Besides, it is to be observed that Nature hath degrees in all her mixtures and temperaments . . . Again, it is to be observed that although Nature hath not made women so strong of body and so clear of understanding as the ablest of men, yet she hath made them fairer, softer, slenderer, and more delicate than they, separating as it were the finer parts from the grosser, which seems as if Nature had made women as purer white manchet [fine wheat bread] for her own table and palate, where men are like coarse household bread which the servants feed on. And if she hath not tempered women's brains to that height of understanding, nor hath put in such strong species of imaginations, yet she hath mixed them with sugar of sweet conceits. And if she hath not planted in their dispositions such firm resolutions, yet she hath sowed gentle and willing obedience, and though she hath not filled the mind with such heroic gallantry, yet she hath laid in tender affections, as love, piety, charity, clemency, patience, humility, and the like, which makes them nearest to resemble angels, which are the perfectest of all her works, where men by their ambitions, extortion, fury and cruelty, resemble to the Devil. But some women are like devils too, when they are possessed with those evils; and the best of men by their heroic, magnanimous minds, by their ingenious and inventive wits, by their strong judgments, by their prudent and wise management, are like to gods.

28 [Bathsua Makin], *Essay to Revive the Antient Education of Gentlewomen* (1673), pp. 3–7, 22–3, 29, 31–2

[Dedicatory Epistle] To All Ingenious and Virtuous Ladies . . .

Custom, when it is inveterate, hath a mighty influence: it hath the force of Nature itself. The barbarous custom to breed women low is grown general amongst us, and hath prevailed so far, that it is verily believed (especially amongst a sort of debauched sots) that women are not endued with such reason as men, nor capable of that improvement by education as they are. It is looked upon as a monstrous thing to pretend to the contrary. A learned woman is thought to be a comet, that bodes mischief whenever it appears. To offer to the world the liberal education of women is to deface the image of God in Man, it will make women so high and men so low; like fire in the housetop it will set the whole world in a flame.

. . . I verily think women were formerly educated in the knowledge of arts and tongues, and by their education many did rise to a great height in learning. Were women thus educated now, I am confident the advantage would be very great. The women would have honour and pleasure, their relations profit, and the whole nation advantage . . .

Were a competent number of schools erected to educate ladies ingenuously, methinks I see how ashamed men would be of their ignorance, and how industrious the next generation would be to wipe off their reproach.

I expect to meet with many scoffs and taunts from inconsiderate and illiterate men, that prize their own lusts and pleasure more than your profit and content. I shall be the less concerned at these so long as I am in your favour, and this discourse may be a weapon in your hands to defend your selves, whilst you endeavour to polish your souls, that you may glorify God and answer to the end of your creation, to be meet helps to your husbands. Let not your ladyships be offended that I do not (as some have wittily done) plead for female pre-eminence. To ask too much is the way to be denied all. God hath made Man the head. If you be educated and instructed as I propose, I am sure you will acknowledge it, and be satisfied that you are helps, that your husbands do consult and advise with you (which, if you be wise, they will be glad of) and that your husbands have the casting voice, in whose determinations you will acquiesce . . .

[Prefatory Epistle] To the Reader

. . . If this way of educating ladies should (as it's like it never will) be generally practised, the greatest hurt that I foresee can ensue is, to put your sons upon greater diligence to advance themselves in arts and languages, that they may be superior to women in parts as well as in place. That is the great thing I design. I am a man myself, that would not suggest a thing prejudicial to our sex. To propose women rivals with us in learning will make us court Minerva more heartily, lest they should be more in her favour . . . It is an easy matter to quibble and droll upon a subject of this nature, to scoff at women kept ignorant on purpose to make slaves. This savours not at all of a manly spirit, to trample upon those that are down. I forbid scoffing and scolding. Let any think themselves aggrieved, and come forth fairly into the field against this feeble sex with solid arguments to refute what I have asserted, I think I may promise to be their champion.

These for My Much Honoured and Worthy Friend [the Author]

Sir,

I have heard you discourse of the education of gentlewomen in arts and tongues. I wonder any should think of so vain a thing.

Women do not much desire knowledge. They are of low parts, fickle natures, they have other things to do [which] they will not mind if they be once bookish. The end of learning is to fit one for public employment, which women are not capable of.

Women must not speak in the church [I Cor. xiv.34–5; I Tim. ii.11–12], it is against custom. Solomon's good housewife is not commended for arts and tongues but for looking after her servants [Prov. xxxi.10–31]. And that which is worst of all, they are of such ill natures, they will abuse their education and be so intolerably proud there will be no living with them. If all these things could be answered, they would not have leisure.

We send our sons to school seven years, and yet not above one in five gets so much of the tongues only so as to keep them, and nothing of the arts.

Girls cannot have more than half the time allotted them. If they were capable, and had time, I cannot imagine what good it would do them. If it would do them good, where should they be instructed? Their converse with boys would do them more hurt than all their learning would do them good.

I have no prejudice against the sex but would gladly have a fair answer to these things, or else shall breed up my daughter as our forefathers did.

Sir, your condescension herein will very much oblige,

Your affectionate friend,

29 May 1673

[From the Author's Essay in Reply]

. . . great is the force of the first tincture anything takes, whether good or bad, as plants in gardens excel those that grow wild, or brutes by due management . . . are much altered. So men, by liberal education, are much bettered as to intellectuals and morals. All conclude great care ought to be taken for the males; but your doubt in your letter is concerning the females. I think the greater care ought to be taken of them because evil seems to be begun here, as in Eve [Gen. iii.1–6], and to be propagated by her daughters. When the sons of God took unto themselves the daughters of men, wickedness multiplied apace [Gen. vi.1–7]. It was the cursed counsel of Balaam to debauch Israel by Balak's idolatrous women [Num. xxv.1–2]. Wretched Jezebel excited Ahab to greater wickedness than he could ever have thought of [I Kgs. xvi.31–3, xxi]. God gave strict commands to the Israelites not to marry heathenish women. When Solomon himself (the wisest of men) did this, they soon drew his heart from God [I Kgs. xi.1–6]. Bad women, weak to make resistance, are strong to tempt to evil. Therefore without all doubt great care ought to be taken, timely to season them with piety and virtue . . .

. . . I do not deny but women ought to be brought up to a comely and decent carriage, to their needles, to neatness, to understand all those things that do particularly belong to their sex. But when these things are competently cared for, and where there are endowments of Nature and leisure, then higher things ought to be endeavoured after. Merely to teach gentlewomen to frisk and dance, to paint their faces, to curl their hair, to put on a whisk, to wear gay clothes, is not truly to adorn but to adulterate their bodies; yea (what is worse), to defile their souls. This (like Circe's cup) turns them to beasts; whilst their belly is their god, they become swine; whilst lust, they become goats; and whilst pride is their god, they become very devils. Doubtless this under-breeding of women began amongst heathen and barbarous people. It continues with the Indians, where they make their women mere slaves, and wear them out in drudgery. It is practised amongst degenerate and apostate Christians, upon the same score, and now is a part of their religion . . .

Had God intended women only as a finer sort of cattle, he would not have made them reasonable. Brutes, a few degrees higher than drills or monkeys (which the Indians use to do many offices) might have better fitted some men's lust, pride and pleasure, especially those that desire to keep them ignorant to be tyrannized over . . .

My intention is not to equalize women to men, much less to make them superior. They are the weaker sex, yet capable of impressions of great things, something like to the best of men . . .

. . . women are not such silly, giddy creatures as many proud, ignorant men would make them, as if they were incapable of all improvement by learning and unable to digest arts that require any solidity of judgement. Many men will tell you they are so unstable and inconstant, borne down upon all occasions with such a torrent of fear, love, hatred, lust, pride, and all manner of exorbitant passions, that they are uncapable to practise any virtues that require greatness of spirit, or firmness of resolution. Let such but look into history, they will find examples enough of illustrious women to confute them . . .

If there be any persons so vain, and are yet pleased with this apish kind of breeding now in use, that desire their daughters should be outwardly dressed like puppets rather than inwardly adorned with knowledge, let them enjoy their humour; but never wonder if such marmosets married to buffoons bring forth and breed up a generation of baboons, that have little more wit than apes and hobby-horses. I cannot say enough against this barbarous rudeness, to suffer one part – I had almost said the better part – of ourselves to degenerate (as far as possible) into brutality.

29 [N.H.], *The Ladies Dictionary* (1694), pp. 18–20

Ability, in some women, why extraordinary: although Man, from the dominion given him in Paradise, may style himself superior and boast of his wonderful abilities, looking on those in women much inferior, yet let us mind him that he frequently runs into mistakes. For, though the strength of body may be different, by reason that of the fair sex is soft and pliable, made for pleasure and charming attraction more than robust actions and suffering hardship, yet we conclude that either souls, proceeding from the same fountain of life, can admit of no difference, or distinction . . . Therefore those that object that the difference is in the organs of the body where the soul actuates in the several faculties may here be mistaken . . . nor can the reasons they would fain seem to draw from the coldness of the woman's constitution be allowed in this case to hinder them from vigour, activity, acuteness, and solid judgement, since experience shows us the contrary . . .

We . . . therefore must be apt to think that men, having gotten the upper hand and engrossed the power, will, right or wrong, have women to be no wiser than they will have them to be and then to be sure they will not allow them to be so wise as themselves . . . We must allow it is in men to endeavour as much as in them lies to keep the fair sex in ignorance that they may reign the more securely without control, and to effect it, possess them, if possible, with a belief of their own incapacity . . . Thus the Turk keeps learning from his subjects that in ignorance they may bear their chains with more content.

5

BEAUTY

'Many have been deceived by the beauty of a woman' (Ecclus. ix.8). The dangers to man of the physical allurements of woman are much canvassed in Old Testament texts. Her beauty arouses lust in the unwary, her enticements lead to shameful incontinence (e.g. Prov. vi.24–6; Ecclus. xxv.17–36). Something of this suspicion of women's bodily beauty continues in the Protestant tradition; on one view, it was his susceptibility to her physical attractiveness which led Adam to follow Eve into sin. So Milton's Adam confesses to the disorientating effect which Eve's beauty has upon him (30), but his regard for Eve owes something also to another, and contrary, tradition: the Neoplatonic vein in seventeenth-century culture. The thought of the fifteenth-century mystical philosopher Marsiglio Ficino was brought to England by early sixteenth-century Humanist scholars. Hence derived a collection of associated ideas which became commonplaces of courtly culture: that love is moved by beauty; that earthly beauty betokens the good and the true and so is a reflection of the divine; that to enjoy and respond to beauty – including woman's beauty – is to respond to an image of the divine and is thus a means to ascend beyond the physical (and sexual) to spiritual bliss. Beauty – of person, manners and dress – hence came to be held in extraordinarily high regard and to enjoy an almost mystical significance. The beauty of a woman is credited with exerting an irresistible and disabling power (31).

These notions received their most influential formulation into a code of behaviour in Baldassare Castiglione's *Il Libro del Cortegiano* (1528), Englished in 1561 by Sir Thomas Hoby as *The Book of the Courtier*. The central contention of this courtly conduct book was that 'no Court, how great soever it be, can have any sightliness or brightness in it, or mirth without women, nor any courtier can be gracious, pleasant or hardy, nor at any time undertake any gallant enterprise of chivalry, unless he be stirred with the conversation and with the love and contentation of women' (for a summary account of Castiglione and his influence see Kelso (1956), pp. 136–224, and the essay 'Did Women have a Renaissance?' in Kelly (1984), pp. 19–50; see also Cropper (1986) and Turner (1993), index). This convention that esteem for women and responsiveness to female beauty were the inspiration of all admirable masculine acts continued to shape courtly and upper-class manners at the Stuart court (Potter (1989), p. 79).

The extract from Burton illustrates that Neoplatonic commonplaces continue to be current in our period (31). Though often ironized and problematized, they inform the lyrical poetry produced by courtier poets, just as the antecedent code of *l'amour courtois* (for which see O'Donoghue (1982)) had shaped Medieval love poetry. The woman's beauty invests her with divine or angelic status which disables the male lover as Milton's Adam was disturbed by Eve. It enchants irresistibly (32). As she is beautiful, so she is of necessity pure, her physical self an image of her inner state (33). It is for this reason that praise of women in this period, whether in a courtly or other context, can rarely avoid crediting them with beauty, for beauty is evidence of goodness. The woman's beauty consequently persuades male love poets that her goodness should prompt the exercise of other 'virtues', mercy, or pity, for the poet conspicuous among them (33, 34; see further chapter 13).

The age rarely forgot the charnel house, adducing the inevitable decay of physical beauty to often gruesomely mortifying purpose, especially earlier in the century; ugliness was conjured to the same moralistic ends (35). Praise of an ugly woman was only possible as parody of received conventions, underlining the equally rhetorical status of such a catalogue of grotesqueries as Suckling's (36) and a blazon such as Herrick's (37). This manipulative contrivance is most evident in the tendency of the male gazer to objectify his ostensible subject. The woman is frequently transmuted into an analogical equivalent, broken down into her constituent parts, or minutely scrutinized. The ingenuity of the poet's invention (38) counts for more than complete portraiture. Women as persons are, in fact, curiously absent from a poetry apparently obsessed with them. And the particularity of its gaze can all too easily become voyeuristic (39) and brutalizing in its desire to undress, grasp and penetrate (see further chapter 13). Suckling recognizes this sexual motivation in a nice parody of Neoplatonic raptures (40). His poem foregrounds the rhetorical construction of the subject; both male poets in the dialogue are observing and speaking of the same (silent) woman. Such disregard for the authentic female self is characteristic of metaphysical poetry which self-reflexively and playfully delights in its dexterous linguistic fashioning of versions of woman. There is no more poised or finer example of the exercise of this male prerogative than the selection of images of woman assembled in Marvell's 'The Gallery' (41).

55

30 John Milton, *Paradise Lost* (1667), VIII.460–78, 521–59

Mine eyes he closed, but open left the cell
Of fancy my internal sight, by which
Abstract as in a trance methought I saw,
Though sleeping, where I lay, and saw the shape
Still glorious before whom awake I stood,
Who stooping opened my left side, and took
From thence a rib, with cordial spirits warm,
And life-blood streaming fresh; wide was the wound
But suddenly with flesh filled up and healed:
The rib he formed and fashioned with his hands;
Under his forming hands a creature grew,
Manlike, but different sex, so lovely fair,
That what seemed fair in all the world, seemed now
Mean, or in her summed up, in her contained
And in her looks, which from that time infused
Sweetness into my heart, unfelt before,
And into all things from her air inspired
The spirit of love and amorous delight . . .
Thus have I told thee all my state, and brought
My story to the sum of earthly bliss
Which I enjoy, and must confess to find
In all things else delight indeed, but such
As used or not, works in the mind no change,
Nor vehement desire, these delicacies
I mean of taste, sight, smell, herbs, fruits, and flowers,
Walks, and the melody of birds; but here
Far otherwise, transported I behold,
Transported touch; here passion first I felt,
Commotion strange, in all enjoyments else
Superior and unmoved, here only weak
Against the charm of beauty's powerful glance.
Or nature failed in me, and left some part
Not proof enough such object to sustain,
Or from my side subducting, took perhaps
More than enough; at least on her bestowed
Too much of ornament, in outward show
Elaborate, of inward less exact.
For well I understand in the prime end
Of nature here the inferior, in the mind
And inward faculties, which most excel,
In outward also her resembling less
His image who made both, and less expressing

56

The character of that dominion given
O'er other creatures; yet when I approach
Her loveliness, so absolute she seems
And in her self complete, so well to know
Her own, that what she wills to do or say
Seems wisest, virtuousest, discreetest, best;
All higher knowledge in her presence falls
Degraded, wisdom in discourse with her
Looses discountenanced, and like folly shows;
Authority and reason on her wait,
As one intended first, not after made
Occasionally; and to consummate all,
Greatness of mind and nobleness their seat
Build in her loveliest, and create an awe
About her, as a guard angelic placed.

31 Robert Burton, *Anatomy of Melancholy* (1621–51, III.ii.2(2) [III.65–87]

Other Causes of Love-Melancholy, Sight, Beauty, from the Face, Eyes, Other Parts, and How it Pierceth

The most familiar and usual cause of love is that which comes by sight, which conveys those admirable rays of beauty and pleasing graces to the heart. Plotinus derives love from sight . . . *Si nescis, oculi sunt in amore duces*, the eyes are the harbingers of love, and the first step of love is sight . . . This amazing, confounding, admirable, amiable beauty, 'than which in all Nature's treasure' (saith Isocrates) 'there is nothing so majestical and sacred, nothing so divine, lovely, precious', 'tis Nature's crown, gold and glory . . . we contemn and abhor generally such things as are foul and ugly to behold, account them filthy, but love and covet that which is fair. 'Tis beauty in all things which pleaseth and allureth us . . . a goddess beauty is, whom the very gods adore . . . Beauty is a dower of itself, a sufficient patrimony, an ample commendation, an accurate epistle . . . young men will adore and honour beauty; nay kings themselves I say will do it, and voluntarily submit their sovereignty to a lovely woman. 'Wine is strong, kings are strong, but a woman strongest' (I Esdras iii.10) . . . When they have got gold and silver, [kings] submit all to a beautiful woman, give themselves wholly to her, gape and gaze on her, and all men desire her more than gold or silver, or any precious thing. They will leave father and mother, and venture their lives for her, labour and travel to get, and bring all their gains to women, steal, fight, and spoil for their mistress' sakes. And no king so strong, but a fair woman is stronger than he is . . .

If you desire to know more particularly what this beauty is, how it doth *influere* [influence], how it doth fascinate (for, as all hold, love is a fascination), thus in brief: 'This comeliness or beauty ariseth from the due proportion of the whole, or from each several part' . . . as Seneca saith, *Ep*. xxxiii, *lib*. IV . . . 'She is no fair woman, whose arm, thigh, etc., are commended, except the face and all the other parts be correspondent'. And the face especially gives a lustre to the rest. The face is it that commonly denominates fair or foul; *arx formæ facies*, the face is beauty's tower; and though the other parts be deformed, yet a good face carries it . . .

Although for the greater part this beauty be most eminent in the face, yet many times those other members yield a most pleasing grace, and are alone sufficient to enamour. An high brow like unto the bright heavens . . . white and smooth like the polished alabaster, a pair of cheeks of vermilion colour, in which love lodgeth . . . a coral lip . . . A white round neck, that *via lactea* [milky way]; dimple in the chin, black eyebrows, *Cupidinis arcus* [Cupid's bow], sweet breath, white and even teeth; [that] which some call the sale-piece, a fine soft round pap, gives an excellent grace . . . and makes a pleasant valley, *lacteum sinum*, between two chalky hills . . .

A flaxen hair: golden hair was ever in great account . . .

A little soft hand, pretty little mouth, small, fine, long fingers . . . a straight and slender body, a small foot, and well-proportioned leg hath an excellent lustre . . . a soft and white skin, etc. have their peculiar graces . . .

Not one in a thousand falls in love, but there is some peculiar part or other which pleaseth most, and inflames him above the rest. A company of young philosophers on a time fell at variance, which part of a woman was most desirable and pleased best? Some said the forehead, some the teeth, some the eyes, cheeks, lips, neck, chin, etc. The controversy was referred to Lais of Corinth to decide; but she, smiling, said they were a company of fools; for suppose they had her where they wished, what would they first seek? . . .

Now, last of all, I will show you by what means beauty doth fascinate, bewitch, as some hold, and work upon the soul of a man by the eye . . . Heliodorus, *lib*. III, proves at large that love is witchcraft . . . The rays, as some think, sent from the eyes, carry certain spiritual vapours with them, and so infect the other party, and that in a moment. I know they that hold *visio fit intra mittendo* [sight comes from receiving the images] will make a doubt of this, but Ficinus proves it . . . But how comes it to pass, then, that a blind man loves, that never saw? We read, in the Lives of the Fathers, a story of a child that was brought up in the wilderness, from his infancy, by an old hermit. Now come to man's estate, he saw by chance two comely women wandering in the woods. He asked the old man, what creatures they were; he told him, fairies. After a while, talking *obiter* [casually], the hermit demanded of him, which was the pleasantest sight that ever he saw in his life? He readily replied, the two fairies he spied in the wilderness. So that, without doubt, there is some secret loadstone in a beautiful woman, a magnetic power, a natural inbred affection, which moves our concupiscence . . .

32 Richard Lovelace, *Lucasta* (1649), pp. 25–6

Gratiana Dancing and Singing

I

See! with what constant motion
Even, and glorious, as the sun,
   Gratiana steers that noble frame,
Soft as her breast, sweet as her voice
That gave each winding law and poise,
   And swifter than the wings of fame.

II

She beat the happy pavement
By such a star made firmament,
   Which now no more the roof envies;
But swells up high with Atlas ev'n,
Bearing the brighter, nobler heav'n,
   And in her, all the deities.

III

Each step trod out a lover's thought
And the ambitious hopes he brought,
   Chain'd to her brave feet with such arts,
Such sweet command, and gentle awe,
As when she ceas'd, we sighing saw
   The floor lay pav'd with broken hearts.

IV

So did she move; so did she sing
Like the harmonious spheres that bring
   Unto their rounds their music's aid;
Which she performed such a way,
As all th'enamour'd world will say
   The Graces danced, and Apollo play'd.

33 Abraham Cowley, *The Works* (1688), pp. 77–8

Clad All in White

1

Fairest thing that shines below,
Why in this robe dost thou appear?
Wouldst thou a white most perfect show,
Thou must at all no garment wear:
Thou wilt seem much whiter so,
Than winter when 'tis clad with snow.

59

2

'Tis not the linen shows so fair:
Her skin shines through, and makes it bright;
So clouds themselves like suns appear,
When the sun pierces them with light:
So lilies in a glass enclose,
The glass will seem as white as those.

3

Thou now one heap of beauty art,
Nought outward, or within is foul:
Condensed beams make every part;
Thy body's clothed like thy soul.
Thy soul, which does itself display,
Like a star plac'd i'th'Milky Way.

4

Such robes the saints departed wear,
Woven all with light divine;
Such their exalted bodies are,
And with such full glory shine.
But they regard not mortals' pain;
Men pray, I fear, to both in vain.

5

Yet seeing thee so gently pure,
My hopes will needs continue still;
Thou wouldst not take this garment sure,
When thou hadst an intent to kill.
Of peace and yielding who would doubt,
When the white flag he sees hung out?

34 Thomas Campion, *The Third and Fourth Booke of Ayres* [1617], pp. 182–3

Are you, what your fair looks express?
      O then be kind:
From law of Nature they digress
      Whose form suits not their mind:
   Fairness seen in th'outward shape,
   Is but th'inward beauty's ape.

Eyes that of earth are mortal made,
      What can they view?
All's but a colour or a shade,
      And neither always true.

Reason's sight, that is etern,
Ev'n the substance can discern.

Soul is the Man; for who will so
    The body name?
And to that power all grace we owe
    That decks our living frame.
What, or how had houses been,
    But for them that dwell therein?

Love in the bosom is begot,
    Not in the eyes;
No beauty makes the eye more hot,
    Her flames the spright surprise:
Let our loving minds then meet,
For pure meetings are most sweet.

35 Thomas Heywood, *Gynækeion* (1624), pp. 164–5

I wish you all to strive that the beauty of your minds may still exceed that of your bodies, because the first apprehends a noble divinity, the last is subject to all frailty. And as the higher powers have bestowed on you fairness above man, to equal that excellency of judgement and wisdom in which man claims justly a priority before you, so it is both behoveful and becoming your sex, that your outward perfections should altogether aim at the inward pulchritude of the mind, since the first is accidental and casual, the last stable and permanent. Besides, if beauty be once branded with impudence or unchastity, it makes that which in itself is both laudable and desired, rejected and altogether despised. For virtue once violated brings infamy and dishonour, not only to the person offending, but contaminates the whole progeny, nay, more, looks back even to the ancestors, be they never so noble: for the mind, as the body, in the act of adultery being both corrupted, makes the action infamous and dishonourable, dispersing the poison of the sin even amongst those from whom she derives her birth; as if with her earthly being they had given her therewith her corruptions, and the first occasion of this her infamy. It extends likewise to the posterity which shall arise from so corrupt a seed, generated from unlawful and adulterate copulation. How chary then ought a fair woman to be, to strengthen her bodily beauty with that of the mind? Of what small continuance it is, and how Nature hath disposed of your age, you should consider: the beauty of your cradle you cannot apprehend, nor of your childhood, and therefore in it you can neither take pride nor delight, or if you could, it is not yet perfect. When you grow ripe for marriage, and that it begins to attract you suitors and servants, it grows to bud, and is then commonly in the blossom, when you have made choice of a husband; as you begin to be the fruitful mother of children, so one by one the leaves fade and fall away. Alas, how swiftly doth age with wrinkles steal upon you, and then where is that admiration it before attracted? Neither is that small season free from the blastings of disease and canker worms of sickness, able to make the fairest amongst you to look aged in her youth. Then may you, the choices of you, with beautiful Laïs, who when she saw the lilies in her brow faded, and the roses in her cheeks withered, the diamonds in her eyes lose their lustre, and the rubies in her lips their colour (as being now grown in years), in these words give up your looking-glasses back to Venus:

> Nunc mihi nullus in hoc usus, quia cernere talem
>   Qualis sum, nolo, qualis eram, nequeo.

> Now there's no use of thee at all,
>   Because I have no will
> To see what I am now, and what
>   I was, I cannot still.

If then this rare ornament be of such small permanence even in the best, how much then is it to be underprized when it is contaminated and spotted with lust and unlawful prostitution? Since it is a maxim that things common are so far from begetting appetite and affection, that they rather engender the seeds of contempt and hatred; for how should anything festered and corrupt please the eye? or that which is rotten and unsound give content unto the palate?

36 Sir John Suckling, *The Last Remains* (1659), pp. 59–60

The Deformed Mistress

I know there are some fools that care
Not for the body, so the face be fair;
Some others, too, that in a female creature
Respect not beauty, but a comely feature;
And others, too, that for those parts in sight
Care not so much, so that the rest be right.
Each man his humour hath, and, faith, 'tis mine
To love that woman which I now define.
First I would have her wainscot foot and hand
More wrinkled far than any pleated band,
That in those furrows, if I'd take the pains,
I might both sow and reap all sorts of grains:
Her nose I'd have a foot long, not above,
With pimples embroider'd, for those I love;
And at the end a comely pearl of snot,
Considering whether it should fall or not:

Provided, next, that half her teeth be out,
Nor do I care much if her pretty snout
Meet with her furrow'd chin, and both together
Hem in her lips, as dry as good whit-leather:
One wall-eye she shall have, for that's a sign
In other beasts the best: why not in mine?
Her neck I'll have to be pure jet at least,
With yellow spots enamell'd; and her breast,
Like grasshopper's wing, both thin and lean,
Not to be touch'd for dirt, unless swept clean:
As for her belly, 'tis no matter, so
There be a belly, and ——
Yet, if you will, let it be something high,
And always let there be a tympany.
But soft! where am I now? here I should stride,
Lest I fall in, the place must be so wide,
And pass unto her thighs, which shall be just
Like to an ant's that's scraping in the dust:
Into her legs I'd have love's issues fall,
And all her calf into a gouty small:
Her feet both thick and eagle-like display'd,
The symptoms of a comely, handsome maid.
As for her parts behind, I ask no more:
If they but answer those that are before,
I have my utmost wish; and, having so,
Judge whether I am happy, yea or no.

37 Robert Herrick, manuscript draft associated with *Hesperides* (1648), pp. 404–6

The Description: Of a Woman

Whose head befringed with bescattered tresses
Seems like Apollo's when the morn he blesses
Or like unto Aurora when she sets
Her long, dishevel'd, rose-crown'd trammelets.
Her forehead smooth, full polished, bright and high
Bears in itself a graceful majesty,
Under the which two crawling eyebrows twine,
Like to the tendrils of a flatt'ring vine
Under whose shades two starry sparkling eyes
Are beautifi'd with fair fring'd canopies.
Her comely nose with uniformal grace
Like purest white stands in the middle place,

Parting the pair, as we may well suppose,
Each cheek resembling still a damask rose
Which like a garden manifestly show
How roses, lilies and carnations grow,
Which sweetly mixed both with white and red,
Like rose leaves, white and red seem mingled.
There Nature for a sweet allurement sets
Two smelling, swelling bashful cherrilets,
The which, with ruby redness being tipp'd,
Do speak a virgin merry, cherry-lipp'd,
Over the which a meet, sweet skin is drawn
Which makes them show like roses under lawn.
These be the ruby portals and divine
Which ope themselves to show an holy shrine,
Whose breath is rich perfume, that to the sense
Smells like the burnt Sabæan frankincense,
In which the tongue, though but a member small,
Stands guarded with a rosy, hilly wall,
And her white teeth which in the gums are set
Like pearl and gold make one rich carcanet.
Next doth her chin with dimpled beauty strive
For his plump, white and smooth prerogative,
At whose fair top to please the sight there grows
The blessed image of a blushing rose,
Mov'd by the chin whose motion causeth this
That both her lips do part, do meet, do kiss.
Her ears, which like two labyrinths are plac'd
On either side with rich, rare jewels grac'd,
Moving a question, whether that by them
The gem is grac'd? or they grac'd by the gem?
But the foundation of this architect
Is the swan-staining, fair, rare, stately neck,
Which, with ambitious humbleness, stands under,
Bearing aloft this rich, round world of wonder,
In which the veins implanted seem to lie
Like loving vines hid under ivory,
So full of claret that whoso pricks a vine
May see it sprout forth streams of muscadine.
Her breast (a place for beauty's throne most fit)
Bears up two globes where love and pleasure sit,
Which, headed with two rich, round rubies, show
Like wanton rose buds growing out of snow.
And in the milky valley that's between
Sits Cupid kissing of his mother Queen,

Fing'ring the paps that feel like sleav'd silk
And press'd a little they will weep new milk.
Then comes the belly, seated next below
Like a fair mountain of Riphean snow
Where nature in a whiteness without spot
Hath in the middle tied a Gordian knot,
Or else that she on that white waxen hill
Hath seal'd the promise of her utmost skill.
But now my Muse hath spied a dark descent
From this so peerless precious prominent,
A milky highway that direction yields
Unto the port mouth of th'Elysian fields,
A place desir'd of all but got by these
Whom Love admits to this Hesperides.
Here's golden fruit that far exceeds all price;
Above the entrance is written this:
'This is the portal to the Bower of Bliss'.
Through midst thereof a crystal stream there flows
Passing the sweet sweat of a musky rose.
Now Love invites me to survey her thighs,
Swelling in likeness like two crystal skies,
With plump, soft flesh of mettle pure and fine,
Resembling shields, both smooth and crystalline.
Hence rise those two ambitious hills that look
Into the middle, most sight-pleasing crook,
Which, for the better beautifying, shrouds
Its humble self 'twixt two aspiring clouds
Which to the knees by Nature fast'ned on
Derive their ever well-grac'd motion.
Her legs, with two clear calves like silver tried,
Kindly swell up with little pretty pride,
Leaving a distance for the beauteous small
To beautify the leg and foot withal.
Then lowly, yet most lovely, stand the feet
Round, short and clear, like pounded spices sweet,
And whatsoever thing they tread upon,
They make it scent like bruised cinnamon.
The lovely shoulders now allure the eye,
To see two tablets of pure ivory,
From which two arms, like branches, seem to spread
With tender rind and silver coloured,
With little hands and fingers long and small
To grace a lute, a viol virginal.
In length each finger doth his next excel,

Each richly headed with a pearly shell
Richer than that fair, precious virtuous horn
That arms the forehead of the unicorn.
Thus every part in contrariety
Meets in the whole and makes a harmony,
As divers strings do single disagree
But form'd by number make sweet melody.
Unto the idol of the work divine
I consecrate this loving work of mine,
Bowing my lips unto that stately root
Whence beauty springs, and thus I kiss thy foot.

38 William Strode, contribution to *Parnassus Biceps* (1656), pp. 28–9

On a Gentlewoman's Blistered Lip

Hide not that sprouting lip, nor kill
The juicy bloom with bashful skill:
Know it is an amorous dew
That swells to court thy coral hew,
And what a blemish you esteem
To other eyes a pearl may seem
Whose watery growth is not above
The thrifty seize that pearls do love,
And doth so well become that part
That chance may seem a secret art.
Doth any judge that face less fair
Whose tender silk a mole doth bear?
Or will a diamond shine less clear
If in the midst a soil appear?
Or else that eye a finer net
Whose glass is ring'd about with jet?
Or is an apple thought more sweet
When honey specks and red do meet?
   Then is the lip made fairer by
   Such sweetness of deformity.
The nectar which men strive to sip
Springs like a well upon your lip,
Nor doth it show immodesty,
But overflowing chastity.
O who will blame the fruitful trees
When too much sap and gum he sees?
Here Nature from her store doth send
Only what other parts can lend;

The bud of love which ere doth grow
Were too too sweet if pluck'd below;
When lovely buds ascend so high
The root below cannot be dry.

39 Robert Herrick, *Hesperides* (1648), pp. 28, 96, 154, 164

Delight in Disorder

A sweet disorder in the dress
Kindles in clothes a wantonness:
A lawn about the shoulders thrown
Into a fine distraction:
An erring lace, which here and there
Enthrals the crimson stomacher:
A cuff neglectful, and thereby
Ribands to flow confusedly:
A winning wave (deserving note)
In the tempestuous petticoat:
A careless shoe-string, in whose tie
I see a wild civility:
Do more bewitch me, than when Art
Is too precise in every part.

Upon Julia's Breasts

Display thy breasts, my Julia, there let me
Behold that circummortal purity:
Between whose glories, there my lips I'll lay,
Ravish'd, in that fair *via lactea*.

To Dianeme

Show me thy feet; show me thy legs, thy thighs;
Show me those fleshly principalities;
Show me that hill (where smiling Love doth sit)
Having a living fountain under it.
Show me thy waist; then let me therewithal,
By the ascension of thy lawn, see all.

Upon the Nipples of Julia's Breasts

Have ye beheld (with much delight)
A red rose peeping through a white?
Or else a cherry (double grac'd)

67

Within a lily's centre plac'd?
Or ever mark'd the pretty beam
A strawberry shows, half drown'd in cream?
Or seen rich rubies blushing through
A pure smooth pearl, and orient too?
So like to this, nay all the rest,
Is each neat niplet of her breast.

40 Sir John Suckling, *Fragmenta Aurea* (1646), pp. 21–2

Upon My Lady Carlisle's Walking in Hampton Court Garden

Dialogue

Thom[as Carew].   J[ohn] S[uckling].

THOM.
Didst thou not find the place inspir'd,
And flowers, as if they had desir'd
No other sun, start from their beds,
And for a sight steal out their heads?
Heard'st thou not music when she talk'd?
And didst not find that, as she walk'd
She threw rare perfumes all about,
Such as bean-blossoms newly out,
Or chafed spices give ——?

J. S.
I must confess those perfumes, Tom,
I did not smell; nor found that from
Her passing by ought sprung up new:
The flowers had all their birth from you;
For I pass'd o'er the selfsame walk,
And did not find one single stalk
Of any thing that was to bring
This unknown after-after-spring.

THOM.
Dull and insensible, could'st see
A thing so near a deity
Move up and down, and feel no change?

J. S.
None and so great were alike strange.
I had all my thoughts, but not your way;
All are not born, sir, to the bay:
Alas! Tom, I am flesh and blood,

And was consulting how I could
In spite of masks and hoods descry
The parts denied unto the eye:
I was undoing all she wore;
And, had she walk'd but one turn more,
Eve in her first state had not been
More naked, or more plainly seen.

THOM.

'Twas well for thee she left the place;
There is great danger in that face;
But, hadst thou view'd her leg and thigh,
And, upon that discovery,
Search'd after parts that are more dear
(As Fancy seldom stops so near),
No time or age had ever seen
So lost a thing as thou hadst been.

41 Andrew Marvell, *Miscellaneous Poems* (1681; written 1650s?), I.31–2

The Gallery

I

Clora come view my soul, and tell
Whether I have contriv'd it well.
Now all its several lodgings lie
Compos'd into one gallery;
And the great arras-hangings, made
Of various faces, by are laid;
That, for all furniture, you'll find
Only your picture in my mind.

II

Here thou are painted in the dress
Of an inhumane murderess;
Examining upon our hearts
Thy fertile shop of cruel arts:
Engines more keen than ever yet
Adorned tyrant's cabinet;
Of which the most tormenting are
Black eyes, red lips, and curled hair.

III

But, on the other side, th'art drawn
Like to Aurora in the dawn;

When in the East she slumb'ring lies,
And stretches out her milky thighs;
While all the morning choir does sing,
And manna falls, and roses spring;
And, at thy feet, the wooing doves
Sit perfecting their harmless loves.

IV

Like an enchantress here thou show'st,
Vexing thy restless lover's ghost;
And, by a light obscure, dost rave
Over his entrails, in the cave;
Divining thence, with horrid care,
How long thou shalt continue fair;
And (when inform'd) them throw'st away,
To be the greedy vulture's prey.

V

But, against that, thou sit'st afloat
Like Venus in her pearly boat.
The halycyons, calming all that's nigh,
Betwixt the air and water fly.
Or, if some rolling wave appears,
A mass of ambergris it bears.
Nor blows more wind than what may well
Convey the perfume to the smell.

VI

These pictures and a thousand more,
Of thee, my gallery does store;
In all the forms thou can'st invent
Either to please me, or torment:
For thou alone to people me,
Art grown a num'rous colony;
And a collection choicer far
Than or Whitehall's, or Mantua's were.

VII

But, of these pictures and the rest,
That at the entrance likes me best:
Where the same posture, and the look
Remains, with which I first was took.
A tender shepherdess, whose hair
Hangs loosely playing in the air,
Transplanting flow'rs from the green hill,
To crown her head, and bosom fill.

70

6

VICES

The weakness of the female so much insisted upon was construed in physical and intellectual terms, as want of strength and judgement, not in psychological terms, as want of character. Women's characters were in no way deemed to be weak. On the contrary, their unruly temperaments were known to be stronger than their wills could control (a point the poet Wither turns sympathetically (42)). It was precisely because what Baxter calls their 'natural imbecility' was believed to be wedded to a passionately determined nature (43) that the century echoes with excoriations of women's vices and reiterations of their duty to submit their wills to masculine guidance. Only in the last decades of the century do we find increasing reference to woman's 'softness' and detect the early stages of the construction of that pallid, almost diaphanously insubstantial, image which was to characterize the heroine of the age of sensibility (Todd (1986), pp. 110–28). Seventeenth-century woman was altogether robuster. The figures of the virago and the Amazon, to which Thomas Heywood devotes one of the nine books of his *Gynækeion* (1624), was at once so fascinating and so appalling since in them woman's nature is both writ large and monstrously masculine (see on this subject Shepherd (1985)).

Woman's innate wilfulness, deceitfulness, cunning and lasciviousness were proverbial throughout the century. Although John Gough's *Academy of Complements* is addressed to gentlewomen in the 1680s it happily prints a series of misogynistic apothegms (44). Early in the century these same charges had been forcibly put in the course of the English contribution to the *querelle des femmes* which engaged Renaissance scholars and wits throughout Europe. Though pursued largely as a rhetorical exercise, its traditional commonplaces, no matter how deftly turned, articulated suspicion, fear and resentment of the female, often viciously. (On the controversy about women, see Beilin (1990); Henderson and McManus (1985), pp. 12–24; Kelly (1984), pp. 65–109; Maclean (1977); Purkiss (1992); Shepherd, ed. (1985), pp. 53–5 and *passim*; and Wright (1958), pp. 465–507.) In England, a conspicuous example is the energetic multiplication of insults by Joseph Swetnam in his enthusiastically adopted persona of woman-hater

(45). The rhetorical energy with which he multiplies insults is so patent that it is perhaps less disturbing than straight-faced homiletic castigations of women's vices.

The flaws in her character and the vices to which she was allegedly prone are those familiar from Medieval (and, indeed, modern) culture. Beilin (1990), p. xiii, quotes Christine de Pisan, *Cité des Dames* in its 1521 English translation *The Cyte of Ladyes*, 'all treatyses of phylosophres, poetes and all rethorycyens . . . speaketh as it were by one mouthe and accordeth all in semble conclusyon determinynge that the condycyons of women ben fully enclyned to all vyces'. So the common opinion continued to hold. Rare is the restraint and fairness of Burton, who, in the course of curing love-melancholy by disabusing male lovers of their high opinion of women, reproduces 'not . . . a tenth of that which might be urged' from his anti-feminist sources, and acknowledges, as does Baxter (43), that 'what is said of the one [sex] . . . may most part be understood of the other' (46); rare, too, his recognition that male possessiveness rather than female viciousness demands that women be controlled and confined (50). More usual is the bias of Alexis Trousset (alias Jacques Olivier), *Alphabet de l'imperfection et malice des femmes*, a relentless collection of Classical dicta, patristic sayings and Biblical exempla to the detriment of women, derived from Medieval models, first published in Paris in 1617. Ingeniously contriving a female vice for each letter of the alphabet, it proved very much to seventeenth-century taste, going into an English translation in 1662. Trousset, like many another commentator, avails himself of the Biblical precedent which was to hand (47). His charges were the staple of the character writers (48, 49) but the stereotypes of the shrew, the scold, the inconstant woman and the whore (on which there is much useful information in de Bruyn (1979), pp. 69–150) are presented in a great variety of genres. Woman's garrulity (43; cf. 98), deceitfulness and inconstancy, wilful assertiveness, acrimony and jealousy (50, 51), pride (52) and lust (53) are incessantly lamented and castigated. Taking their cue from I Tim. ii.9, diatribes against provocative dress and the use of 'paint' or cosmetics (52, 54, 55) betray something of an obsession with lascivious vanity and a dread of female sexuality which readily appropriates the phrasing of the characterization of the whore in Proverbs vii (56, 57). The animus of this misogyny lends force to Esther Sowernam's remarkable retort (58) to Joseph Swetnam that the pollution is in men's minds rather than in women's nature (though we must be cautious before accepting that Sowernam was female (Shepherd, ed. (1985), p. 86)).

At court, the obsession was of a rather different nature. A feature of Renaissance culture had been the status accorded to, and the patronage wielded by, courtesans. The word itself, which entered English from Italian in the early sixteenth century, at once registered this elevation and denoted the only means by which a position analogous to that of the male courtier was customarily attainable by a woman. Rule successively by a queen, a misogynist and homosexual, a morally upright and faithfully married monarch and by a Puritan protector, had in their various ways denied the figure any great play at the English court for a hundred years, but the hedonism of Charles II's court, in libertine reaction against what it took to be the kill-joy hypocrisy of Puritanism, gave a new lease of life to the role of courtesan. The ennoblement of Charles II's own mistresses set the courtesan at the apex of English society. That the aristocracy's casual attitude to sexual indulgence spread much beyond the capital cannot be demonstrated, nor do later seventeenth-century conduct books give any indication that more lax sexual mores obtained in society at large. There can, however, be no doubt that the poor equivalent of the courtesan was common enough in London. Indeed, in the 1690s, John Dunton was able to produce a monthly paper entitled *The Nightwalker, or Evening Rambles in Search of Lewd Women with the Conferences Held with Them*. In contrast to the organized and professional prostitution of the capital, to which Dunton's publication bears dubious witness, prostitution in the provinces appears to have been, in so far as the evidence admits of interpretation, casual and part-time, but not uncommon (Sharpe (1984), pp. 110–11, 114–15). Though disapproved of, it does not appear that prostitution was perceived as a socially disturbing nuisance or scandal (59). Indeed, by the time of Defoe's fictions, if not earlier, the behaviour of a Moll Flanders or Roxana might be seen as socially determined, a woman's only means of survival in a patriarchal world. Certainly, Bunyan was as sympathetically aware as Defoe that men's deceit might betray women into prostitution (60). If the Earl of Rochester's satires similarly show an awareness of the degradation involved in servicing the court's sexual needs and of the hollowness of its pretensions to nobility and dignity (61), they also, more typically and less impressively, seize on the figure of the prostitute as a scapegoat for male loathing and disgust (62).

Upon belief in woman's susceptibility to evil depended the demonization of female power in the figure of the witch. The first and most influential codification of witch lore and law, the *Malleus Maleficarum* (1489, last reprinted in 1669), a handbook for the Holy Inquisition prepared by Jacob Sprenger and Heinrich Kramer, rehearsed the full range of vices and weaknesses attributed to women to show that they were innately more likely than men to become devilish. The seventeenth century's continuing susceptibility to this misogynistic assumption offered it a ready means by which to subdue any woman whose behaviour was transgressive, who aspired to rise above her station, or who displayed exceptional (and challenging) traits of character or mind, particularly in religious or medicinal contexts (Hobby (1988), pp. 5, 34–5, 38, 177–8). The case of Elizabeth Sawyer illustrates the force of prejudice and the lamentable use of evidence to sway even a kindly disposed jury (63; for other cases, see Fraser (1984), pp. 102–18). The farrago of superstition and nonsense assembled around the figure of the witch (64) might seem to have a place amongst the enthusiastic excesses and intellectual extremisms of the Civil War years, when the self-styled Witchfinder General, Matthew Hopkins, was at work (Notestein (1965), pp. 164–205), but it continued to carry weight long after. Sir Matthew Hale, the century's most enlightened, incorruptible and learned judge, and Lord Chief Justice from 1671 to 1676, credited it (Notestein (1965), pp. 261–8); so, too, did Richard Baxter in his *The Certainty of the Worlds of Spirits* published as late as 1691 (Notestein (1965), pp. 336–8). The last execution of a witch in England occurred in 1685, the last conviction for the crime in 1712, and the last trial in 1717 (Fraser (1984), pp. 117–18; Notestein (1965), pp. 324–31).

---

42 George Wither, *Epithalamia* (1612), I.182

Epigram VII

Women, as some men say, inconstant be;
'Tis like enough, and so no doubt are men:
Nay, if their scapes we could so plainly see,
I fear that scarce there will be one for ten.
Men have but their own lusts that tempt to ill;
Women have lusts and men's allurements too:
Alas, if their strengths cannot curb their will,
What should poor women, that are weaker, do?
   Oh, they had need be chaste and look about them,
   That strive 'gainst lust within and knaves without them.

43 Richard Baxter, *A Christian Directory* (1673), II.i [IV.15–16]

And it is no small patience which the natural imbecility of the female sex requireth you to prepare. Except it be very few that are patient and manlike, women are commonly of potent fantasies, and tender, passionate, impatient spirits, easily cast into anger, or jealousy, or discontent; and of weak understandings, and therefore unable to reform themselves. They are betwixt a man and a child: some few have more of the man, and many have more of the child; but most are but in a middle state. Weakness naturally inclineth persons to be froward and hard to please; as we see in children, old people, and sick persons. They are like a sore, distempered body; you can scarce touch them but you hurt them. With too many you can scarce tell how to speak or look but you displease them. If you should be very well versed in the art of pleasing, and set yourselves to it with all your care, as if you made it your very business and had little else to do, yet it would put you hard to it, to please some weak, impatient persons, if not quite surpass your ability and skill. And the more you love them, the more grievous it will be, to see them still in discontents, weary of their condition, and to hear the

74

clamorous expressions of their disquiet minds. Nay the very multitude of words that very many are addicted to, doth make some men's lives a continual burden to them. Mark what the Scripture saith: 'It is better to dwell in a corner of the housetop, than with a brawling woman in a wide house'; 'It is better to dwell in the wilderness, than with a contentious and an angry woman'; 'A continual dropping in a very rainy day, and a contentious woman are alike'; 'One man among a thousand have I found: but a woman among all those have I not found' (Prov. xxi.19, xxv.24, xxvii.15; Eccles. vii.28).

And there is such a meeting of faults and imperfections on both sides [in marriage], that maketh it much harder to bear the infirmities of others aright. If one party only were froward and impatient, the steadfastness of the other might make it the more tolerable: but we are all sick in some measure, of the same disease. And when weakness meeteth with weakness, and pride with pride, and passion with passion, it exasperateth the disease and doubleth the suffering. And our corruption is such, that though our intent be to help one another in our duties, yet we are apter far to stir up one another's distempers.

44 [John Gough], *Academy of Complements* (1684), pp. 76–86, 120–9

*A New School of Love, with Questions and Answers
Resolving the Doubts of Lovers*

Q. How is that there are many more women in the world than men?
A. Women are exempted from the war, and in Nature, the worst things are most plentiful . . .
Q. Why are women more craftily revengeful than men?
A. By reason of the weakness of their natures; what they cannot do by force, they maintain by subtlety . . .
Q. Where are women of best use?
A. *In thalamo, in tumulo*: in the bed and in the tomb . . .
Q. What waters of all other are most deceitful?
A. A woman's tears . . .
Q. How cometh it to pass that women newly married, the first night are so loath to go to bed, yet rise the next day so lusty and joyful?
A. It proceeds from the perfection of the man, which having acquired to themselves, they then know they are women indeed . . .
Q. Wherefore is it that amongst all kind of animals, the females are more subtle and cunning than the males?
A. It is for the most part that they being more weak than the males, Nature to repair the defect hath given them a more wily craft, for the conservation of their lives . . .

75

Q. Who is the most constant in love, the man or the woman?

A. The man, being both in body and spirit more firm and more constant in his persuasions of love affairs . . .

Q. Why do women love fine clothes better than men?

A. Because too often wanting the beauty of their minds, they study the more how to adorn and hide the imperfections of their bodies, which they are therefore the more sensible of . . .

Q. When a man dies, which is the last part of him that stirs, which of a woman?

A. The last part of a man is his heart, of a woman, her tongue . . .

Q. What was the philosopher [Plato] so thankful for?

A. For four things: 1. that he lived in the time of Socrates; 2. that he was a Grecian and not a barbarian; 3. that he was a man and not a beast; 4. that he was a man and not a woman . . .

A Collection of Proverbs and Apothegms

1. A fair wife and a frontier castle breed quarrels.
8. Marry your son when you will, your daughter when you can.
9. Dally not with money nor women.
15. A woman and a glass are ever in danger.
25. Marry a widow before she leaves mourning.
60. A house and a woman suit excellently.
61. Discreet women have neither ears nor eyes.
65. Who lets his wife go to every feast, and his horse drink at every water, shall never have a good wife nor a good horse.
69. In the husband wisdom, in the wife gentleness.
72. Three women make a market.
78. Words are women, deeds are men.
80. A woman conceals what she knows not.
81. He that tells his wife news is but newly married.
85. Mills and wives ever want.
88. A poor beauty finds more husbands than lovers.
105. A ship and a woman are ever repairing.
154. Handsome women without portions find more sweethearts than husbands.

45 [Joseph Swetnam], *The Arraignment of Lewde Women* (1615), *passim*

The lion being bitten with hunger, the bear being robbed of her young ones, the viper being trod on, all these are nothing so terrible as the fury of a woman. A buck may be enclosed in a park, a bridle rules a horse, a wolf may be tied, a tiger may be tamed, but a froward woman will never be tamed. No spur will make her go, nor no bridle will hold her back, for if a woman hold an opinion no man can draw her from it . . .

. . . A man may generally speak of women that for the most part thou shalt find them dissembling in their deeds and in all their actions subtle and dangerous for men to deal withal, for their faces are liars, their beauties are baits, their looks are nets, and their words charms, and all to bring men to ruin . . .

The pride of a woman is like the dropsy, for as drink increaseth in the drought of the one, even so money enlargeth the pride of the other. Thy purse must be always open to feed their fancy, and so thy expenses will be great and yet perhaps thy gettings small. Thy house must be stored with costly stuff, and yet perhaps thy servants starved for lack of meat. Thou must discharge the mercer's book and pay the haberdasher's man, for her hat must continually be of the new fashion, and her gown of finer wool than the sheep beareth any. She must likewise have her jewel box furnished, especially if she be beautiful, for then commonly beauty and pride goeth together. And a beautiful woman is for the most part costly and no good housewife; and if she be a good housewife then no servant will abide her fierce cruelty; and if she be honest and chaste, then commonly she is jealous . . .

It is wonderful to see the mad feats of women, for she will be now merry, then again sad; now laugh, then weep; now sick, then presently whole. All things which like not them is naught, and if it be never so bad if it like them it is excellent. Again, it is death for a woman to be denied the thing which they demand, and yet they will despise things given them unasked.

When a woman wanteth anything, she will flatter and speak fair, not unlike the flattering butcher who gently claweth the ox when he intendeth to knock him on the head. But the thing being once obtained and their desires gained, then they will begin to look big and answer so stately and speak so scornfully, that one would imagine they would never seek help nor crave comfort at thy hands more . . .

It is said that an old dog and a hungry flea bite sore, but in my mind a froward woman biteth more sorer. And if thou go about to master a woman in hope to bring her to humility, there is no way to make her good with stripes except thou beat her to death; for do what thou wilt, yet a froward woman in her frantic mood will pull, haul, swear, scratch and tear all that stands in her way.

For women have a thousand ways to entice thee, and ten thousand ways to deceive thee, and all such fools as are suitors unto them, some they keep in hand with promises, and some they feed with flattery, and some they delay with dalliance, and some they please with kisses. They lay out the folds of their hair to entangle men into their love, betwixt their breasts is the vale of destruction, and in their beds is hell, sorrow and repentance. Eagles eat not men till they are dead, but women devour them alive, for a woman will pick thy pocket and empty thy purse, laugh in thy face and cut thy throat. They are ungrateful, perjured, full of fraud, flouting and deceit, unconstant, waspish, toyish, light, sullen, proud, discourteous and cruel, and yet they were by God created, and by Nature formed, and therefore by policy and wisdom to be avoided, for good things abused are to be refused . . .

. . . Therefore, if all the world were paper, and all the sea ink, and all the trees and plants were pens, and every man in the world were a writer, yet were they not able with all their labour and cunning to set down all the crafty deceits of women.

46 Robert Burton, *Anatomy of Melancholy* (1621–51), III.ii.5(3) [III.214–16]

Cure of Love-Melancholy by Counsel and Persuasion, Foulness of the Fact, Men's, Women's Faults, Miseries of Marriage, Events of Lust, etc.

. . . I will say nothing of the vices of their minds, their pride, envy, inconstancy, weakness, malice, self-will, lightness, insatiable lust, jealousy. 'No malice to a woman's' (Ecclus. xxv.13), 'no bitterness like to hers' (Eccles. vii.26), and as the author urgeth (Prov. xxxi.10), 'Who shall find a virtuous woman?' He makes a question of it . . . I am not willing you see to prosecute the cause against them, and therefore take heed you mistake me not, *matronum nullam ego tango*, I honour the sex, with all good men, and as I ought to do . . . Let . . . Peter Aretine, and such women-haters, bear the blame if aught be said amiss. I have not writ a tenth of that which might be urged out of them and others: *non possunt invectivæ omnes, et satiræ in feminas scriptæ, uno volumine comprehendi* [all the invectives and satires written against women could not be contained in one volume]. And that which I have said (to speak truth) no more concerns them than men, though women be more frequently named in this tract; to apologize once for all, I am neither partial against them, or therefore bitter; what is said of the one, *mutato nomine* [changing the name], may most part be understood of the other . . . If any man take exception at my word, let him alter the name, read him for her, and 'tis all one in effect.

47 Holy Bible, 'Authorized' King James Version (1611)

The Wisdom of Jesus, the Son of Sirach, or Ecclesiasticus

XXV

16. I had rather dwell with a lion and a dragon, than to keep house with a wicked woman.
19. All wickedness is but little to the wickedness of a woman: let the portion of a sinner fall upon her.
24. Of the woman came the beginning of sin, and through her we all die.

XXVI

1.   Blessed is the man that hath a virtuous wife, for the number of his days shall be double.

2.   A virtuous woman rejoiceth her husband, and he shall fulfil the years of his life in peace.

3.   A good wife is a good portion, which shall be given in the portion of them that fear the Lord . . .

7.   An evil wife is a yoke shaken to and fro: he that hath hold of her is as though he held a scorpion.

8.   A drunken woman and a gadder abroad causeth great anger, and she will not cover her own shame.

9.   The whoredom of a woman may be known in her haughty looks and eyelids.

10.   If thy daughter be shameless, keep her in straitly, lest she abuse herself through overmuch liberty.

11.   Watch over an impudent eye: and marvel not if she trespass against thee.

12.   She will open her mouth, as a thirsty traveller when he hath found a fountain, and drink of every water near her: by every hedge will she sit down, and open her quiver against every arrow.

13.   The grace of a wife delighteth her husband, and her discretion will fatten his bones.

14.   A silent and loving woman is a gift of the Lord: and there is nothing so much worth as a mind well instructed.

15.   A shamefaced and faithful woman is a double grace, and her continent mind cannot be valued . . .

22.   An harlot shall be accounted as spittle; but a married woman is a tower against death to her husband.

23.   A wicked woman is given as a portion to a wicked man: but a godly woman is given to him that feareth the Lord.

24.   A dishonest woman contemneth shame; but an honest woman will reverence her husband.

25.   A shameless woman shall be counted as a dog; but she that is shamefaced will fear the Lord.

26.   A woman that honoureth her husband shall be judged wise of all; but she that dishonoureth him in her pride shall be counted ungodly of all.

27.   A loud crying woman and a scold shall be sought out to drive away the enemies.

48 Nicholas Breton, *The Good and the Badde* (1615), pp. 272–4

A Wanton Woman

A wanton woman is the figure of imperfection; in nature an ape, in quality a wagtail, in countenance a witch, and in condition a kind of devil. Her beck is a net, her word a charm, her look an illusion, and her company a confusion. Her life is the play of idleness, her diet the excess of dainties, her love the change of vanities, and her exercise the invention of follies. Her pleasures are fancies, her studies fashions, her delight colours, and her wealth her clothes. Her care is to deceive, her comfort her company, her house is vanity, and her bed is ruin. Her discourses are fables, her vows dissimulations, her conceits subtleties, and her contents varieties. She would she knows not what, and spends she cares not what, she spoils she sees not what, and doth she thinks not what. She is youth's plague and age's purgatory, time's abuse and reason's trouble. In sum, she is a spice of madness, a spark of mischief, a touch of poison, and a fear of destruction.

An Unquiet Woman

An unquiet woman is the misery of man, whose demeanour is not to be described but in extremities. Her voice is the screeching of an owl, her eye the poison of a cockatrice, her hand the claw of a crocodile, and her heart a cabinet of horror. She is the grief of Nature, the wound of wit, the trouble of reason, and the abuse of time. Her pride is unsupportable, her anger unquenchable, her will unsatiable, and her malice unmatchable. She fears no colours, she cares for no counsel, she spares no persons, nor respects any time. Her command is must, her reason will, her resolution shall, and her satisfaction so. She looks at no law and thinks of no lord, admits no command and keeps no good order. She is a cross but not of Christ, and a word but not of grace; a creature but not of wisdom, and a servant but not of God. In sum, she is the seed of trouble, the fruit of travail, the taste of bitterness, and the digestion of death.

49 H[enry?] P[arrot?], *Cures for the Itch* (1626), p. 284

A Scold

Is a much more heard of, than least desired to be seen or known, she-kind of serpent; the venomed sting of whose poisonous tongue, worse than the biting of a scorpion, proves more infectious far than can be cured. She's of all other creatures most untameable, and covets more the last word in scolding than doth a combater the last stroke for victory. She loudest lifts it standing at her door, bidding, with exclamation, flat defiance to any one says black's her eye. She dares appear before any justice, nor is least daunted with the sight of constable, nor at worst threatenings of cucking-stool. There's nothing mads or moves her more to outrage than but the very naming of a wisp, or if you sing or whistle when she is scolding. If any in the interim chance to come within her reach, twenty to one she scratcheth him by the face; or do but offer to hold her hands, she'll presently begin to cry out murder. There's nothing pacifies her but a cup of sack, which taking in full measure of digestion, she presently forgets all wrongs that's done her, and thereupon falls straight a-weeping. Do but entreat her with fair words, or flatter her, she then confesseth all her imperfections, and lays the guilt upon her maid. Her manner is to talk much in her sleep, what wrongs she hath endured of that rogue her husband, whose hap may be in time to die a martyr; and so I leave them.

50 Robert Burton, *Anatomy of Melancholy* (1621–51), III.iii.1(2), III.iii.2 [III.265–6, 282–5]

Causes of Jealousy. Who are most apt . . .

. . . In Friesland the women kiss him they drink to, and are kissed again of those they pledge. The virgins in Holland go hand-in-hand with young men from home, glide on the ice, such is their harmless liberty, and lodge together abroad without suspicion, which rash Sansovinus, an Italian, makes a great sign of unchastity. In France, upon small acquaintance, it is usual to court other men's wives, to come to their houses, and accompany them arm-in-arm in the streets, without imputation. In the most northern countries young men and maids familiarly dance together, men and their wives, which, Siena only excepted, Italians may not abide. The Greeks, on the other side, have their private baths for men and women, where they must not come near, nor so much as see one another; and as Bodine observes, *lib. V de repub.*, 'the Italians could never endure this', or a Spaniard, the very conceit of it would make him mad; and for that cause they lock up their women, and will not suffer them to be near men, so much as in the church, but with a partition between. He telleth, moreover, how that 'when he was ambassador in England, he heard Mendoza the Spanish legate finding fault with it, as a filthy custom for men and women to sit promiscuously in churches together; but Dr. Dale, the Master of the Requests, told him again that it was indeed a filthy custom in Spain, where they could not contain themselves from lascivious thoughts in their holy places, but not with us' . . . we are far from any such strange conceits and will permit our wives and daughters to go to the tavern with a friend . . . *modo absit lascivia* [as long as there is no lewdness], which, as Erasmus writes in one of his epistles, they cannot endure. England is a paradise for women, and a hell for horses: Italy a paradise for horses, hell for women, as the diverb goes. Some make a question whether this headstrong passion rage more in women than men, as

Montaigne, lib. III. But sure it is more outrageous in women, as all other melancholy is, by reason of the weakness of their sex . . .

Symptoms of Jealousy: Fear, Sorrow, Strange Actions, Gestures, Outrages, Locking Up . . .

. . . It is most strange to report what outrageous acts by men and women have been committed in this kind, by women especially, that will run after their husbands into all places and companies . . . But women are sufficiently curbed in such cases; the rage of men is more eminent, and frequently put in practice. See but with what rigour those jealous husbands tyrannize over their poor wives in Greece, Spain, Italy, Turkey, Africa, Asia, and generally over all those hot countries. *Mulieres vestræ terra vestra, arate sicut vultis,* Mahomet in his Alcoran gives this power to men: your wives are as your land, till them, use them, entreat them fair or foul, as you will yourselves. *Mecastor lege dura vivunt mulieres* [By the stars! women's lives are governed by a hard law], they lock them still in their houses, which are so many prisons to them, will suffer nobody to come at them, or their wives to be seen abroad . . . They must not so much as look out. And if they be great persons, they have eunuchs to keep them, as the Grand Seignior among the Turks, the Sophies of Persia, those Tartarian Mogors, and Kings of China . . . The Xeriffs of Barbary keep their courtesans in such a strict manner, that if any man come but in sight of them he dies for it; and if they chance to see a man, and do not instantly cry out, though from their windows, they must be put to death. The Turks have I know not how many black, deformed eunuchs (for the white serve for other ministries) to this purpose sent commonly from Egypt, deprived in their childhood of all their privities, and brought up in the seraglio at Constantinople to keep their wives; which are so penned up they may not confer with any living man . . . I have not yet said all: they do not only lock them up, *sed pudendis seras adhibent* [but they bring bolts for their pudenda] . . . In some parts of Greece at this day, like those old Jews, they will not believe their wives are honest, *nisi pannum menstruatum prima nocte videant* [unless they see a bloody cloth the first night] . . . To what end are . . . such strange absurd trials . . . by stones, perfumes, to make them piss, and confess I know not what in their sleep? Some jealous brain was the first founder of them. And to what passion may we ascribe those severe laws against jealousy (Num. v.14), adulterers (Deut. xxii.22), as amongst the Hebrews, amongst the Egyptians . . . amongst the Athenians of old, Italians at this day, wherein they are to be severely punished, cut in pieces, burned, *vivi-comburio*, buried alive, with several expurgations, etc., are they not as so many symptoms of incredible jealousy?

51 John Taylor, *A Juniper Lecture* (1639), pp. 27–8

On a Woman's Tongue

Things that be bitter, bitterer than gall,
Physicians say are always physical:
Then women's tongues, if into powder beaten,
And in a potion or a pill be eaten,
Nothing more bitter is, I therefore muse,
That women's tongues in physic they ne'er use.
There's many men who live unquiet lives
Would spare that bitter member of their wives.
Then prove them, Doctor, use them in a pill,
Things oft help sick men, that doth sound men kill.

52 Arthur Dent, *The Plaine Mans Path-way to Heaven* (1607), pp. 40–6

Philagathus [an honest man]. I pray you, let us proceed to speak of the outward and gross pride of the world, and, first of all, tell me what you think of pride in apparel.

Theologus [a divine]. I think it to be a vanity of all vanities, and a folly of all follies. For to be proud of apparel is, as if a thief should be proud of his halter, a beggar of his clouts, a child of his gay, or a fool of his bauble.

Phil. Yet we see how proud many (especially women) be of such baubles. For when they have spent a good part of the day in tricking and trimming, pricking and pinning, pranking and pouncing, girding and lacing, and braving up themselves in most exquisite manner, then out they come into the streets with their pedlar's shop upon their back and carry their crests very high, taking themselves to be little angels, or, at least, somewhat more than other women. Whereupon they do so exceedingly swell with pride, that it is to be feared they will burst with it, as they walk in the street. And truly, we may think the very stones in the street, and the beams in the houses do quake and wonder at their monstrous, intolerable and excessive pride. For it seemeth that they are altogether a lump of pride, a mass of pride, even altogether made of pride, and nothing else but pride, pride . . .

Asunetus [an ignorant man]. . . . It was never a good world, since starching and steeling, busks, and whale-bones, supporters, and rebatoes, full moons, and hobby-horses, painting and dying, with selling of favour and complexion, came to be in use . . . what say then to painting of faces, laying open of naked breasts, dying of hair, wearing of periwigs, and other hair coronets and top-gallants? And what say you to our artificial women, which will be better than God hath made them? They like not his handiwork, they will mend it, and have other complexion, other faces, other hair, other bones, other breasts, and other bellies, than God made them.

Theo. This I say, that you and I and all the Lord's people have great and just cause of mourning, weeping and lamentation, because such abomination is committed in Israel . . . It is God's marvellous patience that the Devil doth not carry them away quickly and rid the earth of them . . .

Antilegon [a caviller]. You are too hot in the matters of attire; you make more of them than there is cause . . .

Theo. I know right well, that apparel in its own nature is a thing indifferent; but lewd, wanton, immodest and offensive apparel is not indifferent . . . why should the Lord so plague the proud dames and mincing minions of Jerusalem for their pride and vanity in attire, if there were no evil in such kind of abuses (Isa. iii.[16–24]) . . .

53 Robert Gould, *Love Given O're* (1682), pp. 2–9

Woman! by heav'ns, the very name's a crime,
Enough to blast, and to debauch my rhyme.
Sure, Heaven itself (entranc'd) like Adam lay,
Or else some banished fiend usurp'd the sway
When Eve was form'd; and with her ushered in
Plagues, woes and death, and a new world of sin.
The fatal rib was crooked and unev'n
From whence they have their crab-like nature giv'n
Averse to all the laws of man, and heav'n . . .
    But now, since Woman's boundless lust I name
Woman's unbounded lust I'll first proclaim:
Trace it through all the secret various ways,
Where it still runs in an eternal maze,
And show that our lewd age has brought to view
What impious Sodom and Gomorrah too,
Were they what once they were, would blush to do.
True, I confess that Rome's imperial whore*
(More fam'd for lust than for the crown she wore)
Aspir'd to deeds so impiously high
That their unnatural fame will never die:
Into the public stews (disguis'd) she thrust
To quench the raging fury of her lust:
Her part against th'assembly she made good
And all the sallies of their lust withstood,
And drained 'em dry, exhausted all their store,

*Messalina

84

Yet all could not content th'insatiate whore,
Her c——, like the dull grave, still gap'd for more.
This, this she did, and bravely got her name
Born up for ever on the wings of fame:
Yet this is poor to what our modern age
Has hatch'd, brought forth, and acted on the stage . . .
    And now, if so much to the world's reveal'd,
Reflect on the vast stores that lie conceal'd:
How, when into their closets they retire
Where flaming dil—s does inflame desire
And gentle lap-d—s feed the am'rous fire:
Lap-d—s! to whom they are more kind and free
Than they themselves to their own husbands be.
How curs'd is Man! when brutes his rivals prove
Ev'n in the sacred bus'ness of his love.
Great was the wise man's saying, great as true,
And we well know that he, none better, knew:
Ev'n he himself acknowledg'd the womb
To be as greedy as the gaping tomb:
Take men, dogs, lions, bears, all sorts of stuff,
Yet it will never cry – there is enough . . .
. . . ev'ry one would, could they enact their mind
To their own single share engross ev'n all mankind . . .
That they would have it so their crime assures;
Thus, if they durst, all women would be whores . . .
    Pride is the deity they most adore;
Hardly their own dear selves they cherish more.
When she commands, her dictates they obey
As freely as the lamp that guides the day . . .
Yet, tho' so many crimes of theirs I've nam'd
That's still untold for which they most are fam'd:
A sin! (tall as the pyramids of old)
From whose aspiring top we may behold
Enough to damn a world – what should it be,
But (curse upon the name!) inconstancy? . . .
No more the wind, the faithless wind, shall be
A simile for their inconstancy,
For that is sometimes fix'd; but Woman's mind
Is never fix'd or to one point inclin'd . . .

54 John Bunyan, *Life and Death of Mr. Badman*
(1680), pp. 122–3, 125

Wiseman. . . . For mine own part, I have seen many my self, and those church-members too, so decked and bedaubed with their fangles and toys, and that when they have been at the solemn appointments of God, in the way of his worship, that I have wondered with what face such painted persons could sit in the place where they were without swounding. But certainly the holiness of God, and also the pollution of themselves by sin, must needs be very far out of the minds of such people, what profession soever they make.

I have read of an whore's forehead, and I have read of Christian-shamefacedness; I have read of costly array, and of that which becometh women professing godliness, with good works [Jer. iii.3;I Tim. ii.9; I Pet. iii.1, 2, 3; Jer. xxiii.15]; but if I might speak, I know what I know, and could say, and yet do no wrong, that which would make some professors stink in their places; but now I forbear.

Attentive. Sir, you seem to be greatly concerned at this, but what if I shall say more ? it is whispered, that some good ministers, have countenanced their people in their light and wanton apparel, yea have pleaded for their gold, and pearls, and costly array, &c.

Wise. I know not what they have pleaded for, but 'tis easily seen that they tolerate, or at least wise, wink and connive at such things, both in their wives and children . . . many have their excuses ready; to wit, their parents, their husbands, and their breeding calls for it, and the like: yea, the examples of good people prompt them to it: but all these will be but the spider's web, when the thunder of the Word of the great God shall rattle from heaven against them, as it will at death or judgment; but I wish it might do it before. But alas! these excuses are but bare pretences, these proud ones love to have it so. I once talked with a maid, by way of reproof, for her fond and gaudy garment. But she told me, *The tailor would make it so*: when alas, poor proud girl, she gave order to the tailor so to make it . . .

What can be the end of those that are proud, in the decking of themselves after their antic manner? why are they for going with their bulls-foretops, with their naked shoulders, and paps hanging out like a cow's bag? why are they for painting their faces, for stretching out their necks, and for putting of themselves into all the formalities which proud fancy leads them to? Is it because they would honour God? because they would adorn the Gospel? because they would beautify religion, and make sinners to fall in love with their own salvation? No, no. It is rather to please their lusts, to satisfy their wild and extravagant fancies; and I wish none doth it to stir up lust in others, to the end they may commit uncleanness with them. I believe, whatever is their end, this is one of the great designs of the Devil.

55 [N.H.], *The Ladies Dictionary* (1694), p. 38

Artificial beauty: I do find that *washing* and *painting* is condemned in Holy Writ as the practice of loose, licentious and lascivious women, who, with the deformity of their souls, and polluting their consciences, do use the art for the embellishing their countenances . . . St. Paul and St. Peter prescribed how women should be clad, that is, with modesty, shamefacedness and sobriety [I Tim. ii.9; I Pet. iii. 3–4]; and not with gorgeous apparel, or with braided hair, gold or pearls; and if these things were forbidden, how much more is washing or painting the face?

56 Holy Bible, 'Authorized' King James Version (1611)

Proverbs VII

1. My son, keep my words, and lay up my commandments with thee . . .
4. Say unto wisdom, Thou art my sister; and call understanding thy kinswoman;
5. That they may keep thee from the strange woman, from the stranger which flattereth with her words.
6. For at the window of my house I looked through my casement,
7. And beheld among the simple ones, I discerned among the youths, a young man void of understanding,
8. Passing through the street near her corner; and he went the way to her house,
9. In the twilight, in the evening, in the black and dark night:
10. And, behold, there met him a woman with the attire of an harlot, and subtle of heart.
11. (She is loud and stubborn; her feet abide not in her house:
12. Now is she without, now in the streets, and lieth in wait at every corner.)
13. So she caught him, and kissed him, and with an impudent face said unto him,
14. I have peace offerings with me; this day have I payed my vows.
15. Therefore came I forth to meet thee, diligently to seek thy face, and I have found thee.
16. I have decked my bed with coverings of tapestry, with carved works, with fine linen of Egypt.
17. I have perfumed my bed with myrrh, aloes, and cinnamon.
18. Come, let us take our fill of love until the morning: let us solace ourselves with loves.
19. For the goodman is not at home, he is gone a long journey:
20. He hath taken a bag of money with him, and will come home at the day appointed.
21. With her much fair speech she caused him to yield, with the flattering

of her lips she forced him.

22.   He goeth after her straitway, as an ox goeth to the slaughter, or as a fool to the correction of the stocks;

23.   Till a dart strike through his liver; as a bird hasteth to the snare, and knoweth not that it is for his life.

24.   Hearken unto me now therefore, O ye children, and attend to the words of my mouth.

25.   Let not thine heart decline to her ways, go not astray in her paths.

26.   For she hath cast down many wounded: yea, many strong men have been slain by her.

27.   Her house is the way to hell, going down to the chambers of death.

57 Holy Bible, 'Geneva' Version (1560), marginal gloss on Prov. vii.26

Neither wit nor strength can deliver them that fall into the hands of the harlot.

58 Esther Sowernam, *Ester hath Hang'd Haman* (1617), pp. 109, 113

Philosophers say *nemo leditur nisi a seipso* (no man is hurt but the cause is in himself). The prodigal person amongst the Grecians is called Asotos, as a destroyer, an undoer of himself. When an heart fraughted with sin doth prodigally lavish out a lascivious look out of a wanton eye, when it doth surfeit upon the sight, who is Asotos? Who is guilty of this lascivious disease but himself? *Volenti non fit injuria*: he who is wounded with his own consent hath small cause to complain of another's wrong. Might not a man as easily – and more honestly – when he seeth a fair woman which doth make the best use that she can to set out her beauty, rather glorify God in so beautiful a work than infect his soul with so lascivious a thought? And for the woman . . . is she not to be commended rather that . . . she will . . . set out what she hath received from Almighty God, than to be censured that she doth it to allure wanton and lascivious looks?

The difference is in the minds: things which are called *Adiaphora* (things indifferent), whose qualities have their name from the uses, are commonly so censured and so used as the mind is inclined which doth pass his verdict . . . When men complain of beauty and say that 'women's dressings and attire are provocations to wantonness and baits to allure men', it is a direct means to know of what disposition they are. It is a shame for men in censuring of women to condemn themselves . . .

Our adversary chargeth upon our sex: to be lascivious, wanton and lustful. He saith 'Women tempt, allure and provoke men'. How rare a thing is it for women to prostitute and offer themselves? How common practice is it for men to seek and solicit women to lewdness? What charge do they spare? What travail do they bestow? What vows, oaths and protestations do they spend to make them dishonest? They hire panders, they write letters, they seal them with damnations and execrations to assure them of love when the end proves but lust. They know the flexible disposition of women, and the sooner to overreach them some will pretend they are so plunged in love, that except they obtain their desire, they will seem to drown, hang, stab, poison or banish themselves from friends and country. What motives are these to tender dispositions? some will pretend marriage, another offer continual maintenance; but when they have obtained their purpose, what shall a woman find? – just that which is her everlasting shame and grief: she hath made herself the unhappy subject to a lustful body and the shameful stall of a lascivious tongue. Men may with foul shame charge women with this sin which she had never committed, if she had not trusted; nor had ever trusted, if she had not been deceived with vows, oaths and protestations. To bring a woman to offend in one sin, how many damnable sins do they commit? I appeal to their own consciences. The lewd disposition of sundry men doth appear in this: if a woman or maid will yield unto lewdness, what shall they want? – but if they would live in honesty, what help shall they have? How much will they make of the lewd? how base account of the honest? How many pounds will they spend in bawdy houses? but when will they bestow a penny upon an honest maid or woman, except it be to corrupt them?

59 [N.H.], *The Ladies Dictionary* (1694), pp. 303, 420–1, 478–9 [misnumbered from p. 240]

Nightwalkers and Divers: I join them together as being but one and the same thing; for she that is a diver or pickpocket is an infallible stroller or nightwalker.

This occupation is contrary to all other, for she opens her shop-windows when all other trades are about to shut them. The night approaching, she rigs herself out in the best manner she can, with some apparent outward ensign of her profession. Having weighed anchor, and quitted her port, she steers for some one principal street, as Cheapside or Cornhill. With a gentle breeze she first sails slowly on the one side, and if she meet never a man-of-war between Snowhill and Poultry, she tacks and stands away to the other side. But if she be a tolerably rigged frigate, she is laid aboard before, made fast with grapplings, and presently rummaged in the hold; sometimes she sheers off and leaves my man-of-war on fire. You may know her by her brushing you, staring in your face, often halting in the street by gazing about her, or looking after some or other she hath brushed. But the most infallible sign is asking of questions, as 'What is't o'clock?', or, 'I am a stranger, which is my way to such a place?'. If she is picked up she will make a hard shift but she will give a man something whereby he shall remember her as long as he lives. Besides, it is ten pound to a penny but she plays the diver and picks his pocket . . .

Prostitute Doxies: are neither wives, maids nor widows. They will for good victuals, or for a very small piece of money, prostitute their bodies, and then protest they never did any such thing before, that it was pure necessity that now compelled them to do what they have done, and the like; whereas the jades will have [i.e. be] common hackneys upon every slight occasion. They are dexterous in picking of pockets . . . they are destructive queans, and oftentimes secret murderers of the infants which are illegitimately begotten of their bodies.

Stews: are those places where women of professed incontinency proffer their bodies to all comers; from the French, *estuve*, i.e. a bath or hot-house, because wantons are wont to prepare or rather purge themselves for those venerous acts by often bathing and hot-houses . . . Fly from their embraces, as you would from the Devil, for they have many ways to delude . . . These . . . baits they lay for unthinking men who remember not (what Solomon says), 'that the dead are there and her guests are the depths of Hell' [Prov. ix.18; cf. v.5, vii.27].

60 John Bunyan, *Life and Death of Mr. Badman* (1680), pp. 55–6

Mr. Badman has more fellows than Joseph, else there would not be so many whores as there are. For though I doubt not but that sex is bad enough this way, yet I verily believe that many of them are made whores at first by the flatteries of Badman's fellows. Alas! there is many a woman plunged into this sin at first even by promises of marriage. I say, by these promises they are flattered, yea, forced into a consenting to these villanies, and so being in, and growing hardened in their hearts, they at last give themselves up, even as wicked men do, to act this kind of wickedness with greediness. But Joseph, you see, was of another mind, for the fear of God was in him [Gen. xxxix.7–12].

61 John Wilmot, contribution to *Poems on Affairs of State* (written 1673), pp. 74–5

[*A Satire on Charles II*]

I'th'Isle of Britain long since famous grown
For breeding the best cunts in Christendom,
There reigns and oh long may he reign and thrive
The easiest King and best bred man alive.
Him no ambition moves, to get renown
Like the French fool who wanders up and down
Starving his people, hazarding his crown.
Peace is his aim, his gentleness is such
And love, he loves, for he loves fucking much.

Nor are his high desires above his strength,
His sceptre and his prick are of a length,
And she may sway the one, who plays with th'other
And make him little wiser than his brother.
Restless he rolls about from whore to whore
A merry monarch, scandalous and poor.
Poor prince thy prick like thy buffoons at court
Will govern thee because it makes thee sport.
'Tis sure the sauciest that e're did swive
The proudest peremptoriest prick alive.
Though safety, law, religion, life lay on't,
'Twould break through all to make its way to cunt.
To Carwell the most dear of all his dears
The best relief of his declining years
Oft he bewails his fortunes and her fate
To love so well and be belov'd so late.
For though in her he settles well his tarse
Yet his dull graceless ballocks hang an arse.
This you'd believe had I but time to tell you
The pains it cost the poor laborious Nelly
Whilst she employs hands, fingers, mouth, and thighs
E're she can raise the member she enjoys –
I hate all monarchs, and the thrones they sit on
From Hector of France to the Culley of Britain.

62 John Wilmot, *Poems on Several Occasions* (1680), pp. 44–5

On Mistress Willis

Against the charms our ballocks have
　　How weak all human skill is
Since they can make a man a slave
　　To such a bitch as Willis.

Whom that I may describe throughout
　　Assist me bawdy powers
I'll write upon a double clout
　　And dip my pen in flowers.

Her looks demurely impudent
　　Ungainly beautiful
Her modesty is insolent
　　Her wit both pert and dull.

A prostitute to all the Town
　　And yet with no man friends

She rails and scolds when she lies down
  And curses when she spends.

Bawdy in thoughts, precise in words,
  Ill natured though a whore,
Her belly is a bag of turds,
  Her cunt a common shore.

63 Henry Goodcole, *Discoverie of Elizabeth Sawyer* (1621), sigs A4v–B3v

A True Declaration of the Manner of Proceeding against Elizabeth Sawyer

. . . [it was resolved] to find out by all means they could endeavour, her long and close-carried witchcraft, to explain it to the world, and being descried, to pay in the end such a work of iniquity her wages, and that which she had deserved (namely shame and death [Exod. xxii.18; Rom. vi.23]) from which the Devil, that had so long deluded her, did not come as she said, to show the least help of his unto her to deliver her, but, being descried in his ways and works, immediately he fled, leaving her to shift and answer for herself, with public and private marks on her body as followeth:

1. Her face was most pale and ghost-like, without any blood at all, and her countenance was still dejected to the ground.

2. Her body was crooked and deformed, even bending together, which so happened but a little before her apprehension.

3. That tongue, which by cursing, swearing, blaspheming and imprecating, as afterward she confessed was the occasioning cause of the Devil's access unto her even at that time, and to claim thereby his own, by it discovered her lying, swearing, and blaspheming. As also evident proofs produced against her, to stop her mouth with Truth's authority: at which hearing, she was not able to speak a sensible or ready word for her defence, but sends out in the hearing of the Judge, jury and all good people that stood by, many most fearful imprecations for destruction against herself then to happen, as heretofore she had wished and endeavoured to happen on divers of her neighbours, the which the righteous Judge of Heaven, whom she thus invocated, to judge then and discern her cause, did reveal . . .

On Saturday, being the fourteenth day of April, *Anno Domini* 1621, this Elizabeth Sawyer, late of Edmonton, in the county of Middlesex, spinster, was arraigned and indicted . . . which indictments were, *viz.*

That she . . . by diabolical help did out of her malicious heart (because her neighbours where she dwelt would not buy brooms of her) would therefore thus revenge herself on them in this manner, namely, witch to death their nurse children and cattle . . .

She was also indicted for that she . . . by diabolical help and out of her malice aforethought did witch unto death Agnes Ratcliff, a neighbour of hers . . . because Elizabeth [i.e. Agnes] Ratcliff did strike a sow of hers in her sight for licking up a little soap where she had laid it, and for that Elizabeth Sawyer would be revenged of her and thus threatened Agnes Ratcliff that it should be a dear blow unto her, which accordingly fell out, and suddenly, for that evening Agnes Ratcliff fell very sick . . . the said Agnes Ratcliff, lying on her death-bed . . . said unto her husband . . . that if she died at that time, she, the said Elizabeth Sawyer, was the cause of her death, and maliciously did by her witchery procure the same.

This made some impression in their minds, and caused careful and due and mature deliberation, not trusting their own judgements, what to do, in a matter of such great import, as life, they deemed, might be conserved [concerned?].

The Foreman of the Jury asked of Master Heneage Finch, Recorder, his direction, and advice, to whom he Christianlike replied, namely, 'Do in it as God shall put in your hearts'.

Master Arthur Robinson, a worshipful Justice of Peace dwelling at Tottenham, had often and divers times upon the complaints of the neighbours against this Elizabeth Sawyer, laboriously and carefully examined her, and still his suspicion was strengthened against her, that doubtless she was a witch. An information was given unto him by some of her neighbours that this Elizabeth Sawyer had a private and strange mark on her body, by which their suspicion was confirmed against her; and he sitting in the Court at that time of her trial, informed the Bench thereof, desiring the Bench to send for women to search her presently before the jury did go forth to bring in the verdict . . .

The Bench commanded officers appointed for those purposes to fetch in three women . . . one of the women's names was Margaret Weaver, that keeps the Sessions House for the City of London, a widow of an honest reputation, and two other grave matrons, brought in by the officer out of the street, passing by there by chance, were joined with her in this search of the person named, who, fearing and perceiving she should by that search of theirs be then discovered, behaved herself most sluttishly and loathsomely towards them, intending thereby to prevent their search of her . . . yet nevertheless, niceness they laid aside, and according to the request of the Court . . . they all three severally searched her . . . And they all three said that a little above the fundament of Elizabeth Sawyer . . . [they] found a thing like a teat, the bigness of the little finger, and the length of half a finger, which was branched at the top like a teat, and seemed as though one had sucked it, and that the bottom thereof was blue, and the top of it was red. This view of theirs, and answer that she had such a thing about her, which boldly she denied, gave some insight to the Jury of her, who, upon their consciences, returned the said Elizabeth Sawyer to be guilty by diabolical help of the death of Agnes Ratcliff only, and acquitted her of the other two indictments.

64 Thomas Heywood, *Gynækeion* (1624), pp. 397, 406–7. 445–6

Of Witches

It was never found or known that ever any witch could by exorcisms or incantations add anything to Nature to make herself in any part appear more comely. It is further observed that all such are for the most part stigmatical and ugly, insomuch that it is grown into a common adage *Deformis ut saga*, i.e. as deformed as a witch. Moreover, Cardanus, who was not held the least amongst the magicians (as having his art, or rather diabolical practice, from his father hereditary) confesseth that in all his lifetime, in his great familiarity and acquaintance amongst them, he never knew any one that was not in some part misshapen and deformed. The same author . . . affirms that all those demoniacs or witches after they have had commerce and congress with the Devil, have about them a continual nasty and odious smell, or which (by the ancient writers) they were called *fœtentes*, . . . i.e. of stench; insomuch that women who by nature have a more sweet and refreshing breath than men, after their beastly consociety with Satan, change the property of nature and grow horrid, putrid, corrupt and contagious. For Sprangerus witnesseth (who hath taken the examination of many) they have confessed (a thing fearful to be spoken) to have had carnal copulation with evil and unclean spirits, who no doubt bear the smell of the invisible sulphur about them . . .

All agree that some have made express covenant with the Devil by bond and indenture sealed and delivered; others, by promise and oath only. As likewise that all such have secret marks about them in some private place of their bodies, some in the inside of the lip, some in the hair of the eyebrow, some in the fundament, some in the inside of the thigh, the hollow of the arm or privy parts . . .

Of Witches and the Punishments due to them

The Scripture saith, 'Thou shalt not suffer a witch to live' [Exod. xxii.18]. Bodinus (contrary to Wyerius, who will scarce believe there be any such, accounting all those judges as condemn them to the stake or gallows, no better than executioners and hangmen) he shows divers probable reasons why they ought not to live. The first is, because all witches renounce God and their religion . . . The second is, that having renounced God and their religion, they curse, blaspheme, and provoke the Almighty to anger . . . The third is, that they plight faith and make covenant with the Devil, adore him and make sacrifice to him . . . A fourth thing is (which many have confessed), that they have vowed their children to the Devil . . . A fifth thing is (gathered out of their own confessions), that they have sacrificed infants not yet baptized to the Devil, and have killed them by thrusting great pins into their heads . . . A sixth thing is, that they do not only offer children in the manner of sacrifice . . . but they vow them in the womb. A seventh is, that they are not themselves blasphemers and idolaters only, but they are tied by covenant with the Devil to allure and persuade others to the like abominations . . . An eighth is, that they not only call upon the Devil, but swear by his name . . . A ninth is, that adulterous incests are frequent amongst them . . . A tenth, that they are homicides . . . Next, that they kill children before their baptism, by which circumstance their offence is more capital and heinous. The eleventh, that witches eat of the flesh of infants, and commonly drink their bloods, in which they take much delight . . . A twelfth is,that they kill as oft by poisons, as by powders and magic spells . . . A thirteenth is, that they are the death of cattle . . . A fourteenth, that they blast the corn and grain, and bring barrenness and scarcity . . . A fifteenth, that they have carnal consociety with the Devil . . .

7

VIRTUES

Although Christianity imposes the same moral code upon men and women and offers to each the same promise of grace and salvation the widespread assumption that woman's weaker nature made her more prone than men to certain (if not all) vices required of her the practice of what were seen as preeminently feminine virtues: most especially, obedience and submissiveness were hers (65, 71), for her unreliable intellect and unruly passions stood in need of the guidance of 'masculine and wise counsellors', in Lucy Hutchinson's phrase (127; cf. 26, and see further chapter 9). It is consequently no surprise that the opposed Biblical stereotypes of the whore and the good woman (47) continued to dominate the century's discourse as they had done that of the Middle Ages. Classical texts provided precisely similar types (66). Opposed to the vices outlined in chapter 6 above are their contrary virtues: silence, patience, discretion, piety, modesty and chastity (67, 68, 69). Opposed, too, are the virtues proper to men and to women. The dynamic virtues are masculine, the passive feminine. Courage, magnanimity and authority belong to men; bashfulness, reticence and obedience to women. In the figure of the Amazon Radigund, to whom the knight Artegal yields in combat out of misguided pity, Edmund Spenser represented the monstrosity of female assertiveness (70). 'Virtuous women wisely understand / That they were born to base humility' and should 'obey the 'hests of man's well ruling hand'. For his part, Artegal is 'justly damned' to the punishment of role reversal and the shame of 'woman's weeds' for having permitted this perversion of the natural order through his abdication of his masculine authority.

After the Restoration, and in reaction against the radical sexual politics of the Interregnum (for which see 133–7), this notion of sexual difference is ever more inclined to infer from the softness of women's bodies the softness (that is, sensitivity and compassion) of their natures. The gentler virtues are peculiarly (and 'naturally') theirs. That influential advocate of the refined manners of the new age, Richard Allestree, was in no doubt that to ignore this 'distinction between the masculine and feminine virtues' is both unnatural and ungodly. A woman who fails to exemplify his ideal of passive femininity is frustrating her own nature. Consequently, the indecent, immodest and oafish behaviour expected in, and permitted to, men becomes intolerable and shameful in her; it is not merely morally reprehensible but unwomanly, and so shocking, monstrous (71). By the date of *The Ladies Dictionary* (1694), the demands of gracefulness and elegance further enervate female potential. The *Dictionary* portends the tender hearts and charitable works by which eighteenth-century ladies would seek to give substance to what too easily threatened to become merely decorative lives (72).

Early in the century William Crashaw, Puritan minister and father of the poet, epitomized the 'good woman' in the epitaph and summary of Ussher's funeral sermon with which the volume of elegiac tributes to his wife begins (73); late in the century another minister, Anthony Walker, exemplified very similar virtues in his account of his wife's merits (74). Like the preface (75) to Elizabeth Jocelin's posthumous advice book (for discussion see Beilin (1990), pp. 271–5), they follow Proverbs xxxi (76) in assuming that the good woman is, in the words of the Geneva Bible's page-heading, 'A virtuous wife' (Travitsky (1980), pp. 39–40). Virginity in women was not held in the esteem it enjoyed in early Christianity and in the Roman tradition (see Brown (1988), *passim*, and Castelli (1986), pp. 65–78). For devout Protestants, the marital estate was as much honoured by Mary as was the virgin (68). A Puritan sensibility might go further: Lucy Hutchinson derided celibacy as grounds for Edward the Confessor's claim to sanctity by describing him as that 'superstitious prince, who was sainted for his ungodly chastity' (Hutchinson, *Memoirs of the Life of Colonel Hutchinson*, p. 280). From Gen. ii.8 the Protestant tradition inferred that celibacy was undesirable (cf. Milton in 18); its exemplary women are, like Christiana in Part II of *The Pilgrim's Progress* (1684), wives and mothers (77), faithfully obedient to their husbands (see further chapter 9, and, for dissent from this view, chapter 17).

～

65 Thomas Heywood, *Gynækeion* (1624), p. 268

It is reported of a young woman of Lacena that, a great man sending her rich gifts to corrupt her chastity, she returned him this answer: 'Whilst I was a virgin, I was taught to obey my father, which I accordingly did; and, being a wife, to submit myself to my husband's will. If, then, you desire any courtesy at my hands, get first his consent and you shall after understand my further pleasure'.

66 Robert Herrick, *Hesperides* (1648), p. 283

A Defence of Women

Naught are all women: I say no,
Since for one bad, one good I know:
For Clytemnestra most unkind
Loving Alcestis there we find:
For one Medea that was bad,
A good Penelope was had:
For wanton Lais, then we have
Chaste Lucrece, or a wife as grave:
And thus through womankind we see
A good and bad. Sirs credit me.

67 Nicholas Breton, *The Good and the Badde* (1615), p. 273

A Quiet Woman

A quiet woman is like a still wind, which neither chills the body nor blows dust in the face. Her patience is a virtue that wins the heart of love, and her wisdom makes her will well worthy regard. She fears God and flieth sin, showeth kindness and loveth peace. Her tongue is tied to discretion, and her heart is the harbour of goodness. She is a comfort of calamity and in prosperity a companion, a physician in sickness and a musician in help. Her ways are the walk toward heaven, and her guide is the grace of the Almighty. She is her husband's down-bed, where his heart lies at rest, and her children's glass in the notes of her grace; her servants' honour in the keeping of her house, and her neighbours' example in the notes of a good nature. She scorns fortune and loves virtue, and out of thrift gathereth charity. She is a turtle in her love, a lamb in her meekness, a saint in her heart, and an angel in her soul. In sum, she is a jewel unprizeable and a joy unspeakable, a comfort in nature incomparable, and a wife in the world unmatchable.

68 Dorothy Leigh, *The Mothers Blessing* (1616), pp. 27–43

The names I have chosen you [her children] are these: Philip, Elizabeth, James, Anna, John and Susanna. The virtues of them that bore those names, and the cause why I chose them, I let pass and only mean to write of the last name, Susan, famoused through the world for chastity, a virtue which always hath been and is of great account, not only amongst the Christians and people of God, but even among the heathen and infidels; insomuch that some of them have written that a woman that is truly chaste, is a great partaker of all other virtues, and, contrariwise, that the woman that is not truly chaste hath no virtue in her. The which saying may well be warranted by the Scripture, for who is truly chaste is free from idleness and from all vain delights, full of humility and all good Christian virtues. Who so is chaste is not given to pride in apparel, nor any vanity, but is always either reading, meditating, or practising some good thing which she hath learned in the Scripture. But she which is unchaste, is given to be idle, or, if she do anything, it is for a vain glory, and not for the praise of men, more than for any humble, loving and obedient heart, that she beareth unto God and his Word, who said, 'Six days thou shalt labour' (Exod. xx.9), and so left no time for idleness, pride, or vanity; for in none of these is there any holiness. The unchaste woman is proud, and always decking herself with vanity, and delights to hear the vain words of men, in which there is not only vanity, but also so much wickedness, that the vain words of men, and women's vainness in hearing them, hath brought many women to much sorrow and vexation . . .

An unchaste woman destroyeth both the body and the soul of him she seemeth most to love, and it is almost impossible to set down the mischiefs which have come through unchaste women. Solomon saith that 'her steps lead to hell' (Prov. ii.18). Wherefore, bring up your daughters, as Susanna's parents brought her up . . .

Mary was filled with the Holy Ghost, and with all goodness, and yet is called the blessed Virgin, as if our God should (as he doth indeed) in brief comprehend all other virtues under this one virtue of chastity. Wherefore I desire, that all women, what name soever they bear, would learn of this blessed Virgin to be chaste. For though she were more replenished with grace than any other, and more freely beloved of the Lord, yet the greatest title that she had was, that she was a blessed and pure Virgin; which is a great cause to move all women whether they be maids or wives (both which estates she honoured) to live chastely, to whom for this cause God hath given a cold and temperate disposition, and bound them with these words, 'Thy desire shall be subject to thy husband' (Gen. iii.6). As if God in mercy should say: 'You of your selves shall have no desires, only they shall be subject to your husband's'. Which hath been verified in heathen women, so as it is almost incredible to be believed, for many of them before they would be defiled, have been careless of their lives, and so have endured all those torments, that men would devise to inflict upon them, rather than they would lose the name of a modest maid, or a chaste matron . . .

Some of the Fathers have written that it is not enough for a woman to be chaste, but even so to behave herself that no man may think or deem her to be unchaste . . .

Some godly and reverend men of the Church have gathered this, that there were five women of great virtue in time of the [Mosaic] Law, the first letters of whose names do make her [Mary's] whole name [Maria], to show that she had all their virtues wholly combined in her, as namely: Michal, Abigail, Rachel, Judith, and Anna.

She was as faithful to her husband as Michal, who saved her husband, David, from the fury of Saul, although he were her father and her king, not preferring her own life before the safety of her husband (I Sam. xix.12). She was as wise as Abigail, who is highly commended for her wisdom (I Sam. xxv.3); amiable in the sight of her husband as Rachel (Gen. xxix.17); stout and magnanimous in the time of trouble as Judith [Judith viii.1ff.]; patient and zealous in prayer as Anna [Luke ii.36]. Seeing then, that by this one name so many virtues are called to remembrance, I think it meet that good names be given to all women, that they might call to mind the virtues of those women whose names they bear; but especially above all other moral virtues, let women be persuaded by this discourse to embrace chastity, without which we are mere beasts and no women.

69 Richard Brathwait, *The English Gentlewoman* (1631), pp. 50, 82–9

Behaviour

. . . Women in sundry countries, when they go into any public concourse or press of people, use to wear veils, to imply that secret enscreened beauty which best becomes a woman, *bashful modesty*, which habit our own nation now in later years hath observed, which . . . deserves approvement, because it expresseth in itself *modest shamefastness*, a woman's chief ornament. I second his opinion, who held it for divers main respects a custom very irregular and indecent, that women should frequent places of public resort, as stage-plays, wakes, solemn feasts, and the like. It is occasion that depraves us, company that corrupts us . . .

Decency

. . . It is no hard thing to gather the disposition of our hearts by the dimension of our gate. What a circular gesture we shall observe some use in their pace, as if they were troubled with the vertigo! Others make a tinkling with their feet, and make discovery of their light thoughts by their wanton gait . . . This cannot decency endure . . .

Far be these ways from your walks, virtuous ladies, whose modesty makes you honoured of your sex . . . Though the world be your walk while you sojourn here, heaven should be your aim, that you may repose eternally there. Live devoutly, walk demurely, profess constantly, that devotion may instruct you, your ways direct you, your profession conduct you to your heavenly country . . .

'Thou that art young, speak, if need be, and yet scarcely when thou art twice asked. Comprehend much in few words; in many be as one that is ignorant; be as one that understandeth, and yet hold thy tongue' (Ecclus.

[xxxii.7–8]). The direction is general, but to none more consequently useful than to young ones, whose bashful silence is an ornament to their sex. Volubility of tongue in these, argues either rudeness of breeding or boldness of expression. The former may be reclaimed by a discreet tutor, but the latter, being grounded on arrogancy of conceit, seldom or never. It will beseem you, Gentlewomen, whose generous education hath estranged you from the first, and whose modest disposition hath weaned you from the last, in public consorts to observe rather than discourse. It suits not with her honour for a young woman to be prolocutor; but especially when either men are in presence or ancient matrons, to whom she owes a civil reverence, it will become her to tip her tongue with silence . . .

There is nothing which moves us more to pride it in sin than that which was first given us to cover our shame. The fruit of a Tree made man a sinner; and the leaves of a Tree gave him a cover. In your habit is your modesty best expressed . . . It skills not much for the quality of your habits, whether they be silken or woollen, so they be civil and not wanton . . .

70 Edmund Spenser, *The Faerie Queene* (1590–6), V.v.20–5 [II.213–14]

Then took the Amazon this noble knight,
   Left to her will by his own wilful blame,
   And caused him to be disarmed quite,
   Of all the ornaments of knightly name,
   With which whilom he gotten had great fame:
   Instead whereof she made him to be dight
   In woman's weeds, that is to manhood shame,
   And put before his lap an apron white,
Instead of curiets and bases fit to fight.

So being clad, she brought him from the field,
   In which he had been trained many a day,
   Into a long large chamber, which was sield
   With monuments of many knights' decay,
   By her subdued in victorious fray:
   Amongst the which she caused his warlike arms
   Be hang'd on high, that might his shame bewray;
   And broke his sword, for fear of further harms,
With which he wont to stir up battailous alarms.

There entered in, he round about him saw
   Many brave knights, whose names right well he knew,
   There bound t'obey that Amazon's proud law,
   Spinning and carding all in comely rew,
   That his big heart loath'd so uncomely view.

But they were forc'd through penury and pine,
   To do those works, to them appointed due:
   For nought was given them to sup or dine,
But what their hands could earn by twisting linen twine.

Amongst them all she placed him most low,
   And in his hand a distaff to him gave,
   That he thereon should spin both flax and tow;
   A sordid office for a mind so brave.
   Yet he it took in his own self's despite,
   And thereto did himself right well behave,
   Her to obey, sith he his faith had plight,
Her vassal to become, if she him won in fight.

Who had him seen, imagine might thereby,
   That whilom hath of Hercules been told,
   How for Iole's sake he did apply
   His mighty hands, the distaff vile to hold,
   For his huge club, which had subdu'd of old
   So many monsters, which the world annoyed;
   His lion's skin changed to a pall of gold,
In which forgetting wars, he only joyed
In combats of sweet love, and with his mistress toyed.

Such is the cruelty of womenkind,
   When they have shaken off the shamefast band,
   With which wise Nature did them strongly bind,
   T'obey the 'hests of man's well ruling hand,
   That then all rule and reason they withstand,
   To purchase a licentious liberty.
   But virtuous women wisely understand,
   That they were born to base humility,
Unless the heavens them lift to lawful sovereignty.

71 [Richard Allestree], *The Ladies Calling* (1673), pp. 3–15, 29–30, 36–40, 48, 65, 79

That the obligation to moral and Christian virtues is in itself universal, and not confined to any sex or person, is not to be denied: yet, as in human constitutions there are often precepts which (though not exclusive of any, do yet) more peculiarly and eminently level at some particular rank or order of men, so in the laws of God and Nature, there appears a like distinction . . . This sure is shadowed to us in that particular caution given to the Jews, not to confound the habit of the several sexes, Deut. xii.5, and yet more clearly evinced in the precept which the Apostles address to women, I Tim. ii and I

Pet.iii. Nay, this is granted a truth, that all ages and nations have made some distinction between masculine and feminine virtues, Nature having not only given a distinction as to the beauties of their outward form, but also in their very mould and constitution implanted peculiar aptnesses and proprieties of mind, which accordingly vary the measure of decency; that being comely for one sex, which often is not (at least in the same degree) for the other . . . [In the] first rank of female virtues . . . we shall choose to begin with the virtue of modesty . . . It appears in the face in calm and meek looks, where it so impresses itself, that it seems thence to have acquired the name of shamefacedness. Certainly (whatever the modern opinion is) there is nothing gives a greater lustre to feminine beauty . . .

. . . And as modesty prescribes the manner, so it does also the measure of speaking, restrains all excessive talkativeness, a fault incident to none but the bold. It is indeed universally an insolent unbecoming thing, but most peculiarly so in a woman . . .

And this great indecency of loquacity in women, I am willing to hope is the reason why that sex is so generally charged with it, not that they are all guilty, but that when they are, it appears so unhandsome, as makes it the more eminent and remarkable. Whether it were from that ungracefulness of the thing, or from the propension women have to it, I shall not determine; but we find the Apostle very earnest in his cautions against it, I Cor. xi.35. He expressly enjoins women to 'keep silence in the Church', where he affirms it a shame for them to speak . . . besides this, he has a more indefinite prescription of silence to women, I Tim. ii.11–12 . . .

But besides this assuming sort of talkativeness, there is another usually charged upon the sex, a mere chatting, prattling humour, which maintains itself at the cost of their neighbours . . . This I would fain hope is the voice of the vulgar sort of women, the education of the nobler sort setting them above those mean entertainments . . .

Such a degenerous age do we now live in, that everything seems inverted, even sexes, whilst men fall to the effeminacy and niceness of women, and women take up the confidence and boldness of men, and this too under the notion of good breeding. A blush (though formerly reputed the colour of virtue) is accounted worse manners than those things which ought to occasion it, and such as nothing but the simplicity of a country girl can excuse. But the infirmity for the most part proves very corrigible. A few weeks of the town discipline wears off that piece of rusticity and advances them to a modish assurance. Nor is that designed to terminate in itself, but it is to carry them on, till they arise to a perfect metamorphosis, their gesture, their language, nay sometimes their habit too being affectedly masculine . . .

. . . there are women who think they have not made a sufficient escape from their sex, till they have assumed the vices of men too. A sober modest dialect is too effeminate for them: a blustering ranting style is taken up . . . 'Tis true indeed an oath sounds gratingly out of whatever mouth, but out of a woman's it hath such an uncouth harshness that there is no noise on this side Hell can be more amazingly odious . . .

. . . Modesty [is] . . . the most indispensable requisite of a woman, a thing so essential and natural to the sex, that every the least declination from it, is a proportionable receding from womanhood, but the total abandoning it ranks them among beasts . . .

In the next place we may rank meekness as a necessary feminine virtue; this even Nature seems to teach, which abhors monstrosities and disproportions, and therefore having allotted to women a more smooth and soft composition of body, infers thereby her intention that the mind should correspond . . . But it is not Nature only which suggests this, but the God of Nature also, meekness being not only recommended to all as a Christian virtue, but particularly enjoined to women as a peculiar accomplishment of their sex, I Pet. iii.4 . . .

. . . Meekness . . . lies in . . . submission to . . . the will of God . . . a will regulated by reason in things within its sphere . . . a will duly submissive to lawful superiors . . . And as a will thus resigned to reason and just authority is a felicity all rational natures should aspire to, so especially the feminine sex, whose passions being naturally the more impetuous, ought to be the more strictly guarded and kept under the severe discipline of reason; for where 'tis otherwise, where a woman has no guide but her will, and her will is nothing but her humour, the event is sure to be fatal to herself, and often to others also.

. . . Yet sure God and Nature do attest the particular expediency of this to women, by having placed that sex in a degree of inferiority to the other. Nay, farther, 'tis observable that as there are but three states of life through which they can regularly pass, virginity, marriage and widowhood, two of them are states of subjection, the first to the parent, the second to the husband, and the third, as it is casual, whether ever they arrive to it or no, so if they do, we find it by God himself reckoned as a condition the most desolate and deplorable . . . And since God's assignation has thus determined subjection to be the woman's lot, there needs no other argument of its fitness, or for their acquiescence. Therefore, whenever they oppose it, the contumacy flies higher than the immediate superior, and reaches God himself . . .

Of near affinity to the virtue of meekness is that of mercy or compassion . . .

In the next place we may reckon affability and courtesy, which as it is amiable in all, so it is singularly so in women of quality, and more universally necessary in them than in the other sex; for men have often charges and employments which do justify, nay perhaps require somewhat of sternness and austerity, but women ordinarily have few or no occasions of it . . .

Lastly, to complete and crown all other excellency, nothing is so proper, so necessary as piety and devotion . . .

72 [N.H.], *The Ladies Dictionary* (1694),
pp. 135–7, 174, 305, 327–8, 397, 459 [misnumbered after p. 240]

Compassion and a Merciful Disposition, praiseworthy in the female sex: Compassion is that which inclines us to do good to all, but more especially to those that are in misery and stand in need of our help . . . and this chiefly should reign in the lovely tender breasts of the female sex, made for the seats of mercy and commiseration. They being made of the softest mould, ought to be most pliant and yielding to the impression of pity and compassion, and to redouble the horror of any sad object . . . The application is very obvious, and directs all that own the title of virtuous women, to prefer the necessities of the hungry and needy before their own delicacies . . . there are many ways among those of ability to save out of superfluous expenses that which would warm and fill the hungry . . .

Gracefulness: Grant we that beauty external in woman is exceedingly to be admired, yet more by the vulgar than those who see with clearer eyes into the chief graces and ornaments of the fair sex. As from the well-mixed elements arises bodily temperament, and from the blood mingling with lively humours in the face, beauty, so from a well-tempered spirit ariseth gracefulness . . .

Meekness: meekness may be ranked with humility, and both of them are very comely and adorning to birth and beauty, commanding love and affection from all . . . Meekness is not only enjoined to all as a Christian virtue but is in a more peculiar manner enjoined to women as one main accomplishment of their sex . . .

Natural Modesty: . . . Intemperance is visible in but few of the very worst of females; meekness is seldom disordered in them without great provocation; and as their sex is generally more difficult to be exasperated, they are more easy to forgive than ours: 'tis far the most part our fault if they injure us. *Modesty* is so inherent to their frame, that they cannot divest themselves of it without violence to their nature . . .

Silence: the true virtue of silence cannot be too much commended. It is such a quality that I want words to express its worth . . . Speech enricheth and corrupteth, but silence is poor, but honest. I am not so much against discourse as vain prattling, which consumes time and profiteth nobody . . .

Patience, admirable in either sex: patience is a necessary exercise for everyone that lives in this world, for there is none so free from one cross or other but this virtue will be wanting to render him the more easy in the course of his life. The female sex especially ought to be endued with it, because they have frequent occasion to use it . . .

73 [William Crashaw], *The Honour of Vertue* [1620], sigs A2–A4

The Monument,
To the Honour of Christ Jesus,
To the Praise of Piety,
To the Example of Posterity,
And for the Preservation of the Godly Memory
of
Elizabeth
His most worthily beloved wife,
A woman of a hundred,
Wife of a thousand,
Descended
Of the worshipful families the
Skinners and Emersons.

In whom (by a rare conjunction,
So happy was she, and so highly beloved of God)
Godliness and Comeliness,
Wisdom and Virtue,
Beauty with Chastity
Youth with Discretion,
And Discretion with Devotion,
Were most sweetly combined.

Who, in the prime of her years,
Upon her first child,
By her first husband,
Even in the very birth,
Yielded up by untimely death,
Her soul to God, her life to Nature,
Her body to the earth,
Her memory to the world,
And left
To the pensive father a dear bought son,
To her friends heaviness hard to be removed,
To her husband sorrow, not to be expressed,
And to all that knew her, a longing desire after
Her, never (in this world) to be satisfied.
William Crashaw
Her most sad and sorrowful husband
Unworthy pastor of this Church,
Unworthy husband of such a wife,
Mourning for his own unworthiness,
Yet rejoicing in her happiness,
Most unwilling to part with her,

106

But most willing to honour her, with many sighs and tears,
Dedicated this monument
In assurance of her glorious resurrection.

I know that my Redeemer liveth (Job xix.[25])

The funeral sermon was made by Doctor [James] Ussher of Ireland, then in England, and now Lord Bishop of Meath in Ireland . . .

He useth to be very wary and moderate in commendation. But of her he said, holiness and the truth itself forbad him to be silent. That which he observed in her was:

That besides her piety, charity, devotion, modesty, sobriety, housewifery and other worthy qualities, wherein she excelled the best, peculiarly in these she excelled:

1.   Being young, healthful, and living in great content, and with a husband after her own heart, yet she longed to leave this life and rejoiced to think or speak or hear of the life to come.

2.   Being young, fair, comely, brought up as a gentlewoman, in music, dancing, and like to be of great estate, and therefore much sought after by young gallants and rich heirs, and good jointures offered, yet she chose a divine, twice her own age.

3.   Her extraordinary love, and almost strange affection to her husband, expressed in such excellent and well tempered passages of kindness as is too rare to find in one of her age, person and parts.

4.   Her singular motherly affection to the children of her predecessor. A rare virtue (as he noted) in step-mothers at this day.

5.   Her excellent disposition from her infancy in that, from a child, she never offended her parents, nor was ever heard to swear an oath.

6.   Her husband's discretion being questioned by some, for such a choice, and it being the common conceit that by this marriage they had lost a good preacher, contrariwise, her comeliness in attire and excellency of behaviour graced him everywhere, and her zeal in religion, her kindness to him, her care of his health, and her honourable estimation of his profession, encouraged him to do more than ever he did, insomuch as she was a principal cause of his beginning that morning exercise, for which so many hundred poor souls do daily praise God.

74 [Anthony Walker], *The Holy Life of Mrs. Elizabeth Walker* (1690), pp. 168–200

Acts and Kinds of her Great Charity

. . . she would be overbalanced against her own inclination, if there were *charity* in the case. She was not more averse from any thing than the enlarging our family, loved to have it as small as might be, that it might be still and private, free from disturbing noise and distracting diversions . . . yet was she cheerfully content when charity opened the door, and made the fire and bed . . .

. . . besides what she gave in money, she . . . bought good cloth to clothe poor women and children . . . She used to buy primers, psalters, testaments, Bibles to give away, and other good books . . . she yearly gave to poor women when with child, not only old linen, but a good new blanket every lying-in. She would also be ready to supply the poor with work when she heard they wanted . . .

. . . none ever equalled her . . . to put forth her utmost ability and strength in assisting the sick and infirm; not the meanest neighbour whom she would not visit and help in such circumstances . . . [for] women labouring with child . . . she would rise at any hour of the night to go to, and carry with her what might be useful to them . . . and there was scarcely ever any difficulty in that case round about but recourse was made to her, both for advice and medicine; and, if it might be with convenience, for her presence . . .

. . . her *sympathy* with others, in their sufferings and sorrows . . . was as signal as her *patience* in her own . . .

Several Graces in which She Was Most Eminent

. . . For her *repentance*, it was her daily business to renew it, and approve it to be sincere . . . Her *reverential fear* of God was very remarkable: she could not endure to hear sacred things spoken of with lightness, much less with scorn and ridicule . . . Her *obedience* was very uniform, universal, unreserved, and constant . . . She did not cull out cheap and easy duties . . . but what was God's will commanding, was her will obeying . . . Her *sincerity* was very eminent; she hated guile and hypocrisy with a perfect hatred . . . For her *modesty* . . . I never heard a word proceed from her mouth of unpure defiling sound or sense . . . Her garb and dress, her carriage and gestures, and her whole conversation were all of a piece with her communication, which was always savoury . . . she was as *meek* as a lamb in her own cause, though as bold as a lion in the cause of God . . .

Her care to *improve* that inch of precious time on which so vast an eternity depends, was very signal. She squandered not an hour . . . Her *zeal* was very vigorous and lively. She knew not what it was to be dull and sluggish . . . Nature, which too often is the remora [hindrance] of grace, in her was a nimble and useful handmaid to it. She had an agile, active body, spare and lean, feared to be fat, saying, she hated to be clogged with a foggy bulk of flesh, and of a vivacious sprightly soul . . .

Lastly, she was clothed with *humility* . . . This I might call her dust-gown, for the aptness of the allusion, only that it hung not so loose about her; but was girded on with the girdle of truth about her loins; she wore it constantly.

75 Thomas Good, preface to Elizabeth Jocelin, *The Mothers Legacie* (1624), sigs a2–a5

The Approbation

In her prosecution of the duty of obedience unto parents I view the deep impression, long since, when she was not above six years old, made in her mind by the last words of her own mother, charging her upon her blessing to show all obedience and reverence to her father (Sir Richard Brooke) and to her reverend grandfather [Laurence Chaderton].

In the whole course of her pen, I observe her piety and humility; these her lines scarce showing one spark of the elementary fire of her secular learning, this her candle being rather lighted from the lamp of the Sanctuary.

In her commission of the office of an overseer to her husband (which the printer is pleased to stile by the name of an epistle dedicatory) what eyes cannot behold the flames of her true and unspotted love toward her dearest, who enjoyed her about the space of six years and a half, being all that while both an impartial witness of her virtues and an happy partner of those blessings both transitory and spiritual wherewith she was endowed.

Besides the domestic cares pertaining to a wife, the former part of those years were employed by her in the studies of morality and history, the better by the help of foreign languages, not without a taste and faculty in poetry. Wherein some essay she hath left, ingenious, but chaste and modest, like the author. Of all which knowledge she was very sparing in her discourses, as possessing it rather to hide than to boast of . . .

The many blessings she enjoyed were not without some seasoning of afflictions, which, by the good use she made of them, bred in her a constant temper of patience, and more than womanly fortitude, especially in her later time, when as the course of her life was a perpetual meditation of death, amounting almost to a prophetical sense of her dissolution, even then when she had not finished the 27 year of her age, nor was oppressed by any disease, or danger, other than the common lot of childbirth, within some months approaching. Accordingly, when she first felt herself quick with child (as then travelling with death itself) she secretly took order for the buying of a new winding-sheet . . . And about that time, undauntedly looking death in the face, privately in her closet between God and her, she wrote these pious meditations . . .

76 Holy Bible, 'Authorized' King James Version (1611)

Proverbs XXXI

10. Who can find a virtuous woman? for her price is far above rubies.

11. The heart of her husband doth safely trust in her, so that he shall have no need of spoil.

12. She will do him good and not evil all the days of her life.

13. She seeketh wool, and flax, and worketh willingly with her hands.

14. She is like the merchants' ships; she bringeth her food from afar.

15. She riseth also while it is yet night, and giveth meat to her household, and a portion to her maidens.

16. She considereth a field, and buyeth it: with the fruit of her hands she planteth a vineyard.

17. She girdeth her loins with strength, and strengtheneth her arms.

18. She perceiveth that her merchandise is good: her candle goeth not out by night.

19. She layeth her hands to the spindle, and her hands hold the distaff.

20. She stretcheth out her hand to the poor, yea, she reacheth forth her hands to the needy.

77 Margaret Cavendish, 'A True Relation of My Birth' (1656), pp. 163–5

But not only the family I am linked to [Cavendishes] is ruined, but the family from which I sprung [Lucases], by these unhappy wars. Which ruin my mother [Elizabeth Lucas, née Leighton] lived to see, and then died [1647], having lived a widow many years; for she never forgot my father [Thomas Lucas, d. 1625] so as to marry again. Indeed, he remained so lively in her memory, and her grief was so lasting, as she never mentioned his name, though she spoke often of him, but love and grief caused tears to flow, and tender sighs to rise, mourning in sad complaints. She made her house her cloister, inclosing herself, as it were, therein, for she seldom went abroad, unless to church. But these unhappy wars forced her out, by reason she and her children were loyal to the King; for which they plundered her and my brothers of all their goods, plate, jewels, money, corn, cattle, and the like, cut down their woods, pulled down their houses, and sequestered them from their lands and livings; but in such misfortunes my mother was of an heroic spirit, in suffering patiently where there is no remedy, or to be industrious where she thought she could help. She was of a grave behaviour, and had such a majestic grandeur, as it were continually hung about her, that it would strike a kind of awe to the beholders, and command respect from the rudest (I mean the rudest of civilized people, I mean not such barbarous people as plundered her, and used her cruelly, for they would have pulled God out of heaven, had they had power, as they did royalty out of his throne). Also her beauty was beyond the ruin of time, for she had a well-favoured loveliness in her face, a pleasing sweetness in her countenance, and a well-tempered complexion, as neither too red nor too pale, even to her dying hour, although in years. And by her dying, one might think death was enamoured with her, for he embraced her as she slept, and so gently, as if he were afraid to hurt her. Also she was an affectionate mother, breeding her children with a most industrious care, and tender love; and having eight children, three sons and five daughters, there was not any one crooked, or any ways deformed, neither were they dwarfish, or of a giant-like stature, but every ways proportionable; likewise well-featured, clear complexions, brown hairs (but some lighter than others), sound teeth, sweet breaths, plain speeches, tunable voices . . . But this I dare say, their beauty, if any they had, was not so lasting as my mother's, Time making suddener ruin in their faces than in hers. Likewise my mother was a good mistress to her servants, taking care of her servants in their sickness, not sparing any cost she was able to bestow for their recovery: neither did she exact more from them in their health than what they with ease or rather like a pastime could do. She would freely pardon a fault, and forget an injury, yet sometimes she would be angry; but never with her children, the sight of them would pacify her; neither would she be angry with others but when she had cause, as negligent or knavish servants, that would lavishly or unnecessarily waste, or subtly and thievishly steal. And though she would often complain that her family was too great for her weak management, and often pressed my brother to take it upon him, yet I observe she took a pleasure, and some little pride, in the governing thereof.

Part II
FEMALE ROLES
AND AFFAIRS

8

MARRIAGE, ADULTERY
AND DIVORCE

In what remains one of the most fully documented accounts of its subject Stone (1977) argued that, during the late sixteenth and seventeenth centuries, the 'open lineage' (or extended) family was replaced by the nuclear family and that, correspondingly, the notion of marriage as a matter of duty and parental arrangement yielded to a marital ideal of loving companionship. He further distinguished between the 'patriarchal nuclear family' of the late Elizabethan and early Stuart period and, in what he calls the 'decisive shift' (p. 7), the development in the later seventeenth century of the less hierarchical 'closed domesticated nuclear family'. In itself, this thesis was not novel; historians have long argued that Protestantism introduced a more positive view of the marriage partnership than that held by Medieval Catholicism. Stone's development of it, however, has come in for a good deal of criticism (see Ferguson (1985), p. 40, n. 13, for a succinct listing of texts, of which Houlbrooke (1984) and Ezell (1987) are the most substantial), much of it alleging that he minimizes lacunae and contradictions in the evidence and exaggerates the degree of change which occurred in both the theory and practice of marriage. It is characteristic of his critics to doubt that the extended family ever existed in any meaningful sense (Laslett (1983), pp. 90–6) and to hold, like Houlbrooke (1984), that 'Six hundred years ago the nuclear family was the basic element in English society as it still is today' (pp. 14–15).

Disputing that the idea of marriage was transformed in the early modern period and stressing continuity with the past, Stone's critics point out that, in the Medieval period, 'Affection and obedience were the bases of the performance of familial duties. Mutual love was described as the basis of marriage' (Houlbrooke (1984), p. 21; cf. Davies (1981)). Even so, the weight of Medieval tradition unquestionably preferred celibacy and virginity to marriage and sexual fulfilment and an air of concession and regret consequently hangs over all marriage counsels, of suspicion and disquiet over all discussions of sexual love. In the words of Brooke (1989), 'Medieval clergymen accepted that marriage was of divine institution, but many of them thought it pretty rum – on the most optimistic view a second best' (p. 277), or, as Chaucer's Wife of Bath had tersely remarked, 'it is an impossible / That any clerk wol speke good of wyves' (*The Wife of Bath's Prologue*, l.689). During the sixteenth and seventeenth centuries Protestantism reversed this emphasis (78, 79): marriage became the 'ethical norm' to which Christians aspired (Stone (1977), p. 135). It continued to be held that marriage was instituted for the procreation of children and as a remedy for lust (79, 80), but far more homiletic and expository energy was now devoted to the joys of its fellowship (Maclean (1980), pp. 19–20), setting 'mutual love' at its heart (160). Procreation may be 'one end of marriage yet it is not the only end' (81: II.i§4; cf. 88). Rather than suppose that marriage was either a consequence of the Fall or a concession to human fallibility, divines inferred from Gen. ii.18 that celibacy is undesirable and that marriage was an essential component of prelapsarian bliss (79; cf. 18). In the erotic poetry of the Song of Songs, wherein, as the headnote in the Geneva Bible puts it, 'is declared the singular love of the bridegroom toward his bride', they found evidence not only of the joy and dignity of marriage (81: II.ii§10) but also of both the decency and the desirability of sexual fulfilment. 'If marriage be not a sin, then the duties of marriage are no sin' (79); on the contrary, marital love is increased through sexual intercourse (81: II.ii§9). It was because sexual pleasure is possible when the woman is barren but not when the man is impotent that marriage was admitted in the former case but not the latter (81: II.i§4. See Doriani (1991) and Turner (1987) for evidence and discussion of Puritan attitudes to marital sexual relations, and cf. chapters 3 and 9). The romantic love which Medieval literature had found so hard to accommodate within marriage is now an essential ingredient of it (82); recourse is had to its language even in the midst of financial transactions and the legal business of marriage settlements (83). Love within marriage was to be the *idée fixe* of the novel, the definitive genre of the new age; its experience is movingly rendered in women's contributions to one of the novel's antecedents, the nascent genres of biography and autobiography, which might recount marital difficulties and crosses in love with novelistic attentiveness (84).

Marriage was consequently conceived as women's proper and 'natural' destiny (see chapter 9); their character, education and behaviour were discussed almost exclusively in relation to it. This can be construed as having reduced woman's sphere into a domestically circumscribed space (Hamilton (1978), pp. 50–75; see further introduction to chapter 12), but, if one excludes monasticism, it is doubtful that the Medieval woman was encouraged to exercise herself in a greater variety of roles, arguable that she was not invested with either the dignity or the authority accorded her by Protestant treatises, and certain that she was subject to a more virulent and widespread clerical misogyny. In that the characteristic emphasis of the seventeenth century recognized the necessity of 'mutual liking' in spouses (81: II.i§13) it granted the woman the right to refuse marriage to a man she could not like, and, even as it disapproved of marriages contracted without parental approval or advice, it disapproved of forced marriages.

Despite its centrality to the period's social and religious thought, the legal status of marriage was peculiarly complicated and indefinite (see Stone (1977), pp. 30–7), confused still more by the exigencies of Civil War (Durston (1989), pp. 66–86). Though Roman Catholics had regarded marriage as a sacrament since 1439, it was not until the Council of Trent so ordered in 1563 that the presence of a priest was legally required (Houlbrooke (1984), p. 79). In the Protestant tradition, marriage was never a sacrament. Its inclination to place marriage in the civil sphere reached its apogee in 1653 when the Puritan Barebone's Parliament established marriage as a secular contract before a Justice of the Peace and declared church weddings alone to be no longer legally binding (Durston (1989), pp. 57–8, 69–70). This lapsed at the Restoration, but throughout our period a private contract (*spousal* or *betrothal*) between a man over fourteen and a woman over twelve was sufficient to constitute a legal marriage (if consummation followed), even against parental wishes, and, it seems, without witnesses, though these were desirable to prove the fact (78, 81: II.i§§13–14, 85). A church wedding (or *nuptials*) was a recommended subsequent and distinct public solemnization (78, 80, 81: II.i§21), but not essential. Consequently, the marriages of Quakers and others separated or excluded from the Church of England were quite legal. Sexual relations might be entered into after the spousal, and cohabitation might then commence, but it was more commonly delayed until after the wedding (83; Stone (1977), p. 31; Macfarlane (1986), pp. 124–9, 299–300, 304–5).

One evidence that conceptions of marriage were undergoing a change is the debate on divorce which was especially prominent in the first half of the century. In the Roman Catholic tradition there was no divorce in the modern sense of the word; a properly constituted marriage could not be dissolved. However, an improperly constituted marriage could be annulled. Those seeking divorce had, therefore, to prove that, through some impediment, theirs had never been a true marriage. Although divorce permitting remarriage for the innocent party was allowed in the European Reformed tradition, this was never available in Protestant England, except, very rarely, by Act of Parliament in individual cases (85; Thomas (1959), p. 200; Stone (1977), pp. 37–41; Houlbrooke (1984), pp. 114–18). Remarriage for the innocent party was not available even in cases of adultery, the commonly accepted grounds for what the seventeenth century termed divorce (81: III.§5, 85, 86, 87), that is, *divortium a mensa et thoro*, the legal separation of the married partners from bed and board, which effectively ended a marriage. Although not even this was universally granted, the Puritan insistence that chastity and fidelity obliged both husband and wife (81: II.ii§§1–7; cf. 94, 95) led more liberal spirits to acknowledge in the wife an equal right to the husband's to sue for divorce on the grounds of adultery (87). In some divines, the emphasis on companionship in marriage encouraged sympathy for the idea of divorce (that is, separation of married partners) on the grounds of incompatibility or breakdown in loving relations. The argument was that if loving companionship is as essential as sexual consummation, its absence is as fatal to the being of a marriage as is want of the latter. It was infamously (but not uniquely) developed by Milton into an argument for divorce in the modern sense, that is, separation permitting remarriage (88; for a full and clear account of thinking and legislation on divorce, see Powell (1917), pp. 61–100, and for discussion of Milton's views in particular see Sirluck (1959), pp. 137–58 and Turner (1987), esp. pp. 188–229).

Milton, however, could not bring himself to grant to the wife an equal right to the husband to sue for divorce. No matter how much the mutuality of companionship might be stressed, its potential to foster a relationship of equals was generally held on a tight rein by patriarchal self-interest. This is nowhere more evident than in the toleration of the 'double standard' whereby women were required to be virgin at marriage and to continue sexually faithful as wives while, without serious consequence, men might come to marriage sexually experienced and be adulterous thereafter (Thomas (1959); Stone (1977), pp. 501–7). Like other divines (e.g. 114), Gouge refused to grant the husband greater sexual licence than the wife, yet he cannot but acknowledge that 'more inconveniences may follow upon the woman's default than upon the man's' since a 'man cannot so well know which be his own children as the woman' (81: II.ii§7). Sixty years later, the urbane Halifax is much less troubled by the ways of the masculine world, and advises his daughter simply to put up with them (89).

True sexual equality is to be found, if at all, only among some few radical sects, notably the Quakers (see 134, 135) and perhaps in the libertinism of a few radical Interregnum enthusiasts. Drawing on Titus i.15 ('unto the pure, all things are pure') and Rom. xiv.20 their antinomianism rejected all moral restraint for the 'perfect freedom' of the Spirit (90). It is, however, doubtful that the consequent exchange of marriage partners and promiscuity reported of, and by, the Ranters (91) liberated women from male domination any more than did the libertinism of high culture in the poems and practices of the Cavaliers or the Restoration court: Coppe's (90) rapture and Carew's (160) may not be so far apart as the social and religious gulf between them suggests. (For further cases, see Durston (1989), pp. 12–13, 20, 25, 31, 95–8, 157–8; for the wider cultural context, see Smith (1989)).

78 William Whately, *A Care-cloth* (1624), pp. 3, 29–32

I Cor. vii.28: 'But and if thou marry, thou hast not sinned; and if a virgin marry, she hath not sinned. Nevertheless, such shall have trouble in the flesh. But I spare you.'

. . . The thing then that the Apostle delivers in this verse, is in effect this: that marriage is not to be forborne as a matter sinful, but troublesome, and virginity to be embraced not as a state of life more holy but alone more easeful; and that he dissuadeth marriage, not as if it were in any sort to be reputed unlawful to marry, but alone because it is commonly attended upon with more difficulty than single life . . .

. . . I go forward to note what the Apostle principally teacheth, and that is plain enough in express words. Marriage is a lawful ordinance for all sorts: no unmarried man shall sin by marrying; no maid shall sin in taking a husband. Any bachelor may make himself a husband; any virgin may make herself a wife. And for the act itself, no sin shall be imputed unto them . . .

. . . The Lord would have men and women enter into matrimony, as it were leisurely and with deliberation; and for this cause it is his ordinance that the covenant should be perfected betwixt them in two degrees. The one is espousal, or betrothment, which they call 'Making sure', and is nothing else but a giving the right of each other's bodies, by a solemn and serious promise of marriage hereafter to be consummated. The other is wedding, called also by the name of marriage, and is nothing but a giving of the possession of each other's bodies by a solemn and serious promise to live together during life.

Now the Scripture, in the two and twentieth chapter of Deuteronomy, doth as well call the betrothed woman a wife of him that betrothed her, as the wedded woman of him that wedded her . . . so it is manifest that if any man or woman have betrothed him or herself to any one person, it is become now utterly unlawful for them to marry with any other person, unless the contract be lawfully dissolved . . .

79 Henry Smith, *A Preparative to Marriage* (1591), pp. 1–5, 8–9, 10–11, 13–17, 22–4

Well might Paul say, 'Marriage is honourable' (Heb. xiii.4), for God hath honoured it himself. It is honourable for the author, honourable for the time, and honourable for the place. Whereas all other ordinances were appointed of God by the hands of men, or the hands of angels, marriage was ordained by God himself, which cannot err . . .

Then it is honourable for the time, for it was the first ordinance which God instituted, even the first thing which he did after man and woman were created, and that in the state of innocency before either had sinned, like the finest flower which will not thrive but in a clean ground. Before man had any other calling he was called to be an husband . . .

Then it is honourable for the place, for whereas all other ordinances were instituted out of Paradise, marriage was instituted in Paradise, in the happiest place, to signify how happy they are which marry in the Lord, they do not only marry one another but Christ is married unto them . . .

As Christ honoured marriage with his birth, so he honoured it with his miracles, for the first miracle which Christ did, he wrought at a marriage in Canaan, where he turned the water into wine (John ii.1–11) . . .

To honour marriage more, it is said that God took a rib out of Adam's side and thereof built the woman. He is not said to make man a wife, but to build him a wife, signifying, that man and wife make as it were one house together, and that the building was not perfect until the woman was made as well as the man . . .

Now, it must needs be, that marriage, which was ordained of such an excellent author, and in such a happy place, and of such an ancient time, and after such a notable order, must likewise have some special causes for the ordinance of it. Therefore the Holy Ghost doth show us three causes of this union. One is, the propagation of children, signified in that when Moses saith, 'He created them male and female' (Gen. i.27), not both male, nor both female, but one male, and the other female, as if he created them fit to propagate other . . . For this cause marriage is called *matrimony*, which signifieth *mothers*, because it maketh them mothers which were virgins before . . .

The second cause is to avoid fornication. This Paul signifieth when he saith, 'For the avoiding of fornication, let every man have his own wife' (I Cor. vi.2). He saith not for the avoiding of adultery, but for avoiding of fornication, showing that fornication is unlawful too . . .

. . . if marriage be a remedy against sin, then marriage itself is no sin, for if marriage were a sin, we might not marry for any cause, because we must not do the least evil that the greatest good may come of it (Rom. iii.8). And if marriage be not a sin, then the duties of marriage are no sin, that is, the secret of marriage is not evil, and therefore Paul saith not only 'Marriage is honourable', but the bed is honourable (Heb. xiii.4), that is, even the action of marriage is as lawful as marriage. Besides, Paul saith, 'Let the husband give unto the wife due benevolence' (I Cor. vii.3). Here is a commandment to yield this duty. That which is commanded is lawful, and not to do it is a breach of the commandment. Therefore marriage was instituted before any sin was, to show that there is no sin in it if it be not abused; but because this is rare, therefore after women were delivered, God appointed them to be purified (Lev. xii.4, 5, etc.), showing that some stain or other doth creep into this action, which had need to be repented, and therefore when they prayed, Paul would have them come together, lest their prayers should be hindered (I Cor. vii.5).

The third cause is, to avoid the inconvenience of solitariness, signified in these words, 'It is not good for man to be alone' (Gen. ii.[18]) . . . God coupled two together, that the infinite troubles which lie upon us in this world might be eased with the comfort and help one of an other, and that the poor in the world might have some comfort as well as the rich.

80 Book of Common Prayer (revised 1662)

The Form of the Solemnization of Matrimony

¶ *First the Banns of all that are to be married together must be published in the Church three several Sundays, during the time of Morning Service, or of Evening Service, (if there be no Morning Service,) immediately after the Second Lesson; the Curate saying after the accustomed manner,*

I publish the Banns of Marriage between *M.* of —— and *N.* of ——. If any of you know cause, or just impediment, why these two persons should not be joined together in holy Matrimony, ye are to declare it. This is the first [*second* or *third*] time of asking.

¶ *And if the persons that are to be married dwell in divers Parishes, the Banns must be asked in both Parishes; and the Curate of the one Parish shall not solemnize Matrimony betwixt them, without a Certificate of the Banns being thrice asked, from the Curate of the other Parish.*

¶ *At the day and time appointed for solemnization of Matrimony, the persons to be married shall come into the body of the Church with their friends and neighbours: and there standing together, the Man on the right hand, and the Woman on the left, the Priest shall say,*

Dearly beloved, we are gathered together in the sight of God, and in the face of this congregation, to join together this Man and this Woman in holy Matrimony; which is an honourable estate, instituted of God in the time of man's innocency, signifying unto us the mystical union that is betwixt Christ and his Church; which holy estate Christ adorned and beautified with his presence, and first miracle that he wrought, in Cana of Galilee [John ii.1–11]; and is commended of Saint Paul to be honourable among all men: and therefore is not by any to be enterprised, nor taken in hand, unadvisedly, lightly, or wantonly, to satisfy men's carnal lusts and appetites, like brute beasts that have no understanding; but reverently, discreetly, advisedly, soberly, and in the fear of God; duly considering the causes for which Matrimony was ordained.

First, it was ordained for the procreation of children, to be brought up in the fear and nurture of the Lord, and to the praise of his holy Name.

Secondly, it was ordained for a remedy against sin, and to avoid fornication; that such persons as have not the gift of continency might marry, and keep themselves undefiled members of Christ's body.

Thirdly, it was ordained for the mutual society, help, and comfort, that the one ought to have of the other, both in prosperity and adversity. Into which holy estate these two persons present come now to be joined. Therefore if any man can show any just cause, why they may not lawfully be joined together, let him now speak, or else hereafter for ever hold his peace.

¶ *And also, speaking unto the persons that shall be married, he shall say,*

I require and charge you both, as ye will answer at the dreadful day of judgment when the secrets of all hearts shall be disclosed, that if either of you know any impediment, why ye may not be lawfully joined together in Matrimony, ye do now confess it. For be ye well assured, that so many as are coupled together otherwise than God's Word doth allow are not joined together by God; neither is their Matrimony lawful.

¶ *At which day of Marriage, if any man do allege and declare any impediment, why they may not be coupled together in Matrimony, by God's Law, or the Law of this Realm; and will be bound, and sufficient sureties with him, to the parties; or else put in a Caution (to the full value of such charges as the persons to be married do thereby sustain) to prove his allegations: then the solemnization must be deferred, until such time as the truth be tried.*

¶ *If no impediment be alleged, then shall the Curate say unto the Man*

M. Wilt thou have this Woman to thy wedded wife, to live together after God's ordinance in the holy estate of Matrimony? Wilt thou love her, comfort her, honour, and keep her in sickness and in health; and, forsaking all other, keep thee only unto her, so long as ye both shall live?

¶ *The Man shall answer,*

I will.

¶ *Then shall the Priest say unto the Woman,*

N. Wilt thou have this Man to thy wedded husband, to live together after God's ordinance in the holy estate of Matrimony? Wilt thou obey him, and serve him, love, honour, and keep him in sickness and in health; and, forsaking all other, keep thee only unto him, so long as ye both shall live?

¶ *The Woman shall answer,*

I will.

¶ *Then shall the Minister say,*

122

Who giveth this Woman to be married to this Man?

¶ *Then shall they give their troth to each other in this manner.*
The Minister, receiving the Woman at her father's or friend's hands,
shall cause the Man with his right hand to take the Woman by her right
hand, and to say after him as followeth.

I *M.* take thee *N.* to my wedded wife, to have and to hold from this day
forward, for better for worse, for richer for poorer, in sickness and in health,
to love and to cherish, till death us do part, according to God's holy
ordinance; and thereto I plight thee my troth.

¶ *Then shall they loose their hands; and the Woman, with her right*
hand taking the Man by his right hand, shall likewise say after the
Minister,

I *N.* take thee *M.* to my wedded husband, to have and to hold from this day
forward, for better for worse, for richer for poorer, in sickness and in health,
to love, cherish, and to obey, till death us do part, according to God's holy
ordinance; and thereto I plight thee my troth.

¶ *Then shall they again loose their hands; and the Man shall give unto*
the Woman a Ring, laying the same upon the book with the accustomed
duty to the Priest and Clerk. And the Priest, taking the Ring, shall
deliver it unto the Man, to put it upon the fourth finger of the Woman's
left hand. And the Man holding the Ring here, and taught by the Priest,
shall say,

With this Ring I thee wed, with my body I thee worship, and with all my
worldly goods I thee endow: in the Name of the Father, and of the Son, and
of the Holy Ghost. Amen.

¶ *Then the Man leaving the Ring upon the fourth finger of the*
Woman's left hand, they shall both kneel down; and the Minister shall
say,

Let us pray.
O Eternal God, Creator and Preserver of all mankind, Giver of all
spiritual grace, the Author of everlasting life; send thy blessing upon these
thy servants, this man and this woman, whom we bless in thy Name; that, as
Isaac and Rebecca lived faithfully together, so these persons may surely
perform and keep the vow and covenant betwixt them made, (whereof this
Ring given and received is a token and pledge,) and may ever remain in
perfect love and peace together, and live according to thy laws; through
Jesus Christ our Lord. *Amen.*

¶ *Then shall the Priest join their right hands together, and say,*

123

Those whom God hath joined together let no man put asunder.

¶ *Then shall the Minister speak unto the people.*

Forasmuch as *M*. and *N*. have consented together in holy wedlock, and have witnessed the same before God and this company, and thereto have given and pledged their troth either to other, and have declared the same by giving and receiving of a Ring, and by joining of hands; I pronounce that they be Man and Wife together, in the Name of the Father, and of the Son, and of the Holy Ghost. *Amen* . . .

O God, who . . . by thy mighty power hast made all things of nothing; who also (after other things set in order) didst appoint, that out of man (created after thine own image and similitude) woman should take her beginning; and, knitting them together, didst teach that it should never be lawful to put asunder those whom thou by Matrimony hadst made one: O God, who hast consecrated the state of Matrimony to such an excellent mystery, that in it is signified and represented the spiritual marriage and unity betwixt Christ and his Church; look mercifully upon these thy servants, that both this man may love his wife, according to thy Word, (as Christ did love his spouse the Church, who gave himself for it, loving and cherishing it even as his own flesh,) and also that this woman may be loving and amiable, faithful and obedient to her husband; and in all quietness, sobriety and peace, be a follower of holy and godly matrons. O Lord, bless them both, and grant them to inherit thy everlasting kingdom; through Jesus Christ our Lord. *Amen* . . .

¶ *After which, if there be no Sermon declaring the duties of Man and Wife, the Minister shall read as followeth.*

All ye that are married, or that intend to take the holy estate of Matrimony upon you, hear what the holy Scripture doth say as touching the duty of husbands towards their wives, and wives towards their husbands.

Saint Paul, in his Epistle to the Ephesians, the fifth Chapter, doth give this commandment to all married men: 'Husbands, love your wives, even as Christ also loved the Church, and gave himself for it, that he might sanctify and cleanse it with the washing of water, by the Word; that he might present it to himself a glorious church, not having spot, or wrinkle, or any such thing; but that it should be holy, and without blemish. So ought men to love their wives as their own bodies. He that loveth his wife loveth himself; for no man ever yet hated his own flesh, but nourisheth and cherisheth it, even as the Lord the Church: for we are members of his body, of his flesh, and of his bones. For this cause shall a man leave his father and mother, and shall be joined unto his wife; and they two shall be one flesh. This is a great mystery; but I speak concerning Christ and the Church. Nevertheless, let every one of you in particular so love his wife, even as himself'.

Likewise the same Saint Paul, writing to the Colossians, speaketh thus to all men that are married; 'Husbands, love your wives, and be not bitter against them'.

Hear also what Saint Peter, the apostle of Christ, who was himself a married man, saith unto them that are married: 'Ye husbands, dwell with your wives according to knowledge; giving honour unto the wife, as unto the weaker vessel, and as being heirs together of the grace of life, that your prayers be not hindered'.

Hitherto ye have heard the duty of the husband toward the wife. Now likewise, ye wives, hear and learn your duties toward your husbands, even as it is plainly set forth in holy Scripture.

Saint Paul, in the aforenamed Epistle to the Ephesians, teacheth you thus: 'Wives, submit yourselves unto your own husbands, as unto the Lord. For the husband is the head of the wife, even as Christ is the head of the Church: and he is the Saviour of the body. Therefore as the Church is subject unto Christ, so let the wives be to their own husbands in every thing' . . . And again he saith, 'Let the wife see that she reverence her husband'.

And in his Epistle to the Colossians, Saint Paul giveth you this short lesson: 'Wives, submit yourselves unto your own husbands, as it is fit in the Lord'.

Saint Peter also doth instruct you very well, thus saying: 'Ye wives, be in subjection to your own husbands; that, if any obey not the Word, they also may without the Word be won by the conversation of the wives; while they behold your chaste conversation coupled with fear. Whose adorning, let it not be that outward adorning of plaiting the hair, and of wearing of gold, or of putting on of apparel; but let it be the hidden man of the heart, in that which is not corruptible; even the ornament of a meek and quiet spirit, which is in the sight of God of great price. For after this manner in the old time the holy women also, who trusted in God, adorned themselves, being in subjection unto their own husbands; even as Sarah obeyed Abraham, calling him lord; whose daughters ye are as long as ye do well, and are not afraid with any amazement'.

81 William Gouge, *Domesticall Duties* (1622), *passim*

Treatise II: Part I:

OF HUSBAND AND WIFE, WHO ARE SO TO BE ACCOUNTED

§2. Of Ripeness of Years in Them that are to be Married

. . . Ripeness of years is absolutely necessary for consummating a just and lawful marriage, wherefore as God at first made Adam of full age, so when he sought out a wife for him, he made her of full age too. He made her a woman, not a child . . .

Quest. How long lasteth the flower of age [I Cor. vii.36]?

125

Answw. The civil law, and common law also, set down twelve years for the flower of female age, and fourteen of males; which is the least. For before those years, they can have no need of marriage, nor yet are well fit for marriage, so as if they forbear some years longer, it will be much better for the parties themselves that marry, for the children which they bring forth, for the family whereof they are the head, and for the commonwealth whereof they are members . . .

§4. Of Barrenness, that it Hindereth Not Marriage

Quest. Are such as are barren to be ranked among impotent persons?

Answ. No, there is great difference betwixt impotency and barrenness.

1. Impotency may by outward sensible signs be known and discerned, barrenness cannot . . .

2. Impotent persons cannot yield due benevolence [I Cor. vii.3], but such as are barren can.

3. Impotency is incurable, but barrenness is not simply so . . .

. . .though procreation of children be one end of marriage yet it is not the only end, and so inviolable is the marriage bond that, though it is made for children's sake, yet for want of children it may not be broken . . .

§7. Of the Things which are Absolutely Necessary to Make a Person Fit for Marriage

. . . there must be chosen:

1. *One of the same kind* or nature, for among all the creatures which were made 'there was not found an helpmeet for man' (Gen. ii.20). Therefore, God out of his bone and flesh made a woman of his own nature and kind.

Contrary to this is the detestable sin of buggery with beasts, expressly forbidden by the law, a sin more than beastly, for the brute beasts content themselves with their own kind . . .

2. *One of the contrary sex*: the male must choose a female, the female a male. Thus God having made Adam a male made Eve a female, and joined them in marriage . . .

Contrary are those unnatural commixions of parties of the same sex, which the Apostle reckoneth up as judgements inflicted on the heathen (Rom. i.24–7) . . .

3. *One beyond the degrees of consanguinity and affinity which are forbidden by the law of God*: these degrees are expressed by Moses (Lev. xviii.6, 7 etc.) . . .

Contrary is incest, a sin not only forbidden by God's word, but so horrible even to the heathen as (to use the Apostle's words, I Cor. v.1), 'it is not so much as named among the gentiles' . . .

4. *One that is free*, nor married, nor betrothed to another . . .
Contrary is bigamy and polygamy . . .

§13. Of that Mutual Liking which Must Pass betwixt Marriageable Persons before they be Married

. . . There are in Scripture three steps or degrees commended unto us by which marriageable parties are in order to proceed unto marriage:

I.   A mutual liking.
II.   An actual contract.
III.   A public solemnization of marriage . . .

I.   . . . it is very meet that counsel be taken of wise and understanding friends, that in a matter so weighty as marriage is, there may be the advice of more heads than one, for the preventing of such mischiefs as through rashness might fall out. After a liking is . . . taken by one party of a meet mate, that liking must be moved to the other party so liked, to know whether there be a reciprocal affection of one towards another . . . If at first there be a good liking mutually and thoroughly settled in both their hearts of one another, love is like to continue in them for ever, as things which are well glued, and settled before they be shaken up and down, will never be severed asunder; but if they be joined together without glue, or shaken while the glue is moist, they cannot remain firm.

Mutual love and good liking of each other is as glue . . .

§14. Of a Contract, What It Is?

II.   . . . The right making of a firm contract consisteth in two things:
1.   In an actual taking of each other for espoused man and wife.
2.   In a direct promise of marrying each other within a convenient time. So as a form of contract may be made to this purpose: first, the man taking the woman by the hand to say, *I, A., take thee, B., to my espoused wife, and do faithfully promise to marry thee in time meet and convenient*. And then the woman again taking the man by the hand to say, *I, B., take thee, A., to my espoused husband, and do faithfully promise to yield to be married to thee in time meet and convenient*. This mutual and actual taking of one another for espoused man and wife in the time present, and a direct promise of marrying one another afterward, setteth such a right and property of the one in the other as cannot be alienated without licence had from the great Judge of heaven, who hath by his divine ordinance settled that right . . .

§21. Of a Religious Consecration of Marriage

III.   The last degree of consummating a marriage is the open and public solemnization thereof, which consisteth:

1.   in a religious consecration
2.   in a civil celebration

thereof.

A religious consecration of marriage is performed by the blessing of a public minister of the Word in the open face of the Church in the day time . . .

Treatise II: Part II:
OF COMMON-MUTUAL DUTIES BETWIXT MAN AND WIFE

§1. Of the Heads of those Common-Mutual Duties

. . . Common-mutual duties are either *absolutely necessary* for the *being* and *abiding* of marriage; or needful and requisite for the *well being* and *well abiding* of it, that is, for the good estate of marriage, and for a commendable and comfortable living together.

There are two kinds of the former:

1.   *Matrimonial unity*;
2.   *Matrimonial chastity*.

The latter also may be drawn to two heads . . .

1.   *A loving affection of one to another.*
2.   *A provident care of one for another* . . .

§2. Of Matrimonial Unity

The first, highest, chiefest and most absolutely necessary common-mutual duty betwixt husband and wife is matrimonial unity, whereby husband and wife do account one another to be one flesh, and accordingly preserve the inviolable union whereby they are knit together. This is that duty which the Apostle enjoineth to husbands and wives in these words, 'Let not the wife depart from her husband: let not the husband put away his wife' (I Cor. vii.10, 11) . . .

§4. Of Matrimonial Chastity

The second common-mutual marriage duty is matrimonial chastity. Chastity in a large extent is taken for all manner of purity in soul and body

. . . but in the sense in which we here use it it especially appertaineth to the body: which is that virtue . . . whereby we keep our bodies undefiled.

Chastity thus restrained to the body is of *single life* [or] *wedlock*.

That of single life is opposed to fornication and it is either of such as were never married . . . or of such as are lawfully freed from the bond of marriage . . . Chastity of wedlock is that virtue whereby parties married, observing the lawful and honest use of marriage, keep their bodies from being defiled with strange flesh: thus the Apostle commandeth wives to be chaste, Tit. ii.5 . . .

Hereby we may note the dotage of our adversaries [Roman Catholics] who think there is no chastity but of single persons, whereupon in their speeches and writings they oppose chastity and matrimony one to another as two contraries . . .

§5. Of Adultery

The vice contrary to matrimonial chastity is adultery, one of the most capital vices in that estate, a vice whereby way is made for divorce, as is clear and evident by the determination of Christ himself, concerning that point, first propounded in his sermon on the mount (Matt. v.32) and again repeated in his conference with the Pharisees (Matt. xix.9), where, condemning unjust divorce, he excepteth the divorce made for adultery . . .

§7. Of the Difference of Adultery in a Man and a Woman

Quest. Is the bond of marriage as much violated on the man's part when he committeth adultery as on the woman's part when she doth so?

Answ. Though the ancient Romans and Canonists have aggravated the woman's fault in this kind far above the man's, and given the man more privileges than the woman, yet I see not how the difference in the sin can stand with the tenor of God's word. I deny not but that more inconveniences may follow upon the woman's default than upon the man's, as, greater infamy before men, worse disturbance of the family, more mistaking of legitimate or illegitimate children, with the like. The man cannot so well know which be his own children, as the woman. He may take base children to be his own, and so cast the inheritance upon them, and suspect his own to be basely born, and so deprive them of their patrimony. But the woman is freed from all such mistakings. Yet in regard of the breach of wedlock, and transgression against God, the sin of either party is alike. God's word maketh no disparity betwixt them. At the beginning God said of them both, 'they two shall be one flesh' (Matt. xix.5; [Gen. ii.23]), not the woman only with the man, but the man also with the woman is made *one flesh* (I Cor. vii.3–4). Their power also over one another in this respect is alike. If on just occasion they abstain, it must be with mutual consent (I Cor. vii.5).

If the husband leave his wife she is as free, as he should be, if she left him (I Cor. vii.15). Accordingly the punishment which by God's law was to be inflicted on adulterers is the same, whether the man or the woman be the delinquent (Deut. xxii.22). If difference be made, it is meet that adulterous husbands be so much the more severely punished, by how much the more it appertaineth to them to excel in virtue and to govern their wives by example . . .

§9. Of Remedies against Adultery . . .

For preventing this heinous sin . . . one of the best remedies that can be prescribed to married persons (next to an awful fear of God . . .) is, that husband and wife mutually delight each in other, and maintain a pure and fervent love betwixt themselves, yielding that due obedience (I Cor. vii.2, 3, 5, 9) one to another which is warranted and sanctified by God's word . . . This *due benevolence* (as the Apostle styleth it [I Cor. vii.3]) is one of the most proper and essential acts of marriage, and necessary for the main and principal ends thereof, as for preservation of chastity in such as have not the gift of continency, for increasing the world with a legitimate brood, and for linking the affections of the married couple more firmly together . . .

§10. Of Mutual Love betwixt Man and Wife

. . . A loving affection must pass betwixt man and wife, or else no duty will be well performed: this is the ground of all the rest. In some respects, love is proper and peculiar to an husband . . . But love is also required of wives, and they are commanded to be *lovers of their husbands*, as well as husbands *to love their wives* [Tit. ii.4; Ephes. v.25] . . . and that is true wedlock, when man and wife are linked together by the bond of love. . . . 'Love is the fulfilling of the law' (Rom. xii.10), that is, the very life of all those duties which the law requireth. It is the *bond of perfection* (Col. iii.14), which bindeth together all those duties which pass betwixt party and party . . . the Apostle willeth that 'all things be done in love' (I Cor. xvi.14) . . . Love, as it provoketh the party in whom it ruleth to do all the good it can, so it stirreth up the party loved to repay good for good. It is like fire, which is not only hot in itself, but also conveyeth heat into that which is near it, whence ariseth a reflection of heat from one to another. Note how admirably this is set forth betwixt Christ and his Spouse in the Song of Solomon . . .

§14. Of Husbands and Wives Living Together

From a mutual affection of love proceedeth a mutual provident care in husband and wife one for another . . . The means is *cohabitation*, for a duty it is that man and wife dwell together. The phrase used in setting out the woman's creation (he *built* a woman (Gen. ii.22), whereby the erecting of a family is intimated) implieth as much . . .

82 Anne Bradstreet, *Several Poems* (1678), p. 225

To My Dear and Loving Husband

If ever two were one, then surely we.
If ever man were loved by wife, then thee;
If ever wife was happy in man,
Compare with me, ye women, if you can.
I prize thy love more than whole mines of gold
Or all the riches that the East doth hold.
My love is such that rivers cannot quench,
Nor ought but love from thee, give recompense.
Thy love is such I can no way repay,
The heavens reward thee; manifold, I pray.
Then while we live, in love let's so persevere
That when we live no more, we may live ever.

83 Samuel Jeake, *An Astrological Diary* (written 1694), pp. 149–54

7 June 1680: Resolved to seek Mrs. Elizabeth Hartshorn of the age of 12 years and 8 months in marriage, with the consent of her mother Mrs. Barbara Hartshorn of Rye. And this day about 3.00 p.m. went to her house to mention it; but prevented by company from a convenient opportunity.

8 June: About 1.00 p.m. I went again, and finding Mrs. Barbara Hartshorn alone had a fit opportunity to propose it immediately, which was accepted, and the portion argued, I insisting upon £1,200. She first offered £500 in money, and the house she lived in (one of the best in the town) which she rated at £200 and at last said she would make her fortune to me of £1,000 viz. £700 in money, £100 in household goods and the house valued at £200 . . .

9 June: In the morning I acquainted my father with what I had proposed etc. for his consent . . .

11 June: About 1.00 p.m. I went thither again, and stayed about 4 hours; but we came to no conclusion. In the evening I came to a resolution in my own thoughts, and had my father's consent to proceed as I pleased; and having a fit opportunity of waiting on Mrs. Hartshorn to her own house, I told her about 9.00 p.m. that I had advised with my father, and perceived him satisfied. And that I did comply with those terms she had proposed, and declare myself to be her most humble and most obedient son and servant for ever: which she respectfully accepted with expressions of satisfaction.

14 June: About 1.30 p.m. I went to Mrs. Barbara Hartshorn's, having her consent to propose it to her daughter Mrs. Eliz. Hartshorn; for whom I had an affection from her infancy. My first motion was as I remember to this effect: 'My Dear Lady, the deep impression your person and virtues have made upon my mind oblige me to become your servant, and I beseech you Madam to be pleased to believe the greatness of my affection, to which be pleased to return me the favour of having a place in your heart'. 'Sir' (said she) 'it is so weighty a business that I am not capable of returning you an answer without a long time of consideration' . . .

16 June: About 6.00 p.m. I went to Mrs. Barbara Hartshorn's, and having her approbation before, had now the declared consent of her daughter.

28 June: Having drawn up the terms of the marriage and settlement and shown it to my father I went in the evening to carry it to Mrs. Hartshorn; which when she perused she told me she liked nothing in it, and insisted upon the repayment of £500 if her daughter died without issue; which I not granting she seemed so much averse that I thought she repented of what she had offered . . . [Later] she sent . . . to tell me, that if I had no other discouragement, she did accept of the propositions I had made according to the paper which I had drawn up, wherein was contained a reservation of £40 per annum to her during life, in case her daughter died without issue . . .

12 July: About 2.00 p.m. (the writings concerning the marriage being sealed before by Mrs. Barbara Hartshorn and myself) I was betrothed or contracted to her daughter Mrs. Eliz. Hartshorn in the presence of my father and her mother, Mr. Mich. Cadman and Mr. Tho. Miller, in form following, viz.: taking her by the right hand I said, 'I Samuel take thee Elizabeth to be my betrothed wife, and promise to make thee my wedded wife in time convenient; in token whereof is this our holding by the hand'. Then loosing my hand, she took me by my right hand, repeating the same words *mutatis mutandis*.

1 March 1681: About 9.35 a.m. I was married to Mrs. Elizabeth Hartshorn at Rye by Mr. Bruce . . . The day was cloudy, but calm. The sun shone out just at tying the nuptial knot . . . Devirgination 3 [March] Thursday night.

84 Lucy Hutchinson, *Memoirs of the Life of Colonel Hutchinson* (completed 1671), pp. 17–20

She [Margaret Hutchinson, née Biron, mother of John and mother-in-law of Lucy Hutchinson] was a Lady of a noble family as any in the country, of an incomparable shape and beauty, embellished with the best education those days afforded, and above all had such a generous virtue joined with attractive sweetness, that she captivated the hearts of all that knew her. She was pious, liberal, courteous, patient, kind above an ordinary degree, ingenious to all things she would apply herself, and notwithstanding she had had her education at Court, yet delighted in her own country habitation, and managed all her family affairs better than many of the homespun housewives that had been brought up to nothing else. She was a most observant and affectionate wife, a great lover of her father's house, showing that true honour to parents is the leading virtue, which seldom wants the concomitancy of all the rest of honour's train. She was a wise and bountiful mistress in his family, a blessing to her tenants and neighbourhood, and had an indulgent tenderness to her infants; but death veiled all her mortal glories in the 26th year of her age [1619?] . . .

There is a story of her father [Sir John Biron] and mother [Margaret, née Fitzwilliam] so memorable that . . . I shall here put it in . . . Sir John Biron . . . had an elder brother that had married a private gentleman's daughter in the country and so displeased his father in that match that he intended an equal part of his estate to this Sir John Biron, his younger son, and thereupon married him to a young lady who was one of the daughters of my Lord [Sir William Fitzwilliam], that had been Deputy of Ireland in the reign of Queen Elizabeth, and lived as a prince in that country. This daughter of his having an honourable aspiring to all things excellent, and being assisted by the great education her father gave her, attained to a great degree of learning and languages, to such an excellency in music and poetry that she made rare compositions of both kinds; and there was not any of those extraordinary qualities, which are therefore more glorious because more rare in the female sex, but she was excellent in them; and besides all these ornaments of soul she had a body of an admirable frame and beauty, which justly made her husband so infinitely enamoured of her as never man was more. She could not set too high a value on her self if she compared herself with other women of those times, yet it was an allay to her glories that she was a little grieved that a less woman, the elder brother's wife, was superior to her in regard of her husband, though inferior in regard of her birth and person; but that grief was soon removed by a sad accident. That marriage wherein the father had not been obeyed was fruitless, and the young gentleman himself being given to youthful vanity, as he was one day to go out a hunting with his father, had commanded something should be put under the saddle of a young servingman that was to go out with them, to make sport at his affright when his horse should prove unquiet. The thing succeeded as it was designed, and made them such sport that the young gentleman, in the passion of laughter, died, and turned their mirth into mourning, leaving a sad caveat by his example to take heed of hazarding men's precious lives for a little sport. The younger brother by this means was heir of the family, and father of a numerous and hopeful issue. But while the incomparable mother shined in all the human glory she wished, and had the crown of all outward felicity to the full in the enjoyment of the mutual love of her most beloved husband, God in one moment took it away, and alienated her most excellent understanding in a difficult childbirth, wherein she brought forth two daughters which lived to be married, and one more that died, I think as soon or before it was born; but after that, all the art of the best physicians in England could never restore her understanding. Yet she was not frantic, but had such a pretty deliration that her ravings were more delightful than other women's most rational conversations.

Upon this occasion her husband gave himself up to live retired with her, as became her condition, and made haste to marry his son, which he did so young that I have heard say when the first child was born, the father, mother, and child, could not make one and thirty years old. The daughters and the rest of the children, as soon as they grew up, were married and dispersed. I think I have heard that she had some children after that childbirth which distempered her, and then my Lady [Margaret] Hutchinson must have been one of them, for she was the youngest daughter, and at nine years old so taking, and of such an amiable conversation, that the Lady Arabella [Stuart] would needs take her from her parents along with her to the Court, where she minded nothing but her Lady, and grew up so intimate in all her councils that the Princess was more delighted in her than in many of the women about her; but when she [Lady Arabella] was carried from them to prison [in 1610, as a claimant to the throne], my Lady's brother fetched her home to his house, and there, although his wife, a most prudent and virtuous lady, laboured to comfort her with all imaginable kindness, yet so constant was her friendship to the unfortunate princess, as I have heard her servants say, even after her marriage [to Sir Thomas Hutchinson] she would steal many melancholy hours to sit and weep in remembrance of her. Meanwhile her parents were driving on their age in no less constancy of love to each other, when even that distemper which had estranged her mind in all things else had left her love and obedience entire to her husband, and he retained the same fondness and respect for her after she was distempered as when she was the glory of her age. He had two beds in one chamber, and she being a little sick, two women watched by her some time before she died. It was his custom, as soon as ever he unclosed his eyes, to ask how she did; but one night, he being as they thought in a deep sleep, she quietly departed towards the morning [of 7 March 1623]. He was that day to have gone ahunting, his usual exercise for his health, and it was his custom to have his Chaplain pray with him before he went out: the women, fearful to surprise him with the ill news, knowing his dear affection to her, had stolen out and acquainted the Chaplain, desiring him to inform him of it. Sir John waking, did not as was his custom ask for her that day, but called the Chaplain to prayers, and joining with him, in the midst of the prayer expired, and both of them were buried together in the same grave. Whether he perceived and would not take notice, or whether some strange sympathy in love or nature tied up their lives in one, or whether God was pleased to exercise an unusual providence towards them, preventing them both from that bitter sorrow which such separations cause, it can be but conjectured. That he died in giving up his soul to God in prayer was the most comfortable part of the story . . .

85 [T[homas] E[dgar] (ed.)], *The Lawes Resolutions of Womens Rights* (1632), pp. 51–4, 57, 63–6

Of Marriage, according to the Civil and Common Law

Marriage is defined to be a conjunction of man and woman, containing an inseparable connexion and union of life. But as there is nothing that is begotten and finished at once, so this contract of coupling man and woman together hath an inception first, and then an orderly proceeding. The first beginning of marriage (as in respect of contract, and that which law taketh hold on) is when wedlock by words in the future tense is promised and vowed, and this is but *sponsio* [an engagement], or *sponsalia* [a betrothal]. The full contract of matrimony is when it is made by words *de prælenti*, in a lawful consent, and thus two be made man and wife existing without lying together, yet matrimony is not accounted consummate until there go with the consent of mind and will conjunction of body.

Of Sponsion or First Promising

The first promising and inception of marriage is in two parts, either it is plain, simple and naked, or confirmed and borne by giving of something. The first is when a man and woman bind themselves simply by their word only to contract matrimony hereafter; the second, when there is an oath made, or somewhat taken as an earnest or pledge betwixt them on both parts, or on one part to be married hereafter. There is not here to be stood upon, the age definitely set down for making of marriage irrevocable, but all that are seven years old (betwixt whom matrimony may consist) may make sponsion and promise. But if any that is under the age of seven begin this vow and betrothing, it is esteemed as a mist, and vanisheth as nothing.

Of Public Sponsion

This sponsion (in which as it stands is no full contract of matrimony, nor any more save only an obligation, or being bound in a sort to marry hereafter) may be public or secret. Public, either by the parties themselves, present together, or by messages or letters when they be distant one from another . . .

Of Secret Sponsion

Those spousals which are made when a man is without witness, *solus cum sola* [a man alone with a woman alone] are called secret promising or desponsation, which, though it be tolerated . . . yet it is so little esteemed of (unless it be very manifest) that another promise public made after it shall be preferred and prevail against it. The cause why it is misliked is the difficulty of proof for anything of it . . .

Of Matrimony Contracted in the Present time, and Who may Contract

Those which the Latins call *puberes*, that is, they which are come once to such state, habit and disposition of body, that they may be deemed able to procreate, may contract matrimony by words of the time present, for in contract of wedlock *pubertas* is not strictly esteemed by the number of years, as it is in wardship, but rather by the maturity, ripeness and disposition of body. There is further required in them that contract matrimony a sound and whole mind to consent . . .

The Consummation and Individuity of Marriage

When to the consent of mind there is added copulation of body, matrimony is consummate, the principal end whereof is propagation or procreation . . . the knot whereof is so strait and indissoluble that they which are yoked therein cannot the one without the consent of the other (neither was it ever permitted) abdicate themselves, or enter into religion [i.e. celibate monasticism], for Saint Paul in II Cor. vii.[4] saith plainly that the husband hath not power over his own body, etc. And there cannot chance any fedity or uncleanness of body so great as that for it a man and wife ought perpetually to be segregated, yea, so unpartable be they, that law saith, they may not utterly leave *conjugalem consuetudinem* [marital intercourse], though one of them have the very leprosy itself . . .

Of Divorce

And as no man can be compelled by any convention of pain or penalty to contract matrimony, so is it impossible, when it is once lawfully and evidently contracted, to distract it by any partition, covenant or humane tradition, *Quos Deus conjunxit, homo non separer* [those whom God has joined together man may not separate] . . . But divorce, that only separateth *a consuetudine conjugali* [from marital intercourse] taketh not away the bond of matrimony, and therefore divorces are sometimes perpetual, as long as the parties live, sometimes for a season limited, and sometime, till reconcilement be had. And he that maketh divorce with his wife, being only separated *a toro* [from the marriage bed], is forbidden to take another wife.

Causes of Divorce

The civil law hath many causes of divorce, but by divine and common law, the only sufficient cause is adultery and fornication . . .

86 Henry Smith, *A Preparative to Marriage* (1591), pp. 107–10

. . . because all perform not their wedlock vows, therefore he which appointed marriage hath appointed divorcement, as it were taking our privilege from us when we abuse it (Matt. xviii.8–9). As God hath ordained remedies for every disease, so he hath ordained a remedy for the disease of marriage. The disease of marriage is adultery, and the medicine hereof is divorcement. Moses licensed them to depart for hardness of heart [Deut. xxiv.1], but Christ licenseth them to depart for no cause but adultery (Matt. v.32, xix.8). If they might be separated for discord, some would make a commodity of strife, but now they are not best to be contentious, for this law will hold their noses together till weariness make them leave struggling, like two spaniels which are coupled in a chain, at last they learn to go together because they may not go asunder. As nothing might part friends, but 'if thine eye offend thee, pluck it out' (Matt. xviii.9), that is, if thy friend be a tempter, so nothing may dissolve marriage but fornication, which is the breach of marriage. For marriage is ordained to avoid fornication (I Cor. vii.10), and therefore if the condition be broken, the obligation is void. And beside, so long as all her children are his children, she must needs be his wife, because the father and mother are man and wife: but when her children are not his children, she seems no more to be his wife but the other's, whose children she bears, and therefore to be divorced from him . . . Such care hath God had in all ages and callings to provide for them which live honestly, for divorcement is not instituted for the carnal but for the chaste, least they should be tied to a plague while they live. As for the adulterer and the adulteress he hath assigned death to cut them off ([Deut. xxii.22;] Lev. xx.10), lest their breath should infect others. Thus, he which made marriage did not make it inseparable, for then marriage were a servitude.

87 Richard Baxter, *A Christian Directory* (1673), II.ix [IV.158–61]

Quest. Doth adultery dissolve the bond of marriage, or not? . . .

Answ. . . . the injured man may put away an adulterous wife (in a regular way) if he please; but withal . . . he may continue in the relation if he please. So that his continued consent shall suffice to continue it a lawful relation and exercise; and his will on the contrary shall suffice to dissolve the relation, and disoblige him . . .

Quest. Is it only the privilege of the man, that he may put away an adulterous wife? or also of the woman, to depart from an adulterous husband? The reason of the doubt is, because Christ mentioneth the man's power only, Matt. v.19.

Answ. . . . The reason why Christ speaketh only of the man's case is, because he was occasioned only to restrain the vicious custom of men's causeless putting away their wives, having no occasion to restrain women from leaving their husbands. Men having the rule did abuse it to the woman's injury, which Christ forbiddeth. And as it is an act of power, it concerneth the man alone; but as it is an act of liberty, it seemeth to me to be supposed, that the woman hath the same freedom; seeing the covenant is violated to her wrong. And the Apostle in I Cor. vii, doth make the case of the man and of the woman to be equal in the point of infidelity and desertion . . . I know of no reason to blame those countries whose laws allow the wife to sue out a divorce as well as the husband.

88 John Milton, *Doctrine and Discipline of Divorce* (1643), pp. 235–6, 245–9, 275

The Preface

. . . What thing more instituted to the solace and delight of man than marriage, and yet the misinterpreting of some Scripture [Matt. v.31–2] directed mainly against the abusers of the law for divorce given them by Moses [Deut. xxiv.1] hath changed the blessing of matrimony not seldom into a familiar and co-inhabiting mischief; at least into a drooping and disconsolate household captivity, without refuge or redemption . . . For although God in the first ordaining of marriage [Gen. ii.18] taught us to what end he did it, in words expressly implying the apt and cheerful conversation of man with woman, to comfort and refresh him against the evil of solitary life, not mentioning the purpose of generation till afterwards, as being but a secondary end in dignity, though not in necessity; yet now, if any two be but once handed in the Church, and have tasted in any sort of the nuptial bed, let them find themselves never so mistaken in their dispositions through any error, concealment, or misadventure, that through their differ-ent tempers, thoughts and constitutions, they can neither be to one another remedy against loneliness, nor live in any union or contentment all their days, yet they shall . . . be made, spite of antipathy, to fadge together, and combine as they may to their unspeakable wearisomeness and despair of all sociable delight in the ordinance which God established to that very end. What a calamity is this . . .

Chap. ii: The First Reason of this law . . . That no covenant whatsoever obliges against the main end both of itself and of the parties covenanting

. . . what [God's] chief end was of creating woman to be joined with man, his own instituting words declare, and are infallible to inform us what is marriage, and what is no marriage, unless we can think them set there to no purpose: 'It is not good', saith he, 'that man should be alone; I will make

138

him a help meet for him' [Gen. ii.18]. From which words so plain, less cannot be concluded, nor is by any learned interpreter, than that in God's intention a meet and happy conversation is the chiefest and the noblest end of marriage; for we find here no expression so necessarily implying carnal knowledge, as this prevention of loneliness to the mind and spirit of man . . . And with all generous persons married thus it is, that where the mind and person pleases aptly, there some unaccomplishment of the bodies' delight may be better born with, than when the mind hangs off in an unclosing disproportion, though the body be as it ought; for there all corporal delight will soon become unsavoury and contemptible. And the solitariness of man, which God had namely and principally ordered to prevent by marriage, hath no remedy, but lies under a worse condition than the loneliest single life; for in single life the absence and remoteness of a helper might inure him to expect his own comforts out of himself, or to seek with hope; but here the continual sight of his deluded thoughts without cure, must needs be to him . . . a daily trouble . . . and the aggrieved person shall do more manly, to be extraordinary and singular in claiming the due right [of divorce] whereof he is frustrated, than to piece up his lost contentment by visiting the stews, or stepping to his neighbour's bed, which is the common shift in this misfortune . . .

Chap. vi: The Fourth Reason . . . that God regards love
and peace in the family more than a compulsive
performance of marriage

. . . this is a deep and serious verity . . . that love in marriage cannot live nor subsist, unless it be mutual; and where love cannot be, there can be left of wedlock nothing but the empty husk of an outside matrimony, as undelightful and unpleasing to God, as any other kind of hypocrisy . . .

89 George Savile, *Advice to a Daughter* (1688), pp. 279–80

For your better direction I will give a hint of the most ordinary causes of dissatisfaction between man and wife, that you may be able by such a warning to live so upon your guard that when you shall be married you may know how to cure your husband's mistakes and to prevent your own.

First, then, you are to consider you live in a time which hath rendered some kind of frailties so habitual that they lay claim to large grains of allowance. The world in this is somewhat unequal and our sex seemeth to play the tyrant in distinguishing partially for ourselves, by making that in the utmost degree criminal in the woman which in a man passeth under a much gentler censure. The root and the excuse of this injustice is the preservation of families from any mixture which may bring a blemish to them; and whilst the point of honour continues to be so placed, it seems unavoidable to give your sex the greater share of the penalty.

But if in this it lieth under any disadvantage, you are more than recompensed by having the honour of families in your keeping. The consideration so great a trust must give you maketh full amends, and this power the world hath lodged in you can hardly fail to restrain the severity of an ill husband and to improve the kindness and esteem of a good one. This being so, remember that next to the danger of committing the fault yourself the greatest is that of seeing it in your husband. Do not seem to look or hear that way: if he is a man of sense he will reclaim himself, the folly of it is of itself sufficient to cure him; if he is not so, he will be provoked but not reformed. To expostulate in these cases looketh like declaring war, and preparing reprisals, which to a thinking husband would be a dangerous reflection. Besides, it is a so coarse a reason which will be assigned for a lady's too great warmth upon such an occasion that modesty no less than prudence ought to restrain her, since such an indecent complaint makes a wife more ridiculous than the injury that provoketh her to it. But it is yet worse, and more unskilful, to blaze it in the world, expecting it should rise up in arms to take her part; whereas she will find it can have no other effect than that she will be served up in all companies as the reigning jest at that time . . . Be assured that in these cases your discretion and silence will be the most prevailing reproof.

90 Abiezer Coppe, *A Second Fiery Flying Roule* (1649), pp. 106–8

These are things that are, and must be confounded by *base* things, which St. Paul saith, not God hath connived at, winked at, permitted, tolerated, but God hath *chosen* etc. *base* things [I Cor. i.28].

What base things? Why, Michal took David for a base fellow, and thought he had chosen *base* things, in dancing shamelessly uncovered before handmaids [II Sam. vi.20].

And barren, demure Michal thinks (for I know her heart, saith the Lord) that I chose base things when I sat down, and eat and drank around on the ground with gypsies, and clipped, hugged and kissed them, putting my hand in their bosoms, loving the she-gypsies dearly. 'O base!', saith mincing Michal, 'the least spark of modesty would be as red as crimson or scarlet, to hear this'.

I warrant me, Michal could better have borne this if I had done it to ladies: so I can for a need, if it be my will, and that in the height of honour and majesty, without sin. But at that time when I was hugging the gypsies, I abhorred the thoughts of ladies, their beauty could not bewitch mine eyes, or snare my lips, or entangle my hands in their bosoms. Yet I can, if it be my will, kiss and hug ladies, and love my neighbour's wife as my self, without sin . . .

It's meat and drink to an angel (who knows no evil, no sin) to swear a full-mouthed oath, Rev. x.6 . . .

Hear one word more (whom it hitteth it hitteth): give over thy base nasty stinking, formal grace before meat, and after meat . . . give over thy stinking family duties, and the Gospel ordinances as thou callest them; for under them all there lies snapping, snarling, biting, besides covetousness, horrid hypocrisy, envy, malice, evil surmising.

Give over, give over, or, if nothing else will do it, I'll at a time, when thou least of all thinkest of it, make thine own child the fruit of thy loins, in whom thy soul delights, lie with a whore – before thine eyes, that that plaguy holiness and righteousness of thine might be confounded by that base thing. And thou be plagued back again into thy mother's womb, the womb of eternity, that thou mayest become a little child, and let the mother Eternity, Almightiness, who is universal love, and whose service is perfect freedom [cf. John viii.32], dress thee, and undress thee, swaddle thee, unswaddle, bind, loose, lay thee down, take thee up, etc.

And to such a little child, undressing is as good as dressing, foul clothes as good as fair clothes – he knows no evil, etc. [cf. Tit. i.15] – and shall see evil no more – but he must first lose all his righteousness, every bit of his holiness, and every crumb of his religion, and be plagued, and confounded (by base things) into nothing.

91 Laurence Clarkson, *The Lost Sheep Found* (1660), pp. 180–1

I affirmed that there was no sin, but as man esteemed it sin, and therefore none can be free from sin, till in purity it be acted as no sin, for I judged that pure to me, which to a dark understanding was impure, for to the pure all things, yea all acts were pure. Thus, making the Scripture a writing of wax, I pleaded the words of Paul, 'That I know and am persuaded by the Lord Jesus, that there was nothing unclean, but as man esteemed it' [Rom. xiv.14], unfolding that was intended all acts, as well as meats and drinks, and therefore till you can lie with all women as one woman, and not judge it sin, you can do nothing but sin. Now, in Scripture I found a perfection spoken of, so that I understood no man could attain perfection but this way, at which Mr. Rawlinson was much taken, and Sarah Kullin, being present, did invite me to make trial of what I had expressed, so as I take it, after we parted, she invited me to Mr. Wats in Rood Lane, where was one or two more like herself, as I take it, lay with me that night. Now against next [S]unday it was noised abroad what a rare man of knowledge was to speak at Mr. Brush's, at which day there was a great company of men and women, both young and old; and so from day to day increased, that now I had choice of what before I aspired after . . . I had clients many, that I was not able to answer all desires, yet none knew our actions but ourselves; however, I was careful with whom I had to do . . . indeed, Solomon's writings was the

original of my filthy lust, supposing I might take the same liberty as he did
. . . Now I being as they said, Captain of the Rant, I had most of the
principle women came to my lodging for knowledge. Now in the height of
this ranting, I was made still careful for monies for my wife, only my body
was given to other women . . .

9

WIFELY DUTIES

It is the overriding assumption of the conduct books and guides to godliness of the seventeenth century that it is woman's lot to become a wife, that self-fulfilment lies in her performance of that role, and that upon it her salvation depends (I Tim. ii.15). Eve was created not only a woman but a wife (4, 7, 79). The characterization and celebration of a virtuous woman in Proverbs xxxi (76), which informs all comment on womanly behaviour, takes her to be a wife: she is motivated by concern for her husband's well-being and reputation, and for her children's welfare; her skills and duties are those belonging to efficient household management. Thomas Edgar's summary of woman's legal status (92) is more generally applicable: women 'are understood either married or to be married'. Though upon marriage the woman lost her own separate legal identity and yielded up her estate to her husband (92), it appears that the property rights of a good many married women – and hence their financial security, even independence – were safeguarded through marriage settlements (Erickson (1990). The wife's legal position is summarized by Stone (1977), pp. 195–202; for the common law notion of coverture, see Kanowitz (1969), pp. 35–8.

Familial structure and relations were, like all human societies, to replicate that hierarchical and patriarchal order which Christian orthodoxy held to be divinely ordained. In the model family of the conduct books the man is the head of a little commonwealth or church (either analogy serves (96: I.§§8 & 14–15, 97)), responsible for, and in a governing position over, the other members of the household, namely, wife, children and servants (93, 94, 95). His duties towards each are carefully distinguished and delineated (96: I.§8, 98; for a summary of this advice, see Houlbrooke (1984), pp. 96–119). The wife is accorded a position next to the husband in this hierarchy, and supplies his place if ever he is away, but she is certainly not his equal (95, 96: I.§14). Her very nearness, however, together with her female nature and the husband's duty of love towards her, make her much the most difficult member of the family to govern successfully. Commonly, far more space is devoted to her than to any other member of the family. The husband is reassured that he must exert his authority ('It is not humility but baseness, to be ruled by her whom he should rule' says Whately (95)); the wife is admonished at length that it is her duty to obey (her 'whole duty' is two-fold, says Whately: 'to acknowledge her inferiority . . . to carry herself as inferior' (95; cf. 96: I.§§12 & 93 and III.*passim*)). The frequent iterations of this commonplace in Renaissance drama perhaps occasionally have ironic force (99). Womanly and wifely obedience was one of the duties inferred from Eve's Fall by Bunyan (3); to resent, query or refuse obedience is to challenge God's law; insubordination, that is to say, is evidence of unregeneracy. The only qualification is that wives should not 'fear their husbands more than they fear God' (96: III.§53; cf. the insistence on womanly and wifely obedience and compliance, in, e.g., 65, 70, 71, 150, 127, 129, 138).

Despite a tirelessly reiterated array of Biblical proof texts (e.g. Gen. iii.16; I Cor. xi.5–11; I Tim. ii.9–15; Eph. v.22–3; I Pet. iii.7) there is nothing peculiarly Christian (or Judaic) about this insistence upon woman's subordination to man and her duty of obedience to her superior and 'head', that is, her husband. The notion of the wife's submissive inferiority is there in Aristotle and in the Classical moralists (96: III.§3, 100; Maclean (1980), pp. 19, 50); it is, indeed, a commonplace of civilized cultures, perhaps even a definitive characteristic of them. Its presence in seventeenth-century culture is hence hardly remarkable, though it is repeated wellnigh obsessively by William Gouge in one of the most massive and influential marital guides (96). George (1973), pp. 168–9, argues (with particular reference to Gouge) that the handbooks had so to insist on the inferiority of the wife and upon her duty of obedience 'precisely because these characteristics were so alien to the women of the audience they addressed', and she argues that the domestication of woman in the seventeenth century through insistence upon her wifely role, while it dignified marriage (see chapter 8), actually confined and reduced women. Certainly, Gouge seems not to expect women to take his advice kindly. Though other commentators do not so labour obedience *per se*, all do agree with Gouge on how to recognize it. Essentially, it issued in a submissive, soberly dressed and retiring manner; in a pious and modest habit of mind; and in a hard-working and diligent management of household affairs (93, 95, 96: III.§§7–9, 14–17, 54–6, 97, 98, 101).

There is, however, a pronounced counter-theme in these texts. Stone (1977), pp. 325–404, traces the development in the seventeenth century of what he calls the 'companionative marriage' (see chapter 8) and suggests that 'The increasing stress laid by the early seventeenth-century preachers on the need for companionship in marriage in the long run tended to undercut their own arguments in favour of the maintenance of strict wifely subjection and obedience'. Certainly, Protestant divines did insist upon the mutual duty of love within marriage and that wives were not servants, still less slaves, but helpmeets, 'husbands' yoke-fellows, their flesh and their bones' (97; but contrast 103, 196, 199). This bias was most pronounced in Puritan texts (see further Leverenz (1980), pp. 70–104; Morgan (1966), pp. 29–64; Durston

(1989), *passim*). The point is pressed on her son by Dorothy Leigh with a sympathetic sensitivity for the wife's situation which may be due to her sex (102). Gouge himself demonstrates the essential idealism of the Puritan position. For him, the marital relationship is founded upon loving service, self-denial rather than self-assertion (96: I.§§25 & 93). It is not his intention to deprive the wife of a mind of her own (96: III.§52; cf. the contention of Pollock (1989) that, though it fostered deference, female education was not designed 'to preclude the possibility of independent thought or action' (p. 250)). Treatise IV of his *Domesticall Duties*, which deals with the duties of husbands, is much concerned that they should not abuse their position by mistreatment, unreasonable behaviour, ill-temper, harshness or cruelty. There is consequently often a tension to be detected between, on the one hand, a liberating recognition of the importance of mutual affection and sexual love, and, on the other, a fear that to be too liberal would be to introduce disorder and unseemliness. In Gouge, it is the latter which prevails, leading to a stress upon patriarchal authority (but cf. 81: II.ii §10): the best service the husband can render his wife is to recognize that she is the 'weaker vessel' (I Pet. iii.7). The promise of spiritual equality to male and female in Gal. iii.28 is not permitted by Gouge to compromise this dominion, any more than it is by Bunyan (138); but, then, notwithstanding Gal. iii.28, the sexual politics of the Pauline corpus itself remain uncompromisingly authoritarian (on Pauline teaching on the status of women and sexual relations see Brown (1988), pp. 44–57; Thickstun (1988), pp. 1–36). Many commentators detect in such an emphasis the distinctively Puritan contribution to women's history, arguing that Puritan ideas of the dignity and companionableness of marriage merely reinforced patriarchy and more narrowly circumscribed woman's sphere as domestic (e.g. Hamilton (1978), p. 50–75). In other texts, however, the emphasis falls differently: there is a greater stress on love in Henry Smith, the late sixteenth-century Puritan divine famed as 'silver tongued' for his oratory (93); in William Whately, a Puritan of the next generation, husband and wife are physicians to *each other's* bodies and souls (95); 'men are frail too' acknowledges Baxter, stressing the mutual need for help (98).

By the 1680s, a shift in expectations can be detected. When the century opens, Middleton's Leantio anticipates in his new wife an inclination to rebelliousness (103), and that the insubordinate, wilful and determined nature of women was in need of careful supervision was the assumption of the handbooks which followed. Eighty years later, though much the same advice is being given out (104), it is woman's natural gentleness and yieldingness which is stressed. Her compliance is conceived as a matter less of discipline than of good manners. Disobedience would ill become her. In Halifax's urbane and patronizing image of the marital relationship the woman is possessed of little energy, rebellious or otherwise (105). From being a divinely prescribed duty whose exercise required the discipline to control natural

natural female inclination, wifely submission has become a matter of common sense and convention: she is to 'make [the] best of what is settled by law and custom, and not vainly imagine that it will be changed for your sake'.

~

92 [T[homas] E[dgar] (ed.)], *The Lawes Resolutions of Womens Rights* (1632), pp. 4, 6, 125

Now Man and Woman are One

See here [Gen. iii.16] the reason . . . that women have no voice in Parliament, they make no laws, they consent to none, they abrogate none. All of them are understood either married or to be married and their desires or [are?] subject to their husbands. I know no remedy, though some women can shift it well enough. The common law here shaketh hands with divinity . . .

As soon as a man and woman are knit and fast linked together in bands of wedlock, they are in common parlance . . . yoke-fellows, that in an even participation, must take all fortunes equally. Yet law permits not so great an *intervallum* [space] betwixt them as society . . . rather it affirms them to be *una caro* [one flesh], regarded to many intents merely as one undivided substance . . .

The Woman Marrying Changeth her Name, Dignity, etc

The wife must take the name of her husband, Alice Green becometh Alice Musgrave. She that in the morning was Fairweather, is at night perhaps Rainbow or Goodwife Foul; Sweetheart going to Church, and Hoistbrick coming home . . .

That which the Husband Hath is his Own

But the prerogative of the husband is best discerned in his dominion over all external things in which the wife by combination divesteth herself of propriety in some sort, and casteth upon her governor, for here practice everywhere agrees with the theoric of law, and forcing necessity submits women to the affection thereof. Whatsoever the husband had before coverture [legal responsibility for the protection of his wife] either in goods or lands, it is absolutely his own; the wife hath therein no seisin [legal possession] at all. If anything when he is married be given him, he taketh it by himself distinctly to himself . . .

. . . The very goods which a man giveth to his wife are still his own; her chain, her bracelets, her apparel are all the goodman's goods.

. . . A wife how gallant soever she be, glittereth but in the riches of her husband, as the moon hath no light, but it is the sun's . . .

That which the Wife Hath is the Husband's

. . . If before marriage the woman were possessed of horses, peat, sheep, corn, wool, money, plate and jewels, all manner of moveable substance is presently by conjunction the husband's, to sell, keep or bequeath if he die . . .

93 Henry Smith, *A Preparative to Marriage* (1591), pp. 26–42, 55–87 [misnumbered 67]

In Zechariah, sin is called a woman (Zech. v.7), which showeth that women have many faults; therefore he which chooseth of them, had need have judgment and make an anatomy of their bodies and minds by squire and rule before he say, 'This shall be mine' . . .

For help thereof in I Cor. vii.39 we are taught to marry in the Lord; then we must choose in the Lord too . . . To direct thee to a right choice herein, the Holy Ghost gives thee two rules: *godliness* and *fitness* . . .

There be certain signs of this fitness and godliness, both in the man and the woman. If thou wilt know a godly man or a godly woman, thou must mark five things: the report, the looks, the speech, the apparel, and the companions, which are like the pulses that show whether we be well or ill. The report, because as the market goeth, so they say the market men talk. A good man commonly hath a good name . . .

The next sign is the look, for Solomon saith, 'Wisdom is in the face of a man' (Eccles. viii.7): so, godliness is in the face of a man, and so folly is in the face of a man, and so wickedness is in the face of a man . . .

To show how a modest countenance and a womanly shamefacedness do commend a chaste wife, it is observed that the word *nuptiae*, which signifieth marriage of the woman, doth declare the manner of her marriage, for it importeth a covering, because virgins which should be married, when they came to their husbands, for modesty and shamefastness, did cover their faces, as we read of Rebecca (Gen. xxiv.65) . . .

The third sign is her speech, or rather, her silence, for the ornament of a woman is silence: and therefore the law was given to the man (to Adam first, and to Moses after) rather than to the woman, to show that he should be the teacher, and she the hearer . . .

The fourth sign is the apparel . . . A modest woman is known by her sober attire, as the Prophet Elijah was known by his rough garments (II Kgs. i.8). Look not for better within than thou seest without . . .

The fifth sign is the company, for birds of a feather will fly together, and fellows in sin will be fellows in league, as young Rehoboam chose young companions (I Kgs. xii.8) . . .

* * *

In every state there is some one virtue which belongeth to that calling more than others, as justice to magistrates, and knowledge to preachers, and fortitude to soldiers; so love is the marriage virtue, which sings music to their whole life . . .

To show the love which should be between man and wife, a marriage is called *coniugium*, which signifieth a knitting or joining together, showing that unless there be a joining of hearts, and knitting of affections together, it is not marriage indeed, but in show and name, and they shall dwell in a house like two poisons in a stomach and one shall ever be sick of the other . . .

The man is to his wife in the place of Christ to his Church; therefore, the Apostle requireth such an affection of him toward his spouse as Christ beareth toward his spouse (Ephes. v.25) . . .

His next duty to love is a fruit of his love, that is, to let all things be common between them which were private before. The man and his wife are partners, like oars in a boat; therefore, he must divide offices, and affairs, and goods with her, causing her to be feared and reverenced and obeyed of her children and servants like himself . . .

This is far from civil wars between man and wife; in all his offices is found no office to fight . . . As a kingdom cannot stand if it be divided, so a house cannot stand if it be divided: for strife is like fire which leaves nothing but dust and smoke and ashes behind it . . . Wilt thou strike one in his own house? No more shouldest thou strike thy wife in her house. She is come to thee as to a sanctuary, to defend her from hurt, and canst thou hurt thyself? . . . She is a free citizen in thy house . . .

. . . the woman may learn her duty out of her names. They are called *goodwives*, as goodwife A. and goodwife B. Every wife is called *goodwife*; therefore, if they be not good wives their names do belie them, and they are not worth their titles, but answer to a wrong name as players do upon a stage. This name pleaseth them well; but beside this, a wife is called a *yoke-fellow*, to show that she should help her husband to bear his yoke, that is, his grief must be her grief. And whether it be the yoke of poverty, or the yoke of envy, or the yoke of sickness, or the yoke of imprisonment, she must submit her neck to bear it patiently with him, or else she is not his yoke-fellow . . . who shall bear others' burdens if the wife do not bear her husband's burden? Wicked Jezebel comforted her husband in his sickness (I Kgs. xxi.5) . . . Beside a yoke-fellow, she is called a *helper* (Gen. ii.18), to help him in his business, to help him in his labours, to help him in his troubles, to help him in his sickness, like a woman physician . . .

Beside a helper, she is called a *comforter* too, and therefore the man is bid to rejoice in his wife (Prov. v.18) . . .

Lastly, we call the wife *housewife*, that is, house wife, not a street wife like Tamar (Gen. xxxviii.14), nor a field wife like Dinah (Gen. xxxiv.1), but a house wife, to show that a good wife keeps her house. And therefore Paul biddeth Titus to exhort women that they be chaste and keeping at home (Tit. ii.5); presently after *chaste* he saith *keeping at home*, as though *home* were chastity's keeper. And therefore Solomon, depainting the whore, setteth her at the door, now sitting upon her stalls, now walking in the streets (Prov. vii.12), now looking out of the windows, like curled Jezebel (II Kgs. ix.30), as if she held forth the glass of temptation for vanity to gaze upon. But chastity careth to please but one, and therefore she keeps her closet, as though she were still at prayer . . .

. . . (Husbands should not keep their wives too strait, but wives should not think their house their prison, but as their paradise where they would be.) . . .

As it becometh her to keep home, so it becometh her to keep silence, and always speak the best of her head [i.e. husband]. Others seek their honour in triumph but she must seek her honour in reverence, for it becometh not any woman to set light by her husband, nor to publish his infirmities . . . Because this is the quality of that sex, to overthwart and upbraid, and sue the pre-eminence of their husbands, therefore the philosophers could not tell how to define a wife, but called her *the contrary to a husband*, as though nothing were so cross and contrary to a man as a wife. This is not Scripture, but no slander to many. As David exalteth the love of women above all other loves (II Sam. i.26), so Solomon mounteth the envy of women above all other envies (Prov. xxi.19), stubborn, sullen, taunting, gainsaying, outfacing, with such a bitter humour that one would think they were molten out of the salt pillar into which Lot's wife was transformed (Gen. xix.26). We say not all are alike, but this sect hath many disciples . . .

To her silence and patience she must add the *acceptable obedience* which makes a woman rule while she is ruled. This is the wife's tribute to the husband, for she is not called his head, but he is called her head (Ephes. v.23) . . . The first subjection of woman began at sin, for when God cursed her for seducing her husband, when the serpent had seduced her, he said, 'He shall have authority over thee' (Gen. iii.15). And therefore, as the man named all other creatures (Gen. ii.20), in sign that they should be subject to him, as a servant which cometh when his master calleth him by name, so he did name the woman also in token that she should be subject to him likewise (Gen. ii.23).

94 James VI and I, *Basilikon Doron* (1599), pp. 94–9

. . . beware to marry any but one of your own religion; for how can ye be of one flesh and keep unity betwixt you, being members of two opposite churches? . . . Remember also that marriage is one of the greatest actions that a man doth in all his time, especially in taking of his first wife. And if he marry first basely beneath his rank, he will ever be the less accounted of thereafter. And lastly, remember to choose your wife as I have advised you to choose your servants, that she be of a whole and clean race, not subject to the hereditary sicknesses, either of the soul or the body; for if a man will be careful to breed horses and dogs of good kinds, how much more careful should he be for the breed of his own loins? So shall ye in your marriage have respect to your conscience, honour, and natural weal in your successors. When ye are married, keep inviolably your promise made to God in your marriage, which all standeth in doing of one thing, and abstaining from another, to treat her in all things as your wife and the half of your self, and to make your body (which then is no more yours but properly hers) common with none other. I trust I need not to insist here to dissuade you from the filthy vice of adultery; remember only what solemn promise ye make to God at your marriage. And sen it is only by the force of that promise that your bairns succeed unto you, which otherwise they could not do, equity and reason would ye should keep your part thereof . . . And for your behaviour to your wife, the Scripture can best give you counsel therein. Treat her as your own flesh; command her as her lord; cherish her as your helper; rule her as your pupil; please her in all things reasonable, but teach her not to be curious in things that belongeth her not. Ye are the head, she is your body; it is your office to command and hers to obey, but yet with such a sweet harmony, as she should be as ready to obey as ye to command, as willing to follow as ye to go before, your love being wholly knit unto her, and all her affections lovingly bent to follow your will. And to conclude, keep specially three rules with your wife: first, suffer her never to meddle with the politic government of the commonweal, but hold her at the economic rule of the house, and yet all to be subject to your direction; keep carefully good and chaste company about her, for women are the frailest sex; and be never both angry at once, for when ye see her in passion ye should with reason danton [subdue] yours, for both when ye are settled ye are meetest to judge of her errors, and when she is come to her self, she may be best made to apprehend her offence and reverence your rebuke.

95 [William Whately], *A Bride-Bush* (1617), pp. 1–13, 18–32, 36–43

As for love, it is the life and soul of marriage, without which it is no more itself than a carcass is a man; yea, it is uncomfortable, miserable and a living death . . .

. . . nuptial love of yoke-fellows is a special and peculiar love . . . It is the fixing their hearts in the good liking each of other, as the only fit and good match that could be found under the sun for them. The husband must rest his heart in his wife, as the best wife that the world could have yielded him. The wife must settle her very soul upon her husband as the best husband that might have been had amongst men for her . . . They may lawfully think others better men or women, but none a better husband or wife for them than their yoke-fellow . . .

. . . It was the end of her creation to be an helper; he must be a great helper to her, and do more good, by how much the better his place is better . . . they must both observe the diet, temper and constitution (as I may speak) of each other's soul . . . They must labour to be thus acquainted with the diseases and distemperatures of one another's hearts, not to upbraid, not to disgrace, not to vilify, but to help and support one another, by diligent avoiding all things which will cause such evils to break out, and using whatsoever will heal or mitigate the same . . . But they must be helpful also, and faithful to each other's body, by a free and ready undergoing any cost or pains (to their power) to procure whatsoever diet, physic or other-like necessaries may make for the preserving of health and preventing or remedying of sickness . . .

Now, for the husband's special duties, they may fitly be referred to these two heads: the keeping of his authority, and the using of it. First, he must keep his authority and maintain himself in that place wherein his maker hath set him. Nature hath framed the lineaments of his body to superiority, and set the print of government in his face, which is more stern, less delicate than the woman's. He must not suffer this order of Nature to be inverted. The Lord in his Word calls him the *head* [Ephes. v.23]; he must not stand lower than the shoulders; if he do, that is a deformed family. It is a sin to come lower than God hath set one. It is not humility but baseness, to be ruled by her whom he should rule . . .

. . . The whole duty of the wife is referred to two heads: the first is, to acknowledge her inferiority; the next, to carry herself as inferior. First, then, the wife's judgement must be convinced that she is not her husband's equal, yea, that her husband is her better by far, else there can be no contentment either in her heart or in her house . . . If ever thou purpose to be a good wife, and to live comfortably, set down this with thy self, *My husband is my superior, my better* . . .

Secondly, the wife being resolved that her place is the lower, must carry herself as an inferior. It little boots to confess his authority in word, if she frame not to submission indeed. Now she shall testify her inferiority in a Christian manner by practising those two virtues of reverence and obedience, which are appropriate to the place of inferiors . . .

. . . First, in speeches and gestures unto him. These must carry the stamp of fear upon them, and not be cutted, sharp, sullen, passionate, tetchy, but meek, quiet, submissive, which may show that she considers who herself is and to whom she speaks. The wife's tongue towards her husband must be neither keen, nor loose; her countenance neither swelling nor deriding; her behaviour not flinging, nor puffing, nor discontented, but savouring of all lowliness and quietness of affection . . . we have some women that can chase and scold with their husbands, and rail upon them, and revile them, and shake them together with such terms and carriage as were insufferable towards a servant. Stains of womankind, blemishes of their sex, monsters in

Nature, botches of human society, rude, graceless, impudent, next to harlots, if not the same with them . . .

Secondly, the wife must express reverence towards her husband in her
speeches and gestures before him and in his presence to others. His company
must make her more respective how she carries herself towards any else. Her
words must not be loud and snappish to the children, to the servants, in his
sight . . .

Thirdly, the woman's speeches of her husband behind his back must be
dutiful and respective. She must not call him by light names, nor talk of him
with any kind of carelessness and slightness of speech, much less with
despiteful and reproachful terms . . .

Obedience follows: as concerning which duty a plain text avers it to the
full, saying, 'Let the wife be subject to her husband in all things, in the Lord'
[Ephes. v.22]. What need we further proof? . . . It is laudable, commendable,
a note of a virtuous woman, a dutiful wife, when she submits herself with
quietness, cheerfully, even as a well-broken horse turns at the least turning,
stands at the least check of the rider's bridle, readily going and standing as he
wishes that sits upon his back. If you will have your obedience worth
anything, make no tumult about it outwardly, allow none within.

96 William Gouge, *Domesticall Duties* (1622), *passim*

Treatise I: AN EXPOSITION OF THAT PART OF SCRIPTURE OUT OF WHICH
DOMESTIC DUTIES ARE RAISED

§8. Of the Lawfulness of Private Functions in a Family

Among other particular callings the Apostle maketh choice of those which
God hath settled in private families, and is accurate in reciting the several and
distinct orders thereof, (for a family consisteth of these three orders:

Husbands	*Parents*	*Masters*
Wives	*Children*	*Servants*

all which he reckoneth up [in Ephes. v.22-vi.9]) . . .

The reasons of this doctrine are clear, for the family is a seminary of the
Church and commonwealth. It is as a beehive, in which is the stock, and out
of which are sent many swarms of bees. For in families are all sorts of people
bred and brought up; and out of families are they sent into the Church and
commonwealth. The first beginning of mankind and of his increase, was out
of a family. For first did God join in marriage Adam and Eve, made them
husband and wife, then gave them children . . . That great people of the Jews
which could not be numbered for multitude was raised out of the family of
Abraham. Yea, even to this day have all sorts of people come from families,
and so shall to the end of the world. Whence it followeth, that a conscion-
able performance of domestic and household duties, tend to the good

ordering of Church and commonwealth, as being means to fit and prepare men thereunto.

Besides, a family is a little Church and a little commonwealth, at least a lively representation thereof, whereby trial may be made of such as are fit for any place of authority or of subjection in Church or commonwealth. Or rather, it is as a school wherein the first principles and grounds of government and subjection are learned . . .

§12. Of Wives' Subjection

Ephes. v.22: 'Wives submit yourselves unto your own husbands as unto the Lord'

. . . Under this phrase (*submit yourselves*) all the duties which a wife oweth to her husband are comprised, as I shall afterwards more distinctly show.

§14. How an Husband is his Wife's Head

Ephes. v.23: 'For the husband is the head of the wife, even as Christ is the head of the Church: and he is the Saviour of the body'

The place of an husband . . . is expressed under the metaphor of an *head*, and amplified by his resemblance therein unto Christ . . .

A wife must submit herself to an husband because he is her head, and she must do it as to the Lord, because her husband is to her as Christ is to the Church.

The metaphor of the head declareth two points: 1. the dignity, 2. the duty of an husband . . .

1. As an head is more eminent and excellent than the body, and placed above it, so is an husband to his wife.

2. As an head, by the understanding which is in it, governeth, protecteth, preserveth, provideth for the body, so doth the husband [for] his wife; at least, ought so to do, for that is his office and duty. This is here noted to show the benefit which a wife receiveth by her husband . . .

§25. Of the Sum of Husbands' Duties

Ephes. v.25: 'Husbands love your wives, even as Christ also loved the Church, and gave himself for it'

. . . All the duties of an husband are comprised under this one word *Love*. Wherein that an husband might be the better provoked the forenamed example of Christ and of his love to the Church is very lively set forth, first generally in these words, *even as Christ loved the Church*, and then more particularly in the words following [verses 26–7] . . .

§93. Of the Sum of Husbands' and Wives' Duties

Ephes. v.33: 'Nevertheless, let every one of you in particular so love his wife, even as himself: and the wife see that she reverence her husband'

. . . This verse then containeth a conclusion of the Apostle's discourse, concerning the duties of husbands and wives . . .

Their duties are noted in two words: *Love, Fear.*

These two, as they are distinct duties in themselves, so are they also common conditions which must be annexed to all other duties. *Love* as sugar to sweeten the duties of authority, which appertain to an husband. *Fear* as salt to season all the duties of subjection which appertain to a wife . . .

Treatise III: OF WIVES' PARTICULAR DUTIES

[Ephes. v. 22–24]

§2. Of Wives' Subjection in General

. . . when first the Lord declared unto woman her duty, he set it down under this phrase, 'Thy desire shall be subject to thine husband' (Gen. iii.16). . . . Hereby the Holy Ghost would teach wives that *subjection* ought to be as salt to season every duty which they perform to their husband. Their very opinion, affection, speech, action, and all that concerneth the husband, must savour of *subjection*. Contrary is the disposition of many wives, whom ambition hath tainted and corrupted within and without: they cannot endure to hear of *subjection*; they imagine that they are made slaves thereby . . .

§3. Of an Husband's Superiority over a Wife, to be Acknowledged by a Wife

. . . The proofs are these following:

1.   God . . . hath power to place his image in whom he will, and to whom God giveth superiority and authority, the same ought to be acknowledged to be due unto them. But God said of the man to the woman, 'he shall rule over thee' (Gen. iii.16).

2.   Nature hath placed an eminency in the male over the female, so as where they are linked together in one yoke, it is given by Nature that he should govern, she obey. This did the heathen by the light of Nature observe.

3.   The titles and names whereby an husband is set forth, do imply a superiority and authority in him, as *Lord* (I Pet. iii.6), *Master* (Esther i.17), *Guide* (Prov. ii.17), *Head* (I Cor. xi.3), *Image and glory of God* (I Cor. xi.7).

4.   The persons whom the husband, by virtue of his place, and whom the wife, by virtue of her place, represent, most evidently prove as much: for an husband representeth Christ, and a wife the Church (Eph. v.23).

5.   The circumstances noted by the Holy Ghost as the woman's creation imply no less, as that she was created after man, for man's good and out of man's side (Gen. ii.18, etc.)

6.   The very attire which Nature and custom of all times and places have taught women to put on, confirmeth the same: as long hair, and other coverings over the head. This and the former argument doth the Apostle himself use to this very purpose, I Cor. xi.7 etc.

The point then being so clear, wives ought in conscience to acknowledge as much . . .

§4. Of a Fond Conceit, that Husband and Wife are Equal

Contrary to the forenamed subjection is the opinion of many wives, who think themselves every way as good as their husbands, and no way inferior to them.

The reason whereof seemeth to be that small inequality which is betwixt the husband and the wife: for of all degrees wherein there is any difference betwixt persons and person, there is the least disparity betwixt man and wife. Though the man be as the head, yet is the woman as the heart, which is the most excellent part of the body next the head, far more excellent than any other member under the head, and almost equal to the head in many respects, and as necessary as the head. As an evidence that a wife is to man as the heart to the head, she was at her first creation taken out of the side of man where his heart lieth (Gen. ii.21) . . .; and though the woman was at first 'of the man' created out of his side, yet 'is the man also by the woman' (I Cor. xi.12). Ever since his first creation, man hath been born and brought forth out of the woman's womb . . . They are also 'heirs together of the grace of life' (I Pet. iii.7). Besides, wives are mothers of the same children, whereof their husbands are fathers (for God said to both 'multiply and increase' (Gen. i.28)) and mistresses of the same servants whereof they are masters (for Sarah is called *mistress* (Gen. xvi.4)) and in many other respects there is a common equality betwixt husbands and wives, whence many wives gather that in all things there ought to be a mutual equality.

But . . . even in those things wherein there is a common equity, there is not an equality, for the husband hath ever even in all things a superiority . . .

§5. Of a Wife's Acknowledgement of her own Husband's Superiority

. . . *Object.*   What if a man of mean place be married to a woman of eminent place, or a servant be married to his mistress, or an aged woman to a youth, must such a wife acknowledge such an husband her superior?

Answer.   Yea verily, for in giving herself to be his wife . . . she advanceth him above her self and subjecteth herself unto him. It booteth nothing what either of them were before marriage . . .

Object. 2. But what if a man of lewd and beastly conditions, as a drunkard, a glutton, a profane swaggerer, an impious swearer, and a blasphemer, be married to a wise, sober, religious matron, must she account him her superior, and worthy of an husband's honour?

Answer. Surely she must. For the evil quality and disposition of his heart and life, doth not deprive a man of that civil honour which God hath given him. Though an husband in regard of evil qualities may carry the image of the Devil, yet in regard of his place and office he beareth the image of God . . .

§7. Of a Wife's Inward Fear of her Husband

. . . A wife-like respect of her husband consisteth in two points: 1. *Reverence*; 2. *Obedience*.

The reverence which she oweth to him is: 1. *Inward*; 2. *Outward*.

Inward reverence is an awful respect which a wife in her heart hath of her husband, esteeming him worthy of all honour for his place, and office' sake, because he is her husband . . .

§8. Of a Wife's Base Esteem of her Husband

Contrary to this inward reverence of the heart is a base and vile esteem which many have of their husbands, thinking no better of them than of other men; nay, worse than of others, despising their husbands in their hearts . . . This, as it is in itself a very vile vice, so is it a cause of many other vices, as of presumption, rebellion, yea and of adultery itself many times . . .

It commonly riseth either from self-conceit (whereby wives overween their own gifts, thinking them so excellent as they need no guide or head, but are rather fit to guide and rule both their husbands and all the household, of which proud and presumptuous spirit Jezebel seemeth to be (I Kgs. xxi.7)) . . .

§9. Of Wife-like Sobriety

. . . A wife's outward reverence consisteth in her reverend *gesture* and *speech*.

For the first, that a reverend gesture and carriage of herself to her husband and in her husband's presence beseemeth a wife was of old implied by the veil which the woman used to put on when she was brought unto her husband, as is noted in the example of Rebecca (Gen. xxiv.65) . . . most expressly is this duty set down by Saint Peter who exhorteth wives to order their conversation before their husbands so as it be pure, with reverence (I Pet. iii.1).

This reverend conversation consisteth in a wife-like *sobriety*, *mildness*, *courtesy* and *modesty*.

By *sobriety* I mean such a comely, grave, and gracious carriage as giveth evidence to the husband that his wife respecteth his place and the authority which God hath given him . . .

Contrary to this sobriety is lightness and wantonness which vices in a wife, especially before her husband, argueth little respect, if not a plain contempt of him . . .

§14. Of the Titles which Wives Give their Husbands

As their words must be few, so those few words must be reverend and meek, both which are also implied under the forenamed word *silence*, which in the original signifieth *quietness*.

Reverence hath respect to the titles whereby a wife nameth her husband; *meekness* to the manner of framing her speech to him.

For the titles which a wife in speaking to her husband, or naming him, giveth unto him, they must be such as signify superiority, and so savour of reverence. Such are the titles wherewith husbands are named in Scripture; they are titles of honour . . .

Contrary are those compellations which argue equality or inferiority rather than superiority, as *Brother, Cousin, Friend, Man,* etc. If a stranger be in presence, how can he tell by this manner of compellation that he whom thou speakest unto is thy husband? . . . Not unlike to those are such as these, *Sweet, Sweeting, Heart, Sweet-heart, Love, Joy, Dear,* etc., and such as these, *Ducks, Chicks, Pigsny,* etc., and husband's Christian names, as *John, Thomas, William, Henry,* etc. which, if they be contracted (as many use to contract them thus, *Jack, Tom, Will, Hal*) they are much more unseemly: servants are usually so called.

But what may we say of those titles given to an husband by his wife, not seldom in passion, but usually in ordinary speech, which are not fit to be given to the basest men that be, as *Grub, Rogue,* and the like, which I am even ashamed to name, but that the sins of women are to be cast as dirt on their faces, that they may be more ashamed?

Object. Many of the forenamed titles are titles of amity and familiarity.

Answ. Subjection is that mark which wives are directed to aim at in their thoughts, words, deeds, and whole converse towards their husbands. Such tokens of familiarity as are not withal tokens of subjection and reverence are unbeseeming a wife, because they swerve from that mark.

§15. Of Wives' Meekness in their Speeches

Meekness in a wife's manner of framing her speech to her husband doth also commend her reverend respect of him. This is an especial effect of the meek and quiet spirit which Saint Peter requireth of wives (I Pet. iii.4) . . .

As the form of words which a wife useth in asking or answering questions, or any other kind of discourse which she holdeth with her husband, so her moderation in persisting, arguing, and pressing matters, yea and the mild composition of her countenance in speaking, declare her meekness. If she be desirous to obtain anything of him, fairly she must entreat it, as the Shunammite (II Kgs. iv.10, 22). If she would move him to perform a bounden duty, mildly she must persuade him . . .

Contrary is the waspish and shrewish disposition of many wives to their husbands, who care not how hastily and unadvisedly they speak to them, like Rachel (Gen. xxx.1); nor how angrily and chidingly, like Jezebel (I Kgs. xxi.7); nor how disdainfully and spitefully, like Zipporah (Exod. iv.25–6); nor how scoffingly and trumpingly, like Michal (II Sam. vi.20); nor how reproachfully and disgracefully, like Job's wife (Job ii.9) . . .

§17. Of a Wife's Obedience in General

. . . The first law that ever was given to woman since her fall, laid upon her this duty of *Obedience* to her husband in these words, 'thy desire shall be to thine husband, and he shall rule over thee' (Gen. iii.16). How can an husband rule over his wife if she obey not him? . . .

Contrary is the stoutness of such wives as must have their own will, and do what they list, or else all shall be out of quiet. *Their* will must be done, *they* must rule and over-rule all, *they* must command not only children and servants, but husbands also . . .

§46. Of a Wife's Readiness to Do what her Husband Requireth

A third particular instance of a wife's readiness to yield unto her husband's commandments, is to perform what business he requireth of her. When of a sudden there came three men to Abraham, and he was desirous to entertain them, he bid his wife make ready quickly three measures of meal, etc. (Gen. xviii.6), and she did accordingly . . .

Contrary is the humour of many wives who will not do anything upon command . . .

§52. Of Cases wherein a Wife Ought to Forbear what her Husband Requireth

. . . If an husband require his wife to do that which God hath forbidden she ought not to do it.

Two cautions . . . are . . . to be observed about this point.

First, that she be sure (being truly informed by God's Word) that that which she refuseth to do at her husband's command, is forbidden by God.

Secondly, that she first labour with all meekness and by all good means that she can to dissuade her husband from urging and pressing that upon her which with a good conscience she cannot do . . .

§53. Of Wives' Faults in Showing More Respect to their Husbands than to God

Contrary to this limitation is, on the one side, a fawning flattering disposition of such wives as seek to please their husbands, so as they care not to displease God (Jezebel was such an one: to please her husband most lewdly she did practise Naboth's death (I Kgs. xxi.7 etc.)); and, on the other side, a fainting, timorous heart which maketh them fear their husbands more than they fear God. Sarah, that worthy precedent of good wives in other things, somewhat failed herein (Gen. xii.13 etc.). Did wives duly consider, and always remember, that they have an husband (namely Christ) in heaven, as well as on earth, and that there is greater difference betwixt *that* and *this* husband, than betwixt heaven and earth, and that both in giving reward, and taking revenge, there is no comparison betwixt them, their care of pleasing, or their fear of offending, their husband in heaven would be much more than of pleasing, or offending, their husband on earth . . .

§54. Of the Manner of a Wife's Subjection to her Husband

. . . now to insist in the manner only, there are four virtues which are especially needful hereunto, whereby the Church seasoneth her subjection to Christ and wives also may and must season their subjection to their husbands.

These are the four: 1. *Humility*; 2. *Sincerity*; 3. *Cheerfulness*; 4. *Constancy*.

§55. Of a Wife's Humility in Every Duty

1. Humility is that grace that keeps one from thinking highly of himself about that which is meet . . . so as if humility be placed in a wife's heart, it will make her think better of her husband than of herself, and so make her the more willing to yield all subjection unto him . . .

§56. Of Wives' Pride

Contrary is pride, which puffeth up, and maketh them think there is no reason they should be subject to husbands, they can rule themselves well enough, yea and rule their husbands too, as well as their husbands rule them. No more pestilent vice for an inferior than this: it is the cause of all rebellion, disobedience and disloyalty: 'only by pride cometh contention' (Prov. xiii.10).

97 John Bunyan, *Christian Behaviour* [1663], III. 32–4

The Duty of Wives

. . . First [she should] look upon [her husband] as her head and lord. 'The head of the Woman is the Man. And so Sarah called Abraham Lord' (I Cor. xi.3. I Pet. iii.6).

Secondly, she should therefore be subject to him as is fit in the Lord. The Apostle saith, 'That the wife should submit her self to her husband, as to the Lord' (I. Pet. iii.1; Col. iii.18; Ephes. v.22) . . . Therefore, as the Church is subject to Christ, so let the wives be to their own husbands in every thing, Ephes. v.24.

Now for the performing of this work, thou must first shun these evils.

1. The evil of a wandering and a gossiping spirit: this is evil in Church, and is evil also in a wife, who is the figure of a Church. Christ loveth to have his spouse keep at home; that is, to be with him in the faith and practice of his things, not ranging and meddling with the things of Satan: no more should wives be given to wander and gossip abroad. You know that Prov. vii.11 saith, 'She is loud and stubborn, her feet abide not in her house' . . .

2. Take heed of an idle, talking, or brangling tongue. This also is odious either in maids or wives, to be like parrots, not bridling their tongue; whereas the wife should know, as I said before, that her husband is her lord, and is over her, as Christ is over the Church. Do you think it is seemly for the Church to parrot it against her husband? is she not to be silent before him, and to look to his laws rather than her own fictions? 'Why so', saith the Apostle, 'ought the wife to carry it towards her husband'. 'Let the woman', saith Paul, 'learn in silence with all subjection: but I suffer not a woman to teach, or to usurp authority over the man, but to be in silence', I Tim. ii.11, 12.

It is an unseemly thing to see a woman so much as once in all her life-time, to offer to over-top her husband; she ought in every thing to be in subjection to him, and to do all she doth, as having her warrant, licence and authority from him. And indeed here is her glory, even to be under him, as the Church is under Christ. 'Now she openeth her mouth in wisdom, and in her tongue is the law of kindness', Prov. xxxi.26.

3. Take heed of affecting immodest apparel, or a wanton gait; this will be evil both abroad and at home; abroad it will not only give ill example, but also tend to tempt to lust and lasciviousness; and at home 'twill give an offence to a godly husband, and be cankering to ungodly children &c. 'Wherefore', as saith the Apostle, 'let women's apparel be modest, as becometh women professing godliness with good works', I Tim. ii.10, 'not with broidered hair, or gold, or pearls, or costly array' . . .

But yet, do not think that by the subjection I have here mentioned, that I do intend women should be their husbands' slaves. Women are their husbands' yoke-fellows, their flesh and their bones; and he is not a man that hateth his own flesh, or that is bitter against it, Ephes v.29. Wherefore, 'let every man love his wife as himself: and the wife see that she reverence her husband', Ephes. iii.33.

98 Richard Baxter, *A Christian Directory* (1673), II.iv, II.vii [IV.90–1, 117–18, 145–50]

General Directions for the Holy Government of Families

. . . Let governors maintain their authority in their families. For if once that be lost, and you are despised by those you should rule, your words will be of no effect with them; you do but ride without a bridle; your power of governing is gone, when your authority is lost. And here you must first understand the nature, use and extent of your authority: for as your relations are different to your wife, your children and your servants, so also is your authority. Your authority over your wife, is but such as is necessary to the order of your family, the safe and prudent management of your affairs, and your comfortable cohabitation. The power of love and complicated interest must do more than magisterial commands. Your authority over your children is much greater; but yet only such as conjunct with love, is needful to their good education and felicity. Your authority over your servants is to be measured by your contract with them (in these countries where there are no slaves) in order to your service, and the honour of God . . .

The Mutual Duties of Husbands and Wives towards Each Other

The first duty of husbands is to love their wives (and wives their husbands) with a true, entire conjugal love. 'Husbands love your wives, even as Christ also loved the church, and gave himself for it' (Eph. v.25) . . .

The sub-directions for maintaining conjugal love are such as these. 1. Choose one at first that is truly amiable, especially in the virtues of the mind. 2. Marry not till you are sure that you can love entirely . . . 3. Be not too hasty, but know beforehand all the imperfections which may tempt you afterwards to loathing. But if these duties have been sinfully neglected, yet 4. Remember that justice commandeth you to love one that hath, as it were, forsaken all the world for you, and is contented to be the companion of your labours and sufferings . . . It is worse than barbarous inhumanity to entice such a one into a bond and love and society with you, and then to say, you cannot love her . . . 5. Remember that women are ordinarily affectionate, passionate creatures, and as they love much themselves, so they expect much love from you . . . 8. Take more notice of the good that is in your wives, than of the evil. Let not the observation of their faults make you forget or overlook their virtues. 9. Make not infirmities to

161

seem odious faults, but excuse them as far as lawfully you may, by considering the frailty of the sex, and of their tempers, and considering also your
own infirmities, and how much your wives must bear with you. 10. Stir up
that most in them into exercise which is best, and stir not up that which is
evil . . . 11. Overcome them with love; and then whatever they are in
themselves, they will be loving to you, and consequently lovely . . . A good
husband is the best means to make a good and loving wife . . . 12. Give them
examples of amiableness . . .

The Special Duties of Wives to Husbands

The wife that expecteth comfort in a husband, must make conscience of all
her own duty to her husband: for though it be his duty to be kind and
faithful to her, though she prove unkind and froward, yet 1. Men are frail
and apt to fail in such difficult duties as well as women. 2. And it is so
ordered by God, that comfort and duty shall go together, and you shall miss
of comfort, if you cast duty off.

Direct. 1. Be specially loving to your husbands: your natures give you
the advantage in this; and love feedeth love. This is your special requital for
all the troubles that your infirmities put them to.

Direct. 2. Live in a voluntary subjection and obedience to them. If their
softness or yieldingness cause them to relinquish their authority, and for
peace they are fain to let you have your wills, yet remember that it is God
that hath appointed them to be your heads and governors. If they are so silly
as to be unable, you should not have chosen such to rule you as are unfit: but
having chosen them, you must assist them with your better understanding,
in a submissive, and not a ruling masterly way . . .

*Direct. 3. Learn of your husbands as your appointed teachers, and be not
self-conceited and wise in your own eyes, but ask of them such instructions as
your case requireth.* 'Let your women keep silence in the churches: for it is
not permitted to them to speak; but they are commanded to be under
obedience, as also saith the law: and if they will learn anything, let them ask
their husbands at home' (I Cor. xiv.34–5) . . .

*Direct. 4. Set yourselves seriously to amend all those faults which they
reprove in you* . . .

Direct. 5. Honour your husbands according to their superiority. Behave
not yourselves towards them with unreverence and contempt, in titles,
speeches, or any behaviour: if the worth of the persons deserve not honour,
yet their place deserveth it. Speak not of their infirmities behind their backs,
as some twattling gossips use to do, that know not that their husbands'
dishonour is their own . . .

*Direct. 6. Live in a cheerful contentedness with your condition; and take
heed of an impatient, murmuring spirit.* It is a continual burden to a man to
have an impatient, discontented wife. Many a poor man can easily bear his

poverty himself, that yet is not able to bear his wife's impatience under it. To hear her night and day complaining, and speaking distrustfully, and see her live disquietedly, is far heavier than his poverty itself . . . a contented, cheerful wife doth help to make a man cheerful and contented in every state.

Direct. 7. In a special manner strive to subdue your passions, and to speak and do all in meekness and sobriety. The rather because that the weakness of your sex doth usually subject you more to passions than men: and it is the common cause of the husband's disquietness, and the calamity of your relation . . .

Direct. 8. Take heed of a proud and contentious disposition; and maintain a humble, peaceable temper. Pride will make you turbulent and unquiet with your husbands, and contentious with your neighbours: it will make you foolish and ridiculous, in striving for honour and precedency, and envying those that exceed you, or go before you . . .

Direct. 9. Affect not a childish gaudiness of apparel, nor a vain, or costly, or troublesome curiosity in any thing about you. Uncleanness and nastiness is a fault, but very small in comparison of this pride and curiosity. It dishonoureth your sex and selves to be so childish as to overmind such toyish things. If you will needs be proud, be proud of somewhat that is of worth and proper to a man: to be proud of reason, or wisdom, or learning, or goodness, is bad enough; but this is to be proud of something. But to be proud of fashions and fine clothes, of spots and nakedness, of sumptuous entertainments, and neat rooms, is to be proud of your shame, and not your virtue . . .

Direct 10. Be specially careful in the government of your tongues; and let your words be few, and well considered before you speak them. A double diligence is needful in this, because it is the most common miscarriage of your sex: a laxative running tongue, is so great a dishonour to you, that I never knew a woman very full of words, but she was the pity of her friends, and the contempt of others; who behind her back will make a scorn of her, and talk of her as some crack-brained or half-witted person; yea, though your talk be good, it will be tedious and contemptible, if it be thus poured out, and be too cheap . . .

Direct. 11. Be willing and diligent in your proper part, of the care and labour of the family. As the primary provision of maintenance belongeth most to the husband, so the secondary provision within doors belongeth specially to the wife. Read over the thirty-first chapter of Proverbs; especially the care of nursing your own children, and teaching them, and watching over them when they are young; and also watching over the family at home, when your husbands are abroad, is your proper work.

99 William Shakespeare, *The Taming of the Shrew* (written *c.*1592), V.ii.141–73

Fie, fie, unknit that threat'ning, unkind brow,
And dart not scornful glances from those eyes
To wound thy lord, thy king, thy governor.
It blots thy beauty as frosts do bite the meads,
Confounds thy fame as whirlwinds shake fair buds,
And in no sense is meet or amiable.
A woman moved is like a fountain troubled,
Muddy, ill-seeming, thick, bereft of beauty,
And while it is so, none so dry or thirsty
Will deign to sip or touch one drop of it.
Thy husband is thy lord, thy life, thy keeper,
Thy head, thy sovereign, one that cares for thee,
And for thy maintenance commits his body
To painful labour both by sea and land,
To watch the night in storms, the day in cold,
Whilst thou liest warm at home, secure and safe,
And craves no other tribute at thy hands
But love, fair looks, and true obedience,
Too little payment for so great a debt.
Such duty as the subject owes the prince,
Even such a woman oweth to her husband,
And when she is froward, peevish, sullen, sour,
And not obedient to his honest will,
What is she but a foul contending rebel,
And graceless traitor to her loving lord?
I am ashamed that women are so simple
To offer war where they should kneel for peace,
Or seek for rule, supremacy, and sway
When they are bound to serve, love, and obey.
Why are our bodies soft, and weak, and smooth,
Unapt to toil and trouble in the world,
But that our soft conditions and our hearts
Should well agree with our external parts?

100 Robert Burton, *Anatomy of Melancholy* (1621–51), III.ii.1(2) [III.54]

A good wife, according to Plutarch, should be as a looking-glass to represent her husband's face and passion: if he be pleasant, she should be merry; if he laugh, she should smile; if he look sad, she should participate of his sorrow, and bear a part with him, and so they should continue in mutual love one towards another.

101 Sir Thomas Overbury, *A Wife* (1614), p. 21

A Good Wife

Is a man's best movable, a scion incorporate with the stock, bringing sweet fruit; one that to her husband is more than a friend, less than trouble; an equal with him in the yoke. Calamities and troubles she shares alike, nothing pleaseth her that doth not him. She is relative in all, and he without her but half himself. She is his absent hands, eyes, ears, and mouth; his present and absent All. She frames her nature unto his howsoever; the hyacinth follows not the sun more willingly. Stubbornness and obstinacy are herbs that grow not in her garden. She leaves tattling to the gossips of the town, and is more seen than heard. Her household is her charge; her care to that makes her seldom non-resident. Her pride is but to be cleanly, and her thrift not to be prodigal. By her discretion she hath children, not wantons; a husband without her is a misery in a man's apparel: none but she hath an aged husband, to whom she is both a staff and a chair. To conclude, she is both wise and religious, which makes her all this.

102 Dorothy Leigh, *The Mothers Blessing* (1616), pp. 49–57

Chap. 13. It is Great Folly for a Man to Mislike his own Choice

Methinks I never saw a man show a more senseless simplicity than in misliking his own choice, when God hath given a man almost a world of women to choose him a wife in. If a man hath not wit enough to choose him one whom he can love to the end, yet methinks he should have discretion to cover his own folly; but if he want discretion, methinks he should have policy, which never fails a man to dissemble his own simplicity in this case. If he want wit, discretion and policy, he is unfit to marry a woman. Do not a woman that wrong as to take her from her friends that love her and after a while to begin to hate her. If she have not friends, yet thou knowest not but that she may have a husband that may love her. If thou canst not love her to the end, leave her to him that can. Methinks my son could not offend me in anything, if he served God, except he chose a wife that he could not love to the end. I need not say, if he served God; for, if he served God, he would obey God, and then he would choose a godly wife, and live lovingly and godily with her, and not do as some man [*sic*], who taketh a woman to make her a companion and fellow, and after he hath her, he makes her a servant and drudge. If she be thy wife, she is always too good to be thy servant and worthy to be thy fellow. If thou wilt have a good wife, thou must go before her in all goodness, and show her a pattern of all good virtues by thy godly and discreet life; and especially in patience, according to the counsel of the Holy Ghost: 'Bear with the woman, as with the weaker vessel' (I Pet. iii.7). Here God showeth that it is her imperfection that honoureth thee, and that it is thy perfection that maketh thee to bear with her; follow the counsel of God therefore, and bear with her. God willed a man 'to leave father and mother for his wife' (Gen. ii.24). This showeth what an excellent love God did appoint to be between man and wife. In truth, I cannot set down the excellency of that love; but this I assure you, that if you get wives that be godly and you love them, you shall not need to forsake me; whereas if you have wives that you love not, I am sure I will forsake you. Do not yourselves that wrong, as to marry a woman that you cannot love; show not so much childishness in your sex, as to say, you loved her once, and now your mind is changed . . .

103 Thomas Middleton, *Women Beware Women* (acted *c.*1621), I.i.74–93

I pray do not you teach her to rebel,
When she's in a good way to obedience;
To rise with other women in commotion
Against their husbands, for six gowns a year,
And to maintain their cause, when they're once up,
In all things else that require cost enough.
They are all of 'em a kind of spirits – soon raised
But not so soon laid, mother. As for example,
A woman's belly is got up in a trice:
A simple charge ere it be laid down again:
So ever in all their quarrels, and their courses.
And I'm a proud man, I hear nothing of 'em;
They're very still, I thank my happiness,
And sound asleep; pray let not your tongue wake 'em.
If you can but rest quiet, she's contented
With all conditions that my fortunes bring her to:
To keep close as a wife that loves her husband;
To go after the rate of my ability,
Not the licentious swindge of her own will,
Like some of her old schoolfellows.

104 [N.H.], *The Ladies Dictionary* (1694), pp. 472–4 [misnumbered from p. 240]

Wife, good, her character: . . . We find her then to command her husband in any equal matter by constant obedience to him; for if in his passion he should by his power chance to prejudice his right, she wisely knows, by complying or compounding, how to rectify it again to her praise and advantage. She never crosses her husband in the spring-tide of his anger, but stays till it is ebbing-water, and then she mildly argues the matter . . . gives him reasons . . . and if we over-rule them, she is silent . . . her clothes are rather comely than costly . . . and, though of high parentage, her mind is not puffed up to pride and boasting . . . esteeming her husband, though not rich, equal in her mind to the most rich and powerful, because she is satisfied with his fortune, be what it will . . . We find her an *arcana imperii* [secret place of her lord] wherein her husband's secrets are safely lodged . . . in his absence, she is wife and deputy husband, which induces her to double the files of her diligence, and at his return, he is sure to find all things in so good a state, that he is highly pleased, insomuch that upon view of his affairs, he wonders to see himself in effect at home when he was abroad. We find her carriage exceeding modest and comely, even to that degree that she dashes all amorous pretenders out of countenance . . . Her children (if many in number) are none in noise, governing and ordering them with a nod, or a motion of her eyes, as she pleases, and when they come to understanding, she teaches them not pride but good breeding, industry and frugality.

105 George Savile, *Advice to a Daughter* (1688), pp. 277–9

Husband

That which challengeth the next place in your thoughts is how to live with a husband . . .

It is one of the disadvantages belonging to your sex that young women are seldom permitted to make their own choice; their friends' care and experience are thought safer guides to them than their own fancies, and their modesty often forbiddeth them to refuse when their parents recommend, though their inward consent may not entirely go along with it. In this case there remaineth nothing for them to do but to endeavour to make that easy which falleth to their lot . . .

You must first lay it down for a foundation in general, that there is inequality in the sexes, and that for the better economy of the world the men, who were to be the lawgivers, had the larger share of reason bestowed upon them; by which means your sex is the better prepared for the compliance that is necessary for the better performance of those duties which seem to be most properly assigned to it. This looks a little uncourtly at the first appearance, but upon examination it will be found that Nature is so far from being unjust to you that she is partial on your side. She hath made you such large amends by other advantages for the seeming injustice of the first distribution that the right of complaining is come over to our sex. You have it in your power not only to free yourselves but to subdue your masters, and without violence throw both their natural and legal authority at your feet. We are made of differing tempers, that our defects may the better be mutually supplied: your sex wanteth our reason for your conduct, and our strength for your protection; ours wanteth your gentleness to soften and entertain us. The first part of our life is a good deal subjected to you in the nursery, where you reign without competition, and by that means have the advantage of giving the first impressions. Afterwards you have stronger influences, which, well managed, have more force in your behalf than all our privileges and jurisdictions can pretend to have against you. You have more strength in your looks than we have in our laws, and more power by your tears than we have by our arguments.

It is true that the laws of marriage run in a harsher style towards your sex. Obey is an ungenteel word, and less easy to be digested by making such an unkind distinction in the words of the contract, and so very unsuitable to the excess of good manners which generally goes before it. Besides, the universality of the rule seemeth to be a grievance, and it appeareth reasonable that there might be an exemption for extraordinary women from ordinary rules, to take away the just exception that lieth against the false measure of general equality . . .

But the answer to it in short is, that the institution of marriage is too sacred to admit a liberty of objecting to it; that the supposition of yours being the weaker sex having without all doubt a good foundation maketh it reasonable to subject it to the masculine dominion; that no rule can be so perfect as not to admit some exceptions, but the law presumeth there would be so few found in this case who would have a sufficient right to such a privilege that it is safer some injustice should be connived at in a very few instances than to break into an establishment upon which the order of human society doth so much depend.

You are therefore to make your best of what is settled by law and custom, and not vainly imagine that it will be changed for your sake.

10

MOTHER AND DAUGHTER

As the womb was central to the seventeenth century's physiological conception of woman (see chapters 2 and 3), so it was to social and religious thinking about women. Through marriage and childbirth, the curse on Eve (and woman) is reversed and, even if in a puzzling way, salvation becomes possible (106; cf. 79). There is something monstrous in a woman who does not wish to become a mother (107), still more in one who rejects her own child. Popular pamphleteering found an especial *frisson* of horror in the unnatural breaking of the mother/child bond (108; cf. 109: VI.§10). There is some evidence for the practice of contraception (107; Laslett (1983), p. 117; see generally on this subject Noonan (1965)), but it was universally condemned by medical and ecclesiastical authorities (Eccles (1982), p. 67); procured abortion was regarded as a heinous sin, akin to murder (109: VI.§9).

A married woman might expect to conceive many times, perhaps annually until the menopause if conception were not impeded by breastfeeding (see further chapter 12). Pregnancy and childbirth were occasions of great apprehension. It was commonly thought that the woman bore responsibility for the character of the child she carried since this could be adversely affected during pregnancy (or even at conception) by her own disposition and imagination (14; for further cases see Crawford (1986), p. 27, Eccles (1982), pp. 64–5). Gouge takes a more sensible line on the obligations of antenatal care (109: VI.§9). Miscarriage, parturitional complications and puerperal fever presented great hazards, quite apart from the pain and risk of birth without antiseptics or anaesthetics (110; cf. 84, and see further Eccles (1982), *passim*). The incidence of maternal death, and of still births and infant mortality, was far higher than in modern Europe. Stone (1977), pp. 66–73, sees the 'constant presence of death' as the distinguishing feature of life in the early modern family, but Laslett (1983), p. 112, warns against 'lugubrious statements' about the prevalence of child mortality. Even so, his own statistics show that child mortality (to the age of ten) could approach 25 per cent of births, with 150 per 1,000 dying in the first year. Houlbrooke (1984), p. 129, reckons that an overall maternal mortality rate of 25 per 1,000 births 'seems plausible', though Schofield (1986), pp. 248–50, reckons the figure was nearer 10 per 1,000 births in the first half of the century and 15–16 in the second half. Apprehension consequently marks anticipations of childbirth, thankfulness recollections of a successful delivery. The risks and pain of childbirth were accommodated within a providential context (110, 111), and grief at bereavement was assuaged through recourse to Christian patience and submission to the will of God (110, 112; see further on this whole subject Pollock (1990)).

During our period, men (including the father) were generally excluded from the delivery room, but a number of female friends and neighbours commonly attended, with the midwife (111; cf. 74), who was generally female (see chapter 12). The 'social space of the birth' was hence 'a collective female space, constituted on the one hand by the presence of gossips and midwife, and on the other hand by the absence of men' (Wilson (1990), p. 73). This is not to say that there was medical (113) or male indifference to the demands placed upon women (114) or that all husbands felt it a matter of concern only to their wives. Gouge exhorts husbands to be 'very tender' of their pregnant wives (109: VI.§9) and, as Houlbrooke (1984), pp. 129–30, points out, many men were clearly anguished by the pains of their wives' labour: 'women's deaths in childbirth, sometimes recorded in funeral inscriptions from the fifteenth century onwards, inspired some of the most poignant monuments of the early seventeenth century' (see 73 for an example). After the birth, the mother remained confined to her bed for a period of up to several weeks, before (for communicants of the Church of England) her 'churching', a ceremony of thanksgiving for her preservation 'in the great danger . . . pain and peril of childbirth', ultimately derived from the Hebrew practice of ritual atonement and purification from the taint of childbed (Lev. xxii.1–8; see further Wilson (1990), pp. 78–9).

Throughout the century, breastfeeding was felt to be unbecoming by many, particularly gentlewomen and women of higher rank (Alice Thornton was an exception (110)), who made use of wet-nurses, though divines and physicians strenuously recommended that mothers of all classes should suckle their own children (see chapter 12). The subsequent nursing, care and education of the child (to the age of seven) 'belongeth specially to the wife' (98; cf. 20); she is 'to bring up the children' (97). Her husband recorded Elizabeth Walker's exemplary performance of this duty (115). Some social historians take the view that in pre-industrial families with high child mortality rates parents could not allow themselves to become deeply attached to their young children. Stone (1977), p. 70, for example, instances the practice of giving a new-born child the same name as one who had died earlier as evidence that the prevalence of mortality resulted in 'a lack of sense that a child was a unique being, with its own name'. Crawford (1986), pp. 23–4, cites other examples, but she herself, like Houlbrooke (1984), p. 182, and Macfarlane (1986), pp. 52–3, takes a much more positive view of parental affection. Certainly, it is difficult to doubt the depth of parental, and more particularly, maternal love suggested time and again by the tone of the surviving records.

There is some evidence that mother/daughter bonds were the strongest forged (Houlbrooke (1984), pp. 187–8). Unlike sons, daughters remained at home and their later education (if the family was well-to-do) continued to be the mother's responsibility (Crawford (1990), p. 12). It typically consisted of preparation for married life (116, 117), without much intellectual content, though exceptionally it could be more extensive, even if, in the case of Lucy Hutchinson, without the mother's approval (118). Beilin (1990), pp. 274–5, notes the ambivalence with which Elizabeth Jocelin, conventionally deprecating learning in a woman, 'does not much desire' it in her own daughter, and yet applauds the meeting of learning and wisdom in a virtuous woman (119). Citing the Verney letter of 1652 reproduced here (120), Stone (1977), pp. 202–6, argues that this domestic emphasis marked the end of the Humanist tradition of the learned lady (on the education of women see further Gardiner (1929); Hobby (1988), pp. 190–8; Reynolds (1964)). Stone (1977), pp. 161–74, takes a very grim view of parent/child relations and of the seventeenth-century (and, in his view, especially Puritan) determination to break the will of the child (particularly through frequent whipping and physical punishment), which he believes banished affection until sensibility changed at the end of the century (ibid., pp. 221ff.). His evidence, however, concerns boys, and bears generally on their treatment at school and university rather than at home. Houlbrooke (1984), pp. 6–7, 127–56, rejecting Stone's view, insists on the importance of affection throughout the century. It is true that children were expected to obey and revere their parents to a degree now unfamiliar, but it is also true that the conduct manuals regarded both paternal and maternal love as natural and expected it to be unconditional (109: VI.§2).

Although medical texts did not expect a girl to experience menarche until the age of 14 or 15 (14), the stages of her social and legal development were reached earlier than today (121, 81: II.i.§2). It appears that, though daughters could not expect easily to marry contrary to their parents' wishes (122), they might dissent from a parental marriage choice, at least by the end of the century (123).

---

106 Henry Smith, *A Preparative to Marriage* (1591), pp. 7–8

Further, for the honour of marriage, Paul showeth how by it the curse of the woman was turned into a blessing, for the woman's curse was the pains which she should suffer in her travail (Gen. iii.16). Now, by marriage, this curse is turned into a blessing, for children are the first blessing in all the

Scripture (Gen. i.28). And therefore Christ saith, that so soon as the mother seeth a man child born into the world, she forgetteth all her sorrows, as though her curse were turned into a blessing (John xvi.21). And further, Paul saith that by bearing children, if she continue in faith and patience (for those pains will try her faith), she shall be saved, as though one curse were turned into two blessings (I Tim. ii.15). For first she shall have children, and after she shall have salvation. What a merciful God have we, whose curses are blessings?

107 Ben Jonson, *Epigrams* (1616), p. 53

LXII To Fine Lady Would-Be

Fine Madam Would-be, wherefore should you fear,
That love to make so well, a child to bear?
The world reputes you barren: but I know
Your 'pothecary, and his drug says no.
Is it the pain affrights you? That's soon forgot.
Or your complexion's loss? You have a pot,
That can restore that. Will it hurt your feature?
To make amends, you're thought a wholesome creature.
What should the cause be? Oh, you live at court:
And there's both loss of time, and loss of sport
In a great belly. Write, then on thy womb,
Of the not born, yet buried, here's thy tomb.

108 [Henry Goodcole], *Natures Cruell Step-Dames* (1637), pp. 16–17

A Relation of Anne Willis, the Manner of the Murdering of her Own Child

Upon an inquisition of one of the Coroner's Inquest, for the county of Middlesex, upon the view of the body of her bastard child, taken out of a vault in Rosemary Lane, by Tower Hill, by her therein thrown, being by the Jury made, return unto the Coroner of murder, warrants were immediately sent out unto all parts for the apprehending of the said Anne Willis, who, upon the seventh day of March, 1637, was taken, and brought before Sir Thomas Jay, unto whom she confessed the fact: that the child was born alive; there was two upon oath justified it, that she said it was alive. Oh, cruel monsters of that tender sex! 'Can a woman forget the child of her womb?' (Isa. ix. [*recte* xlix.15]). Heaven's infinite compassion is compared unto the mother and infant [Isa. lxvi.13], the near tie between them, and the entire care of mothers over their children! When I lift up mine eyes towards the Heavens, and again cast them down to the earth, bird, beasts, methinks, do rise up in judgement against these unnatural cruel beasts in women's shapes. The swallow flieth high, and in the towering trees, churches and houses build their nests, to preserve their young ones from hunger. The sparrow watcheth alone on the house-top, as careful what it hath hatched and brought forth. Beasts, such as lions, wolves, tigers and foxes, have secret caves and woods where they hide their young, to preserve and foster them alive. But these bloody dogs degenerate from them. O let therefore the memorial of them perish.

109 William Gouge, *Domesticall Duties* (1662), *passim*

Treatise I: AN EXPOSITION OF THAT PART OF SCRIPTURE OUT OF WHICH DOMESTICALL DUTIES ARE RAISED

§97. Of the Meaning of the Second Verse

Ephes. vi.2: 'Honour thy father and mother (which is the first commandment with promise)'

The very words of the fifth commandment are here alleged by the Apostle as a confirmation of the forenamed reason that it is just and right to obey parents because God in the Mosaical law enjoineth as much. The law is more general than the Apostle's precept, for the law compriseth under it all those duties which all kind of inferiors owe to their superiors, whether they be in family, church, or commonwealth; but the Apostle's precept is given only to one kind of inferiors in the family, yet the argument is very sound and good from a general to a particular, thus: *All inferiors must honour their superiors, therefore children their parents* . . .

Both father and mother are expressly mentioned to take away all pretence from children of neglecting either of them, for, through the corruption of nature we are prone to seek after many shifts to exempt us from our bounden duty, and if not in whole, yet in as great a part as we can. Some might think if they honour their father, who is their mother's head, thy have done what the law requireth; others may think they have done as much if they honour their mother who is the weaker vessel [I Pet. iii.7]; but the law expressing father and mother condemneth him that neglecteth either of them . . .

Treatise VI: THE DUTIES OF PARENTS

§2. Of that Love which Parents owe to their Children

. . . The fountain of parents' duties is *love* (Tit. ii.4). This is expressly enjoined them. Many approved examples are recorded hereof, as Abraham (Gen. xxii.2), Isaac (Gen. xxv.28), Rebecca (Gen. xxv.28), and others.

Great reason there is why this affection should be fast fixed in the heart of parents towards their children. For great is that pain, pains, cost and care, which parents must undergo for their children. But if love be in them, no pain, pains, cost or care will seem too much. Herein appeareth the wise providence of God, who by nature hath so fast fixed love in the hearts of parents, as if there be any in whom it aboundeth not, he is counted unnatural. If love did not abound in parents, many children would be neglected and lost. For if parents look not to their children, who will? If none look to them, they must needs perish, for they are not able to help themselves . . .

§9. Of a Mother's Care over her Child while it is in the Womb

. . . The first part of a child's infancy is while it remaineth in the mother's womb. Here therefore the duty lieth principally upon the mother, who, so soon as she perceiveth a child to be conceived in her womb, ought to have an especial care thereof, that (so much as in her lieth) the child may be safely brought forth. (The heathen philosopher [Aristotle], by light of Nature, observed this to be a duty, and prescribed it to mothers.) A mother then must have a tender care over herself when she is with child, for the child being lodged in her, and receiving nourishment from her (as plants from the earth) her well-being tendeth much to the good and safety of the child, but the hurt that cometh to her maketh the child the worse, if it be not a means to destroy it. Why was the charge of abstaining from wine, strong drink and unclean things given to Manoah's wife (Judges xiii.4) but because of the child which she conceived? . . .

Husbands also in this case must be very tender over their wives, and helpful to them in all things needful both in regard of that duty which they owe to their wives and also of that they owe to their children . . .

They who through violence of passion, whether of grief or anger, or through violent motion of the body, as by dancing, striving, running, galloping on horseback, or the like, or through distemper of the body, by eating things hurtful, by eating too much, by too much abstinence, by too much bashfulness in concealing their desires and longings (as we speak) cause any abortion or miscarriage, fall into the offence contrary to the forenamed duty . . .

But they who purposely take things to make away their children in their womb, are in far higher degree guilty of blood, yea, even of wilful murder. For that which hath received a soul formed in it by God, if it be unjustly cast away, shall be revenged.

So far forth as husbands are careless of their wives being with child, denying them things needful, they are accessary to the hurt, which the woman or child taketh, guilty of the sin, and liable to the judgment.

§10. Of Providing Things Needful for the Child so soon as it is Born,
and of Cruelty contrary thereto

The next degree of a child's infancy is while it is in the swaddling bands, and remaineth a sucking child. In this also the care especially lieth upon the mother, yet so as the father must afford what help he can.

The first duty here required is, that sufficient provision of all things needful for a child in that weakness be beforehand provided. What the particulars be, women better know than I can express. For me, it is sufficient to lay down the duty in general, which is commanded unto us in that worthy pattern of the Virgin Mary who, though she were very poor and forced to travel far, and . . . fain to content herself with a stable in a common inn, yet she provided for her child, for it is said, 'She wrapped him in swaddling clothes' (Luke ii.7).

Contrary is the practice of such lewd and unnatural women as leave their new-born children under stalls, at men's doors, in church porches, yea many times in open fields. It is noted as a point of unnaturalness in the ostrich, to leave her eggs in the earth and in the dust, in which respect she is said to be 'hardened against young ones, as though they were not hers' (Job xxxix.14, 16). Much more hardened are the foresaid women . . . The civil law judgeth this to be a kind of murder.

110 Alice Thornton, *Autobiography* (written *post* 1668), pp. 94–5, 123–5, 164–6

Meditations on the Deliverance of my First Son and Fifth Child . . .
10 December [1657]

It pleased God, in much mercy, to restore me to strength to go to my full time, my labour beginning [being?] three days; but upon the Wednesday, the ninth of December, I fell into exceeding sharp travail in great extremity, so that the midwife did believe I should be delivered soon. But lo! it fell out contrary, for the child stayed in the birth, and came cross with his feet first, and in this condition continued till Thursday morning between two and three a clock, at which time I was upon the rack in bearing my child with such exquisite torment, as if each limb were divided from other, for the space of two hours, when at length, being speechless and breathless, I was by the infinite providence of God in great mercy delivered. But I having had such sore travail in danger of my life so long, and the child coming into the world with his feet first, caused the child to be almost strangled in the birth, only living about half an hour, so died before we could get a minister to baptize him, although he was sent for.

I was delivered of my first son and fifth child on 10th of December 1657. He was buried in Catterick Church the same day by Mr. Siddall. This sweet goodly son was turned wrong by the fall I got in September before, nor had the midwife skill to turn him right, which was the cause of the loss of his life and the hazard of my own . . . The weakness of my body was exceeding great, of long continuance, that it put me into the beginning of a consumption, not expecting for many days together that I should recover . . .

My Delivery of my son William, my Sixth Child, and of his Death, 17 April 1660

It was the good pleasure of God to continue me in the land of the living, and to bring forth my sixth child at St. Nicholas. I was delivered of a very goodly son, having Mrs. Hickeringgill with me, after hard labour and hazardous, yet, through great mercy, I had my life spared, and was blessed with a happy child about 3 or 4 a clock in the morning upon Tuesday the 17th of April 1660. That day also was my child baptized . . . my pretty babe was in good health, sucking his poor mother, to whom my good God had given the blessing of the breast as well as the womb, of that child, to whom it was no little satisfaction, while I enjoyed his life; and the joy of it made me recruit faster, for his sake, that I might do my duty to him as a mother. But it so pleased God to shorten this joy, lest I should be too much transported, that I was visited with another trial; for on the Friday sennight after, he began to be very angry and froward after his dressing in the morning, so that I perceived him not be well; upon which I gave him Gascoyne powder and cordial, lest it should be the red gum, in children usual at that time, to strike it out of his heart at morning after his dressing. And having had three hours' sleep, his face when he awaked was full of red round spots like the smallpox, being of the compass of a halfpenny, and all whealed white over, these continuing in his face till night; and being in a slumber in my arms on my knee he would sweetly lift up his eyes to heaven and smile, as if the old saying was true in this sweet infant, that he saw angels in heaven. But then, whether through cold upon his dressing then, or what else was the cause, the Lord knoweth, the spots struck in, and grew very sick all night, and about nine a clock on Saturday morning he sweetly departed this life, to the great discomfort of his weak mother, whose only comfort is that the Lord, I hope, has received him to that place of rest in heaven where little children beholds [sic] the face of their heavenly Father, to his God and my God; whom I humbly crave to pardon all things in me which he sees amiss, and clean away my sins by the blood of my dearest Saviour and Redeemer . . .

The Birth of my Son Christopher Thornton my Ninth Child, 11 November 1667, and of his Death, 1 December 1667

Of my ninth child it was the pleasure of God to give me a weak and sickly time in breeding, from the February till the 10th of May following [1667], I not having fully recruited my last September weakness; and if it had been good in the eyes of my God I should much rather (because of that) not to have been in this condition. But it is not a Christian's part to choose anything of this nature, but what shall be the will of our heavenly Father, be it never so contrary to our own desires . . . The birth of my ninth child was very perilous to me, and I hardly escaped with my life, falling into pangs of labour about the 4th of November, being ill, continuing that week; and on Monday 11th of November 1667 I fell in travail, being delivered betwixt the hours of ten and eleven a clock at night . . .

After this comfort of my child I recovered something of my weakness, better recovering my breasts and milk, and giving suck, when he thrived very well and grew strong, being a lovely babe. But, lest I should too much set my heart in the satisfaction of any blessing under heaven, it seemed good to the most infinite wise God to take him from me, giving me some apprehensions thereof before any did see it as a change in him. And therefore with a full resignation to his providence I endeavoured to submit patiently and willingly to part with my sweet child to our dear and loving Father, who see [saw?] what was better for me than I could, begging that his will might be mine, either in life or death. When he was about fourteen days old, my pretty babe broke into red spots like the smallpox . . . and at length it pleased his Saviour and mine, after the fifth sick night and day, to deliver him out of this miserable world. He sweetly fell asleep on Sunday at night, being then the 1st of December 1667 . . .

After my dear child's death I fell into a great and long continued weakness by the swelling of my milk, he having sucked last, in his pain, of the left breast, had hurt the nipple, causing it to gangrene, and extreme pain with torment of it made me fall into a fever . . .

111 Ralph Josselin, *Diary* (written 1644–81), pp. 50–1

24 November 1645: I had sought to God for my wife (that was oppressed with fears that she should not do well on this child), that God would order all providences so as we might rejoice in his salvation; I had prayed with confidence of good success to her. About midnight on Monday I rose, called up some neighbours; the night was very light, Goodman Potter willing to go for the midwife, and up when I went; the horse out of the pasture, but presently found; the midwife up at Bures, expecting it had been nearer day; the weather indifferent dry; midwife came, all things even gotten ready towards day. I called in the women by daylight, almost all came; and about 11 or 12 of the clock my wife was with very sharp pains delivered November 25 of her daughter intended for a Jane; she was then twenty-five years of age herself. We had made a good pasty for this hour, and that also was kept well. Wife and child both well, praise be my good and merciful Father.

30 November: God good and gracious to us in my wife's and babe's health, enabling her to nurse . . .

4 December: My dearest very ill, as if she would have even died; she uttered as formerly these words, 'Thou and I must part'; but my God continues us together, praise him.

112 Anne Bradstreet, *Several Poems* (1678), p. 237

On My Dear Grandchild Simon Bradstreet, Who Died on 16 November, 1669, Being but A Month, and One Day Old

No sooner came, but gone, and fall'n asleep,
Acquaintance short, yet parting caused us weep;
Three flowers, two scarcely blown, the last i' th' bud,
Cropp'd by th' Almighty's hand; yet is He good.
With dreadful awe before Him let's be mute,
Such was His will, but why, let's not dispute,
With humble hearts and mouths put in the dust,
Let's say He's merciful as well as just.
He will return and make up all our losses,
And smile again after our bitter crosses
Go pretty babe, go rest with sisters twain,
Among the blest in endless joys remain.

113 Robert Barret, *Companion for Midwives* (1699), pp. 35–6

When the woman dies, and the child is alive in her belly, we sometimes open her up, and take out the child. Some foolish people talk of performing this operation upon living women, in a dangerous labour, to save the child's life; and therefore would call it *Caesarian section*, in imitation of Caesar's birth. 'Tis true there would be some pretext of excuse to make martyrs of poor women to bring a second Caesar, or some great and new prophet into our Western world; but 'tis not known that ever there was any law, Christian or civil, which countenanced the martyrdom of the mother to save the child. Some country gossips will tell you they know such yet living whose sides have been opened to make way for the child; but such stories as these are only fit entertainment for fools and children. A surgeon must never practise this operation whilst the mother is alive; but when she is dead, he ought not to neglect it, and what he does, he must do it quickly, because delay will certainly be the death of the child.

114 Richard Baxter, *A Christian Directory* (1673), II.i [IV.18]

Women especially must expect so much suffering in a married life, that if God had not put into them a natural inclination to it, and so strong a love to their children, as maketh them patient under the most annoying troubles, the world would ere this have been at an end, through their refusal of so calamitous a life. Their sickness in breeding, their pain in bringing forth, with the danger of their lives, the tedious trouble night and day, which they have with their children in their nursing and their childhood; besides their subjection to their husbands, and continual care of family affairs; being forced to consume their lives in a multitude of low and troublesome businesses: all this, and much more would have utterly deterred that sex from marriage, if Nature itself had not inclined them to it.

115 [Anthony Walker], *The Holy Life of Mrs. Elizabeth Walker* (1690), pp. 61–72

Care of the Education of Her Children

God was pleased to give her strength to go out her full time of eleven children, six sons and five daughters, besides some abortive or untimely births . . .

Next to their baptism, properly follows her prudent, pious care in the education of her children; that they might want no accomplishments in this world . . . but especially, to train them up in the true and early knowledge of religion . . . She considered children as the nursery of families, the church, and nation; and that errors in their education were hardly ever corrected after . . . She accounted it not only an indispensable duty to be done, but an high honour to be entrusted by God, with the care of bringing up a child for him . . .

Without vanity, she was completely qualified for this performance, as was possible to be desired or wished. She was mistress of her needle to that degree, that she would blame herself that she had spent so much time and industry to attain it . . . And for household employment, all that knew her wondered she could so soon attain such universal dexterity . . . but she being of very quick natural parts . . . soon made herself mistress of whatever she set herself to, not only in what strictly concerned her maids in cooking, brewing, baking, the dairy, and the ordering of linen . . . but in physic, chirurgery . . . and also in preserving of fruits, and in making all sorts of English wines . . .

. . . Her work and business was to improve their intellectuals; to season their tender hearts with a due sense of religion . . . To promote and forward this, she taught them to read as soon as they could pronounce their letters, yea, before they could speak plain; and sowed the seed of early pious knowledge in their tender minds, by a plain familiar catechism . . . When they could read tolerably well, she caused them to get by heart choice sentences of Scripture, then whole psalms, and chapters . . .

She was also very circumspect, not only to keep their morals untainted from pride, immodesty, lying . . . but also of their gestures and carriage, that they might contract no indecent habitudes, nor uncomely postures, which might expose them to contempt; but above all of this kind, pressing them to cleanliness and neatness.

116 Ann Fanshawe, *Memoirs* (written 1676), p. 110

Now it is necessary to say something of my mother's education of me, which was with all the advantages that time afforded, both for working all sorts of fine works with my needle, and learning French, singing, lute, the virginals, and dancing; and, notwithstanding I learned as well as most did, yet was I wild to that degree that the hours of my beloved recreation took up too much of my time, for I loved riding in the first place, and running, and all active pastimes; and in fine I was that which we graver people call a hoyting girl. But to be just to myself, I never did mischief to myself or people, nor one immodest action or word in my life, but skipping and activity was my delight. But upon my mother's [Margaret Harrison, née Fanshawe] death [in 1640, when her daughter was aged 15] I then begun to reflect, and as an offering to her memory, I flung away those little child-nesses that had formerly possessed me, and by my father's command took upon me the charge of his house and family, which I so ordered by my excellent mother's example, as found acceptance in his sight.

117 Margaret Cavendish, 'A True Relation of My Birth' (1656), pp. 156–8

As for my breeding, it was according to my birth, and the nature of my sex; for my birth was not lost in my breeding. For as my sisters was or had been bred, so was I in plenty, or rather with superfluity. Likewise we were bred virtuously, modestly, civilly, honourably, and on honest principles . . .

  As for our garments, my mother [Elizabeth Lucas, née Leighton] did not only delight to see us neat and cleanly, fine and gay, but rich and costly; maintaining us to the height of her estate, but not beyond it . . . Likewise we were bred tenderly, for my mother naturally did strive, to please and delight her children, not to cross or torment them, terrifying them with threats, or lashing them with slavish whips; but instead of threats, reason was used to persuade us, and instead of lashes, the deformities of vice was discovered, and the graces and virtues were presented unto us. Also we were bred with respectful attendance, every one being severally waited upon, and all her servants in general used the same respect to her children (even those that were very young) as they did to herself; for she suffered not her servants, either to be rude before us, or to dominate over us, which all vulgar servants are apt, and ofttimes which some have leave to do. Likewise she never suffered the vulgar serving-men to be in the nursery among the nursemaids, lest their rude love-making might do unseemly actions, or speak unhandsome words in the presence of her children, knowing that youth is apt to take infection by ill examples, having not the reason of distinguishing good from bad. Neither were we suffered to have any familiarity with the vulgar servants, or conversation: yet caused us to demean ourselves with an humble civility towards them, as they with a dutiful respect to us. Not because they were servants were we so reserved; for many noble persons are forced to serve through necessity; but by reason the vulgar sort of servants are as ill-bred as meanly born, giving children ill examples and worse counsel.

As for tutors, although we had for all sorts of virtues [accomplishments], as singing, dancing, playing on music, reading, writing, working, and the like, yet we were not kept strictly thereto, they were rather for formality than benefit; for my mother cared not so much for our dancing and fiddling, singing and prating of several languages, as that we should be bred virtuously, modestly, civilly, honourably, and on honest principles.

As for my brothers, of which I had three, I know not how they were bred. First, they were bred when I was not capable to observe, or before I was born; likewise the breeding of men were after different manner of ways from those of women. But this I know, that they loved virtue, endeavoured merit, practised justice, and spoke truth: they were constantly loyal, and truly valiant.

118 Lucy Hutchinson, 'Autobiographical Fragment' (written 1640s/1650s?), pp. 287–8

After my mother [Lucy, Lady Apsley] had had three sons she was very desirous of a daughter, and when the women at my birth told her I was one, she receiv'd me with a great deal of joy; and the nurses fancying, because I had more complexion and favour than is usual in so young children, that I should not live, my mother became fonder of me, and more endeavour'd to nurse me. As soon as I was wean'd a French woman was taken to be my dry nurse, and I was taught to speak French and English together. My mother, while she was with child of me, dreamt that she was walking in the garden with my father [Sir Allen Apsley], and that a star came down into her hand, with other circumstances which, though I have often heard, I minded not enough to remember perfectly; only my father told her, her dream signified she should have a daughter of some extraordinary eminency, which thing, like such vain prophecies, wrought as far as it could its own accomplishment; for my father and mother fancying me then beautiful, and more than ordinarily apprehensive, applied all their cares and spar'd no cost to improve me in my education, which procur'd me the admiration of those that flatter'd my parents. By that time I was four years old I read English perfectly, and having a great memory, I was carried to sermons, and while I was very young could remember and repeat them so exactly, and being caress'd, the love of praise tickled me and made me attend more heedfully. When I was about seven years of age, I remember I had at one time eight tutors in several qualities, languages, music, dancing, writing, and needle-work, but my genius was quite averse from all but my books, and that I was so eager of that my mother, thinking it prejudic'd my health, would moder-ate me in it; yet this rather animated me than kept me back, and every moment I could steal from my play I would employ in any book I could find, when my own were locked up from me. After dinner and supper I still had an hour allow'd me to play, and then I would steal into some hole or other to read. My father would have me learn Latin, and I was so apt that I outstripped my brothers who were at school, although my father's chaplain that was my tutor was a pitiful dull fellow. My brothers, who had a great deal of wit, had some emulation at the progress I made in my learning, which very well pleas'd my father, though my mother would have been contented I had not so wholly addicted myself to that as to neglect my other qualities: as for music and dancing I profited very little in them, and would never practise my lute or harpsichords but when my masters were with me, and for my needle, I absolutely hated it; play among other children I despis'd, and when I was forc'd to entertain such as came to visit me, I tir'd them with more grave instructions than their mothers, and plucked all their babies [i.e. dolls] to pieces, and kept the children in such awe that they were glad when I entertain'd myself with elder company, to whom I was very acceptable; and living in the house with many persons that had a great deal of wit, and very profitable serious discourses being frequent at my father's table and in my mother's drawing room, I was very attentive to talk, and gather'd up things that I would utter again to great admiration of many that took my memory and imitation for wit. It pleas'd God through the good instructions of my mother, and the sermons she carried me to, I was convinc'd that the knowledge of God was the most excellent study, and accordingly applied myself to it, and to practise what I was taught . . .

119 Elizabeth Jocelin, *The Mothers Legacie* (1624), sigs B4–B8

To My Truly Loving and Most Dearly Loved Husband, Tourell Jocelin

And (dear Love) as thou must be the overseer, for God's sake, when it [our child] shall fail in duty to God, or to the world, let not thy indulgence wink at such folly, but severely correct it. And that thy trouble may be little when it comes to years, take more care when it is young. First, in providing it a nurse. O make choice not so much for her complexion as for her mild and honest disposition. Likewise, if the child be to remain long abroad after weaning, as near as may be, choose a house where it may not learn to swear or speak scurrilous words . . . It will be a great while ere it will be thought old enough to be beaten for evil words, and by that time it will be so perfect in imperfections, that blows will not mend it. And when some charitable body reproves or corrects it for these faults, let nobody pity it the loss of the mother.

Next, good sweetheart, keep it not from school, but let it learn betimes. If it be a son, I doubt not but thou wilt dedicate it to the Lord as his minister, if he will please of his mercy to give him grace and capacity for that great work. If it be a daughter, I hope my mother Brooke (if thou desirest her) will take it among hers, and let them all learn one lesson.

I desire her bringing up may be learning the Bible, as my sisters do, good housewifery, writing, and good works; other learning a woman needs not. Though I admire it in those whom God hath blessed with discretion, yet I desire not much in my own, having seen sometimes women have greater portions of learning than wisdom, which is of no better use to them than a mainsail to a fly-boat, which runs it under water. But where learning and wisdom meet in a virtuous disposed woman, she is the fittest closet for all goodness. She is like a well-balanced ship that may bear all her sail. She is – indeed, I should but shame myself if I should go about to praise her more.

120 Sir Ralph Verney, letter of 27 July 1652 to his goddaughter Nancy Denton, in Frances Parthenope Verney (ed.), *Memoirs of the Verney Family* (1892–9), iii. 73–4

Nothing but yourself could have been so welcome as your letter, nor have surprized me more, for I must confess I did not think you had been guilty of so much learning as I see you are; and yet it seems you rest unsatisfied or else you would not threaten Latin, Greek and Hebrew too. Good sweetheart, be not so covetous. Believe me, a Bible (with the Common Prayer) and a good plain catechism in your mother tongue, being well read and practised, is well worth all the rest, and much more suitable to your sex. I know your father thinks this false doctrine, but be confident your husband will be of my opinion. In French you cannot be too cunning, for that language affords many admirable books fit for you, as romances, plays, poetry, stories of illustrious (not learned) women, recipes for preserving, making creams and all sorts of cookeries, ordering your gardens, and in brief all manner of good housewifery . . .

121 [T[homas] E[dgar] (ed.)], *The Lawes Resolutions of Womens Rights* (1632), p. 7

The Ages of a Woman

The learning is 35 Hen. VI, fol. 40, that a woman hath divers special ages. At the 7th. year of her age, her father shall have aid of his tenants to marry her. At 9 years age, she is able to deserve and have dower. At 12 years to consent to marriage. At 14 to be *hors du guard* [out of wardship]. At 16 to be past the lord's tender of a husband. At 21 to be able to make a feoffment [i.e. make an endowment, convey property or estate]. And . . . a woman married at 12 cannot disagree afterward, but if she be married younger, she may dissent till she be 14.

122 Henry Smith, *A Preparative to Marriage* (1591), pp. 43–7

Touching the question, whether children may marry without their parents' consent, God saith, 'Honour thy father and thy mother' (Exod. xx.12). Now, wherein canst thou honour them more, than in this honourable action, to which they have preserved thee, and brought thee up, which concerneth the state of thy whole life? Again, in the first institution of marriage, when there was no father to give consent, then our heavenly Father gave his consent. God supplied the place of the father, and brought his daughter unto her husband (Gen. ii.22), and ever since, the father after the same manner hath offered his daughter unto her husband . . .

. . . Therefore in Matt. xxii.30 the wife is said to be bestowed in marriage, which signifieth, that some did give her beside herself . . . It is a sweet wedding when the father and the mother bring a blessing to the feast, and a heavy union which is cursed the first day that it is knit . . . Will you take your father's money and will you not take his instruction? Marriage hath need of many counsellors, and doest thou count thy father too many, which is like the foremost of thy instructors? If you mark what kind of youths they be which have such haste, that they dare not stay for their parents' advice, they are such as hunt for nothing but beauty, and for punishment hereof, they marry to beggary and lose their father and mother for their wife. Therefore, honour thy father and mother, as thou wouldest that thy children should honour thee.

123 [N.H.], *The Ladies Dictionary* (1694), pp. 341–2
[misnumbered from p. 240]

Obedience, in virgins: . . . Obedience in young virgins is very comely . . . nor is it more their duty than their interest to pay obedience where the laws of God and Nature require it. Youth is often heady and would frequently miscarry . . . were not care taken by their parents . . . This obedience then is to extend itself to all things that are good or indifferent, there being no clause of exception but where the commands are themselves unlawful . . .

Obedience we must allow to have a large circumference, yet it does not give parents a power to compel their daughters to marry where they can neither love nor like; for a negative voice in the case is certainly as much their right as their parents. However, 'tis reasonable the virgins should well examine the grounds of her [sic] aversion, and if they prove but fanciful and frivolous, she may endeavour to correct them by sober consideration, but if after all she cannot do it, she ought not to proceed to marry against her inclination . . .

11

HOUSECRAFT, STATECRAFT AND PRIESTCRAFT

'Nothing lovelier can be found / In woman, than to study household good' remarks Milton's Adam (124), in this faithfully reflecting the belief of his author's age. Woman's place was within doors, her business domestic, as befitted her wifely role, and as Aristotle as well as the Bible (56, 76) directed (125; cf. 93). Amongst the socially privileged, the efficient provisioning and running of a largely self-sufficient household with an extensive family, a steady succession of guests (each with their own entourage to be accommodated) and scores of servants, was, of course, far from a casual or undemanding occupation (126), especially when the duties involved also the management of the estate, as they frequently might, particularly in the adverse circumstances of Civil War (132). In humbler circumstances, housework was still more varied and onerous than its modern equivalent. Nevertheless, the prevailing assumption was that work in the house was fit for women because it required little intellectual ability.

Women of evident intelligence themselves accepted this divorce between the private (feminine) and public (masculine) spheres (cf. 92) and, despite the recent precedents of Mary Queen of Scots, Mary Tudor and Elizabeth, they shared the age's 'distaste . . . for the notion of woman's involvement in politics' (Maclean (1980), p. 60). Public affairs were not for her, even when (perhaps especially when) her husband was involved in them (cf. 28, 94). Lucy Hutchinson, herself very well-informed on current affairs and vehemently partisan in her interpretation of them, is nevertheless scathing about 'hands that are made only for distaffs' affecting 'the management of sceptres', discounting the example of Elizabeth (127). Margaret Cavendish wished posterity to believe that it was her bashfulness which commended her to her future husband and is deeply resentful when compelled by the exigencies of the Civil War and its aftermath to act on his behalf in a public arena (128). Just as Lucy Hutchinson is prepared to attribute the outbreak of that war to Henrietta Maria's usurping the dominant masculine role, so Margaret Cavendish ascribes it in large part to the unruliness and insubordination of women: 'temperance and quietness are strangers to our sex'

(129). Cross-dressing appalled precisely because it blurred this clear demarcation of duties and spheres of activity (see chapter 14).

Yet this same Margaret Cavendish can, within a few pages, propound a radically different, and potentially seditious, view of women's political and social position, stressing their marginalization and exclusion: 'the truth is, we are no subjects' of the state (129). Her works are, in fact, fascinated by the prospect of women in general, and herself in particular, wielding political power (most notably in *The New Blazing World*; see 189). Indeed, despite her efforts to accommodate it to her 'bashful' self-construction (188), writing appealed to her precisely because it offered an unlimited control over events. As Gallagher (1988), p. 28, argues, 'exclusion from political subjecthood allows female subjectivity to become absolute', enabling Cavendish to construct an absolute sense of self in her writings analogous to the political absolutism her royalism espoused. During that same visit to England in 1652–3 when (by her account in 128) she was so disinclined to intercede for her husband in public, she ensured that her voice might nevertheless be publicly heard on her own behalf by arranging the printing of her first publication (Jones (1988), pp. 75–6, 89–92).

A similar tension between a wifely, domestic role and a politically active one is evident in other women's memoirs. As the Civil War compelled Ann Fanshawe to take the initiative by separating her from her husband, so she becomes the protagonist of her narrative, passing safely through 'thousands of naked swords' and frustrating the designs of no less a person than Cromwell himself, while her husband and protector 'had no possibility to assist' her (130). Another Royalist, Anne Halkett, was willing and able to dispute political matters with an eminent republican Puritan (131). (For discussion of these texts in these terms, see Keeble (1990a); Keeble (forthcoming)). The letters of the Puritan Brilliana, Lady Harley, written to her son Edward from the family estate at Brampton Castle in Herefordshire in the early 1640s when her husband was absent, trace with telling immediacy the stages by which an affectionate mother and obedient wife might be inexorably compelled by war and her own commitment to assume a masculine role (132). As her sense of isolation and vulnerability grows and acts of hostility against the estate increase (Hereford was a Royalist county and her husband, Sir Robert, a prominent Parliamentarian attending sittings of the Long Parliament), so, too, her resolve not to submit to harassment or to yield the castle to Royalist forces grows more determined. She died in October 1643, shortly after successfully defending the castle against a six-week Royalist siege in July and August that year. (For a somewhat sentimental account, see Fraser (1984), pp. 175–81).

On the Puritan side, such resolution might receive positive encouragement. The eminent Independent divine Jeremiah Burroughes exhorted women to put aside 'womanish fears' (133). The preacher and prophetess

Katherine Chidley, arguing in the Independent manner for toleration of divergencies in religious belief and practice, denied the husband authority over his wife's conscience as she denied the state authority over the subject's conscience (134); the Quaker Margaret Fell refuted the received interpretation of the Pauline texts forbidding women a voice in church assemblies (and, by extension, in public debate; see Thomas (1958) on the involvement of Puritan women in church affairs). She distinguishes between the unregenerate (who should keep silent) and those regenerate women, illuminated by the Spirit, who enjoy spiritual equality with men. In an entirely salutary way, she calls attention to the significant part played by women in the Gospels, to Jesus' acceptance of them as messengers of his word, and to the Biblical fondness for personifying the church as a woman (135; on the 'equality of men and women in spiritual privilege and responsibility' among Quakers, see further Braithwaite (1979), pp. 269–89). The incidence of female petitioners of Parliament during the years 1642–53 is a clear and specific example of the Civil War enabling Puritan women to forgo their customary womanly silence for an 'Amazonian' or 'masculine spirit' (McArthur (1909); Higgins (1973); McEntee (1992)); the activities of prophetesses is another (Mack (1988); Trubowitz (1992); see Durston (1989), pp. 87–109, on the involvement of Puritan women in public affairs). Amongst Puritan enthusiasts symbolic public enactments of liberation from unregeneracy might occasionally take the uninhibited form of which Sir Ralph Burgoyne's letter (136) is an unsympathetic Royalist report.

If the respect granted the female and the rights accorded women in some Puritan congregations and their tolerated political activity make 'the civil war . . . important in the history of women in England' either as marking 'the appearance of a new type of woman' or as providing the 'occasion which permitted latent female potential to be expressed' (Higgins (1973), p. 180), it was a shortlived moment. We might expect Richard Allestree, that spokesman for the genteel taste of the Restoration period, to rebuke as reprehensible boldness any female pretensions to speak or teach in public (71), but even in the Puritan tradition the old liberties were restrained. The Baptist Anne Wentworth, attempting to fulfil the prophetic role after the Restoration and to exercise 'liberty of conscience' despite her husband's opposition to her publishing her opinions, encountered nothing but hostility (137). Although apparently liberating Christiana and Mercy to roam outdoors and become the protagonists of their own narratives in Part II of *The Pilgrim's Progress* (1684), Bunyan in fact inculcates wifely domesticity as their proper role and through them warns that women who stray out of doors bring their misfortunes upon themselves (Keeble (1990b), esp. p. 142; Thickstun (1988), pp. 87–104). When women in his congregation began to hold their own separate meetings in the Quaker manner, he would not tolerate this usurpation of the masculine role; in answer to the arguments put forward in their support by an unidentified 'Mr. K.', he 'laboured to keep them in their place' (138).

~

124 John Milton, *Paradise Lost* (1667), IX.229–34

Well hast thou motioned, well thy thoughts employed
How we might best fulfil the work which here
God hath assigned us, nor of me shalt pass
Unpraised: for nothing lovelier can be found
In woman, than to study household good,
And good works in her husband to promote.

125 Thomas Heywood, *Gynækeion* (1624), p. 180

The sacred institution of marriage was not only for procreation but that man should make choice of a woman, and a woman to make election of a husband, as companions and comforters one of another as well in adversity as prosperity. Aristotle confers the cares and businesses that lie abroad upon the husband, but the domestic actions within doors he assigns to the wife; for he holds it as inconvenient and uncomely for the wife to busy herself about any public affairs, as for the man to play the cotquean at home.

126 [N.H.], *The Ladies Dictionary* (1694), pp. 92, 183, 248–9, 302–3 [misnumbered from p. 240]

Chamber-maids, to persons of honour or quality, or gentlewomen, either in city or country: . . . you must in the first place learn to dress well, that you may be able to supply the place of a waiting-woman should she chance to fall sick or be absent from your Lady; you must also learn to wash fine linen well, and to starch tiffanies, lawns, points, gauzes and laces. You must likewise learn to mend them neatly, and wash white sarsenets, with such like things. Then you must learn to make your Lady's bed well, soft and easy, to lay up her night clothes, and see that her chamber be kept neat and clean, and that nothing be wanting which she desires or requires to be done. Then you must learn to be modest in your deportment or behaviour, to be ready at her call, and to be always diligent, never answering again when she taketh occasion to reprove you, but endeavour to mitigate her anger with pacifying words. Be loving and courteous to your fellow servants, not giggling or idling out your time, or wantoning in the society of men. You will soon find the benefit thereof, for an honest and sober man will rather make that woman his wife whom he seeth employed continually about her business

189

that [i.e. than] one who makes it her business to trifle away her own and others' time.

Housemaids: Your principal office is to make clean the greatest part of the house, and so that you suffer no room to lie foul, that you look well to all the stuff, and see that they be often brushed, and the beds frequently turned. That you be careful for, and diligent to, all strangers, and see that they lack nothing in their chamber, which your mistress or lady will allow; and that your close-stools and chamber-pots be duly emptied and kept clean. That in the afternoon you be ready to help the housekeeper or the waiting-woman in the preserving and distilling.

Keeping House, and the ordering and governing a family, etc.: Keeping a house well ordered, and the family affairs well managed and regulated, is no such easy matter as some ladies imagine it and therefore there is a great reputation to be gained in the prudent performance and discharge of such a care and trust, more especially incumbent on those that are entered into a married state; for it not only turns to advantage but procures a true respect and esteem . . . you shall many times find a worn housekeeper making a better figure in the family than my lady in all her bravery, because the one keeps up, and the other neglect, the government. Good breeding we must allow to be very commendable, yet being carried too high, very much impairs in value, lessening still as it soars, especially where the lady is conceited and proud of it. Many there are that take it for a fine air, to be above encumbering their thoughts with such ordinary things as housekeeping and a family; others fearing wrinkles, keep off cares to preserve their beauty and a mistaken pride makes some again imagine they must keep themselves up in a station above descending to such duties as do not seem enough refined for great ladies. If so they can preserve respect, it is more than great princes can do, when they neglect their business, and give themselves up wholly to their pleasures. And we will not only consider the disesteem of the servants, when she that should govern them is careless and supine, but we will come a little nearer, *viz.* to that of a husband; for what account can he make of a wife, whom he took to assist him in his affairs, or at least as a supervisor with care and diligence to see that part more properly belonging to her inspection, trust, performed as it ought, when he sees instead of a careful woman only an empty airy thing, that sails about the house, and only carelessly sweeps it with her train, moving about to no purpose, and looking in all respects as if she came thither only to pay a visit.

Nursery-maids: . . . you must naturally incline yourself to love young children, otherwise you will soon discover your unfitness to manage that charge. You must be very neat and cleanly about them, and be careful to

keep good hours for them, both to arise and to go to bed, likewise to get
their breakfast and suppers at good and convenient time. Let them not sit
too long, but walk them often up and down, especially those who cannot go
well by themselves. You must also be extraordinary careful and vigilant that
they get not any falls through your neglect, for by such falls many . . . have
grown irrecoverably lame . . . You must be extraordinary careful that you be
not churlish or dogged to the children, but be always merry and pleasant,
and contrive and invent pretty sports and pastimes as will be most suitable
and agreeable to the children's age. Keep their linen and other things always
mended and suffer them not to run too fast to decay. Do not let the children
see that you love any one child above the other, for that will be a means of
dejecting and casting down the other. Be careful to hear them read if it be
imposed upon you, and be not too hasty with them. Have a special care how
you behave yourself before them, neither speaking nor acting misbecom-
ingly, lest your bad example prove the subject of their imitation.

127 Lucy Hutchinson, *Memoirs of the Life of Colonel Hutchinson* (completed 1671), pp. 48–9

But above all these [evil counsellors], the King [Charles I] had another
instigator of his own violent purpose, more powerful than all the rest, and
that was the Queen [Henrietta Maria], who, grown out of her childhood,
began to turn her mind from those vain extravagances she liv'd in at first to
that which did less become her, and was more fatal to the kingdom, which
never is in any place happy where the hands that are made only for distaffs
affect the management of sceptres. If any one object the fresh example of
Queen Elizabeth, let them remember that the felicity of her reign was the
effect of her submission to her masculine and wise counsellors; but wherever
male princes are so effeminate to suffer women of foreign birth and different
religion to intermeddle with the affairs of state, it is always found to produce
sad desolations; and it hath been observed that a French queen never
brought any happiness to England. Some kind of fatality, too, the English
imagin'd to be in her name of Marie, which, 'tis said, the King rather chose
to have her call'd by than her other, Henrietta, because the land should find
a blessing in that name which had been more unfortunate; but it was not in
his power, though a great prince, to control destiny. This lady being by her
priests affected with the meritoriousness of advancing her own religion
[Roman Catholicism], whose principle it is to subvert all other, applied that
way her great wit and parts, and the power her haughty spirit kept over her
husband, who was enslav'd in his affection only to her, though she had no
more passion for him than what serv'd to promote her designs, which
brought her into a very good correspondency with the Archbishop [of
Canterbury, William Laud] and his prelatical crew, both joining in the cruel
design of rooting out the godly [Puritans] out of the land.

191

128 Margaret Cavendish, 'A True Relation of My Birth' (1656), pp. 166–8

From thence he [William Cavendish, Marquis, afterwards Duke, of Newcastle] returned to Brabant, unto the city of Antwerp . . . and in that city my Lord settled himself and family . . . But after we had remained some time therein, we grew extremely necessitated, tradesmen being there not so rich as to trust my Lord for so much, or so long, as those of France . . . But at last necessity enforced me to return into England [in 1652] to seek for relief. For I, hearing my Lord's estate, amongst the rest of many more estates, was to be sold, and that the wives of the owners should have no allowance therefrom, it gave me hopes I should receive benefit thereby. So, being accompanied with my Lord's only brother, Sir Charles Cavendish . . . over I went. But when I came there I found their hearts as hard as my fortunes, and their natures as cruel as my miseries, for they sold all my Lord's estate, which was a very great one, and gave me not any part thereof, or any allowance thereout, which few or no other was so hardly dealt withal. Indeed, I did not stand as a beggar the Parliament door, for I never was at the Parliament House, nor stood I ever at the door, as I do know, or can remember, I am sure, not as petitioner. Neither did I haunt the committees, for I never was at any, as a petitioner, but once in my life, which was called Goldsmiths' Hall [where the Committee for Compounding with Delinquents met], but I received neither gold nor silver from them, only an absolute refusal, I should have no share of my Lord's estate. For my brother, the Lord [John] Lucas, did claim in my behalf such a part of my Lord's estate as wives had allowed them, but they told him that by reason I was married since my Lord was made a delinquent, I could have nothing, nor should have anything, he being the greatest traitor to the State, which was to be the most loyal subject to his King and country. But I whisperingly spoke to my brother to conduct me out of that ungentlemanly place, so without speaking to them one word good or bad, I returned to my lodgings, and as that committee was the first, so was it the last, I ever was at as a petitioner. 'Tis true I went sometimes to Drury House to enquire how the land was sold, but no otherways, although some reported I was at the Parliament House, and at this committee and at that committee, and what I should say, and how I was answered. But the customs of England being changed as well as the laws, where women become pleaders, attorneys, petitioners, and the like, running about with their several causes, complaining of their several grievances, exclaiming against their several enemies, bragging of their several favours they receive from the powerful, thus trafficking with idle words bring in false reports and vain discourse. For the truth is, our sex doth nothing but jostle for the pre-eminence of words (I mean not for speaking well, but speaking much) as they do for the pre-eminence of place, words rushing against words, thwarting and crossing each other, and pulling with reproaches, striving to throw each other down with disgrace, thinking to advance themselves thereby. But if our sex would but well consider, and rationally ponder, they will perceive and find, that it is neither words nor place that can advance them, but worth and merit. Nor can words or place disgrace them, but inconstancy and boldness: for an honest heart, a noble soul, a chaste life, and a true speaking tongue, is the throne, sceptre, crown, and footstool that advances them to an honourable renown. I mean not noble, virtuous, discreet, and worthy persons whom necessity did enforce to submit, comply, and follow their own suits, but such as had nothing to lose, but made it their trade to solicit. But I despairing, being positively denied at Goldsmiths' Hall . . . did not trouble myself or petition my enemies. Besides I am naturally bashful, not that I am ashamed of my mind or body, my birth or breeding, my actions or fortunes, for my bashfulness is my nature, not for any crime, and though I have strived and reasoned with myself, yet that which is inbred I find is difficult to root out.

129 Margaret Cavendish, *CCXI Sociable Letters* (1664), pp. 12–13, 27

IX

. . . our sex in this age is ambitious to be state ladies, that they may be thought to be nice women; but let us do what we can, we shall prove ourselves fools, for wisdom is an enemy to our sex, or rather our sex is an enemy to wisdom. 'Tis true we are full of designs and plots, and ready to side into factions; but plotting, designing factions belong nothing to wisdom, for wisdom never intermeddles therein or therewith, but renounces them. It is only cheating craft and subtlety that are managers thereof; and for deceiving craft, women are well practised therein, and most of them may be accounted politicians. For no question, but women may, can and oftentimes do make wars, especially civil wars; witness our late Civil War, wherein women were great, although not good actors. For though women cannot fight with warring men themselves, yet they can easily inflame men's minds against their governors and governments, unto which men are too apt even without the persuasions of women, as to make innovation through envy and emulation in hopes of advancement in title, fortune or power, of which women are as ambitious as men. But I wish for the honour of our sex that women could as easily make peace as war . . . women in state-affairs can do as they do with themselves, they can, and do often make themselves sick, not well again; so that they can disorder a state, as they do their bodies, but neither can give peace to the one nor health to the other; but their restless minds and insatiable appetites do many times bring ruin to the one and death to the other; for temperance and quietness are strangers to our sex . . .

XVI

. . . as for the matter of government, we women understand them not; yet, if we did, we are excluded from intermeddling therewith, and almost from being subject thereto. We are not tied, nor bound to State or Crown; we are free, not sworn to allegiance, nor do we take the Oath of Supremacy. We are not made citizens of the commonwealth; we hold no offices, nor bear we any authority therein. We are counted neither useful in peace, nor service-able in war. And if we be not citizens in the commonwealth, I know no reason we should be subjects to the commonwealth. And the truth is, we are no subjects, unless it be to our husbands, and not always to them, for sometimes we usurp their authority, or else by flattery we get their good wills to govern. But if Nature had not befriended us with beauty and other good graces, to help us insinuate ourselves into men's affections, we should have been more enslaved than any other of Nature's creatures she hath made; but Nature be thanked, she hath been so bountiful to us, as we oftener enslave men than men enslave us. They seem to govern the world, but we really govern the world, in that we govern men: for what man is he that is not governed by a woman more or less?

130 Ann Fanshawe, *Memoirs* (written 1676), pp. 123–4, 134–5

We remained sometime behind in Ireland . . . During this time I had by a fall of a stumbling horse (being with child), broke my left wrist, which because it was ill set put me to great and long pain; and I was in my bed when Cork revolted [from its allegiance to Charles I]. By chance my husband [Sir Richard Fanshawe] that day was gone upon business to Kinsale. It was in the beginning of [Octo]ber, 16[49], at midnight, I heard the great guns go off, and thereupon I called my family to rise, which they and I did, as well as I could in that condition. Hearing lamentable scricks of men and women and children, I asked at a window the cause. They told me they were all Irish, stripped and wounded, turned out of the town, and the Colonel Jeffreys [for John Gifford], with some others, had possessed themselves of the town for Cromwell. Upon this I immediately writ a letter to my husband, blessing God's providence that he was not there with me, persuading him to patience and hope that I should get safely out of the town by God's assistance, and desired him to shift for himself for fear of a surprise, with promise I would secure his papers. So soon as I had finished my letter, I sent it by a faithful servant, who was let down the garden wall of Red Abbey [her lodging], and sheltered by the darkness of the night he made his escape. Immediately I packed up my husband's cabinet, with all his writings, and near £1,000 in gold and silver, and all other things both of clothes, linen, and household stuff that were portable and of value; and then, about 3 o'clock in the morning, by the light of a taper and in that pain I was in, I went into the market place, with only a man and maid, and, passing through an unruly tumult with their swords in their hands, searched for their chief commander, Jeffreys, who whilst he was loyal [to Charles I] had received many civilities from your father [Sir Richard]. I told him that it was necessary that upon that change I should remove, and desired his pass that would be obey'd, or else I must remain there. I hoped he would not deny me that kindness. He instantly writ me a pass, both for myself, family, and goods, and said he would never forget the respects he owed your father.

With this I came through thousands of naked swords to Red Abbey and hired the next neighbour's cart, which carried all that I could remove. And myself, sister, and little girl Nan, with 3 maids and 2 men, set forth at 5 o'clock in [Octo]ber, having but 2 horses among us all, which we rid on by turns. In this sad condition I left Red Abbey, with as many goods as was worth £100, which could not be removed, and so were plundered. We went 10 miles to Kinsale in perpetual fear of being fetched back again, but by little and little, I thank God, we got safe to the garrison where I found your father the most disconsolate man in the world for fear of his family, which he had no possibility to assist; but his joys exceeded to see me and his darling daughter, and to hear the wonderful escape we through the assistance of God had made.

But when the rebels went to give an account to Cromwell of their meritorious act, he immediately asked where Mr. Fanshawe was. They replied, he was that day gone to Kinsale. Then he demanded where his papers and his family were, at which they all stared at one another, but made no reply. Their General said, 'It was as much worth to have seized his papers as the town; for I did make account by them to have known what these parts of the country were worth'.

* * *

Upon the 2 day of September following [1651] was fought the Battle of Worcester, when the King [Charles II] being missed and nothing of your father being dead or alive for 3 days heard of, it is unexpressible what affliction I was in. I neither eat nor slept, but trembled at every motion I heard, expecting the fatal news which at last came in their newsbook, which mentioned your father a prisoner; then with some hopes immediately I went to London, intending to leave my little girl Nan, the companion of my troubles, there, and so find out my husband wheresoever he was carried.

. . . [At] Whitehall, . . . in a little room yet standing in the bowling green he was kept prisoner, without the speech of any so far as they knew, 10 weeks, and in expectation of death. They often examined him, and at a last he grew so ill in health by the cold and hard marches he had undergone, and being pent up in a room so close and small, that the scurvy brought him almost to death's door. During this time of his imprisonment I failed not constantly to go when the clock struck 4 in the morning, with a dark lantern in my hand, all alone and on foot from my lodging in Chancery Lane at my cousin Young's to Whitehall in at the entry that went out of King's Street into the bowling ground. There I would go under his window and softly call him. He, that after the first time expected me, never failed to put out his head at first call. Thus we talked together, and sometimes I was so wet with rain that it went in at my neck and out at my heels. He directed how I should make my addresses, which I did ever to their General Cromwell, who had a great respect for your father and would have brought him off to his service upon any terms.

Being one day to solicit for my husband's liberty for a time, he bid me bring the next day a certificate from a physician that he was really ill. Immediately I went to Doctor Batters that was by chance both physician to Cromwell and to our family, who gave me one very favourable in my husband's behalf. I delivered it at the Council Chamber door at 3 of the clock that afternoon to his own hand, as he commanded me, and himself moved that seeing they could make no use of his imprisonment whereby to lighten them in their business, that he might have his liberty, upon £4,000 bail, to take a course of physic, he being dangerously ill . . . They hearing their General say so, thought it obliged him, and so ordered him his liberty upon bail.

131 Anne Halkett, *Memoirs* (written 1677–8), pp. 59–61

A little after [1651] there came to Fyvie [Aberdeenshire] three regiments [of Parliamentarian soldiers] with their officers, being commanded by Colonel [Robert] Lilburne, Colonel [Thomas] Fitts [i.e. Fitch] and Colonel [Robert] Overton . . . Colonel Overton sitting by me at dinner said to me that God had wonderfully evidenced his power in the great things he had done. I replied, no doubt God would evidence his power still in the great things he designed to do. I spoke this with more than ordinary earnestness, which made him say, 'You speak my words, but not I think my sense.'

'When I know that sense (said I then), I will tell you whether it be mine or no.'

'I speak', said he, 'of the wonderful works that God hath done by his servants in the late times that are beyond what any could have brought about without the immediate assistance of God and his direction.'

'Sir,' said I, 'if you had not begun this discourse, I had said nothing to you; but since you have desired my opinion (which he did) of the times, I shall very freely give it upon the condition that whatever I say, you may not make use of it to the prejudice of the noble family I live in, for I can hold my tongue but I cannot speak anything contrary to what I think. I cannot but confess you have had great success in all your undertakings, but that's no good rule to justify ill actions. You pretend to great zeal in religion and obedience to God's words. If you can show me in all the Holy Scripture a warrant for murdering your lawful king and banishing his posterity, I will then say all you have done is well and will be of your opinion. But as I am sure that cannot be done, so I must condemn that horrid act and whatever is done in prosecution of its vindication.'

He replied that those who had writ upon the prophecy of Daniel showed that he foretold the destruction of monarchy many years since, and that it was a tyrannical government and therefore fit to be destroyed.

'How comes (said I) you have taken the power from the Parliament and those successive interests that have governed since you wanted the King?'

'Because,' said he, 'we found after a little time they began to be as bad as he, and therefore we changed.'

'And,' said I, 'so you will ever find reason to change whatever government you try till you come to beg of the King to come home and govern you again, and this I am as confident of as I am speaking to you.'

'If I thought that would be true (replied he), I would repent all that I have done.'

'It will come to that, I dare assure you,' said I, 'and the greatest hindrance will be that you think your crimes have been such as is impossible he [Charles II] should forgive you. But to encourage you I can assure you there was never any prince more inclined to pardon nor more easy to be entreated to forgive.'

'Well,' says he, 'if this should come to pass, I will say you are a prophetess.' Here we broke off because we saw the rest of the table take notice of our seriousness.

132 Brilliana Harley, letters from Brampton Bryan, Herefordshire, to her son, Edward Harley, in London (written 1640s), *passim*

from Letter CXXXIV (n.d.): . . . Dear Ned, to see you will much revive me in the midst of many sad thoughts. It has very much troubled me to see the affections of this county so against your father [Sir Robert Harley] that is worth thousands of them; and he has deserved so well of them. But you are in the right. It is for God's cause, and then it is an honour to suffer . . .

from Letter CXXXVI (11 February 1642): . . . You know how your father's business is neglected; and, alas! it is not speaking will serve turn, where there is not abilities to do other ways. Therefore I could wish that your father had one of more understanding to entrust, to look to, if his rents are not paid, and I think it will be so. I could desire, if your father thought well of it, that Mr. Thomas Moore were instructed with it; he knows your father's estate and is an honest man . . . I know it would be some charges to have him and his wife in the house; but I think it would quit the charges. I should be loath to have a stranger, now your father is away. Dear Ned, tell your father what I have written to you, and I pray God direct him in his resolutions; and what he resolves of, I shall be contented with; so do not forget to tell your father . . .

from Letter CXXXVIII (17 February 1642): . . . In Hereford they have turned the table in the cathedral, and taken away the cups and basins and all such things. I hope they begin to see that the Lord is about to purge his church of all such inventions of men. Dear Ned, be careful of yourself . . .

from Letter CXLI (12 March 1642): . . . I have no desire at all that a stranger should come to look to your father's business. Now your father is away, you know that I have nobody I can speak to; and if Pinner go away, who I dare trust with anything, and who I know loves your father and me, I should much want him . . .

from Letter CLXI (4 June 1642): . . . At Ludlow they set up a Maypole, and a thing like a head upon it, and so they did at Croft, and gathered a great many about it, and shot at in derision of Roundheads . . . I acknowledge I do not think myself safe where I am. I lose the comfort of your father's company, and am in but little safety, but that my trust is in God; and what is done in your father's estate pleases him not, so that I wish myself, with all my heart, at London, and then your father might be a witness of what is spent; but if your father think it best for me to be in the country, I am very well pleased with what he shall think best . . .

from Letter CLXV (20 June 1642): . . . Since your father thinks Herefordshire as safe as any other county, I will think so too; but when I considered how long I had been from him, and how this county was affected, my desire to see your father, and my care to be in a place of safety, made me earnestly desire to come up to London; but since it is not your father's will, I will lay aside that desire . . .

from Letter CLXXVI (17 July 1642): . . . dear Ned, I hope you and myself will remember for whose cause your father and we are hated. It is the cause of God, and I hope we shall be so far from being ashamed of it or troubled, that we bear the reproach of it, that we shall bind it as a crown upon us [cf. Heb. xi.26]; and I am confident the Lord will rescue his children from reproach.

I sent Samuel to Hereford to observe their ways . . .

He tells me that they all at Hereford cried out against your father, and not one said anything for him, but one man . . . My dear Ned, I cannot think I am safe at Brampton and by no means would I have you come down. I should be very glad if your father could get some religious and discreet gentleman to come for a time to Brampton, that he might see sometimes what they do in the county . . .

from Letter CLXXVII (19 July 1642): . . . My dear Ned, I am not afraid. It is the Lord's cause that we have stood for, and I trust, though our iniquity testify against us, yet the Lord will work for his own name's sake and that he will show the men of the world that it is hard fighting against heaven. And for our comforts, I think never any laid plots to root out all God's children at once but that the Lord did show himself mighty in saving his servants and confounding his enemies, as he did Pharaoh, when he thought to have destroyed all Israel [Exod. v–xv], and so Haman [Esther iii–ix]. Now, the intention is to root out all that fear God, and surely the Lord will arise to help us . . . I have directed these letters to you . . . because I would not have the county take notice that I send to your father so often; but when such occasions come, I must needs send to him, for I can rely upon nobody's counsel but his . . .

from Letter CLXXIX (22 July 1642): . . . My dear Ned, at first when I saw how outrageously this county carried themselves against your father, my anger was up, and my sorrow, that I had hardly patience to stay; but now I have well considered, if I go away I shall leave all that your father has to the prey of our enemies, which they would be glad of; so that, and please God, I purpose to stay as long as it is possible, if I live; and this is my resolution, without your father contradict it . . .

from Letter CLXXXIII (25 December 1642): . . . Mr. Coningsby is the governor of Hereford, and he sent to me a letter by Mr. Wigmore. I did not let him come into my house, but I went into the garden to him. Your father will show you the letter: they are in a mighty violence against me. They revenge all that was done, upon me, so that I shall fear any more Parliament forces coming into this county . . . My dear Ned, I pray you advise with your father whether he thinks it best that I should put away most of the men that are in my house, and whether it be best for me to go from Brampton, or by God's help to stand it out. I will be willing to do what he would have me do . . .

from Letter CLXXXIV (28 January 1643): . . . My dear Ned, I know it will grieve you to know how I am used. It is with all the malice that can be. Mr. Wigmore will not let the fowler bring me any fowl, nor will not suffer any of my servants to pass. They have forbid my rents to be paid. They drove away the young horses at Wigmore, and none of my servants dare go scarce as far as the town. And dear Ned, if God were not merciful to me, I should be in a very miserable condition. I am threatened every day to be beset with soldiers. My hope is, the Lord will not deliver me nor mine into their hands, for surely they would use all cruelty towards me, for I am told that they desire not to leave your father neither root nor branch. You and I must forgive them . . .

from Letter CLXXXV (14 February 1643): . . . Now they say they will starve me out of my house; they have taken away all your father's rents, and they say they will drive away the cattle, and then I shall have nothing to live upon; for all their aim is to enforce me to let those men I have go, that then they might seize upon my house and cut our throats by a few rogues, and then say, they knew not who did it . . .

from Letter CXCI (8 March 1643): . . . here I have sent you a copy of the summons was sent me. I wish with all my heart that everyone would take notice what way they take: that if I do not give them my house, and what they would have, I shall be proceeded against as a traitor . . . I hear there are 600 soldiers appointed to come against me . . .

133 Jeremiah Burroughes, *The Glorious Name of God* (1643), pp. 78–81

The name of God is a strong antidote to drive fear out of the hearts of the weakest. Upon what we see in this title of God, we may well say to the fearful in heart, 'be strong, fear not', as we have it, Isa. xxxv.4. Let women and all such as are naturally fearful, take heed of sinful fear. The fearfulness of women hanging about their husbands, and children, and friends, crying out when they should go forth in this service, and going up and down wringing their hands and making doleful outcries, may do abundance of hurt, and exceedingly hinder the work that the Lord hath now in hand. Let women take heed they be not hindrances, but let them learn to exercise faith and take spirit to themselves, that they may further their husbands, children and friends in this work of the Lord of Hosts. Mark that scripture, I Pet. iii.6: 'Ye are the daughters of Sarah so long as you do well, and be not afraid with any amazement'. Yea, would all willingly be accounted the daughters of Sarah! Observe how the Holy Ghost puts it upon this, that you 'be not afraid with any amazement': it may be Nature may cause some fear, but grace must keep it that it be not with any amazement . . . it seems Sarah . . . in those difficulties that Abraham went through, she was no hindrance but a furtherance to him. She did not cry out to him . . . but . . . rather was a help to him, and an encourager of him. So, says Peter, who, speaking to Christians who lived in troublesome and dangerous times, 'You shall show yourselves the daughters of Sarah', if you have such a spirit as Sarah had . . . not through your inordinate fear either hinder yourselves, your husbands, or any other in the service of the Lord . . . And that a spirit may be put even into women in these times that call for all to be above sinful fears, let them consider three things . . .

. . . first, the first time that ever any speaking to God called him by his name the Lord of Hosts, it was a woman, and that was Hannah, I Sam. i.11.

Secondly, one of the principal psalms, wherein this title of the Lord of Hosts is most magnified, is a psalm tuned to that musical instrument that virgins and women use to play on, from whence the Psalm hath its title, *A Song upon Alamoth*, Ps. xlvi, which is as much as *A Song upon the Virginals*, . . .

3. The most brave expression of a strong, valiant spirit, triumphing over enemies in time of battle, is from a woman (Jud. v). It is the speech of Deborah . . .

134 Katherine Chidley, *Justification of the Independent Churches of Christ* (1641), p. 26

'O! how will this [toleration] take away that power which God hath given to husbands, fathers and masters over wives, children and servants'. To this I answer, O! that you would consider the text in I Cor. vii.[13] which plainly declares that the wife may be a believer, and the husband an unbeliever; but if you have considered this text, I pray you tell me, what authority this unbelieving husband hath over the conscience of his believing wife? It is true he hath authority over her in bodily and civil respects, but not to be a lord over her conscience; and the like may be said of fathers and masters, and it is the very same authority which the sovereign hath over all his subjects, and therefore it must needs reach to families: for it is granted that the King hath power (according to the law) over the bodies, goods, and lives of all his subjects; yet it is still Christ the King of Kings that reigneth over their consciences, and thus you may see it taketh away no authority which God hath given to them.

135 [Margaret Fell], *Womens Speaking Justified* (1666), pp. 3–8

. . . it hath been an objection in the minds of many, and several times hath been objected by the clergy, or ministers, and others, against women speaking in the churches . . . the ground of which objection is taken from the Apostle's words, which he wrote in his first epistle to the Corinthians, xiv.34–5. And also what he writ to Timothy in the first epistle, ii.11–12. But how far they wrong the Apostle's intentions in these scriptures we shall show . . .

It is true 'The serpent that was more subtle than any other beast of the field' [Gen. iii.1] came unto the woman . . . there the temptation got into her . . . [but] see what the Lord saith, verse 15: 'I will put enmity between thee and the woman, and between thy seed and her seed' . . .

Let this word of God . . . stop the mouths of all that oppose women's speaking in the power of the Lord: for he hath put enmity between the woman and the serpent, and if the seed of the woman speak not, the seed of the serpent speaks . . .

Moreover, the Lord is pleased when he mentions his Church to call her a woman, by his prophets (Isa. liv.[5–7]) . . . and David (Ps. xlv.13) . . . And also King Solomon (Song of Sol. i.8, v.9) . . .

Thus much may prove that the Church of Christ is a woman, and those that speak against women's speaking, speak against the Church of Christ, and the seed of the woman, which seed is Christ. That is to say, those that speak against the power of the Lord, and the Spirit of the Lord speaking in a woman, simply by reason of her sex, or because she is a woman, not regarding the seed, and Spirit and power that speaks in her, such speak against Christ . . .

Jesus, when he came to the city of Samaria, where Jacob's well was, where the woman of Samaria was, you may read in John iv how he was pleased to preach the everlasting Gospel to her, and when the woman said unto him 'I know . . . the Messiah . . . cometh . . . ', Jesus saith unto her, 'I that speak unto thee am he'. This is more than ever he said in plain words to man or woman (that we read of) before he suffered . . .

Also, there were many women which followed Jesus in Galilee . . .

Thus we see that Jesus owned the love and grace that appeared in women, and did not despise it; and by what is recorded in the Scripture, he received as much love, kindness, compassion and tender dealing towards him from women, as he did from any other, both in his lifetime, and also after they had exercised their cruelty upon him. For Mary Magdalen, and Mary the mother of James beheld where he was laid . . . Mark xvi.1–4, Luke xxiv.1–2 . . . Matt. xviii.1–7 . . .

It was Mary Magdalen, and Joanna, and Mary the mother of James, and the other women that were with them, which told these things to the Apostles, and their words seemed unto them as idle tales, and they believed them not [Luke xxiv.10–11]. Mark this, ye despisers of the weakness of women, and [who?] look upon your selves to be so wise; but Christ doth not so, for he makes use of the weak, for when he met the women after he was risen, he said unto them 'All hail' [Matt. xxviii.9], and they came and held him by the feet and worshipped him. Then said Jesus unto them, 'Be not afraid; go tell my brethren that they go into Galilee and there they shall see me', Matt xxviii.10 . . . Mark this, you that despise and oppose the message of the Lord God, that he sends by women: what had become of the redemption of the whole body of mankind, if they had not believed the message that the Lord Jesus sent by these women, of and concerning his redemption? And if these women had not thus, out of their tenderness and bowels of love . . . if their hearts had not been so united and knit unto him in love, that they could not depart as the men did but sat watching and waiting and weeping about the sepulchre until the time of his resurrection, and so were ready to carry his message, as is manifested, else how should the disciples have known, who were not there? . . .

And now . . . the ground of the great objection against women's speaking . . . I Cor. xiv.[34–5] . . . the Apostle is there exhorting the Corinthians unto charity, and . . . not to speak in an unknown tongue . . . for God is not the author of confusion, but of peace. And then he saith, 'Let your women keep silence in the Church', etc. Where it doth plainly appear that the women, as well as others, that were among them, were in confusion; for he saith, 'How is it, brethren? when ye come together, every one of you hath a psalm, hath a doctrine, hath a tongue, hath a revelation, hath an interpretation? Let all things be done to edifying' [verse 26]. Here was no edifying, but all was in confusion, speaking together. Therefore he saith, 'If any man speak in an unknown tongue, let it be by two, or at most by three, and that by course; and let one interpret. But if there be no interpreter, let him keep silence in the church' [verses 27–8]. Here the man is commanded to keep silence as well as the woman, when they are in confusion and out of order . . . But the Apostle saith further, 'they are commanded to be in obedience, as also saith the Law' [cf. Gen. iii.16]; and 'if they will learn anything, let them ask their husbands at home; for it is a shame for a woman to speak in the church'. Here the Apostle clearly manifests his intent, for he speaks of women that were under the Law, and in that transgression as Eve was [cf. I Tim. ii.14], and such as were to learn, and not to speak publicly, but they must first ask their husbands at home; and it was a shame for such to speak in the Church . . . and what is all this to women's speaking, that have the everlasting Gospel to preach, and upon whom the promise of the Lord is fulfilled, and his Spirit poured upon them according to his Word, Acts ii.16–18? And if the Apostle would have stopped such as had the Spirit of the Lord poured upon them, why did he say just before, 'if anything be revealed to another that sitteth by, let the first hold his peace'? and, 'you may all prophesy one by one' [I Cor. xiv.30–1]? Here he did not say that such women should not prophesy as had the revelation and Spirit of God poured upon them; but as their women that were under the Law, and in the transgression, and were in strife, confusion and malice in their speaking . . .

136 Sir Ralph Burgoyne, letter to Sir Ralph Verney, 28 July 1652, in Frances Parthenope Verney (ed.), *Memoirs of the Verney Family* (1892–9), III.47–8

On Sunday last sennight a woman in silk being in Whitehall at the sermon, the subject of that discourse being the Resurrection, she perfectly stripped herself of all her apparel, and, as she came into the world from top to toe, she ran into the middle of the congregation, over against the pulpit, and cried, 'Welcome the Resurrection'. She was taken out by the soldiers and what's become of her since I know not; some say it was a great piece of self-denial, but for that I shall leave you to judge of. This is the naked truth of the business.

137 Anne Wentworth, *Vindication* (1677), pp. 183–8

The great searcher of hearts [I Chron. xxviii.9] has seen, neither is it unknown to several Christians in and about this city of London, or to the consciences of my very enemies, what severe and cruel persecutions I have sustained for the space of eighteen years from the unspeakable tyrannies of an hard-hearted yoke-fellow, and since, from the bitter zeal of several eminent professors of religion, commonly called Baptists, who have most unjustly and unchristianlike caused all their pretended church power to wait upon and serve the wrath of my oppressors . . .

And because the mouth of iniquity is opened against me . . . representing me as a proud, passionate, revengeful, discontented and mad woman, and as one that has unduly published things to the prejudice and scandal of my husband, and that have wickedly left him . . . I do . . . hereby solemnly declare:

That I am not conscious to myself of any spiritual pride in this matter, nor in the least desirous to have any appearance or to make any noise in this world. Nor durst I for ten thousand worlds pretend to come in the name of God, or in the pride and forwardness of my own spirit put myself into this work, without his express command concerning it, and his spirit and presence with me in it . . . And however the spirit of prophecy in a poor weak woman shall be despised by the wise and prudent [Matt. xi.25; Luke x.21] of this world, yet Wisdom is justified of her children [Matt. xi.19; Luke vii.35]. And that God who has commanded me to go forth in his name will by a divine power go before me, making way for me, and subduing the spirits before me which I am to deal with, and will also by a divine presence support me in the midst of all those sufferings his work can bring me into. 'Out of the mouth of babes and sucklings God has ordained strength, because of his enemies, that he might quell the enemy and the avenger,' Ps. viii.2.

And I declare, I have no wrath, discontent or revenge in my spirit against the person of my husband, or any of his abettors, but am taught by the forgiveness of God freely to forgive all the injuries he has done me; and my heart's desire and prayer to God, who can alone change the heart, is that he may be converted and saved . . .

And however I am censured and reproached by persons who judge only according to outward appearance, but not righteous judgment, that I have unduly left my husband, I do for the satisfaction of all plain-hearted ones that may be offended at their reports herein declare, first: that it would be very easy for me, from the great law of self-preservation to justify my present absence from my earthly husband to all persons who have learnt to judge of good and evil, not only according to the outward act, but the inward spirit and principle, and who have tenderness enough duly to weigh the various tempers of minds, and the different circumstances of bodies. Forasmuch as the natural constitution of my mind and body, being both considered, he has in his barbarous actions towards me a many times over done such things as not only in the spirit of them will be one day judged a murdering of, but had long since really proved so, if God had not wonderfully supported and preserved me. But my natural life, through the springing up of a better, not being otherwise considerable, then as it is my duty to preserve it in a subserviency to the will and service of that God whose I am in spirit, soul and body, I will not urge anything of this nature as my defence upon this occasion, having learnt through the mercy of God not to be afraid of him who can only kill the body, but can do no more. I do therefore secondly, in the fear of him who can kill both soul and body, further declare that I was forced to fly to preserve a life more precious than this natural one, and that it was necessary to the peace of my soul to absent myself from my earthly husband in obedience to my heavenly bridegroom, who called and commanded me, in a way too terrible, too powerful to be denied, to undertake and finish a work which my earthly husband in a most cruel manner hindered me from performing, seizing and running away with my writings. And however man judges me in this action, yet I am satisfied that I have been obedient to the heavenly vision [Acts xxvi.19] herein, not consulting with flesh and blood [Gal. i.16] . . . I am not afraid or ashamed to say my soul's beloved [Christ] has abundantly owned me in this matter. And whilst men have done all they can to break my heart, he has bound up my soul in the bundle of life [I Sam. xxv.29] and love, and he pleads my cause and takes my part and has spoken by his word with power and authority from heaven, saying I shall abide with him, and he will abide with me [John xv.4] . . . And I do further declare that in the true reason of the case I have not left my husband, but he me. That I do own every law and command of God in the letter of his word to be right and true, and do submit to every rule given forth by the spirit of God to govern the relation of man and wife in the Lord. And that I always stand ready to return to my husband, or to welcome him to me, and have signified so much to him by several Christian friends, provided I may have my just and necessary liberty to attend a more than ordinary call and command of God to publish the things which concern the peace of my own soul and of the whole nation. In which work I stand not in my own will, but in the will of him who has sent and sealed me, as the day will very quickly declare, and decide this matter between me and my husband and all his abettors . . .

138 John Bunyan, *A Case of Conscience Resolved* (1683), IV. 295, 302–3, 306–8, 321–3, 325–6, 329

The Epistle Dedicatory to those Godly Women concerned in the following treatise

Honoured Sisters,

'Tis far from me to despise you, or to do anything to your reproach. I know you are beloved of God for the sake of Christ, and that you stand fixed for ever by faith upon the same foundation with us. I also know that the Lord doth put no difference betwixt male and female, as to the communications of his saving graces, but hath often made many of your sex eminent for piety; yea, there hath been of you, I speak now of ordinary Christians, that for holiness of life have outgone many of the brethren, nor can their virtuous lives but be renown and glory to you, and conviction to those of us that have come behind you in faith and holiness. The love of women in spirituals, as well as naturals, ofttimes outgoes that of men.

When Christ was upon earth, we read not that any man did to, and for him, as did the woman that was a sinner, Joanna, Susanna, and many others (Luke vii.36–8, viii.1–3). And as they have showed themselves eminent for piety, so for Christian valour and fortitude of mind, when called of God to bear witness to, and for his name in the world, as all histories of that nature doth sufficiently testify. They were women, as I take it, as well as men, that were tortured, and that would not accept of deliverance, that they might obtain a better resurrection (Heb. xi.35). Wherefore I honour and praise your eminency in virtue; and desire to be provoked by the exceeding piety of any of you, in all holy conversation and godliness . . .

[Mr. Bunyan's Answer]

. . . I shall now come more directly to discourse of the question itself, to wit, whether, where a church of Christ is situate, it is the duty of the women of that congregation, ordinarily and by appointment, to separate themselves from their brethren, and as so separate, to assemble together to perform divine worship [and] prayer, without their men? . . . my reasons for dissenting from [Mr. K.], they are these:

First, to appoint meetings for divine worship, either in the whole church or in the parts of it, is an act of power: which power resideth in the elders in particular, or in the church in general. But never in the women as considered by themselves . . .

Thirdly, the Holy Ghost doth particularly insist upon the inability of women as to their well managing of the worship now under consideration, and therefore it ought not to be presumed upon by them. They are forbidden to teach, yea to speak in the church of God. And why forbidden, but because of their inability? They cannot orderly manage that worship to God, that in assemblies is to be performed before him; I speak now of our ordinary believing ones, and I know none extraordinary among the churches. They are not builded to manage such worship, they are not 'the image and glory of God', as the men are (I Cor. xi.7). They are placed beneath, and are called 'the glory of the man'. Wherefore they are weak, and not permitted to perform public worship to God. When our first mother, who was not attended with those weaknesses, either sinful or natural, as our women now are, stepped out of her place but to speak a good word for worship, you see how she was baffled, and befooled therein; she utterly failed in the performance, though she briskly attempted the thing. Yea she so failed thereabout, that at one clap she overthrew not only, as to that, the reputation of women for ever, but her soul, her husband, and the whole world besides (Gen. iii.1–7).

The fallen angel knew what he did when he made his assault upon the woman. His subtlety told him that the woman was the weaker vessel [I Pet. iii.7]. He knew also that the man was made the head in worship, and the keeper of the garden of God. The Lord God took the man, said unto the man, commanded the man, and made him keeper of the garden (Gen. ii.15–17). Wherefore the management of worship belonged to him. This, the serpent, as I said, was aware of. And therefore he comes to the woman, says to the woman, and deals with the woman about it, and so overcomes the world. Wherefore it is from this consideration that Paul tells Timothy that he permitted not a woman to teach, nor to usurp authority over the man, but to be in silence . . . If children are not thought fit to help to guide the ship with the mariners, shall they be trusted so much as with a boat at sea alone? . . .

Fifthly, if this worship may be managed by the sisterhood of the churches being congregated together in the absence of their men, of what signification is it that man is made head of the woman as well in worship as in Nature (I Cor. xi.3, 7)? Yea, more, why are the elders of the churches called watchmen, overseers, guides, teachers, rulers, and the like, if this kind of worship may be performed without their conduct and government (Ezek. iii.17, xxxiii.7; Acts xx.28; Eph. iv.11; Ps. lxxviii.72; Heb. xiii.17)? . . .

And now to give the reader a cautionary conclusion . . . by all that I have said I never meant to intimate in the least but that believing women are saints as well as men, and members of the body of Christ. And I will add, that as they and we are united to Christ, and made members of his mystical body, the fullness of him that fills all in all, so there is no superiority, as I know of, but we are all one in Christ. For, the man is not without the woman, nor 'the woman without the man, in the Lord' (I Cor. xi.11) nor are we counted 'as male or female in him' (Gal. iii.28; Eph. i.23). Only we must observe that this is spoken of that church which is his true mystical body, and not of every particular congregation of professing Christians . . .

As Christ then has a body mystical, which is called his members, his flesh, and his bones (Eph. v.30), so he has a body politic, congregations modelled by the skill that his ministers have in his word . . . In this [earthly and visible] church, order and discipline, for the nourishing up of the true mystical body of Christ, has been placed from the foundation of the world . . .

Now, where there is order and government by laws and statutes, there must, of necessity, be also a distinction of sex, degrees, and age. Yea, offices and officers must also be there, for our furtherance and joy of faith. From which government and rule our ordinary women are excluded by Paul . . .

. . . Wherefore, my beloved sisters, this inferiority of yours will last but a little while. When the day of God's salvation is come, to wit, when our Lord shall descend from heaven, with a shout, with the voice of the archangel, and a trump of God, these distinctions of sexes shall be laid aside, and every pot shall be filled to the brim . . .

Methinks, holy and beloved sisters, you should be content to wear this power, or badge of your inferiority, since the cause thereof arose at first from yourselves. 'Twas the woman that at first the serpent made use of, and by whom he then overthrew the world: wherefore the woman, to the world's end, must wear the tokens of her underlingship in all matters of worship. To say nothing of that which she cannot shake off, to wit, her pains and sorrows in child-bearing, which God has rivetted to her nature, there is her silence, and shame, and a covering for her face, in token of it, which she ought to be exercised with, whenever the church comes together to worship (Gen. iii.16; I Tim. ii.9, 15; I Cor. xi.13).

Do you think that God gave the woman her hair, that she might deck herself, and set off her fleshly beauty therewith? It was given her to cover her face with, in token of shame and silence, for that by the woman sin came into the world (I Tim. ii.9) . . . Modesty and shamefacedness becomes women at all times, especially in times of public worship, and the more of this is mixed with their grace and personage, the more beautiful they are both to God and men. But why must the women have shamefacedness, since they live honestly as the men? I answer, in remembrance of the fall of Eve . . .

In what I have said about the women's meetings, I have not at all concerned myself about those women that have been extraordinary ones, such as Miriam [Exod. xv.20], Deborah [Judges iv.4], Huldah [II Kgs. xxii.14; II Chron. xxxiv.22], Anna [Luke ii.36], or the rest, as the daughters of Philip the evangelist [Acts xxi.8–9], Priscilla [Acts xviii.2, 18, 26], the women that Paul said laboured with him in the gospel [Phil. iv.3], or such like; for they might teach, prophesy, and have power to call the people together so to do . . .

Nor do I think that any woman that is holy and humble will take offence at what I have said; for I have not in anything sought to degrade them, or to take from them what either Nature or grace, or an appointment of God, hath invested them with: but have laboured to keep them in their place. And doubtless to abide where God has put us, is that which not only highly concerns us, but that which becomes us best. Sisters, I have said what I have said to set you right, and to prevent your attempting to do things in such sort unto which you are not appointed. Remember what God did to Miriam, and be afraid [Numb. xii; Deut. xxiv.9].

12

MIDWIFERY AND
WET-NURSING

Since its first formulation over seventy years ago by Clark (1992), the prevailing view of women's economic and social position in the seventeenth century has been that enclosure and the development of capitalism during the period (on which the classic study is Tawney (1938)) destroyed the self-sufficiency of the Medieval household and, by separating public work from private domesticity, severely restricted the female sphere, reducing the possibilities open to women and eroding their status. By the century's end women who, in the Medieval household, had been both productive and economically indispensable were confined to a domestic role, economically dependent upon their husbands and denied access to those agricultural, nursing, culinary and cloth-making occupations which had traditionally been theirs. The point may be neatly made by observing that it is during this period that the word *spinster*, which in Medieval usage had referred to a person gainfully employed (*one who spins*), comes in legal terminology to be the designation of an unmarried woman and in common usage to refer to an unmarried, and implicitly useless, woman. Critics of Clark's thesis have argued that it both idealizes the Medieval household and overstates the degree of change during the seventeenth century (Houlbrooke (1984), p. 8, for example, believes Clark exaggerated the decline of productive domestic partnerships and the deterioration in the working life of women, while Prest (1991), p. 170, doubts her contention that the law increasingly marginalized women), but her line is still commonly followed (not necessarily with a Marxist emphasis); see, for example, George (1973); Hamilton (1978); O'Malley (1933), esp. pp. 15–53; Perry (1980), pp. 27–62; and Wiesner (1986). (For an account of the reception of Clark's work, and a full bibliography of relevant studies, see Amy Louise Erickson in Clark (1992), pp. vii–lv.)

The argument that woman was increasingly identified with her wifely and motherly roles may perhaps find support in the fact that, of the occupations traditionally associated with women, it was obstetrics which continued to be very largely a female province. Midwives were generally women (Eccles (1982), p. 91), if not exclusively so (*pace* the famous Chamberlen family of male midwives). Though male midwives grew commoner (especially amongst those attending the upper classes) in the last part of the century, they remained unusual, as the tenacity of the term *midwife* suggests. Except for the years 1642–60, when the licensing of midwives was carried out by the College of Physicians, the only regulation of midwives during our period was ecclesiastical which, having scant regard to medical skill or experience, concerned itself with the character of the woman applying for a licence (Forbes (1964)). As a result, in the view of Schofield (1986), p. 235, midwives 'may have provided a reassuring social setting for childbirth, but few possessed the knowledge to intervene effectively in a difficult labour'. Medical skills do not figure very high on William Sermon's list of desirable attributes, though the advice he gives for behaviour in the delivery room is sensible and sympathetic (139; for a detailed survey of midwives' handbooks and a summary of obstetric theory and practice, see Eccles (1982)).

The *Oxford English Dictionary*'s first citation for the noun *wet-nurse* is from 1620. The practice of wet-nursing, though by no means peculiar to the seventeenth century, appears then to have become particularly fashionable and to have spread throughout the upper classes of society. This disinclination among women of higher rank to breastfeed was strongly deprecated by physicians and divines (Stone (1977), pp. 426–32; Houlbrooke (1984), pp. 132–4; Durston (1989), pp. 122–4) and, occasionally, by titled women (Travitsky (1980), p. 36. See on this whole subject Fildes (1986), pp. 81–210, and Fildes (1988), pp. 79–110). They not only disapproved of the indulgence of personal vanity (breastfeeding was thought to impair looks and to lead to premature ageing) but also appreciated something of the importance of bonding and had an intimation, at least, of the immunity benefits of the mother's own milk (140, 141, 142; see further Crawford (1986), pp. 31–2). This line of thought was especially pronounced in the Puritan tradition (see, for example, the advocacy of breastfeeding in [Elizabeth Clinton], *The Countesse of Lincolnes Nurserie* (Oxford, 1622)). Save among Puritan women, however, advocates of breastfeeding made little headway; 'throughout the seventeenth century women of any status rarely breastfed their own children' (Fildes (1988), pp. 83–5; see Leverenz (1980), pp. 138–61, for a discussion of mothering, breastfeeding and suckling in Puritan discourse). This may have been in part because of the Galenic notion that the milk of a nursing mother was spoiled by sexual intercourse; employing a wet-nurse kept a wife sexually available to her husband (Stone (1977), p. 427). Furthermore, the contraceptive effects of lactation were appreciated and it may be that the husband's desire to sire heirs contributed to maintain a custom which could result in annual pregnancies (Crawford (1986), p. 34; Fildes (1988), p. 83). The frequency of physical disability after a birth without analgesics or anaesthetics may also have played a part (Fildes (1988), p. 90), as will have the attraction of freedom from the troubles of childcare available to women who could afford wet-nurses.

Assessment of character played the largest part in deciding whether a lactating woman was suitable as a wet-nurse (Eccles (1982), pp. 97–100). It was believed that the child could imbibe not only physical ailments but psychological character from the milk (142, 143). The wet-nurse should be healthy, but it was quite as important that she was of good behaviour and habits (142, 144, 145). It was customary for the child to be sent to the wet-nurse's home (Fildes (1988), pp. 79–83, citing the case of Mary Verney, 146), where neglect and maltreatment were possible (142). The commonest hazard appears to have been suffocation in bed (Fildes (1988), pp. 98–9, citing the cases of Alice Thornton and John Evelyn, 147, 148).

139 William Sermon, *The Ladies Companion* (1671), pp. 5–7, 93–6, 101–2

What Manner of Women Ought to be Midwives

As concerning their persons, they must be neither too young nor too old, but of an indifferent age between both; well-composed, not being subject to diseases, nor deformed in any part of their body; comely and neat in their apparel, their hands small, their fingers long, not thick, but clean, their nails pared very close; they ought to be very cheerful, pleasant, and of a good discourse, strong, not idle, but accustomed to exercise, that they may be the more able (if need requires) to watch, etc.

Touching their deportment: they must be mild, gentle, courteous, sober, chaste, and patient, not quarrelsome, nor choleric; neither must they be covetous, nor report anything whatsoever they hear or see in secret, in the person or house of whom they deliver . . .

As concerning their minds: they must be wise and discreet, able to flatter, and speak many fair words, to no other end, but only to deceive the apprehensive women, which is a commendable deceit . . .

But above all things, midwives ought to know that Nature, the handmaid of the great God, hath given to everything a beginning, increase, state, perfection, and declination, which he doth manifestly and chiefly demonstrate (as Galen saith) in the birth of a child when the mother brings it forth; for Nature surpasseth all . . . certainly it is a thing worth consideration . . . to observe how in a little space of time, in the very twinkling of an eye, the neck of the womb, which during the time of the nine months was so exactly and perfectly closed or shut up, that the very point of a needle could not enter therein, how in an instant it is opened and enlarged, to give way for the child to come forth, which (as Galen saith) cannot be comprehended, but wondered at and admired . . .

What Women Ought to Observe when they Find Themselves near their Time

. . . As soon as they shall feel themselves moved and provoked with pains and throws let them walk about the chamber, and sometimes lie down and then walk again, and after lie down in the bed made warm, and afterwards rise up again and walk, till the water be gathered, and the womb become open. But if by lying in bed they happen to take some rest, they may continue, by which means the mother may gather strength, and the child better enabled to come forth at the time appointed . . .

If the labour happen to be long, they may take some broth, or the yolk of eggs with butter, or anything of light digestion . . .

It is commonly known that women are not all delivered after one manner: for some are delivered sitting in a chair, others in their beds; some standing, being supported and held up by their friends, or else leaning upon the side of a bed, table, etc.; others kneeling, and held up by their arms. But certainly the safest and best way of all is to be delivered in their bed . . .

First, women in labour ought to be laid flat upon their backs, having their heads raised somewhat high, with pillows placed under their backs . . . and also under their buttocks . . .

Let their thighs and knees be stretched forth and laid open, and their legs bowed and drawn upward, their heels and feet pressing hard against the piece of wood laid cross the bed for the same purpose.

Some cause a swathe to be put under the back four double, which must come round about; which swathe ought to be . . . so long that it may be held by two women, being placed on each side the bed, therewith to lift up the woman in labour, pulling it easily towards them, and especially when their throws come upon them . . .

Besides the two women that hold the swathe, there must be two more to take them by the hands, therewith to crush them when their throws come, and the other hand they must lay upon the top of their shoulders, that they may not rise too much upward . . . as they thrust their feet against the piece of wood . . .

Women in labour being thus ordered must have a good heart, and strain themselves as much as possible, and when their throws come, make them double and increase by stopping their mouths, holding of their breath, and framing themselves as if they were going to the stool . . .

The great care of midwives must be such that they presume to do nothing . . . rashly or too hastily, to enlarge the passage for the child, much less to let forth the waters, or to tear the membrane that contains it, but with patience wait till it break of its own accord.

For some there are (not for want of ignorance) being over-hasty to busy themselves in matters they know not, destroy poor women by tearing the membrane with their nails, and so let forth the water (at least) to the great danger and hurt not only of the woman but the child . . .

140 Henry Smith, *A Preparative to Marriage* (1591), pp. 99–101

The first duty is the mother's, to nurse her child at her own breasts, as Sarah did Isaac (Gen. xxi.7). And therefore Isaiah joineth the nurse's name and the mother's both in one, and calleth them *nursing mothers*, showing that mothers should be nurses [Isa. xlix.23]. So when God chose a nurse for Moses, he led the handmaid of Pharaoh's daughter to his mother, as though God would have none to nurse him but his mother (Exod. ii.8). After, when the Son of God was born, his father thought none fit to be his nurse but the Virgin his mother (Matt. ii.14). The fountains of the earth are made to give water, and the breasts of women are made to give suck. Every beast and every fowl is bred of the same that did bear it; only women love to be mothers, but not nurses. Therefore, if their children prove unnatural, they may say, thou followest thy mother, for she was unnatural first in locking up her breasts from thee, and committing thee forth like a cuckoo to be hatched in the sparrow's nest . . . yet they which have no milk can give no milk; but whose breasts have this perpetual drought? Forsooth, it is like the gout, no beggars may have it but citizens or gentlewomen. In the 9 of Hosea, dry breasts are named for a curse (Hos. ix.14); what lamentable hap have gentlewomen to light upon this curse more than other? Sure, if their breasts be dry as they say, they should fast and pray together that this curse might be removed from them.

141 William Gouge, *Domesticall Duties* (1622), *passim*

Treatise VI: THE DUTIES OF PARENTS

§11. Of Giving Suck to Children

Among needful things, the milk of the breast is fit for young babes, and with it they are to be nourished. I think none doubt of the equity of this. It hath in all ages, and in all countries, been accounted the best food that can be for young babes. The metaphor which Saint Peter useth, taken from young infants (in these words, 'as new-born babes desire the sincere milk of the word' (I Pet. ii.2)) confirmeth as much. So doth the desire which such infants have to the milk of the breast and the ability and promptness which is in them to suck; and God's providence in causing a woman's breasts to yield forth milk; and the constant manner of nourishing little infants after this manner, commended in the Scripture; and (to conclude) the natural instinct which many unreasonable creatures have thus to nourish their young ones . . .

213

§12. Of Mothers Giving Suck to their Own Children

Of nourishing children with breast milk there is no great question; therefore I have with a touch passed it over. The chiefest question of doubt is concerning the party who is bound to this duty, namely, whether the mother be bound to do it herself or no.

Many strong arguments there be to press it upon the conscience of mothers and to show that (as far as they are able) they are bound to give suck to their own children . . .

These arguments we have from the light of God's Word; other we may have from God's works and the light of Nature.

1. God hath given to women two breasts fit to contain and hold milk, and nipples unto them fit to have milk drawn from them. Why are these thus given? To lay them forth for ostentation? There is no warrant for that in all God's Word. They are directly given for the child's food that cometh out of the womb. Anon after it is born, milk ordinarily floweth into the breasts; yea, a great part of the meat which they eat turneth into milk . . .

2. That nourishment whereon the child fed in the mother's womb, and whereby it was there sustained, turneth into milk, and cometh into the breasts when the child cometh out of the womb. Whence we may gather that of all women's milk, that woman's milk is fittest for the child out of whose womb the child came.

3. Together with the milk passeth some smacks of the affection and disposition of the mother, which maketh mothers to love such children best as they have given suck unto; yea, and ofttimes such children as have sucked their mother's breasts love their mothers best. Yea, we may observe many who have sucked others' milk to love those nurses all the days of their life.

4. Other things are nourished by the same that they are bred. The earth out of which plants grow ministereth nourishment to the said plants . . . unreasonable creatures, and among them the most savage wild beasts, as tigers and dragons, yea sea-monsters, give suck to their young ones . . .

5. Shall I add another argument which daily experience confirmeth, namely, God's blessing upon this motherly duty? Commonly, such children as are nursed by their mothers prosper best. Mothers are most tender over them, and cannot endure to let them lie crying out, without taking them up and stilling them, as nurses will let them cry and cry again, if they be about any business of their own. For who are commonly chosen to be nurses? Even poor country women which have much work to do and little help, and so are forced to let the child lie and cry, many times till it burst again. Children nursed by their mothers are for the most part more cleanly and neatly brought up, freer from diseases, not so many die; I am not sure so many through negligence cast away. The number of nurse children that die every year is very great. It hath been observed in many country villages, that the most part that from time to time die there are nurse children. Are not

mothers that might have nursed their own children if they would, accessary to the death of those that are cast away by the nurse's negligence?

On these and other like reasons heathen women, and very savages, have in all ages been moved to nurse their own children. And some heathen philosophers have urged and pressed the necessity of this duty. Never was it more neglected than among those that bear the name of Christians.

§13. Of the Objections for Putting Children forth to Nurse

Object. 1. Many nurses are mentioned in Scripture, as Rebecca's nurse (Gen. xxiv.59), Mephibosheth's nurse (II Sam. iv.4), Joash his nurse (II Kgs. xi.2), and others.

Answ. Such nurses mentioned in Scripture were commonly dry nurses. Rebecca's nurse was with her before she was married: how can it be thought that she was a milk nurse? . . .

Object. 5. Mothers that are of great wealth and high place cannot endure the pain of nursing, nor take the pains in handling young children as they must be handled.

Answ. 1. The greatest that be must set themselves to do that duty which God requireth at their hands, though it be with pain and pains . . .

2. By this it appeareth that if other women could bear their children in the womb nine months and endure the pain of travail for them, they would hire them to do it . . .

3. If women would with cheerfulness set themselves to perform this duty, much of the supposed pain and pains would be lessened.

4. Though they put not forth their children to nurse, they may for their ease entertain a nurse, so they give suck themselves.

Object. 6. A mother that hath a trade, or that hath the care of an house, will neglect much business by nursing her child, and her husband will save more by giving half a crown a week to a nurse, then if his wife gave the child suck.

Answ. No outward business appertaining to a mother can be more acceptable to God than the nursing of her child. This is the most proper work of her special calling; therefore all other businesses must give place to this, and this must not be left for any other business. As for the husband saving by putting the child forth to nurse, no gain may give dispensation against a bounden duty.

Object. 7. It will break tender fair women, and make them look old too soon.

Answ. 1. God's ordinance must not give place to women's niceness . . .

2. Drying up a woman's milk will more break her than her child's sucking of it, for it is a means both of better health and also of greater strength, as to bear children, so to give them suck. Barren women and bearing women which put forth their children to suck, are most subject to

sickness and weakness. The drawing forth of a woman's milk by her child is a means to get and preserve a good stomach, which is a great preservative of good health.

Object. 8. Husbands are disturbed in the night time, and hindered of their sleep by their wives giving suck to their children.

Answ. 1. By this reason neither mothers nor other nurses which have husbands should give suck.

2. Seeing children come from the loins of the father, as well as out of the womb of the mother, they must be content to endure some disturbance as well as their wives and so much the rather that they may the more pity their wives, and afford unto them what help they can.

Object. 9. Many husbands will not suffer their wives to nurse their children themselves.

Answ. Because it is a bounden duty wives must use all the means they can by themselves or others to persuade their husbands to let them perform it . . . if their husbands will stand upon their authority and be persuaded by no means . . . they must be mere patients in suffering the child to be taken away.

Object. 10. Many poor women maintain their house by nursing other folks' children.

Answ. If they were not that way employed they might take pains in some other thing. But the gain of one may but make another neglect her duty . . .

§14. Of the Father's duty in Encouraging his Wife to Nurse her Child

The duty which on a father's part in this respect is required is that he encourage his wife and help her with all needful things for the performance of this duty . . .

142 Henry Newcome, *The Compleat Mother* (1695), pp. 6–7, 52–3, 56–7, 64–6, 68–9, 71–2, 81–2, 86–8

. . . the children of our nobility and gentry . . . in their infancy generally are more unhappy than the sons of country peasants. The poor tenant's child is for the most part nursed in its mother's bosom, and cherished by her breasts, whilst the landlord's heir is turned out, exiled from his mother's embraces as soon as from her womb, and assigned to the care of some stranger, who hath no other endearments toward it, than what are owing solely to her interest. And such as work for wages are usually not so careful how they do their work, as to get their stipend, nor is a mercenary nurse much concerned how the infant improves, provided she have a good place of it. Thus the infants of the best families are most hardly used, and vast numbers of them undoubtedly destroyed . . .

. . . it is very unlikely that those mothers who transfer the nursing of their children to others, should ordinarily love them as tenderly as those that make them their own care. When the infant is exiled from its mother's sight, that warmth of love, which receives new vigour from the frequent view of its object, cools by degrees and languishes whilst the interposition of other objects soon weans her from that poor exile, who becomes abroad almost as much forgotten as if it had been laid in the grave. It is not rare to observe that foster-children are more dear to their nurses than their mothers; and mothers for the most part are fondest of those whom they have nursed themselves.

. . . this is the way to alienate the child's affections from its mother. Some grammarians derive the Latin word *lac* (milk) from *lacio* (to allure) as concluding no way so likely to allure the child to love its mother as nursing it with her milk. She performs indeed but half the office, and consequently earns but half of that love which otherwise is due to a mother who only bears her child and then turns it off . . .

A mercenary nurse is not likely to take so much care of the child as its own mother . . . how can it be expected that a hireling should endure all the tediousness and inconveniences attending the nursing of a little, helpless, perhaps froward infant when the mother, to whom natural affection should have endeared the employment, out of softness and luxury declines it as a burden? Or why hath God generally inspired the mother with a greater tenderness toward the child, but for this very end, that thereby she may be enabled to digest more easily the little unhandsomenesses . . . which others will nauseate, and submit to those fatigues that none else will for its preservation, whilst her care and patience are doubled by her affection? . . .

But if a child nursed by a stranger be not killed by her neglect, yet secondly it may be very much injured in its health by the unsuitable nourishment which it derives from her breast. It is agreed upon by ancient and modern physicians that the nourishment which infants receive in the womb is of the same nature with the milk which, soon after the birth, Nature provides for it in the breasts. And it is another approved rule among them, that a sudden alteration of diet is oft fatal, always dangerous . . .

But the danger is much greater, lest mercenary nurses transmit some desperate contagion into their nurseries. The mother's distemper is the most plausible pretence for the declining of this office, and all conclude it very reasonable that in that case she forbear to nurse, lest her infant suck death from her breast whose womb gave it life, and she propagate her diseases to it, together with her milk, impregnated with the vicious qualities of her blood. But then the argument is as strong to oblige an healthful mother to nurse, lest she should commit it to a mercenary infected with some latent disease.

. . . It ought further to be considered whether the suck of a mercenary nurse may not corrupt the dispositions of the infant's soul and deprave its manners, for whoever impartially considers it will find great reason to fear lest the child imbibe the nurse's ill conditions together with her milk. Though virtue is a supernatural perfection, added to our nature in this state of depravation by the influences of divine grace, yet some inclinations to it may be owing to the temper of the body, and propagated by a communication of spirits in nourishment. Much more may vicious dispositions, which are natural, and depend more upon the temper of the blood and spirits . . .

. . . there is neither reason nor experience on their side who pretend nursing to be the decay of a woman's health or beauty. The contrary is generally observed, that it helps the appetite and digestion, which is more likely to preserve both, than destroy either . . . on the other hand, women very commonly run apparent hazards of destroying not their health only but their lives. The unnatural stopping up of these fountains occasions the corrupting of the milk, and that corrupted milk infecting the blood, oft raises such a ferment as produces a fever, or some other fatal distemper, and none can think it prudence to throw themselves into immature death to avoid wrinkles.

143 Robert Burton, *Anatomy of Melancholy*
(1621–51), I.ii.4(1) [I.330–2]

From a child's nativity, the first ill accident that can likely befall him . . . is a bad nurse, by whose means alone he may be tainted with this malady [of melancholy] from his cradle. Aulus Gellius, lib. 12, cap. i, brings in Favorinus, that eloquent philosopher, proving this at large, 'that there is the same virtue and property in the milk as in the seed, and not in men alone, but in all other creatures: he gives instance in a kid and lamb, if either of them suck of the other's milk, the lamb of the goat's, or the kid of the ewe's, the wool of the one will be hard, and the hair of the other soft'. Gerald of Wales's *Welsh Journey*, lib. I, cap. ii, confirms this by a notable example which happened in his time. A sow pig by chance sucked a brach, and when she was grown, 'would miraculously hunt all manner of deer, and that as well, or rather better, than any ordinary hound'. His conclusion is, 'that men and beasts participate of her nature and condition, by whose milk they are fed'. Favorinus urgeth it farther, and demonstrates it more evidently, that if a nurse be 'misshapen, unchaste, dishonest, impudent, drunk, cruel', or the like, the child that sucks upon her breast will be so too. All other affections of the mind, and diseases, are almost engraffed, as it were, and imprinted into the temperature of the infant, by the nurse's milk, as pox, leprosy, melancholy, etc. Cato for some such reason would make his servants' children suck upon his wife's breast, because by that means they would love him and his the better, and in all likelihood agree with them. A more evident example that the minds are altered by milk, cannot be given than that of Dion which he relates of Caligula's cruelty. It could neither be imputed to father or mother, but to his cruel nurse alone, that anointed her paps with blood still when he sucked, which made him such a murderer, and to express her cruelty to an hair: And that of Tiberius, who was a common drunkard because his nurse was such a one . . . For bodily sickness there is no doubt to be made. Titus, Vespasian's son, was therefore sickly because his nurse was so . . . And if we may believe physicians, many times children catch the pox from a bad nurse . . . For these causes Aristotle *Politics*, lib. I, cap. xvii, Favorinus and Marcus Aurelius would not have a child put to nurse at all, but every mother to bring up her own, of what condition so ever she be . . . the mother will be more careful, loving and attendant, than any servile woman, or such hired creatures, this all the world acknowledgeth . . . if it be so, as many times it is, they must be put forth, the mother be not fit or well able to be a nurse, I would then advise such mothers . . . that they make choice of a sound woman, of a good complexion, honest, free from bodily diseases, if it be possible, all passions and perturbations of the mind, as sorrow, fear, grief, folly, melancholy. For such passions corrupt the milk and alter the temperature of the child . . . And if such a nurse may be found out, that will be diligent and careful withal, let Favorinus and M. Aurelius plead how they will against it, I had rather accept of her in some cases than the mother herself . . . For why may not the mother be naught, a peevish drunken flirt, a waspish choleric slut, a crazed piece, a fool (as many mothers are) unsound as soon as the nurse? There is more choice of nurses than mothers; and therefore except the mother be most virtuous, staid, a woman of excellent good parts, and of a sound complexion, I would have all children in such cases committed to discreet strangers.

144 Nicholas Culpeper, *Directory for Midwives* (1662), pp. 225–6

Of the Choice of the Nurse

The blood that nourished the child in the womb is turned into milk to nourish him after he is born, because he can eat no solid meats. And because from weakness or disease the mother sometimes cannot suckle her child, she must have a nurse of good habit of body, and red complexion, which is the sign of the best temper. And let her not differ much from the temper of the mother, unless it be for the better. Let her be between twenty and thirty, well bred, and peaceable, not angry, melancholy, or foolish, not lecherous, not a drunkard. Let it not be after her first child, and let not her milk be too old or too new, often months old at the most. Let her breasts be well fashioned, with good nipples, that the child may take them with pleasure.

Let her keep a good diet, and abstain from hard wine and copulation and passions: these chiefly trouble the milk and bring diseases upon the child.

145 Robert Barret, *Companion for Midwives* (1699), pp. 77–9

Character and Duty of a Nurse

. . . First, let her be young and healthy, for if ye give very stale milk, and from an infirm woman, the child forever may suffer . . . In the next place, choose one lively, witty and of a meek temper. Galen and other Greek physicians were very curious in this particular: to make choice of a nurse of good education and wit. Some nurses are humoursome, still complaining, peevish and fretful . . . Now, since the child partakes much of a nurse's complexion and humour, by sucking her milk, we ought to be very cautious in choosing a nurse endowed with the same qualities as we wish in our children . . . their very example and company is influencive upon children, who are generally more led by the eye than the ear. Besides they are liable to be infected not only by their external words and actions but by the internal bias and inclinations of their minds, be what they will, by reason of the affinity intercedes betwixt the qualities of the milk and the disposition of the person that gives it. A nurse also ought to be diligent and careful, some are huffing and bouncing about, and do not mind the poor child, but let it sit or lie half a day in a wet condition, starving and crippling. 'Tis a great abuse, too frequent and common among them; mothers ought to take care to surprise nurses at their own houses, when they are not aware, and find out the miscarriages of these she-murderers, that they may not go unpunished.

146 Mary Verney, letters to her steward, late June 1647, and to her husband Sir Ralph, autumn 1647, in Frances Parthenope Verney (ed.), *Memoirs of the Verney Family* (1892–9), II.269, 294

Upon Tuesday next I intend to send my child [Ralph, born 3 June 1647] to St. Albans [from London], the [wet]-nurse is most extremely desirous to be at home; so, if you can possibly, I would have you be there one Tuesday night and go to Tring on Wednesday. The nurse saith her husband hath a very easy-going horse, and she thinks it will be best for him to carry the child before him upon pillows, because she cannot ride between two panniers and hold the child. When you come there, you will quickly find which will be the best way to carry it. Pray provide for both ways and bring a footman to go by it. If her husband doth carry the child, she cannot ride behind him, so you must provide a horse for her. My sister Mary goes down with them, so you must bring up a pillion to carry her down behind you . . . Pray do you see that they take great care of the child, and that they go very softly, for the weather is very hot; if he carries the child before him it must be tied about him with a garter, and truly, I think it will be a very good way, for the child will not endure to be long out of one's arms.

* * *

She [the second wet-nurse for Ralph] looks like a slattern, but she saith that if she takes the child she will have a mighty care of it, and truly she hath two as fine children of her own as ever I saw. [The nurse is] to have 4s. a week and two loads of wood; truly, 'tis as little as we can offer her . . . for nurses are much dearer than they ever were . . . poor child, I pray God bless him and make him a happy man, for he hath had but a troublesome beginning, yet I praise God he thrives well, and is a lovely baby.

147 Alice Thornton, *Autobiography* (written *post* 1668), p. 91

It was the pleasure of God to give me but a weak time after my daughter Alice her birth [3 January 1654], and she had many preservations from death in the first year, being one night delivered from being overlaid by her nurse, who laid in my dear mother's [Alice Wandesford's] chamber a good while. One night my mother was writing pretty late and she heard my dear child make a groaning troublesomely, and stepping immediately to nurse's bed-side, she saw the nurse fallen asleep, with her breast in the child's mouth, and lying over the child; at which she, being affrighted, pulled the nurse suddenly off from her, and so preserved my dear child from being smothered.

148 John Evelyn, *Diary* (written 1640–1706), III.371

26 March 1664: It pleased God to take away my son Richard, being now a month old [born 10 January 1664], yet without any sickness of [or?] danger perceivable, being to all appearances a most likely child; so as we suspected much the nurse had overlain him, to our extreme sorrow, being now reduced to one. God's will be done.

13

MISTRESS AND MUSE

Since antiquity, sources of inspiration in the Western artistic and intellectual tradition have been represented by female images. Poets invoked a female Muse and embodied excellence in female form: Ben Jonson's Celia is in a line from Helen of Troy (149). Addressing this preponderance of female images in our cultural store, Heywood reveals deep disquiet lest it disturb the sexual hierarchy (150). Wither is equally anxious to maintain the binary opposition of masculine and feminine despite its evidence (151). They had some cause for concern: the excesses of poets, drawing upon Classical precedent, privileged the female in ways of which, in Heywood's view, it were far better women remained ignorant, but upon which Esther Sowernam gleefully seized (152). The ironic and subversive potential of 'such witty encomiums writ in our commendation', when women were generally held so 'contemptible', was realized by *The Women's Sharp Revenge* (153).

The common protestation in 'such witty encomiums' is of a Platonic devotion which accords the woman the status of divine revelation, a being 'all ethereal' (even if, 'In thy immortal part / Man' (155; cf. chapter 5)). Such poems purport to celebrate a spiritual love which, 'Inter-assured of the mind' in Donne's phrase (154), does not depend upon sexual fulfilment. However, this poetry is rarely unproblematic or univocal; more commonly it self-reflexively scrutinizes its own assumptions and subjects its avowals and ideals to ironic and searching scrutiny as it seeks to accommodate sexual desire. After all, undeniably 'something 'tis that differs *Thee* and *Me*' (155). The verse registers deepening degrees of discontent with Platonic protestations (155, 156) on a scale which presents an increasingly harsh image of woman as sexual object, culminating in such sentiments as those of Lovelace's 'La Bella Bona Roba' (157).

As these examples indicate, there is an Ovidian and libertine strain in seventeenth-century poetry which celebrates what Rochester called the 'generosity' of mere lust (on Ovid's influence see Sowerby (1994)). It is a strain convinced that the woman desires sexual gratification as much as man; she is inhibited merely by outmoded and 'Affected rules of honour', fidelity and chastity (158). Within the fiction of the poems, wooer and wooed are each knowingly engaged in a game of courtship, a game which resonates through Restoration drama and, it seems, affected the manners of social intercourse between the sexes. The hypocrisy of its elaborate and posturing rhetoric was derided by *The Women's Sharp Revenge* (159). This courtship game had no truck with the marital and domestic values of the conduct books, or, indeed, traditional Christian values, which are often mocked or subverted. 'Quaint honour' (165), figured as a 'giant', 'vast idol', and 'goblin' in Carew's libertine 'Rapture' (160), is the target; what is called the woman's 'coyness' (165) is to be overcome. As the conduct books return to Genesis for their proof texts, so this celebration of liberty from moral restraint recalls the Classical myth of the Golden Age (161; but note the masturbatory self-awareness of fantasy in this poem's final stanza). Its sexual antinomianism presents an ever more reductive image of woman as sexual object. She is naturally lascivious, available to titillate the poet (162), to be stripped, possessed and conquered (163), annihilated (164), and, in the desperation of Marvell's nihilistic version of the *carpe diem* theme, raped (165).

---

149 Ben Jonson, *Underwoods* (1640), pp. 164–5

XXVII: An Ode

Helen, did Homer never see
Thy beauties, yet could write of thee?
Did Sappho on her seven-tongued lute,
So speak (as yet it is not mute)
Of Phao's form? Or doth the boy
In whom Anacreon once did joy,
Lie drawn to life, in his soft verse,
As he whom Maro did rehearse?
Was Lesbia sung by learned Catullus?
Or Delia's graces, by Tibullus?
Doth Cynthia, in Propertius' song
Shine more, than she the stars among?
Is Horace his each love so high
Rapt from the earth, as not to die?
With bright Lycoris, Gallus' choice,
Whose fame hath an eternal voice?
Or hath Corinna, by the name
Her Ovid gave her, dimmed the fame
Of Caesar's daughter, and the line
Which all the world then styled divine?
Hath Petrarch since his Laura raised
Equal with her? Or Ronsard praised

His new Cassandra, 'bove the old,
Which all the fate of Troy foretold?
Hath our great Sidney, Stella set,
Where never star shone brighter yet?
Or Constable's ambrosiac muse
Made Dian not his notes refuse?
Hath all these done (and yet I miss
The swan so relished Pancharis)
And shall not I my Celia bring,
Where men may see whom I do sing?
Though I, in working of my song,
Come short of all this learned throng,
Yet sure my tunes will be the best,
So much my subject drowns the rest.

150 Thomas Heywood, *Gynækeion* (1624), pp. 60–1

It may now lastly be demanded by those that are studious of antiquities, why the Virtues, Disciplines, the Muses, the devisers and patrons of all good arts, with divers of the like nature, should rather be comprehended under the feminine sex, by the names of virgins and women, as also their pictures drawn to the portraitures of damsels, than either by masculine nomination or according to the effigies of men, the rather since not only the ethics and moral men [i.e. Classical philosophers], but even Christians and theologians themselves, in all their books and writings which they commit to posterity, still continue them under this same gender? For who is ignorant that *Sophia*, which signifies wisdom, was not from the beginning, and before the world [Ecclus. i.4, xxiv.9], who is said to be the mother of the three theological virtues, Faith, Hope and Charity, and these represented as women? Why should the seven liberal arts be expressed in women's shapes? Why the nine Muses be the daughters of Jupiter, as all writers agree? Why is wisdom called the daughter of the highest, and not rather the son, as witnesseth the Book of Wisdom [Ecclus. xxiv.1–3]? Why Pallas, otherwise called Minerva, not the son but the daughter of Jove (of whose brain she was born)? And why the most curious and diligent inquisitors into these curiosities figure the liberal Arts and Disciplines like women and not rather like men? Or by what reason the Muses should be personated rather like damsels than young men, strenuous and excellent in masculine virtue? To all these objections, it is briefly answered by Lilius Gregorius, as likewise by Cornatus, whom some call Pharnutus: that by the symbol or semblance of such women much science is begot and besides much fruit ariseth from the judgement of the soul; besides, it was a custom of old for virgins to play and dance in companies, which excellently fitted the coupling and sisterhood of the sciences . . . in Beroaldus' commentaries upon the *Golden Ass* [by

Apuleius], he adds this one thing, worthy observation, to the great honour and commendation of the feminine sex: the four parts of the world have their denominations from women. Asia was so called of the nymph Asia, from whom and Iapethus, Prometheus descended; Europe, of Europa, the daughter of Ægenor; Lybia, which is Africa, of Lybia the daughter of Epaphus; in like manner America (since discovered) beareth the like female figure: which (as Beroaldus saith) if the women of our age did fully apprehend and truly understand, how insolently would they boast of their worth and dignity? How would they glory in vain boasts and ostentations, how much continual chidings would they upbraid their husbands, still casting in their dishes their own virtues and goodness, still commemorating and urging that women bear the names of all the four parts of the divided world; that Wisdom and the theological Virtues are personated under the sex of women; that the Arts, the Disciplines, the Muses, the Graces, and almost whatsoever is good, are deciphered both by the names and in the persons of women. Therefore (I fear) this had been better kept as secret as mysteries in sanctuaries, and not to have been published to them in their own mother's tongue, in which they are so nimble and voluble, lest, calling a council about this argument, it may add to their insolency, who have too great an opinion of their worths already.

151 George Wither, *Fair-Virtue* (1622), ii.174

Of the Invention of the Nine Muses

The acts of ages past doth Clio write,
The tragedy's Melpomene's delight,
Thalia is with comedies contented,
Euterpe first the shepherd's pipe invented,
Terpsichore doth song and lute apply,
Dancing Erato found geometry,
Calliope on loving verses dwells,
The secrets of the stars Urania tells,
Polymnia with choice words the speech doth trim,
And great Apollo shares with all of them.
Those thrice three feminines we Muses call;
But that one masculine is worth them all.

152 Esther Sowernam, *Ester hath Hang'd Haman* (1617), pp. 99–100, 101–2

The feminine sex is exceedingly honoured by poets in their writings. They have gods as well for good things as for bad; but they have no women goddesses but in things which are especially good. They have Bacchus for a drunken god but no drunken goddess. They have Priapus the lustful god of gardens but no garden goddesses, except of late in the garden-alleys. They will object here unto me Venus: she indeed is the goddess of love, but it is her blind son [Cupid] which is the god of lust . . .

I will not say that women are better than men, but I will say that men are not so wise as I would wish them to be, to woo us in such fashion as they do; except they should hold an account of us as their betters.

What travail, what charge, what study do not men undertake to gain our good-will, love and liking? What vehement suits do they make unto us? With what solemn vows and protestations do they solicit us? They write, they speak, they send, to make known what entire affection they bear unto us: that they are so deeply engaged in love, except we do compassion them with our love and favour they are men utterly cast away . . . What? will they say that we are baser than themselves? Then they wrong themselves exceedingly to prefer such vehement suits to creatures inferior to themselves . . . To what obsequious duty and service do men bind themselves to obtain favour from their devoted mistress? – which if he may obtain he thinketh himself to be much honoured, and puts in place of most noted view that the world may take note. He weareth in his hat or on his breast or upon his arm the glove, the scarf or ring of his mistress. If these were not relics from saintly creatures, men would not sacrifice so much devotion upon them.

153 Mary Tattle-well and Jon Hit-him-home [John Taylor?], *The Women's Sharp Revenge* (1640), pp. 171–2

If we be so contemptible grown either in quality and condition, in conversation or deportment, in name or nature, how comes it that so many elaborate pens have been employed in our praise, and there have been such witty encomiums writ in our commendation? – such as have swelled volumes and enriched libraries. What odes, hymns, love-songs and laudatories, in all kind of sweet measure and number, have not been by poets devised to extol the beauties and virtues of their mistresses? What powers have they not called upon? And what muse not invoked, that they might give them their full meed and merit? By which only, divers have attained to the honour of the laurel amongst all nations, tongues and language, in all frequency from antiquity. Were it a thing new or rare, or of late birth, it perhaps might be called into some suspicion and question: but carrying with it the reverence of age, antiquity and custom, what can we hold him but some novice in knowledge and child in understanding, that shall presume or dare any kind of way to contradict it? . . .

Further, if we were such toys and trifles, or so vile and vicious, as our adversary striveth to make the world believe we are, how comes this seeking, this suing; this courting, this cogging; this prating, this protesting; this vowing, this swearing – but only to compass a smile, a kind look, a favour or a good word from one of us? Can any be so simple to seek his affliction? Or so sottish to sue for his own ruin? What fool would trouble himself to find his own torment? Or what coxcomb pursue his own confusion? Is he not worse than frantic that desires his own fall? And more than a mad man that hunteth after his own misery? Then, by consequence, if we be apish and waggish, wilful and wanton, such cares, such burdens, such troubles, such torments, such vexation, such serpents, such sirens, or such may-games, or rather monsters, as you would make of us – why cannot you let us alone and leave us to our own weakness and imperfections?

154 John Donne, *Poems* (1633; written 1590–1612?), pp. 84–5

A Valediction: Forbidding Mourning

As virtuous men pass mildly away,
    And whisper to their souls, to go,
Whilst some of their sad friends do say,
    The breath goes now, and some say, no:

So let us melt, and make no noise,
    No tear-floods, nor sigh-tempests move,
'Twere profanation of our joys
    To tell the laity our love.

Moving of th'earth brings harms and fears,
    Men reckon what it did and meant,
But trepidation of the spheres,
    Though greater far, is innocent.

Dull sublunary lovers' love
    (Whose soul is sense) cannot admit
Absence, because it doth remove
    The things which elemented it.

But we by a love so much refined,
    That our selves know not what it is,
Inter-assured of the mind,
    Care less, eyes, lips, and hands to miss.

Our two souls therefore, which are one,
    Though I must go, endure not yet
A breach, but an expansion,
    Like gold to aery thinness beat.

If they be two, they are two so
    As stiff twin compasses are two,
Thy soul the fixed foot, makes no show
    To move, but doth, if th'other do.

And though it in the centre sit,
   Yet when the other far doth roam,
It leans, and hearkens after it,
   And grows erect, as that comes home.

Such wilt thou be to me, who must
   Like th'other foot, obliquely run;
Thy firmness makes my circle just,
   And makes me end where I begun.

155 Abraham Cowley, *The Works* (1668), pp. 75–6

Platonic Love

I
Indeed I must confess,
When souls mix 'tis an happiness;
But not complete till bodies too combine,
And closely as our minds together join;
But half of heaven the souls in glory taste,
   'Till by love in heaven at last,
   Their bodies too are plac'd.

II
In thy immortal part
Man, as well as I, thou art.
But something 'tis that differs *Thee* and *Me*;
And we must one even in that difference be.
I thee, both as a man, and woman prize;
   For a perfect Love implies
   Love in all capacities.

III
Can that for true love pass,
When a fair woman courts her glass?
Something unlike must in Love's likeness be,
His wonder is, one, and variety.
For he, whose soul nought but a soul can move,
   Does a new Narcissus prove,
   And his own image love.

IV
That souls do beauty know,
'Tis to the bodies' help they owe;
If when they know't, they straight abuse that trust,

And shut the body from't, 'tis as unjust,
 As if I brought my dearest friend to see
   My mistress, and at th'instant he
     Should steal her quite from me.

156 William Cartwright, *The Works* (1651), pp. 494–5

No Platonic Love

Tell me no more of minds embracing minds,
  And hearts exchang'd for hearts;
That spirits spirits meet, as winds do winds,
  And mix their subtlest parts;
That two unbodi'd essences may kiss,
And then like angels twist and feel one bliss.

I was that silly thing that once was wrought
  To practise this thin love:
I climbed from sex to soul, from soul to thought;
  But thinking there to move,
Headlong I roll'd from thought to soul, and then
From soul I lighted at the sex again.

As some strict down-look'd men pretend to fast,
  Who yet in closets eat,
So lovers who profess they spirits taste
  Feed yet on grosser meat;
I know they boast they souls to souls convey:
Howe'er they meet, the body is the way.

Come, I will undeceive thee: they that tread
  Those vain aërial ways
Are like young heirs and alchemists misled
  To waste their wealth and days;
For searching thus to be for ever rich
They only find a med'cine for the itch.

157 Richard Lovelace, *Lucasta* (1649), p. 96

La Bella Bona Roba

I cannot tell who loves the skeleton
Of a poor marmoset, nought but bone, bone.
Give me nakedness with her clothes on:

Such whose white satin upper coat of skin,
Cut upon velvet rich incarnadine,
Has yet a body (and of flesh) within.

229

Sure it is meant good husbandry in men,
Who do incorporate with airy lean,
T' repair their sides, and get their rib again.

Hard hap unto that huntsman that decrees
Fat joys for all his sweat, whenas he sees,
After his 'ssay, nought but his keeper's fees.

Then, love, I beg, when next thou tak'st thy bow,
Thy angry shafts, and dost heart-chasing go,
Pass rascal deer, strike me the largest doe.

158 John Wilmot, *Poems on Several Occasions* (1680), p. 20

To Corinna. A Song

1

What cruel pains Corinna takes,
    To force that harmless frown:
When not one charm her face forsakes,
    Love cannot lose his own.

2

So sweet a face, so soft a heart,
    Such eyes so very kind,
Betray, alas! the silly art
    Virtue had ill design'd.

3

Poor feeble tyrant! who in vain
    Would proudly take upon her,
Against kind Nature to maintain
    Affected rules of honour.

4

The scorn she bears so helpless proves,
    When I plead passion to her,
That much she fears, (but more she loves,)
    Her vassal should undo her.

159 Mary Tattle-well and Joan Hit-him-home [John Taylor?], *The Women's Sharp Revenge* (1640), pp. 174–5

When I was a young maid of the age of fifteen, there came to me in the wooing way very many of those fly-blown, puff-paste suitors. Amongst the rest, one of them was as brave a gentleman as any tailor could make him . . . he would swear that his life or death were either in my accepting or rejecting his suit; he would lie and flatter in prose, and cog and foist in verse most shamefully. He would sometimes salute me with most delicious sentences, which he always kept in syrup, and he never came to me empty-mouthed or handed. For he was never unprovided of stewed anagrams, baked epigrams, soused madrigals, pickled roundelays, broiled sonnets, parboiled elegies, perfumed posies for rings, and a thousand other such foolish flatteries and knavish devices – which I suspected; and the more he strived to overcome me or win me with oaths, promises and protestations, still the less I believed him: so that at last he grew faint at the siege, gave over to make any more assaults and, vanquished with despair, made a final retreat. In like manner I wish all women and maids in general to beware of their gilded glosses: an enamoured toad lurks under the sweet grass, and a fair tongue hath been too often the varnish or embroidery of a false heart. What are they but lime-twigs of lust and school-masters of folly? Let not their foolish fancy prove to be your brain-sick frenzy. For if you note them, in all their speech or writings, you shall seldom or never have any word or syllable in the praise of goodness or true virtue to come from them. Their talk shall consist either of wealth, strength, wit, beauty, lands, fashions, horses, hawks, hounds, and many other trivial and transitory toys; which, as they may be used, are blessings of the left hand, wherewith they entice and entrap poor silly, young, tender-hearted females to be enamoured of their good parts (if they had any). But if men would lay by their tricks, sleights, falsehoods and dissimulations, and, contrarily, in their conversing with us use their tongues and pens in the praise of meekness, modesty, chastity, temperance, constancy and piety, then surely women would strive to be such as their discourses did tend unto. For we do live in such an age of pollution that many a rich wicked man will spend willingly and give more to corrupt and make spoil of the chastity and honour of one beautiful untainted virgin, than they will bestow, in charity, towards the saving of an hundred poor people from perishing by famine here or from perdition in a worser place.

160 Thomas Carew, *Poems* (1640), pp. 49–53

A Rapture

I will enjoy thee now my Celia, come
And fly with me to Love's Elysium:
The giant, Honour, that keeps cowards out,
Is but a masquer, and the servile rout
Of baser subjects only, bend in vain
To the vast idol, whilst the nobler train
Of valiant lovers, daily sail between
The huge colossus' legs, and pass unseen
Unto the blissful shore; be bold, and wise,

And we shall enter, the grim Swiss denies
Only tame fools a passage, that not know
He is but form, and only frights in show
The duller eyes that look from far; draw near,
And thou shalt scorn, what we were wont to fear.
We shall see how the stalking pageant goes
With borrowed legs, a heavy load to those
That made, and bear him; not as we once thought
The seed of gods, but a weak model wrought
By greedy men, that seek to enclose the common,
And within private arms empale free woman.
   Come then, and mounted on the wings of love
We'll cut the flitting air, and soar above
The monster's head, and in the noblest seats
Of those bless'd shades, quench, and renew our heats.
There, shall the Queen of Love, and Innocence,
Beauty and Nature, banish all offence
From our close ivy twines, and there I'll behold
Thy bared snow, and thy unbraided gold.
There, my enfranchis'd hand, on every side
Shall o'er thy naked polish'd ivory slide.
No curtain there, though of transparent lawn,
Shall be before thy virgin-treasure drawn;
But the rich mine, to the enquiring eye
Expos'd, shall ready still for mintage lie,
And we will coin young Cupids. There, a bed
Of roses, and fresh myrtles, shall be spread
Under the cooler shade of cypress groves:
Our pillows, of the down of Venus' doves,
Whereon our panting limbs we'll gently lay
In the faint respites of our active play;
That so our slumbers, may in dreams have leisure,
To tell the nimble fancy our past pleasure;
And so our souls that cannot be embrac'd,
Shall the embraces of our bodies taste.
Meanwhile the bubbling stream shall court the shore,
Th'enamoured chirping wood-choir shall adore
In varied tunes the Deity of Love;
The gentle blasts of Western winds, shall move
The trembling leaves, and through their close boughs breath
Still music, whilst we rest ourselves beneath
Their dancing shade; till a soft murmur, sent
From souls entranc'd in amorous languishment
Rouse us, and shoot into our veins fresh fire,

232

Till we, in their sweet ecstasy expire.
  Then, as the empty bee, that lately bore,
Into the common treasure, all her store,
Flies 'bout the painted field with nimble wing,
Deflow'ring the fresh virgins of the Spring;
So will I rifle all the sweets, that dwell
In my delicious paradise, and swell
My bag with honey, drawn forth by the power
Of fervent kisses, from each spicy flower.
I'll seize the rose-buds in their perfum'd bed,
The violet knots, like curious mazes spread
O'er all the garden, taste the rip'ned cherry,
The warm, firm apple, tipp'd with coral berry:
Then will I visit, with a wand'ring kiss,
The vale of lilies, and the bower of bliss;
And where the beauteous region doth divide
Into two milky ways, my lips shall slide
Down these smooth alleys, wearing as I go
A tract for lovers on the printed snow;
Thence climbing o'er the swelling Appenine,
Retire into thy grove of eglantine;
Where I will all those ravish'd sweets distil
Through Love's alembic, and with chemic skill
From the mix'd mass, one sovereign balm derive,
Then bring the great elixir to thy hive.
  Now in more subtle wreaths I will entwine
My sinewy thighs, my legs and arms with thine;
Thou like a sea of milk shalt lie display'd,
Whilst I the smooth, calm ocean, invade
With such a tempest, as when Jove of old
Fell down on Danae in a storm of gold:
Yet my tall pine, shall in the Cyprian strait
Ride safe at anchor, and unload her freight:
My rudder, with thy bold hand, like a tried,
And skilful pilot, thou shalt steer, and guide
My bark into Love's channel, where it shall
Dance, as the bounding waves do rise or fall:
Then shall thy circling arms, embrace and clip
My willing body, and thy balmy lip
Bathe me in juice of kisses, whose perfume
Like a religious incense shall consume,
And send up holy vapours, to those powers
That bless our loves, and crown our sportful hours,
That with such halcyon calmness, fix our souls

233

In steadfast peace, as no affright controls.
There, no rude sounds shake us with sudden starts,
No jealous ears, when we unrip our hearts
Suck our discourse in, no observing spies
This blush, that glance traduce; no envious eyes
Watch our close meetings, nor are we betray'd
To rivals, by the bribed chambermaid.
No wedlock bonds unwreath our twisted loves;
We seek no midnight arbour, no dark groves
To hide our kisses, there, the hated name
Of husband, wife, lust, modest, chaste, or shame,
Are vain and empty words, whose very sound
Was never heard in the Elysian ground.
All things are lawful there, that may delight
Nature, or unrestrained appetite;
Like, and enjoy, to will, and act, is one,
We only sin when Love's rites are not done . . .
    Come then my Celia, we'll no more forbear
To taste our joys, struck with a panic fear,
But will depose from his imperious sway
This proud usurper and walk free, as they
With necks unyok'd; nor is it just that he
Should fetter your soft sex with chastity,
Which Nature made unapt for abstinence;
When yet this false imposter can dispense
With human justice, and with sacred right,
And maugre both their laws command me fight
With rivals, or with emulous loves, that dare
Equal with thine, their mistress' eyes, or hair:
If thou complain of wrong, and call my sword
To carve out thy revenge, upon that word
He bids me fight and kill, or else he brands
With marks of infamy my coward hands,
And yet religion bids from blood-shed fly,
And damns me for that act. Then tell me why
This goblin Honour which the world adores,
Should make men atheists, not women whores.

161 Richard Lovelace, *Lucasta: Posthume Poems* (1659), pp. 146–8

Love Made in the First Age: To Chloris

1

In the nativity of time,
Chloris! it was not thought a crime
  In direct Hebrew for to woo.
Now we make love, as all on fire,
Ring retrograde our loud desire,
  And court in English backward too.

2

Thrice happy was that golden age,
When compliment was constru'd rage,
  And fine words in the centre hid;
When cursed *No* stain'd no maid's bliss,
And all discourse was summ'd in *Yes*,
  And nought forbad, but to forbid.

3

Love then unstinted, Love did sup,
And cherries pluck'd fresh from the lip,
  On cheeks and roses free he fed;
Lasses like autumn plums did drop,
And lads, indifferently did crop
  A flower, and a maidenhead.

4

Then unconfined each did tipple
Wine from the bunch, milk from the nipple,
  Paps tractable as udders were,
Then equally the wholesome jellies,
Were squeez'd from olive trees, and bellies,
  Nor suits of trespass did they fear.

5

A fragrant bank of strawberries,
Diaper'd with violets' eyes,
  Was table, tablecloth, and fare;
No palace to the clouds did swell,
Each humble princess then did dwell
  In the piazza of her hair.

6

Both broken faith, and th'cause of it,
All damning gold was damn'd to th'pit,
  Their troth seal'd with a clasp and kiss,

Lasted until that extreme day,
In which they smil'd their souls away,
   And in each other breath'd new bliss.

7

Because no fault, there was no tear;
No groan did grate the granting ear,
   No false foul breath their del'cate smell:
No serpent kiss poison'd the taste,
Each touch was naturally chaste,
   And their mere sense a miracle.

8

Naked as their own innocence,
And embroider'd from offence
   They went, above poor riches, gay;
On softer than the cygnet's down,
In beds they tumbled of their own,
   For each within the other lay.

9

Thus did they live: thus did they love,
Repeating only joys above;
   And angels were, but with clothes on,
Which they would put off cheerfully,
To bathe them in the galaxy
   Then gird them with the heavenly zone.

10

Now, Chloris! miserably crave,
The offer'd bliss you would not have;
   Which evermore I must deny,
Whilst ravish'd with these noble dreams,
And crown'd with mine own soft beams,
   Enjoying of my self I lie.

162 William Cartwright, *Sportive Wit* (1656), pp. 467–8

A Song of Dalliance

Hark, my Flora; Love doth call us
To that strife that must befall us:
He has robb'd his mother's myrtles,
And hath pull'd her downy turtles.
See, our genial posts are crowned,
And our beds like billows rise;
Softer combat's nowhere found,

And who loses, wins the prize.

Let not dark nor shadows fright thee;
Thy limbs of lustre they will light thee:
Fear not any can surprise us,
Love himself doth now disguise us.
From thy waist thy girdle throw:
Night and darkness both dwell here;
Words or actions who can know,
When there's neither eye nor ear?

Show thy bosom, and then hide it;
License touching and then chide it;
Give a grant, and then forbear it;
Offer something, and forswear it:
Ask where all our shame is gone;
Call us wicked wanton men:
Do as turtles, kiss and groan;
Say, 'We ne'er shall meet again'.

I can hear thee curse, yet chase thee;
Drink thy tears, yet still embrace thee.
Easy riches is no treasure:
She that's willing, spoils the pleasure.
Love bids learn the restless fight,
Pull and struggle whilst ye twine:
Let me use my force tonight,
The next conquest shall be thine.

163 John Donne, *Poems* (1635; written 1590–1612?), pp. 124–6

Elegy 19: To his Mistress Going to Bed

Come, Madam, come, all rest my powers defy,
Until I labour, I in labour lie.
The foe oft-times having the foe in sight,
Is tired with standing though they never fight.
Off with that girdle, like heaven's zone glistering,
But a far fairer world encompassing.
Unpin that spangled breastplate which you wear,
Unlace yourself, for that harmonious chime
Tells me from you, that now 'tis your bed time.
Off with that happy busk, which I envy,
That still can be, and still can stand so nigh.
Your gown going off, such beauteous state reveals,

As when from flowery meads th'hill's shadow steals.
Off with that wiry coronet and show
The hairy diadem which on you doth grow;
Now off with those shoes, and then safely tread
In this Love's hallowed temple, this soft bed.
In such white robes heaven's angels used to be
Received by men; thou angel bring'st with thee
A heaven like Mahomet's paradise; and though
Ill spirits walk in white, we easily know
By these angels from an evil sprite,
Those our hairs but these our flesh upright.
    License my roving hands, and let them go
Before, behind, between, above, below.
O my America, my new found land,
My kingdom, safeliest when with one man manned,
My mind of precious stones, my empery,
How blessed am I in this discovering thee!
To enter in these bonds, is to be free;
Then where my hand is set, my seal shall be.
    Full nakedness, all joys are due to thee.
As souls unbodied, bodies unclothed must be,
To taste whole joys. Gems which you women use
Are like Atlanta's balls, cast in men's views,
That when a fool's eye lighteth on a gem,
His earthly soul may covet theirs, not them.
Like pictures, or like books' gay coverings made
For laymen, are all women thus arrayed;
Themselves are mystic books, which only we
Whom their imputed grace will dignify
Must see revealed. Then since I may know
As liberally as to a midwife, show
Thyself: cast all, yea, this white linen hence,
Here is no penance, much less innocence.
    To teach thee, I am naked first, why then
What needst thou have more covering than a man?

164 William Cartwright, *The Works* (1651), p. 471

Women

Give me a girl (if one I needs must meet)
Or in her nuptial, or her winding sheet;
I know but two good hours that women have,
One in the bed, another in the grave.

Thus of the whole sex all I would desire,
Is to enjoy their ashes, or their fire.

165 Andrew Marvell, *Miscellaneous Poems* (1681; written 1650s?), I.27–8

To His Coy Mistress

Had we but world enough and time,
This coyness lady were no crime.
We would sit down, and think which way
To walk, and pass our long love's day.
Thou by the Indian Ganges' side
Should'st rubies find: I by the tide
Of Humber would complain. I would
Love you ten years before the Flood:
And you should if you please refuse
Till the Conversion of the Jews.
My vegetable love should grow
Vaster than empires, and more slow.
An hundred years should go to praise
Thine eyes, and on thy forehead gaze.
Two hundred to adore each breast:
But thirty thousand to the rest.
An age at least to every part,
And the last age should show your heart.
For Lady you deserve this state;
Nor would I love at lower rate.
    But at my back I always hear
Time's winged chariot hurrying near:
And yonder all before us lie
Deserts of vast eternity.
Thy beauty shall no more be found;
Nor, in thy marble vault, shall sound
My echoing song: then worms shall try
That long preserv'd virginity:
And your quaint honour turn to dust;
And into ashes all my lust.
The grave's a fine and private place,
But none I think do there embrace.
    Now therefore, while the youthful hue
Sits on thy skin like morning dew,
And while thy willing soul transpires
At every pore with instant fires,
Now let us sport us while we may;

And now, like am'rous birds of prey,
Rather at once our time devour
Than languish in his slow-chapt pow'r.
Let us roll all our strength, and all
Our sweetness, up into one ball:
And tear our pleasures with rough strife
Through the iron gates of life.
Thus, though we cannot make our sun
Stand still, yet we will make him run.

Part III
'FEMINISMS'

14

CROSS-DRESSING

'The woman shall not wear that which pertaineth unto a man, neither shall a man put on a woman's garment: for all that do so are abominations unto the Lord thy God' (Deut. xxii.5). This Biblical prohibition fuelled the outrage felt at the practice of cross-dressing by either sex: it blurred the God-given demarcation between the sexes. For a man, it was demeaning and shaming since it reduced him to a lesser level (70); in women, it betokened insubordinate self-assertiveness; in either, it was a monstrosity. Despite this, there is some evidence that in the later sixteenth and earlier seventeenth centuries, in particular, there was a marked increase in the practice among women (Faderman (1985), p. 48). James VI and I certainly thought so, and was appalled by it (166), as was the pamphlet *Hic Mulier: or, The Man-Woman* (167). Indeed, it may be that the practice was always more widespread than historians have recognized. Dekker & van de Pol (1989), p. 115, n. 3, believe so, arguing that, while instances of men dressing as women are rare (save on the stage), female cross-dressing amounted almost to a tradition in Northern Europe, particularly among the lower classes, with the great majority of cases involving life as a sailor or soldier (pp. 1, 9, 11, 54).

Usually, the evidence is too slight to determine whether the motivation was romantic, necessitous, criminal or psychosexual, but contemporaries appreciated well enough the political dimension of the practice. In the few discovered, and consequently recorded, cases of lesbian transvestism, the impersonation of a man appears to have been regarded more seriously than the sexual transgression (Faderman (1985), pp. 51–2). This is the burden of Thomas Dekker and Thomas Middleton's dramatization in *The Roaring Girl* (c.1608) of the case of the famous thief Moll Frith, whose defiance and emancipation from social restraint, rather than sexual proclivities, are represented in her masculine dress. By the early seventeenth century the adoption of masculine disguise by troubled heroines (played, of course, by boys) had become a standard comic convention (168, 169), faithfully reflecting the fact that male attire might be tolerated for travelling as both more practical and safer (Dekker and van de Pol (1989), pp. 8, 27). There was also an element of eroticism, both heterosexual and homosexual (Jardine (1983), pp. 9–33). Women were for the first time admitted on to the stage after the Restoration, but in equivocal roles, with 'extraordinary frequency' in 'breeches parts' (Pearson (1988), pp. 100–18; Faderman (1985), pp. 57–8), again offering the male spectator a titillating spectacle (see further Howe (1992)).

In the exceptional circumstances of Civil War, disguise was a commonly adopted temporary expedient, which might be accompanied by a sense of liberation, as it was for Ann Fanshawe (170). It was as a plea for just such an invigorating liberation from constraint and custom that the pamphlet *Hæc-Vir* defended female cross-dressing (171), in answer to the tract *Hic Mulier*. Unhappily, its advocacy is problematized by Hic-Mulier's concluding concession that she would rather dress as a woman would men but dress in their proper habits, which prompts in Hæc-Vir a resolution to reform his manners. *Hæc-Vir*, it seems, is after all quite as convinced as *Hic Mulier* that women should no more dress as men than men as women. It may very well be that both these popular pamphlets were in fact exercises in journalistic opportunism from the same pen, coming as they do in the year of King James's admonition to his clergy.

~

166 John Chamberlain, extract from a letter of 25 January 1620, in *The Chamberlain Letters* (written 1597–1626), p. 271

Yesterday the Bishop of London [John King] called together all his clergy about this town and told them he had express commandment from the King [James I] to will them to inveigh vehemently and bitterly in their sermons against the insolency of our women and their wearing of broad-brimmed hats, pointed doublets, their hair cut short or shorn, and some of them stilettos or poniards, and such other trinkets of like moment, adding withal that if pulpit admonitions will not reform them he would proceed by another course. The truth is the world is very far out of order, but whether this will mend it God knows.

167 Anon, *Hic Mulier* (1620), sigs A3–B4

. . . Come, then, you masculine women, for you are my subject, you that have made admiration an ass, and fooled him with a deformity never before dreamed of, that have made yourselves stranger things than ever Noah's Ark unloaded, or Nile engendered . . . whose like are not found in any antiquary's study, in any seaman's travel, nor in any painter's cunning, you that are stranger than strangeness itself . . . 'Tis of you I entreat, and of your monstrous deformity, you that have made your bodies like antic boscage or crotesco work, not half man, half woman; half fish, half flesh; half beast, half monster; but all odious, all devil, that have cast off the ornaments of your sex, to put on the garments of shame, that have laid by the bashfulness of your natures, to gather the impudence of harlots; that have buried silence, to revive slander; that are all things but that which you should be and nothing less than friends to virtue and goodness . . . exchanging the modest attire of the comely hood, caul, coise [?], handsome dress or kerchief, to the cloudy ruffianly broad-brimmed hat and wanton feather; the modest upper parts of a concealing straight gown to the loose, lascivious civil embracement of a French doublet, being all unbuttoned to entice, all of one shape to hide deformity, and extreme short waisted to give a most easy way to every luxurious action; the glory of a fair large hair to the shame of most ruffianly short locks; the side, thick gathered and close guarding safe-guards to the short, weak, thin, loose and every hand entertaining short bases; for needles, swords; for prayer books, bawdy jigs; for modest gestures, giant-like behaviours; and for women's modesty, all mimic and apish incivility . . .

. . . did ever these mermaids, or rather mer-monsters . . . ever know comeliness or modesty? Fie, no, they never walked in those paths . . . this deformity hath no agreement with goodness, nor no difference [defence?] against the weakest reason. It is all base, all barbarous. Base, in respect it offends man in the example, and God in the most unnatural use. Barbarous, in that it is exorbitant from Nature, and an antithesis to kind, going astray (with ill-favoured affectation) both in attire, in speech, in manners, and (it is to be feared) in the whole courses and stories of their actions. What can be more barbarous than with the gloss of mumming art to disguise the beauty of their creations? To mould their bodies to every deformed fashion, their tongues to vile and horrible profanations, and their hands to ruffianly and uncivil actions? To have their gestures as piebald and as motley various as their disguises, their souls fuller of infirmities than a horse or prostitute, and their minds languishing in those infirmities? If this be not barbarous, make the rude Scythian, the untamed Moor, the naked Indian, or the wild Irish, lords and rulers of well-governed cities . . .

It is an infection that emulates the plague, and throws itself amongst women of all degrees, all deserts, and all ages . . .

. . . such as are able to buy all at their own charges, they swim in the excess of these vanities, and will be man-like not only from the head to the waist but to the very foot, and in every condition: man in bodily attire, man in behaviour by rude compliment, man in nature by aptness to anger, man in action by pursuing revenge, man in wearing weapons, man in using weapons. And, in brief, so much man in all things, that they are neither men, nor women, but just good for nothing . . .

Remember how your Maker made for our first parents coats, not one coat but a coat for the man and a coat for the woman; coats of several fashions, several forms, and for several uses: the man's coat fit for his labour, the

woman's fit for her modesty. And will you lose the model left by this great
workmaster of heaven?

168 William Shakespeare, *As You Like It* (registered 1600), I.iii.105–37

Rosalind	Why, whither shall we go?
Celia	To seek my uncle in the forest of Arden.
Rosalind	Alas, what danger will it be to us,
	Maids as wee are, to travel forth so far!
	Beauty provoketh thieves sooner than gold.
Celia	I'll put myself in poor and mean attire,
	And with a kind of umber smirch my face.
	The like do you, so shall we pass along
	And never stir assailants.
Rosalind	Were it not better,
	Because that I am more than common tall,
	That I did suit me all points like a man,
	A gallant curtal-axe upon my thigh,
	A boar-spear in my hand, and in my heart,
	Lie there what hidden woman's fear there will.
	We'll have a swashing and a martial outside,
	As many other mannish cowards have,
	That do outface it with their semblances . . .
	Let's away,
	And get our jewels and our wealth together,
	Devise the fittest time and safest way
	To hide us from pursuit that will be made
	After my flight. Now go we in content,
	To liberty, and not to banishment.

169 William Shakespeare, *Cymbeline* (written 1610–11?), III.iv.144–68

Pisanio	. . . Now if you could wear a mind
	Dark as your fortune is, and but disguise
	That which t'appear itself must not yet be
	But by self-danger, you should tread a course
	Pretty and full of view . . .
Imogen	O, for such means,
	Though peril to my modesty, not death on't,
	I would venture.
Pisanio	Well, then, here's the point:
	You must forget to be a woman; change

Command into obedience, fear and niceness –
The handmaids of all women, or more truly
Woman it pretty self – into a waggish courage,
Ready in gibes, quick-answered, saucy and
As quarrelous as the weasel. Nay, you must
Forget that rarest treasure of your cheek,
Exposing it – but O! the harder heart! –
Alack, no remedy – to the greedy touch
Of common-kissing Titan, and forget
Your laboursome and dainty trims wherein
You made great Juno angry.

Imogen   Nay, be brief.
I see into thy end, and am almost
A man already.

170 Ann Fanshawe, *Memoirs* (written 1676), pp. 127–8

We pursued our voyage [in 1650, from Galway to Malaga] with prosperous winds, but with a most tempestuous master, a Dutchman, which is enough to say, but truly I think the greatest beast I ever saw of this kind. When we had just passed the Straits [of Gibraltar], we saw coming towards us, with full sail a Turkish galley well mann'd, and we believed we should all be carried away slaves, for this man had so loaden his ship with goods for Spain that his guns were useless, though the ship carried 60 guns. He called for brandy, and after he had well drunken and all his men, which were near 200, he called for arms and cleared the deck as well as he could, resolving to fight rather than lose his ship that was worth £30,000. This was sad for us passengers, but my husband bid us be sure to keep in the cabin and not appear (no woman), which would make the Turks think we were a man-of-war; but if they saw women, they would take us for merchants and board us. He went upon the decks and took a gun and bandoliers and sword, and with the rest of the ship's company stood on the deck expecting the arrival of the Turkish man-of-war. This beast captain had locked me up in the cabin. I knocked and called long to no purpose, until at length a cabin boy came and opened the door. I, all in tears, desired him to be so good as to give me his blue throm cap he wore and his tarred coat, which he did, and I gave him half a crown, and putting them on and flinging away my night's clothes, I crept up softly and stood upon the deck at my husband's side as free from sickness and fear as, I confess, from discretion; but it was the effect of that passion which I could never master. By this time the 2 vessels were engaged in parley and so well satisfied with speech and sight of each other's forces that the Turk's man-of-war tacked about and we continued our course. But when your father saw it convenient to retreat, looking upon me he blessed himself and snatched me up in his arms, saying, 'Good God, that love can make this change!' And though he seemingly chid me, he would laugh at it as often as he remembered that voyage.

171 Anon, *Hæc-Vir* (1620), sigs A3–C4

Hæc-Vir: The Womanish-Man
Hic-Mulier: The Man-Woman

Hæc-Vir. . . . In that book [*Hic Mulier*] you are arraigned and found guilty first, of baseness, in making your self a slave to novelty and the poor invention of every weak brain that hath but an embroidered outside; next, of unnaturalness, to forsake the creation of God, and customs of the kingdom, to be pieced and patched up by a French tailor, an Italian baby-maker, and a Dutch soldier . . .; then, of shamelessness, in casting off all modest softness, and civility, to run thorough every desert and wilderness of men's opinions, like careless untamed heifers or wild savages; lastly, of foolishness, in having no moderation or temper, either in passion or affections . . .

Hic-Mulier.   Well, then, to the purpose. First, you say, I am base, in being a slave to novelty. What slavery can there be in freedom of election? Or what baseness to crown my delights with those pleasures which are most suitable to mine affections? Bondage or slavery is a restraint from those actions which the mind (of its own accord) doth most willingly desire, to perform the intents and purposes of others' dispositions, and that not but by mansuetude or sweetness of entreaty, but by the force of authority and strength of compulsion. Now, for me to follow change according to the limitations of mine own will and pleasure, there cannot be a greater freedom. Nor do I in my delight of change otherwise than as the whole world doth, or as becometh a daughter of the world to do. For what is the world, but a very shop or warehouse of change? Sometimes winter, sometimes summer; day and night; they hold sometimes riches, sometimes poverty, sometimes health, sometimes sickness; now pleasure, presently anguish; now honour, then contempt; and to conclude, there is nothing but change which doth surround and mix withal our fortunes. And will you have poor woman such a fixed star, that she shall not so much as move or twinkle in her own sphere? That were true slavery indeed, and baseness beyond the chains of the worst servitude . . .

But you will say, it is not change but novelty from which you deter us . . . Alas (soft Sir) what can you christen by that new imagined title when the words of the wise man are, 'that what was done, is but done again: all things do change, and under the cope of heaven is no new thing' [Eccles. i.9]. So that whatsoever we do or imitate, it is neither slavish, base nor a breeder of novelty.

Next, you condemn me of unnaturalness in forsaking my creation and contemning custom. How do I forsake my creation, that do all the rights and offices due to my creation? I was created free, born free, and live free; what lets me then so to spin out my time, that I may die free?

To alter creation were to walk on my hands with my heels upward, to feed myself with my feet, or to forsake the sweet sound of sweet words for the hissing noise of the serpent. But I walk with a face erected, with a body clothed, with a mind busied and with a heart full of reasonable and devout cogitations. Only oftentimes in attire, in as much as it is a stranger to the curiosity of the present times, and an enemy to custom. Are we then bound to be the flatterers of time, or the dependents on custom? O miserable servitude, chained only to baseness and folly! For than custom nothing is more absurd, nothing more foolish . . .

But you say we are barbarous and shameless and cast off all softness to run wild through a wilderness of opinions. In this you express more cruelty than in all the rest, because I stand not with my hands on my belly like a baby at Bartholomew Fair, that move not my whole body when I should but only stir my head like Jack of the Clock house which hath no joints, that am not dumb when wantons court me, as if ass-like I were ready for all burdens, or because I weep not when injury grips me, like worried deer in the fangs of many curs: am I therefore barbarous or shameless? He is much injurious that so baptised us. We are as free-born as men, have as free election, and as free spirits, we are compounded of like parts, and may with like liberty make benefit of our creations. My countenance shall smile on the worthy, and frown on the ignoble; I will hear the wise, and be deaf to idiots, give counsel to my friend but be dumb to flatterers; I have hands that shall be liberal to reward desert, feet that shall move swiftly to do good offices, and thoughts that shall ever accompany freedom and severity. If this be barbarous, let me leave the city and live with creatures of like simplicity . . .

Hæc-Vir. You have wrested out some wit to wrangle forth no reason, since everything you would make for excuse approves your guilt still more ugly. What baser bondage, or what more servile baseness, than for the flattering and soothing of an unbridled appetite or delight, to take a wilful liberty to do evil, and to give evil example? This is to be Hell's apprentice, not Heaven's free woman. It is disputable amongst our divines whether upon any occasion a woman may put on man's attire, or no. All conclude it is unfit, and the most indifferent will allow it but only to escape persecution. Now, you will not only put it on, but wear it continually, and not wear it, but take pride in it . . .

. . . So that notwithstanding your elaborate plea for freedom, your severe condemnation of custom, your fair promises of civil actions, and your temperate avoiding of excess, whereby you would seem to hug and embrace discretion, yet . . . you shall never lose the title of baseness, unnaturalness, shamelessness and foolishness . . . if you will walk without difference, you

249

shall live without reverence; if you will contemn order, you must endure the shame of disorder; and if you will have no rulers but your wills, you must have no reward but disdain and disgrace . . .

Hic-Mulier. . . . till you will be pleased to be cleansed of that leprosy which I see apparent in you, give me leave to doubt whether mine infection be so contagious as your blind severity would make it.

Therefore to take your proportion in a few lines (my dear Feminine Masculine) tell me what character, prescription or right of claim you have to those things you make your absolute inheritance? Why do you curl, frizzle and powder your hairs . . .? Why do you rob us of our ruffs, of our earrings, carcanets and mamillions, of our fans and feathers, our busks and French bodices . . .? . . . Fie, you have gone a world further, and even ravished from us our speech, our actions, sports and recreations . . . where are the tilts and tourneys, and lofty galliards that were danced in the days of old? . . . Tut, tut, all's forsaken, all's vanished . . . To see one of your gender either show himself . . . at a playhouse, or public assembly, how (before he dare enter) . . . he takes a full survey of himself, from the highest sprig in his feather to the lowest spangle that shines in his shoe-string, how he prunes and picks himself like a hawk set a weathering . . . to see him pluck and tug everything into the form of the newest received fashion . . . and lastly, to see him cast himself amongst the eyes of the people (as an object of wonder) with more niceness than a virgin goes to the sheets of her first lover, would make patience herself mad . . .

Now, since according to your own inference, even by the laws of Nature, by the rules of religion and the customs of all civil nations, it is necessary there be a distinct and special difference between man and woman, both in their habit and behaviour, what could we poor, weak women do less (being far too weak by force to fetch back those spoils you have unjustly taken from us) than to gather up those garments you have proudly cast away, and therewith to clothe both our bodies and our minds . . .? . . . Hence, we have preserved (though to our own harms) those manly things which you have forsaken, which would you again accept, and restore to us the blushes we laid by, when first we put on your masculine garments, doubt not but chaste thoughts and bashfulness will again dwell in us . . .

. . . Cast then from you our ornaments and put on your own armours. Be men in shape, men in show, men in words, men in actions, men in counsel, men in example; then will we love and serve you; then will we hear and obey you; then will we like rich jewels hang at your ears to take our instructions, like true friends follow you through all dangers, and like careful leeches pour oil into your wounds. Then shall you find delight in our words, pleasure in our faces, faith in our hearts, chastity in our thoughts, and sweetness both in our inward and outward inclinations. Comeliness shall be our study, fear our armour, and modesty our practice. Then shall we be all your most excellentest thoughts can desire, and have nothing in us less than impudence and deformity.

Hæc-Vir. Enough. You have both raised mine eyelids, cleared my sight, and made my heart entertain both shame and delight at an instant: shame in my follies past; delight in our noble and worthy conversion. Away from me these light vanities, the only ensigns of a weak and soft nature, and come you grave and solid pieces which arm a man with fortitude and resolution. You are too rough and stubborn for a woman's wearing. We will here change our attires, as we have changed our minds, and with our attires, our names. I will no more be *Hæc-Vir* but *Hic Vir*, nor you *Hic-Mulier* but *Hæc Mulier*. From henceforth, deformity shall pack to Hell . . .

15

WIDOWHOOD, CELIBACY AND FEMALE FRIENDSHIP

In the Roman Catholic tradition virginity and monasticism offered women a possible, and highly esteemed, alternative to the role of wife and mother; no such clearly recognized alternative existed in Protestant England. Provided she did not betray a lustful nature by seeking remarriage (172), a widow enjoyed some status (for an exemplary widowhood, see 88), and some independence, being vested in common law with dower, a third of her husband's estate (173), until this was abolished by statute in 1692 (Houl-brooke (1984), p. 210), but an unmarried woman was an anomaly with no defined role or position. 'Old maid' was a name of 'scorn' (179), as was noted by Richard Allestree, an episcopalian who rather regretted the abolition of the monasteries at the Reformation (174; contrast Burton in 17). Celibacy and the attractions of female company and friendship do, however, become marked literary themes from the 1650s onward, allowing the contemplation, if not the enjoyment, of an alternative emotional and social order. By the early eighteenth century, a tradition of romantic female friendship was a fact of higher class life as well as of letters (Faderman (1985), pp. 65–143). The key figure in establishing this tradition of Platonic affection was Katherine Philips, 'the matchless Orinda', both through her 'Society of Friendship', a literary coterie of Royalists who in the 1650s continued the ideals of Platonic love, honour and elaborate manners fostered at court by Henrietta Maria (on which see Thomas, ed. (1990–2), i.7–12), and, more influentially, through the celebration of female friendship in her poetry. Hers is a poetry which explicitly prefers virginity to heterosexual love, celibacy to marriage (175). It finds in the 'happy quiet' of female friendship a security and emotional fulfilment which the changing and inconstant patriarchal world cannot provide (176).

Exalting female friendship might be a way of expressing lesbian feelings in a culture which could barely conceive, and hardly had a word for, sexual relations between women. The *Oxford English Dictionary* can find only one citation for *tribade* before the late nineteenth century (Dekker and van de Pol (1989), pp. 55–8). Evidence for lesbian relationships in this period is consequently very scarce (see Mueller (1993), p. 192). Faderman (1985), p. 68, is confident that had Philips lived in the twentieth century her poetry 'would undoubtedly have been identified as "lesbian"'. Philips can address women in the ardent manner of the seventeenth-century heterosexual love lyric (177; Faderman (1985), pp. 69–71), often echoing Donne, but there is an inescapably Platonic insistence in her poetry that female friendship is attractive precisely because its experience is 'calm as a virgin' (178).

In the last decades of the century these concepts and motifs are deployed by other female poets, sometimes with a sharper satirical and political edge (179). The pastoral tradition was particularly serviceable to them: as in Renaissance pastoral the male lover had retreated to idyllic scenes for emotional solace after disappointment by women, so now women escape from the impositions of men (180). The desire to escape 'tyrant man' leads Anne Finch into something very like a Romantic preference for Nature over society in a poem of (at this date) extraordinary particularity and sensitivity to natural phenomena (181).

172 Sir Thomas Overbury, *A Wife* (1614), pp. 70–2

A Virtuous Widow

Is the palm-tree, that thrives not after supplanting of her husband. For her children's sake she first marries; for she married that she might have children; and for their sakes she marries no more. She is like the purest gold, only employed for princes' medals: she never receives but one man's impression. The largest jointure moves her not, titles of honour cannot sway her. To change her name were (she thinks) to commit a sin should make her ashamed of her husband's calling. She thinks she hath travelled all the world in one man; the rest of her time, therefore, she directs to heaven. Her main superstition is, she thinks her husband's ghost would walk, should she not perform his will. She would do it were there no prerogative Court. She gives much to pious uses, without any hope to merit by them; and as one diamond fashions another, so is she wrought into works of charity, with the dust or ashes of her husband. She lives to see herself full of time; being so necessary for earth, God calls her not to heaven till she be very aged, and even then, though her natural strength fail her, she stands like an ancient pyramid, which, the less it grows to man's eyes, the nearer it reaches to heaven. This latter chastity of hers is more grave and reverend than that ere she was married, for in it is neither hope, nor longing, nor fear, nor jealousy. She ought to be a mirror for our youngest dames to dress themselves by, when she is fullest of wrinkles. No calamity can now come near her, for in suffering the loss of her husband she accounts all the rest trifles. She hath laid his dead body in the worthiest monument that can be: she hath buried it in her one heart. To conclude, she is a relic, that, without any superstition in the world, though she will not be kissed, yet may be reverenced.

An Ordinary Widow

Is like the herald's hearse-cloth; she serves to many funerals, with a very little altering the colour. The end of her husband begins in tears, and the end of her tears begins in a husband. She uses to cunning women to know how many husbands she shall have, and never marries without the consent of six midwives. Her chiefest pride is in the multitudes of her suitors, and by them she gains; for one serves to draw on another, and with one at last she shoots out another, as boys do pellets in eldern guns. She commends to them a single life, as horse-coursers do their jades, to put them away. Her fancy is to one of the biggest of the Guard, but knighthood makes her draw in in a weaker bow. Her servants or kinsfolk are the trumpeters that summon any to this combat. By them she gains much credit, but loseth it again in the old proverb, *Fama est mendax*. If she live to be thrice married, she seldom fails to cozen her second husband's creditors. A churchman she dare not venture upon, for she hath heard widows complain of dilapidations; nor a soldier, though he had candle-rents in the city, for his estate may be subject to fire; very seldom a lawyer, without he shows his exceeding great practice, and can make her case the better; but a knight with the old rent may do much, for a great coming in is all in all with a widow, ever provided that most part of her plate and jewels (before the wedding) be concealed with her scrivener. Thus, like a too-ripe apple, she falls off herself; but he that hath her is lord but of a filthy purchase, for the title is cracked. Lastly, while she is a widow, observe her, she is no morning woman; the evening, a good fire and sack may make her listen to a husband, and if ever she be made sure, 'tis upon a full stomach to bedward.

173 [T[homas] E[dgar] (ed.], *The Lawes Resolutions of Womens Rights* (1632), pp. 90, 93, 106–7

Of Dower

I have hitherto handled only those gifts [dowries] . . . which come from women or their ancestors, as if English men were so dainty and coy that they must be enticed, or our women so unamiable that unless it were by purchase, they could have no husbands. But I could never hear of any woman that needed [to] buy new boots to ride on wooing. Contrariwise, so sweet, fair and pleasing are they, or so very good and prudent . . . that though some men get lands by them, most men are fain to assure part, or all of such lands as they have (in jointure or otherwise) to them, ere they can win their love, and where there is no such assurance, the Christian custom and law of the realm giveth every good wife part of her husband's lands to live on when he is dead, which we call dower . . .

How Much and How a Woman shall Hold in Dower

The Common Law alloweth for dower the third part of that whereof the husband during coverture has such seisin as is before declared to have and hold (if it be in land) by limits and bounds . . .

Less or more than a Third Part

Though by the Common Law a woman is to have no less than a third part, yet if a widow will be so foolish as to accept a fourth or fifth part or moiety of her husband's inheritance . . . it is a good assignment . . .

174 [Richard Allestree], *The Ladies Calling* (1673), p. 145

As for the religious orders of virgins in the present Roman Church, though some and those very great abuses have crept in, yet I think it were to be wished, that those who suppressed them in this nation, had confined themselves within the bounds of a reformation, by choosing rather to rectify and regulate than abolish them. But though there be not among us such societies, yet there may be nuns who are not professed . . . But . . . women are so little transported with this zeal of voluntary virginity, that there are few can find patience for it when necessary. An old maid is now thought such a curse, as no poetic fury can exceed, looked on as the most calamitous creature in Nature . . . but sure the original of that misery is from the desire, not the restraint, of marriage: let them but suppress that once, and the other will never be their infelicity.

175 Katherine Philips, *Poems* (1667), I.254

A Married State

A married state affords but little ease:
The best of husbands are so hard to please.
This in wives' careful faces you may spell,
Tho' they dissemble their misfortunes well.
A virgin state is crown'd with much content,
It's always happy as it's innocent.
No blustering husbands to create your fears,
No pangs of child birth to extort your tears,
No children's cries for to offend your ears,
Few worldly crosses to distract your prayers.

Thus are you freed from all the cares that do
Attend on matrimony and a husband too.
Therefore, madam, be advised by me:
Turn, turn apostate to love's levity.
Suppress wild nature if she dare rebel,
There's no such thing as leading apes in hell.

176 Katherine Philips, *Poems* (1667), I.97–8

A Retired Friendship, to Ardelia

1

Come, my Ardelia, to this bower,
  Where kindly mingling souls a while,
Let's innocently spend an hour,
  And at all serious follies smile.

2

Here is no quarrelling for crowns,
  Nor fear of changes in our fate;
No trembling at the great ones' frowns,
  Nor any slavery to state.

3

Here's no disguise, nor treachery,
  Nor any deep conceal'd design;
From blood and plots this place is free,
  And calm as are those looks of thine.

4

Here let us sit, and bless our stars
  Who did such happy quiet give,
As that remov'd from noise of wars
  In one another's hearts we live.

5

Why should we entertain a fear?
  Love cares not how the world is turn'd:
If crowds of dangers should appear,
  Yet friendship can be unconcern'd.

6

We wear about us such a charm,
  No horror can be our offence;
For mischief's self can do no harm
  To friendship and to innocence.

7

Let's mark how soon Apollo's beams
   Command the flocks to quit their meat,
And not entreat the neighbour-streams
   To quench their thirst, but cool their heat.

8

In such a scorching age as this,
   Whoever would not seek a shade
Deserve their happiness to miss,
   As having their own peace betray'd.

9

But we (of one another's mind
   Assur'd,) the boisterous world disdain:
With quiet souls, and unconfin'd,
   Enjoy what princes wish in vain.

177 Katherine Philips, *Poems* (1667), I.121–2

To My Excellent Lucasia, on our Friendship. 17th. July 1651

I did not live until this time
   Crown'd my felicity,
When I could say without a crime,
   I am not thine, but thee.
This carcass breath'd, and walk'd, and slept,
   So that the world believ'd
There was a soul the motions kept;
   But they were all deceiv'd.
For as a watch by art is wound
   To motion, such was mine:
But never had Orinda found
   A soul till she found thine;
Which now inspires, cures and supplies,
   And guides my darken'd breast:
For thou art all that I can prize,
   My joy, my life, my rest.
Nor bridegrooms nor crown'd conqu'rors' mirth
   To mine compar'd can be:
They have but pieces of this earth,
   I've all the world in thee.
Then let our flame still light and shine,
   (And no bold fear control)
As innocent as our design,
   Immortal as our soul.

178 Katherine Philips, *Poems* (1667), I.150–1

Friendship

Let the dull brutish world that know not love
Continue heretics, and disapprove
That noble flame; but the refined know
'Tis all the heaven we have here below.
Nature subsists by love, and they tie
Things to their causes but by sympathy.
Love chains the differing elements in one
Great harmony, link'd to the heavenly throne;
And as on earth, so the blest choir above
Of saints and angels are maintain'd by love;
That is their business and felicity,
And will be so to all eternity.
That is the ocean, our affections here
Are but streams borrow'd from the fountain there;
And 'tis the noblest argument to prove
A beauteous mind, that it knows how to love.
Those kind impressions which fate can't control,
Are heaven's mintage on a worthy soul;
For love is all the arts epitome,
And is the sum of all divinity.
He's worse than beast that cannot love, and yet
It is not bought by money, pains or wit;
So no chance nor design can spirits move,
But the eternal destiny of love.
  For when two souls are chang'd and mixed so,
It is what they and none but they can do;
And this is friendship, that abstracted flame
Which creeping mortals know not how to name.
All love is sacred and the marriage tie
Hath much of honour and divinity;
But lust, design, or some unworthy ends
May mingle there, which are despis'd by friends.
Passion hath violent extremes, and thus,
All oppositions are contiguous.
So when the end is serv'd the love will bate,
If friendship make it not more fortunate:
Friendship! that love's elixir, that pure fire
Which burns the clearer 'cause it burns the higher;
For love, like earthly fires (which will decay
If the material fuel be away)
Is with offensive smoke accompanied,

258

And by resistance only is supplied:
But friendship, like the fiery element,
With its own heat and nourishment content,
(Where neither hurt, nor smoke, nor noise is made)
Scorns the assistance of a foreign aid.
Friendship (like heraldry) is hereby known:
Richest when plainest, bravest when alone;
Calm as a virgin, and more innocent
Than sleeping doves are, and as much content
As saints in visions; quiet as the night,
But clear and open as the summer's light;
United more than spirits faculties,
Higher in thoughts than are the eagle's eyes;
Free as first agents are true friends, and kind,
As but themselves I can no likeness find.

179 Jane Barker, *Poetical Recreations* (1688), pp. 360–1

A Virgin Life

Since gracious heaven, you have bestow'd on me
So great a kindness for virginity,
Suffer me not, to fall into the power,
Of man's, almost omnipotent amour.
But in this happy state, let me remain,
And in chaste verse, my chaster thoughts explain.
Fearless of twenty-five and all its rage,
When time and beauty endless wars engage,
And fearless of the antiquated name*,
Which oft makes happy maid turn helpless dame,
The scorn fix'd to that name our sex betray,
And often makes us fling ourselves away.
Like harmless kids which are pursu'd by men,
For safety run into a lion's den.
Ah lovely state how strange it is to see,
What mad conceptions, some have made of thee.
As if thy being was all wretchedness,
Or foul deformity i'th'ugliest dress,
Whereas thy beauty's pure, celestial,
Thy thoughts divine, thy words angelical:
And such ought all thy votaries to be,
Or else they're so, but for necessity
A virgin bears the impress of all good,

---

* old maid

Under that name, all virtue's understood.
To equal all her looks her mien, her dress
That nought but modesty, seems in excess.
When virgins any treats or visits make,
'Tis not for tattle, but for friendships sake,
The neighbouring poor are her adopted heirs,
And less she cares, for her own good than theirs.
And by obedience testifies she can
Be's good a subject as the stoutest man.
She to her church, such filial duty pays,
That one would think she'd liv'd i'th'pristine days.
Her whole life's business, she drives to these ends,
To serve her God, her neighbour, and her friends.

180 [Anne Finch], *Miscellany Poems* (1713; written *post* 1685), pp. 33–49

From: *The Petition for an Absolute Retreat*

Give me, O indulgent Fate!
Give me but before I die
A sweet, but absolute retreat,
'Mongst paths so lost and trees so high
That the world may ne'er invade
Through such windings and such shade
My unshaken liberty.

   No intruders thither come
Who visit but to be from home;
None who their vain moments pass
Only studious of their glass . . .
Be no tidings thither brought,
But silent as a midnight thought
Where the world may ne'er invade
Be those windings and that shade! . . .

   Give me there (since Heaven has shown
It was not good to be alone)
A partner suited to my mind,
Solitary, pleased and kind;
Who partially may something see
Preferred to all the world in me;
Slighting, by my humble side,
Fame and splendour, wealth and pride.
When but two the earth possessed,
'Twas their happiest days, and best;

They by business, nor by wars,
They by no domestic cares,
From each other e'er were drawn,
But in some grove or flowery lawn
Spent the swiftly flying time,
Spent their own and Nature's prime,
In love: that only passion given
To perfect man, whilst friends with Heaven.
Rage, and jealousy, and hate,
Transports of his fallen state,
(When by Satan's wiles betrayed)
Fly those windings, and that shade!

   Thus, from crowds and noise removed,
Let each moment be improved . . . . . .
Friendship still has been designed,
The support of human-kind;
The safe delight, the useful bliss,
The next world's happiness, and this.
Give then, O indulgent Fate!
Give a friend in that retreat
(Though withdrawn from all the rest)
Still a clue, to reach my breast.
Let a friend be still convey'd
Through those windings, and that shade! . . .

   Give me, O indulgent Fate!
For all the pleasures left behind
Contemplations of the mind.
Let the fair, the gay, the vain,
Courtship and applause obtain;
Let th'ambitious rule the earth;
Let the giddy fool have mirth;
Give the epicure his dish,
Every one their several wish;
Whilst my transports I employ
On that more extensive joy,
When all Heaven shall be surveyed
From those windings, and that shade.

181 [Anne Finch], *Miscellany Poems* (1713; written *post* 1685), pp. 291–3

A Nocturnal Reverie

In such a night, when every louder wind
Is to its distant cavern safe confined;

And only gentle zephyr fans his wings,
And lonely Philomel, still waking, sings;
Or from some tree, famed for the owl's delight,
She, hollowing clear, directs the wanderer right;
In such a night, when passing clouds give place,
Or thinly veil the heaven's mysterious face;
When in some river, overhung with green,
The waving moon and trembling leaves are seen;
When freshened grass now bears itself upright,
And makes cool banks to pleasing rest invite,
Whence springs the woodbine and the bramble-rose,
And where the sleepy cowslip sheltered grows;
Whilst now a paler hue the foxglove takes,
Yet chequers still with red the dusky brakes:
When scattered glow-worms, but in twilight fine,
Show trivial beauties watch their hour to shine;
Whilst Salisbury stands the test of every light,
In perfect charms and perfect virtue bright.
When odours which declined repelling day,
Through temperate air uninterrupted stray;
When darkened groves their softest shadows wear,
And falling waters we distinctly hear;
When through the gloom more venerable shows
Some ancient fabric, awful in repose,
While sunburnt hills their swarthy looks conceal,
And swelling haycocks thicken up the vale:
When the loosed horse now, as his pasture leads,
Comes slowly grazing through th' adjoining meads,
Whose stealing pace, and lengthened shade we fear,
Till torn-up forage in his teeth we hear:
When nibbling sheep at large pursue their food,
And unmolested kine rechew the cud;
When curlews cry beneath the village walls,
And to her straggling brood the partridge calls;
Their short-lived jubilee the creatures keep,
Which but endures whilst tyrant man does sleep:
When a sedate content the spirit feels,
And no fierce light disturbs, whilst it reveals;
But silent musings urge the mind to seek
Something, too high for syllables to speak;
Till the free soul to a composedness charmed,
Finding the elements of rage disarmed,
O'er all below a solemn quiet grown,
Joys in th' inferior world, and thinks it like her own:

In such a night let me abroad remain,
Till morning breaks, and all's confused again;
Our cares, our toils, our clamours are renewed,
Or pleasures, seldom reached, again pursued.

16

AUTHORSHIP

Women who appeared in print in the seventeenth century almost invariably prefaced their texts with some form of apology for their transgression in speaking with a public voice when silent retirement was proper and becoming a woman. 'I am', admits Anne Bradstreet, 'obnoxious to each carping tongue / Who says my hand a needle better fits' (182). Apology was needed also since female authors were only too well aware that by education and upbringing, if not by sex, they had been ill-fitted for essaying this role. Even when fulfilling a maternal duty, Elizabeth Jocelin feels it necessary to explain why, knowing her 'weakness', she nevertheless appears as an author (183). A similar apprehensiveness prompts the preface to her posthumous book to reassure readers that her literary endeavours were 'chaste and modest' and to insist that they did not detract from her proper fulfilment of her wifely role (75). Dorothy Leigh similarly explains why she has had the 'boldness' to do something 'so unusual among us' as to change 'the usual order of women' by writing (184). She tactfully concedes to men 'the first and chief place', just as Anne Bradstreet seeks to win a hearing by judiciously conceding the inevitability of male pre-eminence (182). Evidence of hostility towards women who, in Lovelace's phrase (perhaps with reference to Margaret Cavendish), prostituted themselves in public (185), is not hard to locate. 'Whore is scarce a more reproachful name, / Than poetess' declares Rochester (186). Anne Killigrew learned that publication by a woman brought 'shame', not 'honour', and, since she was a woman, also the charge of plagiarism (187). Ezell (1987) argues, however, that literary composition was a more generally available option for women than this hostility to publication and their own printed apologias might suggest (see esp. pp. 62–100).

The difficulties of self-conception and self-awareness confronted by a woman who published are exemplified by the inconsistencies in the persona of Margaret Cavendish's autobiographical essay (188). She seeks to present herself as a traditionally compliant and retiring wife even as the act of writing demonstrates her to be nothing of the sort. Though she states that hers is mere 'scribble' compared to her husband's 'writing', though she claims to find happiness only in his company and to prefer 'contemplation' to communication, she nevertheless grants herself a public voice and escapes from the domestic sphere through the act of publication. In truth, she prefers 'to write with the pen than to work with a needle' but there is no socially acceptable way to articulate that preference; the author must finally justify herself not as a writer but as her husband's wife (see further Gallagher (1988), pp. 25–33; Keeble (forthcoming)). She much more confidently empowers herself as an author in her fiction *The New Blazing World*, not only through the scheme of the narrative in which the Duchess herself appears as the Platonic friend and soul-mate of an Empress who assumes and exercises supreme political power, but also in her explicit prefatory aspiration to become 'Margaret the First', in the imaginative freedom with which she 'makes a world of her own invention' within the text, and in the absolute authority the epilogue grants her as 'Authoress of a whole world' (189; see further Lilley (1992)).

Margaret Cavendish was not much regarded by her own age, save as unusually preposterous even for a woman. With Katherine Philips (probably Lovelace's Sappho (185)) it was different. Although in the 1680s and 1690s Anne Killigrew still encountered hostility (187) and Anne Finch had still to apologize for her temerity as a woman 'attempting the pen' (190), the example of Orinda did much to make writing, if not publishing, especially in verse, respectable for women later in the century (191), since hers were such unexceptionably virtuous texts. The preface to the first edition of her poems had prudently stressed her virtue as much as her poetic skills (192). The inspiration she was to other women poets is illustrated by 'Philo-Philippa', though her improbable characterization of Orinda as 'fearless' and 'manly' serves satiric and subversive purposes which would have appalled Philips herself (193). (The standard account of seventeenth-century English women's authorship in all genres is Hobby (1988), where see pp. 1–25 for a description of the cultural context, on which Ezell (1987) should also be consulted; for poetry, see Greer *et al.* (1988), pp. 1–31; and for biography and fiction, see Perry (1980); Spencer (1986), esp. pp. 3–74; Spender (1986), esp. pp. 11–111; Todd (1989), esp. pp. 13–98. Wilson and Warnke (1989), pp. xi–xxiii, discuss women's writing throughout Europe.)

---

182 Anne Bradstreet, *The Tenth Muse* (1650), pp. 15–17

The Prologue

To sing of wars, of captains, and of kings
Of cities founded, commonwealths begun,
For my mean pen are too superior things:
Or how they all, or each their dates have run

Let poets and historians set these forth,
My obscure line shall not so dim their worth.

But when my wond'ring eyes and envious heart
Great Bartas' sugared lines do but read o'er,
Fool I do grudge the Muses did not part
'Twixt him and me that overfluent store;
A Bartas can do what a Bartas will
But simple I according to my skill.

From schoolboy's tongue no rhet'ric we expect,
Nor yet a sweet consort from broken strings,
Nor perfect beauty where's a main defect:
My foolish, broken, blemished Muse so sings,
And this to mend, alas, no art is able,
'Cause nature made it so irreparable.

Nor can I, like that fluent sweet tongued Greek,
Who lisped at first, in future times speak plain.
By art he gladly found what he did seek,
A full requital of his striving pain.
Art can do much, but this maim's most sure:
A weak or wounded brain admits no cure.

I am obnoxious to each carping tongue
Who says my hand a needle better fits,
A poet's pen all scorn I should thus wrong;
For such despite they cast on female wits:
If what I do prove well, it won't advance,
They'll say it's stol'n, or else it was by chance.

But sure the antique Greeks were far more mild
Else of our sex, why feigned they those nine
And poesy made Calliope's own child;
So 'mongst the rest they placed the arts divine:
But this weak knot they will full soon untie,
The Greeks did nought, but play the fools and lie.

Let Greeks be Greeks, and women what they are
Men have precedency and still excel,
It is but vain unjustly to wage war;
Men can do best, and women know it well.
Pre-eminence in all and each is yours;
Yet grant some small acknowledgement of ours.

And oh ye high flown quills that soar the skies,
And ever with your prey still catch your praise,
If e'er you deign these lowly lines your eyes,

Give thyme or parsley wreath, I ask no bays;
This mean and unrefined ore of mine
Will make your glist'ring gold but more to shine.

183 Elizabeth Jocelin, *The Mothers Legacie* (1624), sigs B1–B3v

To My Truly Loving and Most Dearly Loved Husband, Tourell Jocelin

Mine own dear love, I no sooner conceived an hope that I should be made a mother by thee, but with it entered the consideration of a mother's duty, and shortly after followed the apprehension of danger that might prevent me from executing that care I so exceedingly desired, I mean in religious training our child. And in truth, death appearing in this shape was doubly terrible unto me. First, in respect of the painfulness of that kind of death, and next of the loss my little one should have in wanting me . . .

Yet still I thought there was some good office I might do for my child more than only to bring it forth (though it should please God to take me). When I considered our frailty, our apt inclination to sin, the Devil's subtlety, and the world's deceitfulness, against these how much desired I to admonish it? But still it came into my mind that death might deprive me of time if I should neglect the present. I knew not what to do. I thought of writing, but then mine own weakness appeared so manifestly that I was ashamed, and durst not undertake it. But when I could find no other means to express my motherly zeal, I encouraged my self with these reasons:

First, that I wrote to a child, and though I were but a woman, yet to a child's judgement, what I understood might serve for a foundation to better learning.

Again, I considered it was to my own, and in private sort, and my love to my own might excuse my errors.

And lastly, but chiefly, that my intent was good, and that I was well assured God is the prosperer of good purposes.

Thus resolved, I writ this ensuing letter to our little one, to whom I could not find a fitter hand to convey it than thine own . . .

184 Dorothy Leigh, *The Mothers Blessing* (1616), pp. 1–6, 17

Chap. 1. The Occasion of Writing this Book was the Consideration of the Care of Parents for their Children

My children, when I did truly weigh, rightly consider, and perfectly see the great care, labour, travail and continual study which parents take to enrich their children . . . I thought good (being not desirous to enrich you with transitory goods) to exhort and desire you to follow the counsel of Christ: 'First seek the kingdom of God . . .' (Matt. vi.33).

Chap. 2. The First Cause of Writing is a Motherly Affection

But lest you should marvel, my children, why I do not, according to the usual custom of women, exhort you by word and admonitions, rather than by writing, a thing so unusual among us, and, especially in such a time, when there be so many godly books in the world . . . know . . . that it was the motherly affection that I bear unto you all, which made me now (as it often hath hitherto) forget myself in regard of you: neither care I what you or any shall think of me, if among many words I may write but one sentence which may make you labour for the spiritual good of the soul . . .

Chap. 5. The Third Cause is to Move Women to be Careful of their Children

The third is to encourage women (who, I fear, will blush at my boldness) not to be ashamed to show their infirmities, but to give men the first and chief place, yet let us labour to come in the second; and because we must needs confess that sin entered by us into our posterity, let us show how careful we are to seek to Christ to cast it out of us and our posterity, and how fearful we are that our sin should sink any of them to the lowest part of the earth. Wherefore, let us call upon them to follow Christ, who will carry them to the height of heaven.

185 Richard Lovelace, *Lucasta: Posthume Poems* (1659), pp. 199–200

From: *On Sannazar's being Honoured with Six Hundred Duckets by the Clarissimi of Venice, for composing an Elegiac Hexastich of the City*

A SATIRE

. . . Arise thou rev'rend shade, great Jonson rise!
Breakthrough thy marble natural disguise . . .
How would thy masc'line spirit, father Ben,
Sweat to behold basely deposed men,
Jostled from the prerog'tive of their bed,
Whilst wives are per'wig'd with their husbands' head.
Each snatches the male quill from his faint hand
And must both nobler write and understand,
He to her fury the soft plume doth bow,
O Pen, ne'er truly justly slit till now!
Now as her self a poem she doth dress,
And curls a line as she would do a tress;
Then prostitutes them both to public air.
Nor is't enough that they their faces blind
With a false dye, but they must paint their mind;
In metre scold, and in scann'd order brawl,
Yet there's one Sappho left may save them all.

186 John Wilmot, extract from *A Letter from Artemiza in the Town*
to Chloe in the Country **(1679), p. 83 (ll. 1–31)**

Chloe, in verse by your command I write;
Shortly you'll bid me ride astride, and fight.
These talents better with our sex agree,
Than lofty flights of dang'rous poetry.
Amongst the men (I mean) the men of wit
(At least they passed for such, before they writ)
How many bold advent'rers for the bays
(Proudly designing large returns of praise)
Who durst that stormy pathless world explore,
Were soon dash'd back, and wreck'd on the dull shore,
Broke of that little stock, they had before?
How would a woman's tott'ring bark be toss'd,
Where stoutest ships (the men of wit) are lost?
When I reflect on this I straight grow wise,
And my own self thus gravely I advise.
Dear Artemiza, poetry's a snare:
Bedlam has many mansions: have a care.
Your Muse diverts you, makes the reader sad;
You fancy, you're inspired, he thinks, you mad.
Consider too, 'twill be discreetly done,
To make yourself the fiddle of the Town,
To find th'ill-humour'd pleasure at their need,
Curs'd, if you fail, and scorn'd, though you succeed.
Thus, like an arrant woman, as I am,
No sooner well convinc'd, writing's a shame,
That whore is scarce a more reproachful name,
Than poetess:
Like men, that marry, or like maids, that woo,
'Cause 'tis the very worst thing they can doe,
Pleas'd with the contradiction, and the sin,
Methinks, I stand on thorns, till I begin . . .

187 Anne Killigrew, *Poems* **(1686), pp. 44–7**

Upon the Saying that my Verses were Made by Another

Next heaven my vows to thee (O sacred Muse!)
I offer'd up, nor didst thou them refuse.

   O Queen of Verse, said I, if thou'lt inspire,
And warm my soul with thy poetic fire,
No love of gold shall share with thee my heart,

Or yet ambition in my breast have part,
More rich, more noble I will ever hold
The Muses' laurel, than a crown of gold.
An undivided sacrifice I'll lay
Upon thine altar, soul and body pay;
Thou shalt my pleasure, my employment be,
My All I'll make a holocaust to thee.

    The Deity that ever does attend
Prayers so sincere, to mine did condescend.
I writ, and the judicious prais'd my pen:
Could any doubt ensuing glory then?
What pleasing raptures fill'd my ravish'd sense?
How strong, how sweet, Fame, was thy influence?
And thine, false Hope, that to my flatter'd sight
Didst glories represent so near, and bright?
By thee deceiv'd, methought, each verdant tree,
Apollo's transform'd Daphne seem'd to be;
And ev'ry fresher branch, and ev'ry bough
Appear'd as garlands to impale my brow.
The learn'd in love say, 'Thus the Winged Boy
Does first approach, dress'd up in welcome joy;
At first he to the cheated lovers' sight
Nought represents, but rapture and delight,
Alluring hopes, soft fears, which stronger bind
Their hearts, than when they more assurance find'.

    Embolden'd thus, to fame I did commit,
(By some few hands) my most unlucky wit.
But, ah, the sad effects that from it came!
What ought t'have brought my honour, brought me shame!
Like Æsop's painted jay I seem'd to all.
Adorn'd in plumes, I not my own could call:
Rifl'd like her, each one my feathers tore,
And, as they thought, unto the owner bore.
My laurels thus another's brow adorn'd,
My numbers they admir'd, but me they scorn'd:
Another's brow, that had so rich a store
Of sacred wreaths, that circled it before;
Where mine quite lost, (like a small stream that ran
Into a vast and boundless ocean)
Was swallow'd up, with that it join'd and drown'd,
And that abyss yet no accession found.

    Orinda, (Albion's and her sex's grace)
Ow'd not her glory to a beauteous face,

It was her radiant soul that shone within,
Which struck a lustre through her outward skin;
That did her lips and cheeks with roses dye,
Advanc'd her height, and sparkled in her eye.
Nor did her sex at all obstruct her fame,
But higher 'mong the stars it fix'd her name;
What she did write, not only all allow'd,
But ev'ry laurel, to her laurel, bow'd!

   Th'envious age, only to me alone,
Will not allow, what I do write, my own,
But let 'em rage, and 'gainst a maid conspire,
So deathless numbers from my tuneful lyre
Do ever flow; so Phoebus I by thee
Divinely inspired and possess'd may be;
I willingly accept Cassandra's fate,
To speak the truth, although believ'd too late.

188 Margaret Cavendish, 'A True Relation of My Birth' (1656), pp. 171–8

I made the more haste to return to my Lord [Marquis of Newcastle], with whom I had rather be as a poor beggar, than to be mistress of the world absented from him . . . howsoever our fortunes are, we are both content, spending our time harmlessly, for my Lord pleaseth himself with the management of some few horses, and exercises himself with the use of the sword . . . Also here [Antwerp] creates himself with his pen, writing what his wit dictates to him, but I pass my time rather with scribbling than writing, with words than wit. Not that I speak much, because I am addicted to contemplation, unless I am with my Lord, yet then I rather attentively listen to what he says, than impertinently speak. Yet when I am writing any sad feigned stories, or serious humours, or melancholy passions, I am forced many times to express them with the tongue before I can write them with the pen, by reason those thoughts that are sad, serious, and melancholy are apt to contract, and to draw too much back, which oppression doth as it were overpower or smother the conception in the brain. But when some of those thoughts are sent out in words, they give the rest more liberty to place themselves in a more methodical order, marching more regularly with my pen on the ground of white paper; but my letters seem rather as a ragged rout than a well-armed body, for the brain being quicker in creating than the hand in writing or the memory in retaining, many fancies are lost, by reason they ofttimes outrun the pen, where I, to keep speed in the race, write so fast as I stay not so long as to write my letters plain, insomuch as some have taken my handwriting for some strange character, and being accustomed so to do, I cannot now write very plain, when I strive to write my best; indeed my ordinary handwriting is so bad as few can read it, so as to write it fair for the press; but however, that little wit I have, it delights me to scribble it out, and disperse it about. For I being addicted from my childhood to contemplation rather than conversation, to solitariness rather than society, to melancholy rather than mirth, to write with the pen than to work with a needle, passing my time with harmless fancies, their company being pleasing, their conversation innocent (in which I take such pleasure as I neglect my health, for it is as great a grief to leave their society as a joy to be in their company), my only trouble is, lest my brain should grow barren, or that the root of my fancies should become insipid, withering into a dull stupidity for want of maturing subjects to write on . . . Yet I must say this in the behalf of my thoughts, that I never found them idle; for if the senses bring no work in, they will work of themselves, like silk-worms that spins out of their own bowels . . . And though I desire to appear to the best advantage, whilst I live in the view of the public world, yet I could most willingly exclude myself, so as never to see the face of any creature but my Lord as long as I live, inclosing myself like an anchorite, wearing a frieze gown, tied with a cord about my waist. But I hope my readers will not think me vain for writing my life, since there have been many that have done the like, as Caesar, Ovid, and many more, both men and women, and I know no reason I may not do it as well as they: but I verily believe some censuring readers will scornfully say, why hath this Lady writ her own life? since none cares to know whose daughter she was or whose wife she is, or how she was bred, or what humour or disposition she was of. I answer that it is true, that 'tis to no purpose to the readers, but it is to the authoress, because I write it for my own sake, not theirs. Neither did I intend this piece for to delight, but to divulge; not to please the fancy, but to tell the truth, lest after-ages should mistake, in not knowing I was daughter to one Master [John] Lucas of St. Johns, near Colchester, in Essex, second wife to the Marquis of Newcastle; for my Lord having had two wives, I might easily have been mistaken, especially if I should die and my Lord marry again.

189 Margaret Cavendish, *The New Blazing World* (1666), pp. 124, 183–6, 188, 224–5

To The Reader

. . . [this fiction] is a description of a *new world* . . . a world of my own creating, which I call the *Blazing World* . . . which if it add any satisfaction to you, I shall account myself a happy *creatoress*; if not, I must be content to live a melancholy life in my own world; I cannot call it a poor world, if poverty be only want of gold, silver, and jewels; for there is more gold in it than all the chemists ever did, and (as I verily believe) will ever be able to make. As for the rocks of diamonds, I wish with all my soul they might be shared amongst my noble female friends, and upon that condition, I would willingly quit my part; and of the gold I should only desire so much as might suffice to repair my noble lord and husband's [the Duke of Newcastle's] losses [in the Civil War]: for I am not covetous, but as ambitious as ever any of my sex was, is, or can be; which makes, that though I cannot be Henry the Fifth or Charles the Second, yet I endeavour to be *Margaret the First*; and although I have neither power, time nor occasion to conquer the world as Alexander and Caesar did; yet rather than not to be mistress of one, since Fortune and Fates would give me none, I have made a world of my own: for which nobody, I hope, will blame me, since it is in every one's power to do the like.

* * *

One time, when the Duchess her soul was with the Empress, she seemed to be very sad and melancholy; at which the Empress was very much troubled, and asked her the reason of her melancholic humour? 'Truly', said the Duchess to the Empress (for between dear friends there's no conceal-ment, they being like several parts of one united body) 'my melancholy proceeds from an extreme ambition'. The Empress asked, what the height of her ambition was? The Duchess answered, that neither she herself, nor no creature in the world was able to know either the height, depth or breadth of her ambition; 'but', said she, 'my present desire is, that I would be a great princess . . . as you are, that is, an Empress of a world, and I shall never be at quiet until I be one'. 'I love you so well', replied the Empress, 'that I wish with all my soul, you had the fruition of your ambitious desires, and I shall not fail to give you my best advice how to accomplish it; the best informants are the immaterial spirits, and they'll soon tell you, whether it be possible to obtain your wish' . . . 'If you will but direct me', said the Duchess to the spirits, 'which world is easiest to be conquered, her Majesty will assist me with means, and I will trust to fate and fortune; for I had rather die in the adventure of noble achievements, than live in obscure and sluggish security; since by the one, I may live in a glorious fame, and by the other I am buried in oblivion'. The spirits answered, that the lives of fame were like other lives; for some lasted long, and some died soon. ''Tis true', said the Duchess, 'but yet the shortest-lived fame lasts longer than the longest life of man'. 'But', replied the spirits, 'if occasion does not serve you, you must content yourself to live without such achievements that may gain you a fame: but we wonder', proceeded the spirits, 'that you desire to be Empress of a terrestrial world, whenas you can create yourself a celestial world if you please'. 'What', said the Empress, 'can any mortal be a creator?' 'Yes', answered the spirits, 'for every human creature can create an immaterial world fully inhabited by immaterial creatures, and populous of immaterial subjects, such as we are, and all this within the compass of the head or skull; nay, not only so, but he may create a world of what fashion and government he will, and give the creatures thereof such motions, figures, forms, colours, perceptions, etc., as he pleases . . . And since it is in your power to create such a world, what need you to venture life, reputation and tranquillity, to conquer a gross material world? For you can enjoy no more of a material world than a particular creature is able to enjoy, which is but a small part, considering the compass of such a world; and you may plainly observe it by your friend the Empress here, which although she possesses a whole world, yet enjoys she but a part thereof; neither is she so much acquainted with it, that she knows all the places, countries and dominions she governs. The truth is, a sovereign monarch has the general trouble, but the subjects enjoy all the delights and pleasures in parts; for it is impossible, that a kingdom, nay, country should be enjoyed by one person at once, except he takes the pains to travel into every part, and endure the inconveniences of going from one place to another; wherefore, since glory, delight and pleasure lives but in other men's opinions, and can neither add tranquillity to your mind, nor give ease to your body, why should you desire to be Empress of a material world and be troubled with the cares that attend government? whenas by creating a world within yourself, you may enjoy all both in whole and in parts, without control or opposition, and may make what world you please, and alter it when you please, and enjoy as much pleasure and delight as a world can afford you?' 'You have converted me', said the Duchess to the spirits, 'from my ambitious desire; wherefore I'll take your advice, reject and despise all worlds without me, and create a world of my own' . . .

. . . which world after it was made, appeared so curious and full of variety, so well ordered and wisely governed, that it cannot possibly be expressed by words, nor the delight and pleasure which the Duchess took in making this world of her own.

* * *

The Epilogue to the Reader

By this poetical description, you may perceive, that my ambition is not only to be Empress, but Authoress of a whole world; and that the worlds I have made . . . are framed and composed of the most pure, that is, the rational parts of matter, which are the parts of my mind; which creation was more easily and suddenly effected, than the conquests of the two famous monarchs of the world, Alexander and Caesar; neither have I made such disturbances, and caused so many dissolutions of particulars, otherwise named deaths, as they did . . . And in the formation of those worlds, I take more delight and glory, than ever Alexander or Caesar did in conquering this terrestrial world; and though I have made my Blazing World a peaceable world, allowing it but one religion, one language, and one government, yet I could make another world, as full of factions, divisions, and wars, as this is of peace and tranquillity; and the rational figures of my mind might express as much courage to fight, as Hector and Achilles had; and be as wise as Nestor, as eloquent as Ulysses, and as beautiful as Helen. But I esteeming peace before war, wit before policy, honesty before beauty, instead of the figures of Alexander, Caesar, Hector, Achilles, Nestor, Ulysses, Helen etc., chose rather the figure of honest Margaret Newcastle, which now I would not change for all this terrestrial world; and if any should like the world I have made, and be willing to be my subjects, they may imagine themselves such, and they are such, I mean, in their minds, fancies or imaginations; but if they cannot endure to be subjects, they may create worlds of their own, and govern themselves as they please . . .

190 Anne Finch, *Poems* (written *post* 1685), pp. 24–5

The Introduction

Did I my lines intend for public view,
How many censures would their faults pursue!
Some would, because such words they do affect,
Cry they're insipid, empty, incorrect.
And many have attained, dull and untaught,
The name of wit, only by finding fault.
True judges might condemn their want of wit;
And all might say, they're by a woman writ.
Alas! a woman that attempts the pen,
Such an intruder on the rights of men,
Such a presumptuous creature is esteemed,
The fault can by no virtue be redeemed.
They tell us we mistake our sex and way;
Good breeding, fashion, dancing, dressing, play,
Are the accomplishments we should desire;
To write, or read, or think, or to enquire,
Would cloud our beauty, and exhaust our time,
And interrupt the conquests of our prime;
While the dull manage of a servile house
Is held by some out utmost art and use.

    Sure, 'twas not ever thus, nor are we told
Fables, of women that excelled of old;
To whom, by the diffusive hand of heaven,
Some share of wit and poetry was given . . .

      How are we fallen! fallen by mistaken rules,
And Education's, more than Nature's fools;

Debarred from all improvements of the mind,
And to be dull, expected and designed,
And if some one would soar above the rest,
With warmer fancy, and ambition pressed,
So strong the opposing faction still appears,
The hopes to thrive can ne'er outweigh the fears.
Be cautioned, then, my Muse, and still retired;
Nor be despised, aiming to be admired;
Conscious of wants, still with contracted wing,
To some few friends, and to thy sorrows sing.
For groves of laurel thou wert never meant:
Be dark enough thy shades, and be thou there content.

191 [N. H.], *The Ladies Dictionary* (1694), pp. 417–20 [misnumbered from p. 240]

Poetesses: . . . in this art, that has foiled and puzzled a number of wise and learned men, the fair sex has been very famous. Their beauties and virtues have not only been the glorious subjects of poetry, and inspired it . . . but themselves have been very commendably the authoresses of many curious pieces wherein their ingenuity has been livelier displayed and raised them as lasting monuments as men can pretend to . . . so that we may see, would ladies bend their talents this way, they might be capable of equalling, if not exceeding, the men; and one main advantage they would gain by it, by being armed for the encountering their satires, pasquils, lampoons, etc., and by matching them, not only in vindicating their sex, but in exposing the folly and malice of their adversaries, they would keep them in such awe, that the number of false aspersions and calumnies would be lessened, and dwindling away by degrees they would at length be disencumbered of all unjust reproaches . . . Poetry at leisure hours is a very curious recreation, if it be on worthy subjects; nay, it elevates and illuminates the mind to a high degree of refining it . . . therefore, ladies, if it be used as you ought, you cannot have a better companion, except divinity, in your retirement.

192 Preface to Katherine Philips, *Poems* (1667), I.22–3

Some of them would be no disgrace to the name of any man that amongst us is most esteemed for his excellency in this kind, and there are none that may not pass with favour, when it is remembered that they fell hastily from the pen but of a woman. We might well have called her the English Sappho, she of all the female poets of former ages, being for her verses and her virtues both, the most highly to be valued; but she has called herself ORINDA, a name that deserves to be added to the number of the Muses, and to live with honour as long as they. Were our language as generally known to the world as the Greek and Latin were anciently, or as the French is now, her verses could not be confined within the narrow limits of our islands, but would spread themselves as far the continent has inhabitants, or as the seas have any shore. And for her virtues, they as much surpassed those of Sappho as the theological do the moral (wherein yet Orinda was not her inferior) or as the fading immortality of an earthly laurel, which the justice of men cannot deny to her excellent poetry, is transcended by that incorruptible and eternal crown of glory, wherewith the mercy of God hath undoubtedly rewarded her more eminent piety.

193 'Philo-Philippa', from 'To the Excellent Orinda', commendatory poem on Katherine Philips' translation of Corneille's *La Mort de Pompée* prefixed to Katherine Philips, *Poems* (1667), pp. 204–7

Let the male poets their male Phoebus choose,
Thee I invoke, Orinda, for my Muse;
He could but force a branch, Daphne her tree
Most freely offers to her sex and thee,
And says to verse, so unconstrain'd as yours,
Her laurel freely comes, your fame secures:
And men no longer shall with ravish'd bays
Crown their forc'd poems by as forc'd a praise.
 Thou glory of our sex, envy of men,
Who are both pleas'd and vex'd with thy bright pen:
Its lustre doth entice their eyes to gaze,
But men's sore eyes cannot endure its rays;
It dazzles and surprises so with light,
To find a noon where they expected night:
A woman translate *Pompey*! which the fam'd
Corneille with such an art and labour fram'd! . . .
Yes, that bold work a woman dares translate,
Not to provoke, nor yet to fear men's hate.
And now resolves to recompense that wrong:
Phoebus to Cynthia must his beams resign,
The rule of Day, and wit's now feminine.
 That sex, which heretofore was not allow'd
To understand more than a beast, or crowd;
Of which problems were made, whether or no
Women had souls; but to be damn'd, if so;
In men's esteem, no higher than the glass;
And all the painful labours of their brain,
Was only how to dress and entertain:
Or, if they ventur'd to speak sense, the wise

Made that, and speaking ox, like prodigies.
From these thy more than masculine pen hath rear'd
Our sex; first to be prais'd, next to be feared.
And by the same pen forc'd men now confess,
To keep their greatness, was to make us less.
   Men know of how refin'd and rich a mould
Our sex is fram'd, what sun is in our gold:
They know in lead no diamonds are set,
And jewels only fill the cabinet.
Our spirits purer far than theirs, they see;
By which even men from men distinguish'd be:
By which the soul is judg'd, and does appear
Fit or unfit for action, as they are.
   When in an organ various sounds do stroke,
Or grate the ear, as birds sing, or toads croak;
The breath, that voices every pipe, 's the same,
But the bad metal doth the sound defame.
So, if our souls by sweeter organs speak,
And theirs with harsh, false notes the air do break;
The soul's the same, alike in both dwell,
'Tis from her instruments that we excel.
Ask me not then, why jealous men debar
Our sex from books in peace, from arms in war;
It is because our parts will soon demand
Tribunals for our persons, and command.
   Shall it be our reproach, that we are weak,
And cannot fight, nor as the school-men speak?
Even men themselves are neither strong nor wise,
If limbs and parts they do not exercise.
   Train'd up to arms, we Amazons have been,
And Spartan virgins strong as Spartan men:
Breed women but as men, and they are these;
Whilst sybarite men are women by their ease.
Why should not brave Semiramis break a lance,
And why should not soft Ninias curl and dance?
Ovid in vain bodies with change did vex,
Changing her form of life, Iphis changed sex.
Nature to females freely doth impart
That, which the males usurp, a stout, bold heart.
Thus hunters female beasts fear to assail:
And female hawks more mettl'd than the male:
Men ought not then courage and wit engross,
Whilst the fox lives, the lion, or the horse.
Much less ought men both to themselves confine,

Whilst women, such as you, Orinda, shine.
    That noble friendship brought thee to our coast,
We thank Lucasia, and thy courage boast.
Death in each wave could not Orinda fright,
Fearless she acts that friendship she did write:
Which manly virtue to their sex confin'd,
Thou rescuest to confirm our softer mind;
For there's requir'd (to do that virtue right)
Courage, as much in friendship as in fight.
The dangers we despise, doth this truth prove,
Though boldly we not fight, we boldly love.
    Engage us unto books, Sappho comes forth,
Though not of Hesiod's age, of Hesiod's worth.
If souls no sexes have, as 'tis confessed,
'Tis not the he or she makes poems best:
Nor can men call these verses feminine,
Be the sense vigorous and masculine.
'Tis true, Apollo sits as judge of wit
But the nine female learned troop are it . . .
Something of grandeur in your verse men see,
That they rise up to it as majesty . . .
If that all Egypt, for to purge its crime,
Were built into one pyramid o'er him,
Pompey would lie less stately in the hearse,
Than he doth now, Orinda, in thy Verse . . .

17

'TYRANT CUSTOM,
WHY MUST WE OBEY'?

Throughout the seventeenth century examples can be found of dissatisfaction with the educational exclusion, social marginalization and political impotence of women. Such discontent is voiced in popular pamphlets, plays and poems, though often by men and with doubtful intent. Less problematically, individual women adumbrated feminist arguments in their rejection of the obedient marital role prescribed for them (for a survey of such opinions, see Smith (1982)). Although it would be anachronistic and tendentious to speak of a feminist movement in this period, there was a significant increase in the publication of such sentiments in the last quarter of the century. Such names as Aphra Behn, Mary, Lady Chudleigh, Sarah Egerton, 'Ephelia', Anne Finch, Bathsua Makin, Hannah Woolley, constitute a notable roll-call of critical and dissident voices (all are noticed in Todd (1987)), repudiating the 'childish things' prescribed for women (194), the ignorance in which they were confined (195), the 'slavery' of marriage (196) and the 'tyranny' of custom (197). Conspicuous amongst them is Mary Astell whose analysis of 'woman's place' is the most sustained and important in English before Mary Wollstonecraft's (see Hill (1986), pp. 1–62, and Perry (1986)). Insisting that the 'oft-remarked incapacity of women' is 'acquired not natural', her *Serious Proposal to the Ladies* (1694; Part II, 1697) argued for the establishment of residential female academies to which women of means might withdraw for study and religious meditation (198). More radical was her second publication, *Some Reflections upon Marriage* (1700), which recognized the potentially tyrannical nature of the authority vested in husbands and urged great circumspection and caution in women contemplating marriage. The most that can be hoped for is that the experience will prove 'tolerable', but since marriage is founded on the exploitation and servitude of women, it is unlikely to be even that (199). The long apologetic preface to the third edition of 1706 is finely ironic: 'If all men are born free, how is it that all women are born slaves?'. Acuity and a rhetorically dexterous pen would be needed to formulate that question in any period; to have posed it in 1706 required besides an astonishing independence of mind.

---

194 *Triumphs of Female Wit, in some Pindarick Odes* (1683), pp. 309–12

The Emulation: a Pindaric Ode

I

Ah! tell me why, deluded Sex, thus we
    Into the secret beauty must not pry
    Of our great Athenian deity.
Why do we Minerva's blessings slight,
    And all her tuneful gifts despise;
    Shall none but the insulting sex be wise?
    Shall they be blest with intellectual light?
    Whilst we drudge on in ignorance's night?
    We've souls as noble, and as fine a clay,
And parts as well compos'd to please as they.
    Men think perhaps we best obey,
    And best their servile business do,
    When nothing else we know
But what concerns a kitchen or a field,
    With all the meaner things they yield.
    As if a rational unbounded mind
Were only for the sordid'st task of life design'd.

II

    They let us learn to work, to dance, or sing,
    Or any such like trivial thing,
Which to their profit may increase or pleasure bring.
    But they refuse to let us know
    What sacred sciences doth impart
    Or the mysteriousness of art.
In learning's pleasing paths denied to go,
    From knowledge banish'd, and their schools;
    We seem design'd alone for useful fools,
    And foils for their ill shapen sense, condemn'd to prize
    And think 'em truly wise,
    Being not allow'd their follies to despise.
Thus we from ignorance to wonder run,
(For admiration ceases when the secret's known)
    Seem witty only in their praise
    And kind congratulating lays.
Thus to the repute of sense they rise,
And thus through the applauder's ignorance are wise.
    For should we understand as much as they,
    They fear their empire might decay.

281

For they know women heretofore
Gain'd victories, and envied laurels wore:
    And now they fear we'll once again
    Ambitious be to reign
And to invade the dominions of the brain.
And as we did in those renowned days
Rob them of laurels, so we now will take their bays.

III

But we are peaceful and will not repine,
They still may keep their bays as well as wine.
    We've no Amazonian hearts,
They need not therefore guard their magazine of arts.
    We will not on their treasure seize,
A part of it sufficiently will please:
    We'll only so much knowledge have
    As may assist us to enslave
    Those passions which we find
    Too potent for the mind.
'Tis o'er them only we desire to reign,
And we no nobler, braver, conquest wish to gain.

IV

We only so much will desire
As may instruct us how to live above
Those childish things which most admire,
And may instruct us what is fit to love.
We covet learning for this only end,
That we our time may to the best advantage spend:
    Supposing 'tis below us to converse
    Always about our business or our dress;
As if to serve our senses were our happiness.
    We'll read the stories of the ancient times,
To see, and then with horror hate their crimes.
But all their virtues with delight we'll view,
    Admir'd by us, and imitated too.
    But for rewarding sciences and arts,
    And all the curious products which arise
    From the contrivance of the wise,
We'll tune and cultivate our fruitful hearts.
    And should Man's envy still declare,
    Our business only to be fair;
    Without their leave we will be wise,
And beauty, which they value, we'll despise.

Our minds, and not our faces, we'll adorn,
For that's the employ to which we are born.
The Muses gladly will their aid bestow,
And to their sex their charming secrets show.
Whilst Man's brisk notions owe their rise
To an inspiring bottle, wench, or vice,
Must be debauch'd and damn'd to get
The reputation of a wit.
To Nature only, and our softer Muses, we
Will owe our charms of wit, of parts, and poetry.

195 Mary, Lady Chudleigh, from *The Ladies Defence* (1701), pp. 2–3

'Tis hard we should be by the men despised,
Yet kept from knowing what would make us prized;
Debarred from knowledge, banished from the schools,
And with the utmost industry bred fools;
Laughed out of reason, jested out of sense,
And nothing left but native innocence;
Then told we are incapable of wit,
And only for the meanest drudgeries fit;
Made slaves to serve their luxury and pride,
And with innumerable hardships tried,
Till pitying heaven release us from our pain,
Kind heaven, to whom alone we dare complain.
Th'ill-natured world will no compassion show:
Such as are wretched it would still have so.
It gratifies its envy and its spite:
The most in others' miseries take delight.
While we are present, they some pity spare,
And feast us on a thin repast of air;
Look grave and sigh, when we our wrongs relate,
And in a compliment accuse our fate;
Blame those to whom we our misfortunes owe,
And all the signs of real friendship show,
But when we're absent, we their sports are made,
They fan the flame, and our oppressors aid;
Join with the stronger, the victorious side,
And all our sufferings, all our griefs deride.
Those generous few whom kinder thoughts inspire,
And who the happiness of all desire,
Who wish we were from barbarous usage free,
Exempt from toils and shameful slavery,

Yet let us, unreproved, mis-spend our hours,
And to mean purposes employ our nobler powers.
They think, if we our thoughts can but express,
And know but how to work, to dance and dress,
It is enough, as much as we should mind,
As if we were for nothing else designed,
But made, like puppets, to divert mankind.
O that my sex would all such toys despise,
And only study to be good and wise;
Inspect themselves, and every blemish find,
Search all the close recesses of the mind,
And leave no vice, no ruling passion there,
Nothing to raise a blush, or cause a fear;
Their memories with solid notions fill,
And let their reason dictate to their will;
Instead of novels, histories peruse,
And for their guides the wiser ancients choose;
Through all the labyrinths of learning go,
And grow more humble, as they more do know.
By doing this they will respect procure,
Silence the men, and lasting fame secure;
And to themselves the best companions prove,
And neither fear their malice, nor desire their love.

196 Mary, Lady Chudleigh, *Poems on Several Occasions* (1703), p. 3

To the Ladies

Wife and servant are the same,
But only differ in the name:
For when that fatal knot is tied,
Which nothing, nothing can divide,
When she the word *Obey* has said,
And man by law supreme has made,
Then all that's kind is laid aside,
And nothing left but state and pride.
Fierce as an eastern prince he grows,
And all his innate rigour shows:
Then but to look, to laugh, or speak,
Will the nuptial contract break,
Like mutes, she signs alone must make,
And never any freedom take,
But still be governed by a nod,

And fear her husband as her god:
Him still must serve, him still obey,
And nothing act, and nothing say,
But what her haughty lord thinks fit,
Who, with the power, has all the wit.
Then shun, oh! shun that wretched state,
And all the fawning flatterers hate.
Value yourselves, and men despise:
You must be proud, if you'll be wise.

197 Sarah Egerton, *Poems on Several Occasions* (1703), pp. 31–2

The Emulation

Say, tyrant Custom, why must we obey
The impositions of thy haughty sway?
From the first dawn of life unto the grave,
Poor womankind's in every state a slave,
The nurse, the mistress, parent and the swain,
For love she must, there's none escape that pain.
Then comes the last, the fatal slavery:
The husband with insulting tyranny
Can have ill manners justified by law,
For men all join to keep the wife in awe.
Moses, who first our freedom did rebuke,
Was married when he writ the Pentateuch.
They're wise to keep us slaves, for well they know,
If we were loose, we soon should make them so.
We yield like vanquished kings whom fetters bind,
When chance of war is to usurpers kind;
Submit in form; but they'd our thoughts control,
And lay restraints on the impassive soul.
They fear we should excel their sluggish parts,
Should we attempt the sciences and arts;
Pretend they were designed for them alone,
So keep us fools to raise their own renown.
Thus priests of old, their grandeur to maintain,
Cried vulgar eyes would sacred laws profane;
So kept the mysteries behind a screen:
Their homage and the name were lost had they been seen.
But in his blessed age such freedom's given,
That every man explains the will of heaven;
And shall we women now sit tamely by,

Make no excursions in philosophy,
Or grace our thoughts in tuneful poetry?
We will our rights in learning's world maintain;
Wit's empire now shall know a female reign.
Come, all ye fair, the great attempt improve,
Divinely imitate the realms above:
There's ten celestial females govern wit,
And but two gods that dare pretend to it.
And shall these finite males reverse their rules?
No, we'll be wits, and then must men be fools.

198 [Mary Astell], *Serious Proposal to the Ladies* (1694–7), pt I, pp. 6–8, 14–17, 19–20, 24, 27–8, 36

This is a matter infinitely more worthy your [women readers'] debates than what colours are most agreeable, or what's the dress becomes you best. Your glass will not do you half so much service as a serious reflection on your own minds . . . No solicitude in the adornation of your selves is discommended, provided you employ your care about that which is really your *self*, and do not neglect that particle of divinity within you, which must survive, and may (if you please) be happy and perfect, when it's unsuitable and much inferior companion is mouldering in the dust . . . Remember, I pray you, the famous women of former ages, the Orindas of late, and the more modern heroines, and blush to think how much is now, and will hereafter be said of them, when you your selves . . . must be buried in silence and forgetfulness! . . . How can you be content to be in the world like tulips in a garden, to make a fine show, and be good for nothing . . .

Although it has been said by men of more wit than wisdom, and perhaps of more malice than either, that women are naturally incapable of acting prudently, or that they are necessarily determined to folly, I must by no means grant it . . .

The incapacity, if there be any, is acquired not natural; and none of their follies are so necessary, but that they might avoid them if they pleased themselves . . .

. . . Women are from their very infancy debarred those advantages with the want of which they are afterwards reproached, and nursed up in those vices which will hereafter be upbraided to them. So partial are men as to expect brick where they afford no straw; and so abundantly civil as to take care we should make good that obliging epithet of *ignorant*, which out of an excess of good manners they are pleased to bestow on us! . . .

. . . seeing it is ignorance, either habitual or actual, which is the cause of all sin, how are they like to escape *this*, who are bred up in *that*? That therefore women are unprofitable to most, and a plague and dishonour to some men is not much to be regretted on account of the *men*, because 'tis the product of their own folly, in denying them the benefits of an ingenious and liberal education, the most effectual means to direct them into, and to secure their progress in, the ways of virtue.

For that ignorance is the cause of most feminine vices, may be instanced in that pride and vanity which is usually imputed to us, and which I suppose, if thoroughly sifted, will appear to be some way or other, the rise and original of all the rest. These, though very bad weeds, are the product of a good soil, they are nothing else but generosity degenerated and corrupted . . .

Whence is it but from ignorance, from want of understanding to compare and judge of things, to choose a right end, to proportion the means to the end, and to rate everything according to its proper value, that we quit the substance for the shadow, reality for appearance, and embrace those very things which if we understood we should hate and fly . . . Thus ignorance and a narrow education lay the foundation of vice, and imitation and custom rear it up. Custom, that merciless torrent that carries all before it, and which indeed can be stemmed by none but such as have a great deal of prudence and a rooted virtue. For 'tis but decorous that she who is not capable of giving better rules, should follow those she sees before her, lest she only change the instance and retain absurdity. 'Twould puzzle a considerate person to account for all that sin and folly that is in the world . . . did not Custom help to solve the difficulty . . . 'Tis Custom, therefore, that Tyrant Custom, which is the grand motive to all those irrational choices which we daily see made in the world, so very contrary to our present interest and pleasure, as well as to our future . . .

Now as to the Proposal, it is to erect a monastery, or if you will . . . we will call it a religious retirement, and such as shall have a double aspect, being not only a retreat from the world for those who desire that advantage, but likewise, an institution and previous discipline, to fit us to do the greatest good in it . . .

. . . one great end of this institution shall be to expel that cloud of ignorance which Custom has involved us in, to furnish our minds with a stock of solid and useful knowledge, that the souls of women may no longer be the only unadorned and neglected things.

199 [Mary Astell], *Some Reflections upon Marriage* (1700; 3rd edn 1706), pp. 11–12, 22, 26–7, 31, 36–7, 60, 66

The Preface [in defence of the publication in 1700 of
Some Reflections upon Marriage]

. . . 'Tis true, through want of learning and of that superior genius which men, as men, lay claim to, she [i.e. Mary Astell in the 1700 text] was ignorant of the *natural inferiority* of our sex, which our masters lay down as a self-evident and fundamental truth. She saw nothing in the reason of things, to make this either a principle or a conclusion, but much to the contrary; it being sedition at least, if not treason, to assert it in this reign [of Queen Anne]. For if by the *natural superiority of their sex* they mean that *every* man is by nature superior to *every* woman, which is the obvious meaning, and that which must be stuck to if they would speak sense, it would be a sin in *any* woman to have dominion over *any* man, and the greatest queen ought not to command but to obey her footman, because no municipal law can supersede or change the Law of Nature . . .

If they mean that *some* men are superior to *some* women, this is no great discovery; had they turned the tables they might have seen that *some* women are superior to *some* men. Or had they been pleased to remember their oaths of allegiance and supremacy, they might have known that *one* woman is superior to *all* the men in these nations . . .

. . . if absolute sovereignty be not necessary in a state, how comes it to be so in a family? or if in a family, why not in a state, since no reason can be alleged for the one that will not hold more strongly for the other? If the authority of the husband so far as it extends is sacred and inalienable, why not of the prince? The domestic sovereignty is without dispute elected, and the stipulations and contract are mutual; is it not then partial in men to the last degree to contend for, and practise, that arbitrary dominion in their families which they abhor and exclaim against in the state? For if arbitrary power is evil in itself, and an improper method of governing rational and free agents, it ought not to be practised anywhere; nor is it less but rather more mischievous in families than in kingdoms, by how much 100,000 tyrants are worse than one. What though a husband can't deprive a wife of life without being responsible to the law, he may however do what is much more grievous to a generous mind, render her life miserable, for which she has no redress, scarce pity which is afforded to every other complainant. It being a wife's duty to suffer everything without complaint. *If all men are born free, how is it that all women are born slaves?*

. . . if reason is only allowed us by way of raillery, and the secret maxim is that we have none, or little more than brutes, 'tis the best way to confine us with chain and block to the chimney-corner, which probably might save the estates of some families and the honour of others . . .

Some Reflections upon Marriage

. . . if marriage be such a blessed state, how comes it, you may say, that there are so few happy marriages? Now in answer to this, it is not to be wondered that so few succeed, we should rather be surprised to find so many do, considering how imprudently men engage, the motives they act by, and the very strange conduct they observe throughout.

For pray, what do men propose to themselves in marriage? What qualifications do they look after in a spouse? 'What will she bring?' is the first enquiry, 'How many acres?' . . .

Few men have so much goodness as to bring themselves to a liking of what they loathed merely because it is their duty to like; on the contrary, when they marry with an indifferency to please their friends or increase their fortune, the indifferency proceeds to an aversion, and perhaps even the kindness and complaisance of the poor abused wife shall only serve to increase it . . .

If . . . it is a woman's hard fate to meet with a disagreeable temper . . . she is as unhappy as anything in this world can make her. For when a wife's temper does not please, if she makes her husband uneasy, he can find entertainments abroad, he has an hundred ways of relieving himself, but neither prudence nor duty will allow a woman to fly out, her business and entertainment are at home, and though he makes it ever so uneasy to her she must be content and make her best on't. She who elects a monarch for life, who gives him an authority she cannot recall however he misapply it, who puts her fortune and person entirely in his powers . . . had need be very sure that she does not make a fool her head, nor a vicious man her guide and pattern . . .

. . . the woman has in truth no security but the man's honour and good nature, a security that in this present age no wise person would venture much upon . . .

. . . since God has placed different ranks in the world, put some in a higher and some in a lower station, for order and beauty's sake, and for many good reasons, though it is both our wisdom and duty not only to submit with patience, but to be thankful and well-satisfied when by his providence we are brought low, yet there is no manner of reason for us to degrade our selves; on the contrary, much why we ought not. The better our lot is in this world and the more we have of it, the greater is our leisure to prepare for the next; we have the more opportunity to exercise that god-like quality, to taste that divine pleasure, doing good to the bodies and souls of those beneath us. Is it not then ill manners to Heaven, and an irreligious contempt of its favours, for a woman to slight that nobler employment, to which it has assigned her, and thrust herself down to a meaner drudgery, to what is in the very literal sense a caring for the things of the world, a caring not only to please, but to maintain a husband? . . .

. . . how can a man respect his wife when he has a contemptible opinion of her and her sex? When from his own elevation he looks down on them as void of understanding and full of ignorance and passion, so that folly and a woman are equivalent terms with him? Can he think there is any gratitude due to her whose utmost services he exacts as strict duty? Because she was made to be a slave to his will, and has no higher end than to serve and obey him! . . .

She then who marries ought to lay it down for an indispensable maxim, that her husband must govern absolutely and entirely, and that she has nothing else to do but to please and obey. She must not attempt to divide his authority, or so much as dispute it (to struggle with her yoke will only make it gall the more) but must believe him wise and good and in all respects the best, at least he must be so to her. She who can't do this is no way fit to be a wife, she may set up for that peculiar coronet [for virginity] the ancient Fathers talked of, but is not qualified to receive that great reward which attends the eminent exercise of humility and self-denial, patience and resignation, the duties that a wife is called to.

BIBLIOGRAPHY

1 PRIMARY SOURCES

The numbers of the extracts taken from the following titles are given in square brackets.

[Allestree, Richard] (1673). *The Ladies Calling*. Oxford: at the Theater. [71, 174]

[Astell, Mary] (1694–7). *A Serious Proposal to the Ladies . . . by a lover of her sex*. Pt I, 4th edn; pt II, 1st edn. London: for R. Wilkin, 1697. [198]

[——] (1700; 3rd edn 1706). *Some Reflections upon Marriage*. 5th edn, Dublin, 1730. [199]

Barker, Jane (1688). *Poetical Recreations*, taken from Germaine Greer, Jeslyn Medoff, Melinda Sansone and Susan Hastings (eds), *Kissing the Rod: An anthology of seventeenth-century women's verse*. London: Virago, 1988. [179]

Barret, Robert (1699). *A Companion for Midwives, Child-Bearing Women and Nurses*. London: for Thomas Ax. [113, 145]

Baxter, Richard (1673). *A Christian Directory*, in William Orme (ed.), *The Practical Works*, 23 vols. London: James Duncan, 1830. [20, 43, 87, 98, 114]

Bible, Holy, 'Authorized' King James Version (1611). Oxford: Oxford University Press, n.d. [1, 47, 56, 76]

Bible, Holy, 'Geneva' Version (1560). Facsimile edn, introd. Lloyd E. Berry. Madison, Milwaukee and London: University of Wisconsin Press, 1969. [6, 57]

Bradstreet, Anne (1650). *The Tenth Muse*, taken from Jeannine Hensley (ed.), *The Works*. Cambridge, Mass.: Belknap Press of Harvard University Press, 1967. [182]

—— (1678). *Several Poems*, taken from Jeannine Hensley (ed.), *The Works*. Cambridge, Mass.: Belknap Press of Harvard University Press, 1967. [82, 112]

Brathwait, Richard (1631). *The English Gentlewoman, drawne out to the full body: expressing what habilliments do best attire her, what ornaments do best adorn her, what complements do best accomplish her*. London: for Michael Sparke. [69]

[——] (1640). *Ar't Asleepe Husband? A Boulster Lecture; stored with all variety of witty jeasts, merry tales and other pleasant passages*. London: for R. B. [9]

Breton, Nicholas (1615). *The Good and the Badde*, taken from Henry Morley (ed.), *Character Writing of the Seventeenth Century*. London: Routledge, 1891. [48, 67]

Bunyan, John ([1663]). *Christian Behaviour*, taken from Roger Sharrock (gen. ed.), *Miscellaneous Works*, 13 vols, in progress. Oxford: Clarenden Press, 1976–94. [97]

—— (1680). *The Life and Death of Mr. Badman*, eds James F. Forrest and Roger Sharrock. Oxford: Clarendon Press, 1988. [54, 60]

—— (1683). *A Case of Conscience Resolved; Viz. Whether, where a Church of Christ is situate, it is the duty of the women of that congregation ordinarily and by appointment to separate themselves from their brethren, and so to assemble together to perform some parts of divine worship, as prayer, etc., without their men?*, taken from Roger Sharrock (gen. ed.), *Miscellaneous Works*, 13 vols. in progress. Oxford: Clarendon Press, 1976–94. [138]

— (1692; written 1680s?). *An Exposition on the First Ten Chapters of Genesis*, taken from George Offor (ed.), *The Works*, 3 vols. Glasgow, Edinburgh and London: Blackie,1860–2. [3]

Burroughes, Jeremiah (1643). *The Glorious Name of God, The Lord of Hosts. Opened in two sermons at Michaels Cornhill, London*. London: for R. Dawlinson. [133]

Burton, Robert (1621–51). *The Anatomy of Melancholy*, ed. Holbrook Jackson, 3 vols. London: Dent, 1932. [11, 17, 31, 46, 50, 100, 143]

Campion, Thomas [1617]. *The Third and Fourth Booke of Ayres*, taken from Percival Vivian (ed.), *The Works*. Oxford: Clarendon Press, 1909. [34]

Carew, Thomas (1640). *Poems*, taken from Rhodes Dunlap (ed.), *The Poems*. Oxford: Clarendon Press, 1949. [160]

Cartwright, William (1651). *The Works*, taken from G. Blakemore Evans (ed.), *The Plays and Poems*. Madison: University of Wisconsin Press, 1951. [156, 164]

— (1656). *Sportive Wit*; taken from G. Blakemore Evans (ed.), *The Plays and Poems*. Madison: University of Wisconsin Press, 1951. [162]

Cavendish, Margaret, Duchess of Newcastle (1655). *The Worlds Olio*. London: for J. Martin and J. Allestrye. [27]

— (1656). 'A True Relation of My Birth, Breeding and Life', in *Nature's Pictures*, taken from C. H. Firth (ed.), *The Life of William Cavendish, Duke of Newcastle. To which is added the True Relation of My Birth, Breeding and Life*. London: Routledge [1906]. [77, 117, 128, 188]

— (1664). *CCXI Sociable Letters*. London: by William Wilson. [129]

— (1666). *The Description of a New World called The Blazing World, and other writings*, ed. Kate Lilley. London: William Pickering, 1992. [189]

Chamberlain, John (written 1597–1626). *The Chamberlain Letters: a selection of the letters of John Chamberlain concerning life in England from 1597 to 1626*, ed. Elizabeth McClure Thomson. London: John Murray, 1965. [166]

Chidley, Katherine (1641). *The Justification of the Independent Churches of Christ. Being an answer to Mr. Edwards his book which he hath written against . . . toleration of Christs public worship*. London: for William Larnar. [134]

Chudleigh, Mary, Lady (1701). *The Ladies Defence*, taken from Roger Lonsdale (ed.), *Eighteenth-century Women Poets*. Oxford: Oxford University Press, 1990. [195]

— (1703). *Poems on Several Occasions*, taken from Roger Lonsdale (ed.), *Eighteenth-century Women Poets*. Oxford: Oxford University Press, 1990. [196]

Clarkson, Laurence (1660). *The Lost Sheep Found: or, the prodigal returned to his fathers house*,taken from Nigel Smith (ed.), *A Collection of Ranter Writings from the 17th Century*. London: Junction Books, 1983. [91]

Common Prayer, Book of (revised 1662). [80]

Coppe, Abiezer (1649). *A Second Fiery Flying Roule*, taken from Nigel Smith (ed.), *A Collection of Ranter Writings from the 17th Century*. London: Junction Books, 1983. [90]

Cowley, Abraham (1668). *The Works*, taken from A. R. Waller (ed.), *Poems*. Cambridge: Cambridge University Press, 1905. [33, 155]

[Crashaw, William] [1620]. *The Honour of Vertue. Or, The Monument Erected by the Sorrowful Husband, and the Epitaphs Annexed by Learned and Worthy Men, to the Immortall Memory of that Worthy Gentle-Woman Mrs. Elizabeth Crashawe. Who died in child-birth and was buried in Whit-Chappell: Octob. 8. 1620. In the 24 yeare of her age.* [n.p.] [73]

BIBLIOGRAPHY

Culpeper, Nicholas (1662). *Culpeper's Directory for Midwives. Or, a Guide for Women: the second part. Discovering . . . Diseases*. London: by Peter Cole. [14, 144]

Dent, Arthur (1607). *The Plaine Mans Path-way to Heaven: wherein every man may cleerly see, whether he shall be saved or damned. Set forth dialogue-wise*. London: for Edward Bishop, 9th impression. [52]

Donne, John (1633; written 1590–1612?). *Poems*, taken from A. J. Smith (ed.), *The Complete English Poems*. Harmondsworth: Penguin, 1971. [154]

—— (1635; written 1590–1612?). *Poems*, taken from A. J. Smith (ed.), *The Complete English Poems*. Harmondsworth: Penguin, 1971. [163]

—— (1652; written 1603–10). *Paradoxes, Problemes, Essayes and Characters*, ed. Helen Peters. Oxford: Clarendon Press, 1980. [23]

[E[dgar], T[homas] (ed.)] (1632). *The Lawes Resolutions of Womens Rights: Or, The Lawes Provision for Woemen. A methodicall collection of such statutes and customes, with the cases, opinions, arguments and points of learning in the law, as doe properly concerne women*. London: by the assigns of John More. [21, 85, 92, 121, 173]

Egerton, Sarah (1703). *Poems on Several Occasions*, taken from Roger Lonsdale (ed.), *Eighteenth-century Women Poets*. Oxford: Oxford University Press, 1990. [197]

Evelyn, John (written 1640–1706). *The Diary*, ed. E. S. de Beer, 6 vols. Oxford: Clarendon Press, 1955. [148]

Fanshawe, Ann (written 1676). *The Memoirs of . . . Ann, Lady Fanshawe*, ed. John Loftis. Oxford: Clarendon Press, 1979. [116, 130, 170]

[Fell, Margaret] (1666). *Womens Speaking Justified, Proved and Allowed of by the Scriptures, All Such as Speak by the Spirit and Power of the Lord Jesus. And how women were the first that preached the tidings of the resurrection of Jesus*. London: [n.p.]. [135]

[Finch, Anne, Countess of Winchilsea] (1713; written *post* 1685). *Miscellany Poems on Several Occasions: written by a lady*. London: for J. B. [180, 181]

—— (written *post* 1685). *Poems by Anne, . . . Countess of Winchilsea, 1661–1720*, ed. John Middleton Murry. London: Cape, 1928. [190]

Fox, George (dictated 1675). *The Journal*, ed. John L. Nickalls. London: Religious Society of Friends, 1975. [24]

Galen (1586). *Certain Workes of Galens, called Methodus Medendi*, trs. Thomas Gale. London: by Thomas East. [10]

[Gibson, Thomas] (1682). *The Anatomy of Humane Bodies Epitomized. Wherein all parts of man's body, with their actions and uses, are succinctly described, according to the doctrine of the most accurate and learned modern authorities*. London: for T. Flesher. [12]

Goodcole, Henry (1621). *The Wonderfull Discoverie of Elizabeth Sawyer a Witch, late of Edmonton, her Conviction and Condemnation and Death. Together with the relation of the Divels access to her, and their conversation together*. London: for William Butler. [63]

[——] (1637). *Natures Cruell Step-Dames: or, matchless monsters of the female sex, Elizabeth Barnes and Anne Willis . . .* London: for Francis Coules. [108]

Gouge, William (1622). *Of Domesticall Duties: Eight Treatises*. London: for William Bladen. [81, 96, 109, 141]

[Gough, John] (1684). *The Academy of Complements, with many new additions of songs and catches a-la-mode. Stored with variety of complemental and elegant expressions of love and courtship . . . Composed for the use of ladies and gentlewomen*. London: for R. Parker. [44]

Gould, Robert (1682). *Love Given O're: or, a satyr against the pride, lust, and inconstancy, &c. of woman*. London: for Andrew Green. [53]

[H., N.] (1694). *The Ladies Dictionary; being a General Entertainment for the Fair Sex*. London: for John Dunton. [15, 29, 55, 59, 72, 104, 123, 126, 191]

Hæc-Vir: or The Womanish-Man: being an answer to a late book intituled Hic-Mulier. Expressed in a brief dialogue between Hæc-Vir the Womanish-Man and Hic-Mulier the Man-Woman (1620). London: for I. T. [171]

Halkett, Anne (written 1677–8). *The Memoirs of Anne, Lady Halkett . . .*, ed. John Loftis. Oxford: Clarendon Press, 1979. [131]

Harley, Lady Brilliana (written 1640s). *Letters of the Lady Brilliana Harley, Wife of Sir Robert Harley*, ed. Thomas Taylor Lewis. London: for the Camden Society, 1854. [132]

Herrick, Robert (1648). *Hesperides*, taken from L. C. Martin (ed.), *The Poetical Works*. Oxford: Clarendon Press, 1963. [37, 39, 66]

Heywood, Thomas (1624). *Gynækeion: or, Nine Books of Various History concerning Women*. London: by Adam Islip. [35, 64, 65, 125, 150]

Hic Mulier: or, The Man-Woman: being a medicine to cure the coltish disease of the staggers in the masculine-feminine of our times. Expressed in a brief declamation (1620). London: for J. T[rundle]. [167]

Hutchinson, Lucy (written 1640s?). *On The Principles of the Christian Religion* [ed. Julius Hutchinson]. London: Longman, Hurst, Rees, Orme & Brown, 1817. [26]

—— (written 1640s/1650s?). 'Autobiographical Fragment', included in *Memoirs of the Life of Colonel Hutchinson*, ed. James Sutherland. London: Oxford University Press, 1973. [118]

—— (completed 1671). *Memoirs of the Life of Colonel Hutchinson*, ed. James Sutherland. London: Oxford University Press, 1973. [84, 127]

James VI of Scotland and I of England (1599). *Basilikon Doron*. Edinburgh: for R. Walde-grace. [94]

Jeake, Samuel (written 1694). *An Astrological Diary of the Seventeenth Century*, eds Michael Hunter and Annabel Gregory. Oxford: Clarendon Press, 1988. [83]

Jocelin, Elizabeth (1624). *The Mothers Legacie to her Unborn Childe*. London: for William Barret. [75, 119, 183]

Jonson, Ben (1616). *Epigrams*, taken from George Parfitt (ed.), *The Complete Poems*. Harmondsworth: Penguin, 1975. [107]

—— (1640). *Underwoods*, taken from George Parfitt (ed.), *The Complete Poems*. Harmondsworth: Penguin, 1975. [149]

Josselin, Ralph (written 1644–81). *The Diary of Ralph Josselin 1616–83*, ed. Alan Macfarlane. London: Oxford University Press for the British Academy, 1976. [111]

Killigrew, Anne (1686). *Poems by Mrs. Anne Killigrew*. London: for Samuel Lowndes. [187]

Leigh, Dorothy (1616). *The Mothers Blessing. Or The Godly Counsel of a Gentlewoman not long since Deceased, left behind her for her Children*. London: for John Budge. [68, 102, 184]

Lovelace, Richard (1649). *Lucasta*, taken from C. H. Wilkinson (ed.), *The Poems*. Oxford: Clarendon Press, 1930. [32, 157]

—— (1659). *Lucasta: Posthume Poems*, taken from C. H. Wilkinson (ed.), *The Poems*. Oxford: Clarendon Press, 1980. [161, 185]

[Makin, Bathsua] (1673). *An Essay to Revive the Antient Education of Gentlewomen, in Religion, Manners, Arts & Tongues. With an Answer to the Objections against this Way of Education (1673)*, introd. Paula L. Barbour. University of California, Los Angeles: Augustan Reprint Society, 1980. [28]

Marvell, Andrew (1681; written 1650s?). *Miscellaneous Poems*, taken from H. M.

Margoliouth (ed.), rev. Pierre Legouis and E. E. Duncan-Jones, *The Poems and Letters*, 2 vols. Oxford: Clarendon Press, 1971. [41, 165]

Middleton, Thomas (acted *c*.1621). *Women Beware Women*, ed. Roma Gill. London: Benn, 1968. [103]

Milton, John (1643). *The Doctrine and Discipline of Divorce* (1643), taken from Ernest Sirluck (ed.), *Complete Prose Works*, vol. II. New Haven and London: Yale University Press and Oxford University Press, 1959. [88]

—— (1667). *Paradise Lost*, taken from John Carey and Alastair Fowler (eds), *The Poems*. London and New York: Longman, 1980. [2, 18, 30, 124]

Montaigne, Michel de (1603). *The Essayes, or Morall Politike and Militarie Discourses of Lo: Michaell de Montaigne, Knight*, trs. John Florio. London: for Edward Blount. [22]

Newcome, Henry (1695). *The Compleat Mother. Or, an earnest persuasive to all mothers (especially those of rank and quality) to nurse their own children*. London: for J. Wyat. [142]

Overbury, Sir Thomas (1614). *A Wife . . . whereunto are added Many Witty Characters*, taken from W. J. Paylor (ed.), *The Overburian Characters*. Oxford: Blackwell, 1936. [4, 101, 172]

P[arrot?], H[enry?] (1626). *Cures for the Itch: Characters, Epigrams, Epitaphs*, taken from Henry Morley (ed.), *Character Writings of the Seventeenth Century*. London: Routledge, 1891. [49]

Philips, Katherine (1667). *Poems by the Most Deservedly Admired Mrs. Katherine Philips The Matchless Orinda*, taken from Patrick Thomas (ed.), *The Collected Works*, 2 vols. Stump Cross, Essex: Stump Cross Books, 1990–2. [175, 176, 177, 178, 192]

'Philo-Philippa' (1667). 'To the Excellent Orinda', commendatory poem on Katherine Philips' translation of Corneille's *La Mort de Pompée* prefixed to Katherine Philips, *Poems* (1667), taken from Germaine Greer, Jeslyn Medoff, Melinda Sansone and Susan Hastings (eds), *Kissing the Rod: An anthology of seventeenth-century women's verse*. London: Virago, 1988. [193]

Savile, George, Marquess of Halifax (1688). *The Lady's New Year's Gift: or, Advice to a Daughter*, taken from J. P. Kenyon (ed.), *Halifax: Complete Works*. Harmondsworth: Penguin, 1969. [89, 105]

Sermon, William (1671). *The Ladies Companion, or The English Midwife, wherein is demonstrated the manner and order how women ought to govern themselves during the whole time of their breeding children*. London: for Edward Thomas. [13, 139]

Shakespeare, William (written *c*.1592). *The Taming of the Shrew*, taken from Stanley Wells and Gary Taylor (eds), *The Complete Works*, compact edn. Oxford: Clarendon Press, 1988. [99]

—— (registered 1600). *As You Like It*, taken from Stanley Wells and Gary Taylor (eds), *The Complete Works*, compact edn. Oxford: Clarendon Press, 1988. [168]

—— (written 1610–11?). *Cymbeline*, taken from Stanley Wells and Gary Taylor (ed.), *The Complete Works*, compact edn. Oxford: Clarendon Press, 1988. [19, 169]

Smith, Henry (1591). *A Preparative to Marriage. The summe whereof was spoken at a contract, and inlarged after*. London: for Thomas Man. [79, 86, 93, 106, 122, 140]

Sowernam, Esther (1617). *Ester hath Hang'd Haman*, taken from Simon Shepherd (ed.), *The Women's Sharp Revenge: Five women's pamphlets from the Renaissance*. London: Fourth Estate, 1985. [7, 58, 152]

Speght, Rachel (1617). *A Mouzell for Melastomus*, taken from Simon Shepherd (ed.), *The Women's Sharp Revenge: Five women's pamphlets from the Renaissance*. London: Fourth Estate, 1985. [8]

BIBLIOGRAPHY

Spenser, Edmund (1590–6). *The Faerie Queene*, ed. J. C. Smith, 2 vols. Oxford: Clarendon Press, 1909. [70]

Strode, William (1656). Contribution to *Parnassus Biceps: or, Severall Choice Pieces of Poetry*, taken from Bertram Dobell (ed.), *The Poetical Works*. London: published by the editor, 1907. [38]

Suckling, Sir John (1646). *Fragmenta Aurea*, taken from A. Hamilton Thompson (ed.), *The Works*. London: Routledge, 1910. [40]

—— (1659). *The Last Remains*, taken from A. Hamilton Thompson (ed.), *The Works*. London: Routledge, 1910. [36]

[Swan, John] (1635). *Speculum Mundi: or, A Glass Representing the Face of the World; showing both that it did begin and must also end: the manner how, and time when, being largely examined.* Cambridge: by printers to the University. [5]

[Swetnam, Joseph] (1615). *The Arraignment of Lewde, Idle, Froward and Unconstant Women: Or, the vanity of them, choose you whether. With a commendation of wise, virtuous and honest women. Pleasant for married men, profitable for young men, and hurtful to none.* London: for Thomas Archer. [45]

Tattle-well, Mary, and Hit-him-home, Joan [Taylor, John?] (1640). *The Women's Sharp Revenge*, taken from Simon Shepherd (ed.), *The Women's Sharp Revenge: Five women's pamphlets from the Renaissance*. London: Fourth Estate, 1985. [153, 159]

Taylor, John (1639). *A Juniper Lecture. With the description of all sorts of women, good, and bad.* London: for William Ley. [51]

Thornton, Alice (written *post* 1668). *The Autobiography of Mrs. Alice Thornton of East Newton, Co. York*, [ed. Christopher Jackson]. Durham, Edinburgh and London: Andrews, Whittaker and Blackwood, for the Surtees Society, 1875. [110, 147]

Triumphs of Female Wit, in some Pindarick Odes (1683), taken from Germaine Greer, Jeslyn Medoff, Melinda Sansone and Susan Hastings (eds), *Kissing the Rod: An anthology of seventeenth-century women's verse*. London: Virago, 1988. [194]

Verney, Frances Parthenope, ed. (1892–9). *Memoirs of the Verney Family*, 4 vols. London: Longman's, Green. [120, 136, 146]

Wentworth, Anne (1677). *A Vindication of Anne Wentworth*, taken from Elspeth Graham *et al.* (eds), *Her Own Life: Autobiographical writings by seventeenth-century Englishwomen*. London and New York: Routledge, 1989. [137]

[Walker, Anthony] (1690). *The Holy Life of Mrs. Elizabeth Walker*. London: for John Leake. [74, 115]

[Whately, William] (1617). *A Bride-Bush, or Wedding Sermon: compendiously describing the duties of married persons.* London: for Nicholas Bourne. [16, 95]

—— (1624). *A Care-cloth: or a treatise of the cumbers and troubles of marriage.* London: for Thomas Man. [78]

Wilmot, John, Earl of Rochester (written 1673). Contribution to *Poems on Affairs of State* (1697), taken from Keith Walker (ed.), *The Poems*. Oxford: Blackwell, 1984. [61]

—— (1679). *A Letter from Artemiza in the Town to Chloe in the Country*, taken from Keith Walker (ed.), *The Poems*. Oxford: Blackwell, 1984. [186]

—— (1680). *Poems on Several Occasions*, taken from Keith Walker (ed.), *The Poems*. Oxford: Blackwell, 1984. [62, 158]

Winthrop, John (written 1630–49). *Journal*, taken from Perry Miller & Thomas H. Johnson (eds), *The Puritans: A sourcebook of their writings*, 2 vols. New York: Harper & Row, 1963. [25]

Wither, George (1612). *Epithalamia*, taken from Frank Sidgwick (ed.), *The Poetry of George Wither*, 2 vols. London: Bullen, 1902. [42]

—— (1622). *Fair-Virtue*, taken from Frank Sidgwick (ed.), *The Poetry of George Wither*, 2 vols. London: Bullen, 1902. [151]

2 SECONDARY SOURCES AND STUDIES

Beilin, Elaine V. (1990). *Redeeming Eve: Women writers of the English Renaissance*. Princeton, NJ: Princeton University Press.

Bell, Maureen, Parfitt, George, and Shepherd, Simon (1990). *A Biographical Dictionary of English Women Writers 1580–1720*. Hemel Hempstead: Harvester Wheatsheaf.

Belsey, Catherine (1985). *The Subject of Tragedy: Identity and difference in Renaissance drama*. London and New York: Methuen.

Braithwaite, William C. (1979). *The Second Period of Quakerism*. York: William Sessions.

Brink, J. R. (1980). 'Bathsua Makin: Educator and linguist', in J. R. Brink (ed.), *Female Scholars: A tradition of learned women before 1800*, pp. 86–100. Montreal: Eden Press.

Brooke, Christopher N. L. (1989). *The Medieval Idea of Marriage*. Oxford: Oxford University Press.

Brown, Peter (1988). *The Body and Society: Men, women and sexual renunciation in Early Christianity*. London: Faber.

Castelli, Elizabeth (1986). 'Virginity and its Meaning for Women's Sexuality in Early Christianity', *Journal of Ecclesiastical History*, 11: 61–87.

Clark, Alice (1992). *Working Life of Women in the Seventeenth Century*, with a new introduction by Amy Louise Erickson. London and New York: Routledge.

Crawford, Patricia (1986). '"The Sucking Child": Adult attitudes to child care in the first year of life in seventeenth-century England', *Continuity and Change*, 1: 23–51.

—— (1990). 'The Construction and Experience of Maternity in Seventeenth-century England', in Valerie Fildes (ed.), *Women as Mothers in Pre-Industrial England*, pp. 3–38. London and New York: Routledge.

Cropper, Elizabeth (1986). 'The Beauty of Woman: Problems in the rhetoric of Renaissance portraiture', in Margaret W. Ferguson, Maureen Quilligan and Nancy J. Vickers. (eds), *Rewriting the Renaissance: The discourses of sexual difference in early modern Europe*, pp. 175–90. Chicago and London: University of Chicago Press.

Davies, K. M. (1981). 'Continuity and Change in Literary Advice on Marriage', in R. B. Outhwaite (ed.), *Marriage and Society: Studies in the social history of marriage*. pp. 58–80. London: Europa.

Davies, Stevie (1986). *The Idea of Woman in Renaissance Literature: The feminine reclaimed*. Brighton: Harvester.

de Bruyn, Lucy (1979). *Woman and the Devil in Sixteenth-Century Literature*. Tisbury, Wilts: Compton Press.

Dekker, Rudolph M. and van de Pol, Lotte (1989). *The Tradition of Female Transvestism in Early Modern Europe*. London: Macmillan.

Delaney, Janice, Lupton, Mary Jane and Toth, Emily (1976). *The Curse: A cultural history of menstruation*. New York: Dutton.

Doriani, Daniel (1991). 'The Puritans, Sex and Pleasure', *Westminster Theological Journal*, 53: 125–43.

Durston, Christopher (1989). *The Family in the English Revolution*. Oxford: Blackwell.

Dusinberre, Juliet (1975). *Shakespeare and the Nature of Women*. London: Macmillan.

Easlea, Brian (1980). *Witch-hunting, Magic and the New Philosophy: An introduction to debates of the scientific revolution, 1450–1750*. Brighton: Harvester.

Eaton, Sarah J. (1987). 'Presentation of Women in the English Popular Press', in Carole Levin and Jeannie Watson (eds), *Ambiguous Realities: Women in the Middle Ages and Renaissance*, pp. 165–83. Detroit, MI: Wayne State University Press.

Eccles, Audrey (1982). *Obstetrics and Gynaecology in Tudor and Stuart England*. London: Croom Helm.

Ehrenreich, Barbara, and English, Deirdre (1973). *Witches, Midwives and Nurses*. Detroit: Black & Red.

Erickson, Amy Louise (1990). 'Common Law versus Common Practice: The use of marriage settlements in early modern England', *Economic History Review*, 2nd series, 43: 21–39.

Ezell, Margaret J. M. (1987). *The Patriarch's Wife: Literary evidence and the history of the family*. Chapel Hill and London: University of North Carolina Press.

Faderman, Lilian (1985). *Surpassing the Love of Men: Romantic friendship and love between women from the Renaissance to the present*. London: The Women's Press.

Ferguson, Moira, ed. (1985). *First Feminists: British women writers 1578–1799*. Bloomington, Ind. and Old Westbury, NY: Indiana University Press and The Feminist Press.

Fildes, Valerie (1986). *Breasts, Bottles and Babies: A history of infant feeding*. Edinburgh: Edinburgh University Press.

—— (1988). *Wet Nursing: A history from antiquity to the present*. Oxford: Blackwell.

Forbes, Thomas R. (1964). 'The Regulation of English Midwives in the Sixteenth and Seventeenth Centuries', *Medical History*, 8: 235–44.

Fraser, Antonia (1984). *The Weaker Vessel: Woman's lot in seventeenth-century England*. London: Weidenfeld & Nicolson.

French, Marilyn (1982). *Shakespeare's Division of Experience*. London: Cape.

Gallagher, Catherine (1988). 'Embracing the Absolute: The politics of the female subject in seventeenth-century England', *Genders*, 1: 24–39.

Gardiner, Dorothy (1929). *English Girlhood at School*. London: Oxford University Press.

George, Margaret (1973). 'From "Goodwife" to "Mistress": The transformation of the female in bourgeois culture', *Science and Society*, pp. 152–77.

Greer, Germaine, Medoff, Jeslyn, Sansone, Melinda and Hastings, Susan, eds (1988). *Kissing the Rod: An anthology of seventeenth-century women's verse*. London: Virago.

Hamilton, Roberta A. (1978). *The Liberation of Women: A study of patriarchy and capitalism*. London: Allen & Unwin.

Harralson, David M. (1975). 'The Puritan Art of Love: Henry Smith's "A Preparative to Marriage"', *Ball State University Forum*, 16: 46–55.

Henderson, Katherine Usher, and McManus, Barbara F. (1985). *Half Humankind: Contexts and texts of the controversy about women in England, 1540–1640*. Urbana and Chicago, Ill.: University of Illinois Press.

Higgins, Patricia (1973). 'The Reactions of Women, with Special Reference to Women Petitioners', in Brian Manning (ed.), *Politics, Religion and the English Civil War*, pp. 179–222. London: Arnold.

Hill, Bridget, ed. (1986). *The First English Feminist . . . writings by Mary Astell*. Aldershot: Gower.

Hobby, Elaine (1988). *Virtue of Necessity: English women's writing 1649–88*. London: Virago.

Houlbrooke, Ralph A. (1984). *The English Family 1450–1700*. London and New York: Longman.

—— , ed. (1988). *English Family Life, 1576–1716: An anthology from diaries.* Oxford: Blackwell.

Howe, Elizabeth (1992). *The First English Actresses.* Cambridge: Cambridge University Press.

Jardine, Lisa (1983). *Still Harping on Daughters: Women and drama in the age of Shakespeare.* Brighton: Harvester.

Jones, Ann Rosalind (1987). 'Nets and Bridles: Early modern conduct books and sixteenth-century women's lyrics', in Nancy Armstrong and Leonard Tennenhouse (eds), *The Ideology of Conduct: Essays on literature and the history of sexuality,* pp. 39–72. New York and London: Methuen.

Jones, Kathleen (1988). *A Glorious Fame: The life of Margaret Cavendish, Duchess of Newcastle.* London: Bloomsbury.

Kahn, Coppelia (1986). 'The Absent Mother in *King Lear*', in Margaret W. Ferguson, Maureen Quilligan and Nancy J. Vickers. (eds), *Rewriting the Renaissance: The discourses of sexual difference in early modern Europe,* pp. 33–49. Chicago and London: University of Chicago Press.

Kanowitz, Leo (1969). *Women and the Law: the unfinished revolution.* Albuquerque, N.Mex.: University of New Mexico Press.

Keeble, N. H. (1990a). '"The Colonel's Shadow": Lucy Hutchinson, women's writing and the Civil War', in Thomas Healy and Jonathan Sawday (ed.), *Literature and the English Civil War,* pp. 227–47. Cambridge: Cambridge University Press.

—— (1990b). '"Here is her glory, even to be under him": The feminine in the thought and work of John Bunyan', in Anne Laurence, W. R. Owens and Stuart Sim (eds), *John Bunyan and his England 1628–88,* pp. 131–47. London: Hambledon Press.

—— (forthcoming). 'Obedient Subjects? The loyal self in some later seventeenth-century Royalist women's memoirs', in Gerald MacLean (ed.), *Literature, Culture and Society in the Stuart Restoration.* Cambridge: Cambridge University Press.

Kelly, Joan (1984). 'Did Women have a Renaissance?' and 'Early Feminist Theory and the *Querelle des Femmes,* 1400–1789', in Joan Kelly, *Women, History & Theory,* pp. 19–50, pp. 65–109. Chicago and London: University of Chicago Press.

Kelso, Ruth (1956). *Doctrine for the Lady of the Renaissance.* Urbana, Ill.: University of Illinois Press.

Laqueur, Thomas (1986). 'Orgasm, Generation and the Politics of Reproductive Biology', *Representations,* 14: 1–41.

—— (1990). *Making Sex: Body and gender from the Greeks to Freud.* Cambridge, Mass.: Harvard University Press.

Laslett, Peter (1983). *The World We Have Lost Further Explored.* 3rd edn. London: Methuen.

Leverenz, David (1980). *The Language of Puritan Feeling.* New Brunswick, NJ: Rutgers University Press.

Lilley, Kate (1992). 'Blazing Worlds: Seventeenth-century women's Utopian writing', in Claire Brant and Diane Purkiss (eds), *Women, Texts and Histories, 1575–1760,* pp. 102–33. London and New York: Routledge.

McArthur, Ellen (1909). 'Women Petitioners and the Long Parliament', *English Historical Review,* 24: 698–709.

McEntee, Ann Marie (1992). '"The [Un]Civill-Sisterhood of Oranges and Lemons": Female petitioners and demonstrators, 1642–53', in James Holstun (ed.), *Pamphlet Wars: Prose in the English Revolution,* pp. 92–111. London: Frank Cass.

Macfarlane, Alan (1986). *Marriage and Love in England: Modes of reproduction, 1300–1800.* Oxford: Blackwell.

Mack, Phyllis (1982). 'Women as Prophets during the English Civil War', *Feminist Studies,* 8: 19–45.

— (1988). 'The Prophet and her Audience: Gender and knowledge in the world turned upside down', in Geoff Eley and William Hunt (eds), *Reviving the English Revolution: Reflections and elaborations on the work of Christopher Hill*, pp. 139–52. London: Verso.

Maclean, Ian (1977). *Woman Triumphant: Feminism in French literature, 1610–1652*. Oxford: Clarendon Press.

— (1980). *The Renaissance Notion of Woman: A study in the fortunes of scholasticism and medical science in European intellectual life*. Cambridge: Cambridge University Press.

Mahl, Mary R. and Koon, Helene, eds (1977). *The Female Spectator: English women writers before 1800*. Bloomington, Ind. and Old Westbury, NY: Indiana University Press and The Feminist Press.

Morgan, Edmund S. (1966). *The Puritan Family: Religion and domestic relations in seventeenth-century New England*. New York: Harper & Row.

Mueller, Janel (1993). 'Troping Utopia: Donne's brief for lesbianism', in James Grantham Turner (ed.), *Sexuality and Gender in Early Modern Europe*, pp. 182–207. Cambridge: Cambridge University Press.

Noonan, J. T. (1965). *Contraception: A history of its treatment by the Catholic theologians and canonists*. Cambridge, Mass.: Belknap Press of Harvard University Press.

Notestein, Wallace (1965). *A History of Witchcraft in England from 1558 to 1718*. New York: Russell & Russell.

O'Donoghue, Bernard, ed. (1982). *The Courtly Love Tradition*. Manchester: Manchester University Press.

O'Malley, I. B. (1933). *Women in Subjection: A study of the lives of Englishwomen before 1832*. London: Duckworth.

Pearson, Jacqueline (1988). *The Prostituted Muse: Images of women and women dramatists, 1642–1737*. New York: St Martin's Press.

Perry, Ruth (1980). *Women, Letters and the Novel*. New York: AMS Press.

— (1986). *The Celebrated Mary Astell: An early English feminist*. Chicago and London: University of Chicago Press.

Philips, John A. (1984). *Eve: The History of an Idea*. San Francisco: Harper & Row.

Pollock, Linda (1989). ' "Teach her to live under obedience": The making of women in the upper ranks of early modern England', *Continuity and Change*, 4: 231–58.

— (1990) 'Embarking on a Rough Passage: The experience of pregnancy in early-modern society', in Valerie Fildes (ed.), *Women as Mothers in Pre-Industrial England*, pp. 39–67. London and New York: Routledge.

Potter, Lois (1989). *Secret Rites and Secret Writing: Royalist literature, 1641–1660*. Cambridge: Cambridge University Press.

Powell, Chilton Latham (1917). *English Domestic Relations, 1487–1653: A study of matrimony and family life*. New York: Columbia University Press.

Prest, W. R. (1991). 'The Law and Women's Rights in Early Modern England', *The Seventeenth Century*, 6: 169–87.

Purkiss, Diane (1992). 'Material Girls: The seventeenth-century woman debate', in Claire Brant and Diane Purkiss (eds), *Women, Texts and Histories, 1575–1760*, pp. 69–101. London and New York: Routledge.

Reynolds, Myra (1964). *The Learned Lady in England, 1650–1760*. Boston and New York: Houghton Mifflin.

Schoenfeldt, Michael C. (1993). 'Gender and Conduct in *Paradise Lost*', in James Grantham Turner (ed.), *Sexuality and Gender in Early Modern Europe*, pp. 310–38. Cambridge: Cambridge University Press.

Schofield, Roger (1986). 'Did the Mothers Readily Die? Three centuries of maternal mortality in "The World We Have Lost"', in Lloyd Bonfield, Richard M. Smith and Keith Wrightson (eds), *The World We Have Gained*, pp. 231–60. Oxford: Blackwell.

Sharpe, J. A. (1984). *Crime in Early Modern England, 1550–1750*. London and New York: Longman.

Shepherd, Simon (1985). *Amazons and Warrior Women: Varieties of feminism in seventeenth-century drama*. Brighton: Harvester.

—— ed. (1985) The Women's Sharp Revenge: Five women's pamphlets from the Renaissance. London: Fourth Estate.

Siraisi, Nancy (1990). *Medieval and Early Renaissance Medicine: An introduction to knowledge and practice*. Chicago and London: University of Chicago Press.

Sirluck, Ernest, ed. (1959). *John Milton: Complete Prose Works*, vol. II. New Haven and London: Yale University Press and Oxford University Press.

Sizemore, Christine W. (1976). 'Early Seventeenth-Century Advice Books: The female viewpoint', *South Atlantic Bulletin*, 41: 41–9.

Skinner, John (1930). *A Critical and Exegetical Commentary on Genesis*, 2nd edn. Edinburgh: T. & T. Clark.

Smith, Hilda (1976). 'Gynaecology and Ideology in Seventeenth-century England', in Bernice A. Carroll (ed.), *Liberating Women's History*, pp. 97–114. Urbana, Ill.: University of Illinois Press.

—— (1982). *Reason's Disciples: Seventeenth-century English Feminists*. Urbana, Ill.: Illinois University Press.

Smith, Nigel (1989). *Perfection Proclaimed: Language and literature in English radical religion, 1640–1660*. Oxford: Clarendon Press.

Sowerby, Robin (1994). *The Classical Legacy in English Renaissance Poetry*. Harlow: Longman.

Speiser, E. A. (1964). *Genesis: Introduction, translation and notes*. Garden City, New York: Doubleday.

Spencer, Jane (1986). *The Rise of the Woman Novelist: From Aphra Behn to Jane Austen*. Oxford: Blackwell.

Spender, Dale (1986). *Mothers of the Novel: 100 good women writers before Jane Austen*. London and New York: Pandora.

Stone, Lawrence (1977). *The Family, Sex and Marriage in England, 1500–1800*. London: Weidenfeld & Nicolson.

Tawney, R. H. (1938). *Religion and the Rise of Capitalism*. Harmondsworth: Penguin.

Temkin, Owsei (1973). *Galenism: Rise and decline of medical philosophy*. Ithaca, NY and London: Cornell University Press.

Thickstun, Margaret Olofson (1988). *Fictions of the Feminine: Puritan doctrine and the representation of women*. Ithaca, NY and London: Cornell University Press.

Thomas, Keith (1958). 'Women and the Civil War Sects', *Past and Present*, 13: 42–62.

—— (1959). 'The Double Standard', *Journal of the History of Ideas*, 20: 195–216.

—— (1978). 'The Puritans and Adultery: The Act of 1650 reconsidered', in Donald Pennington and Keith Thomas (eds), *Puritans and Revolutionaries: Essays . . . presented to Christopher Hill*, pp. 257–82. Oxford: Clarendon Press.

Thomas, Patrick, ed. (1992–2). *The Collected Works of Katherine Philips*, 2 vols. Stump Cross, Essex: Stump Cross Books.

Tickner, F. W. (1981). *Women in English Economic History*. Westport, Conn.: Hyperion Press.

Todd, Janet (1986). *Sensibility: An introduction*. London: Methuen.

——, ed. (1987). *A Dictionary of British and American Women Writers 1660–1800*. London: Methuen.

—— (1989). *The Sign of Angellica: Women, writing and fiction, 1660–1800*. London: Virago.

Travitsky, Betty S. (1980). 'The New Mother of the English Renaissance: Her writings on motherhood', in Cathy N. Davidson and E. M. Broner (eds), *The Lost Tradition: Mothers and daughters in literature*, pp. 33–43. New York: Frederick Ungar.

Trevor-Roper, Hugh (1969). *The European Witch-craze of the 16th and 17th Centuries*. Harmondsworth: Penguin.

Trubowitz, Rachel (1992). 'Female Preachers and Male Wives: Gender and authority in Civil War England', in James Holstun (ed.), *Pamphlet Wars: Prose in the English Revolution*, pp. 112–33. London: Frank Cass.

Turner, James Grantham (1987). *One Flesh: Paradisal marriage and sexual relations in the age of Milton*. Oxford: Clarendon Press.

——, ed. (1993). *Sexuality and Gender in Early Modern Europe: Institutions, texts, images*. Cambridge: Cambridge University Press.

Walker, Julia M., ed. (1988). *Milton and the Idea of Woman*. Urbana and Chicago, Ill.: University of Illinois Press.

Warner, Marina (1976). *Alone of All Her Sex: The myth and cult of the Virgin Mary*. London: Weidenfeld & Nicolson.

Wiesner, Merry E. (1986). 'Spinsters and Seamstresses: Women in cloth and clothing production', in Margaret W. Ferguson, Maureen Quilligan and Nancy J. Vickers (eds), *Rewriting the Renaissance: The discourses of sexual difference in early modern Europe*, pp. 191–205. Chicago and London: University of Chicago Press.

Wilson, Adrian (1990). 'The Ceremony of Childbirth and its Interpretation', in Valerie Fildes (ed.), *Women as Mothers in Early Modern England*, pp. 68–107. London and New York: Routledge.

Wilson, Katharina M., & Warnke, Frank J., eds (1989). *Women Writers of the Seventeenth Century*. Athens, Ga. and London: Georgia University Press.

Wiseman, Susan (1992). '"Adam, the Father of All Flesh": Porno-political rhetoric and political theory in and after the English Civil War', in James Holstun (ed.), *Pamphlet Wars: Prose in the English Revolution*, pp. 134–57. London: Frank Cass.

Wood, Charles T. (1981). 'The Doctors' Dilemma: Sin, salvation and the menstrual cycle in medieval thought', *Speculum*, 56: 710–27.

Wright, Louis B. (1958). *Middle-Class Culture in Elizabethan England*. Ithaca, NY: Cornell University Press.

INDEX

Note: The authors of extracts are not included in this index. Reference should be made to the bibliography to identify extracts from any particular writer.

Swetnam, Joseph 71–2

Thornton, Alice 211
Tiberius, Emperor 219
Titus, son of Vespasian 219
Trent, Council of 117
Trousset, Alexis (alias Jacques Olivier)
72

ugliness 55, 62–3
Ussher, James, Archbishop of Armagh
97

Verney, Mary 211
Verney, Sir Ralph 171
Vesalius, Andreas 17
Vespasian, Emperor 219
vices of women: deceit 76–8; as evil 73;
jealousy 82; lasciviousness 71–2,
88–9; loquacity 103–4; lust 84–5;
scolds 80–1; unquietness 80;
wantonness 80; wilfulness,
deceitfulness, cunning 71–2; see also
courtesans; prostitutes; witches
virago 18, 71
Virgil 41
virgins 259–60
virtues of women: charitableness 107–8;
chasteness 99, 117; decency 100–1;
faithfulness 100; gracefulness 105;
humility 108–9; meekness 104–5, 108,

157–8; modesty 100, 104–5, 108;
obedience 96, 97, 108–9, 184–5;
passivity 96–7; patience 105;
quietness 98; silence 105; of a
wife 8

Walker, Anthony 97
Walker, Elizabeth 170
Weaver, Margaret, a widow 93
Wentworth, Anne 188
wet-nurses 210–11, 215, 217–18, 219–21
Whately, William 19, 145
whores see prostitutes
widows 252, 253–4
Wilmot, John, Earl of Rochester 73,
222, 264
Winthrop, John 44
witches 73–4, 92–5
Wither, George 71
wives, duties of 143, 186, 289;
companionship 144–5; domestic
148–9, 152–3, 154, 163, 190;
obedience 144, 148, 152, 158, 162;
subordination 144
Wollstonecraft, Mary 280
woman: inferiority of i–ii, 1–2, 207–8,
288; natural imbecility of 71, 74–5
womb, the 19, 21, 23–4, 28–30, 33, 41,
169
Woolley, Hannah 280
Wyerius, Johannes 94